OECD Insurance Statistics 2022

OECD
BETTER POLICIES FOR BETTER LIVES

Please cite this publication as:
OECD (2023), *OECD Insurance Statistics 2022*, OECD Publishing, Paris,
https://doi.org/10.1787/0512c106-en.

ISBN 978-92-64-52744-7 (print)
ISBN 978-92-64-35623-8 (pdf)

OECD Insurance Statistics
ISSN 2307-8421 (print)
ISSN 2307-843X (online)

Corrigenda to OECD publications may be found on line at: *www.oecd.org/about/publishing/corrigenda.htm*.

Table of contents

Conventional signs and abbreviations

Signs and abbreviations

c	Confidential data
..	Not available
.	Decimal point
|	Break in series

ISO country codes and abbreviations for currency

	ISO code	Currency	Abbreviation
Australia	AUS	dollar	AUD
Austria	AUT	euro	EUR
Belgium	BEL	euro	EUR
Canada	CAN	dollar	CAD
Chile	CHL	peso	CLP
Colombia	COL	peso	COP
Costa Rica	CRI	colon	CRC
Czech Republic	CZE	koruna	CZK
Denmark	DNK	krone	DKK
Estonia	EST	euro	EUR
Finland	FIN	euro	EUR
France	FRA	euro	EUR
Germany	DEU	euro	EUR
Greece	GRC	euro	EUR
Hungary	HUN	forint	HUF
Iceland	ISL	króna	ISK
Ireland	IRL	euro	EUR
Israel	ISR	sheqel	ILS
Italy	ITA	euro	EUR
Japan	JPN	yen	JPY
Korea	KOR	won	KRW
Latvia	LVA	euro	EUR
Lithuania	LTU	euro	EUR
Luxembourg	LUX	euro	EUR
Mexico	MEX	peso	MXN
Netherlands	NLD	euro	EUR
New Zealand	NZL	dollar	NZD
Norway	NOR	krone	NOK
Poland	POL	zloty	PLN
Portugal	PRT	euro	EUR
Slovak Republic	SVK	euro	EUR
Slovenia	SVN	euro	EUR
Spain	ESP	euro	EUR
Sweden	SWE	krona	SEK
Switzerland	CHE	franc	CHF
Türkiye	TUR	lira	TRY
United Kingdom	GBR	pound	GBP
United States	USA	dollar	USD

Common definitions and notes

Notes on data sources

All the data in the statistical tables of each jurisdiction have been reported by the relevant national insurance authorities. Regarding comparative tables of indicators, the data are mainly drawn from the tables by jurisdiction. Data on exchange rates are taken from the IMF International Financial Statistics database. Data on population are taken from the IMF publication *World Economic Outlook*. Data on GDP come from the OECD Annual National Accounts database for OECD jurisdictions and from the IMF publication *World Economic Outlook* for all the other jurisdictions.

To achieve greater clarity, the number of variables selected and displayed in this publication has been limited. Data have been extracted from the Global Insurance Statistics database. The complete database can be accessed online at the following link:

OECD Insurance Statistics, *http://dx.doi.org/10.1787/ins-data-en.*

A significant effort has been made to achieve comparability among jurisdictions. Definitions, classifications, calculation methods, and units have been standardised as far as possible.

General notes

a) Life and non-life categories follow the definitions used in national law. However, the premiums for accident and sickness insurance underwritten by life companies should be included in non-life figures.

b) Up until 2008, the insurance business is broken down between life and non-life business. As of 2009, the insurance business is broken down between the business of pure life, pure non-life and composite undertakings. The insurance business of composite undertakings is further broken down between life and non-life components. Some jurisdictions do not allow for insurance undertakings to be active in both life and non-life insurance business and therefore composite insurance undertakings do not exist in these jurisdictions. In other jurisdictions (e.g., Austria, Hungary, Mexico, Spain) however, composite insurance undertakings account for more than 25% of all insurance undertakings operating in these jurisdictions. Therefore, to have comparable data across years for life business data (respectively non-life), one has to sum up the life (respectively non-life) business of pure life (respectively non-life) undertakings and the life (respectively non-life) business of composite undertakings as of 2009.

c) Figures provided for the number of companies and for insurance premiums should include all insurance companies licensed or authorised in the reporting jurisdiction, *including* professional reinsurers, whether or not these are controlled, but *excluding* any statutory system of social security administered by the State.

d) *Domestic companies* means those companies incorporated under national law, together with those companies in the reporting jurisdiction which are unincorporated, but excluding the branches and agencies of foreign companies.

e) *Foreign-controlled companies* means those domestic companies controlled by foreign interests, such "control" being defined according to national law (see the definition of foreign controlled companies in notes by jurisdiction). The data of *foreign-controlled companies* are part of those of *Domestic companies*.

f) *Foreign companies* means companies incorporated outside the reporting jurisdiction.

In 2016, a new supervisory framework for insurance and reinsurance companies was implemented in the European Union (EU) and the European Economic Area (EEA). This framework includes harmonised reporting requirements across EU/EEA jurisdictions. These requirements led to changes in national data collection, which may hamper the data comparability with the ones collected before 2016 for some jurisdictions which only collect data with the Solvency II framework.

International Comparisons:

Detailed metadata at: *http://metalinks.oecd.org/ins/20190221/0f8b*.

Country tables

In this part, the main insurance statistics are presented through separate tables for each OECD member jurisdiction. Figures refer to the calendar year. The premiums and other amounts are described in millions of the national currency unit.

International comparisons

Table 1. Balance sheet and income, direct insurance (All insurance companies)

2021

Million US dollars

	Gross claims payments	Gross operating expenses	Commissions	Outstanding claims provision (changes)	Total assets	Gross technical provisions	Gross technical provisions unit-linked	Shareholders' equity	Net income
Argentina	6 282	2 776	1 744	270	21 052	5 288	..	6 070	232
Australia	41 424	10 302	3 040	..	176 954	122 211	9 227	32 777	1 919
Austria	18 655	..	..	..	..	..	..	..	..
Belgium	31 508	3 490	4 416	2 743	379 814	311 800	58 102	19 421	2 427
Bermuda	..	..	..	..	..	..	..	..	..
Bolivia	464	242	52	..	1 219	499	..	343	5
Brazil	11 522	10 172	5 527	1 155	248 438	221 524	180 979	16 605	2 134
Bulgaria	783	593	362	90	4 016	2 551	411	430	171
Canada	..	..	..	..	..	..	..	..	..
Chile	9 748	1 771	887	-715	68 853	57 633	6 242	6 931	1 332
Colombia	5 355	3 096	770	-474	24 839	18 401	..	3 810	232
Costa Rica	727	305	226	31	4 300	1 531	0	2 023	257
Cuba	..	..	..	..	..	..	..	..	..
Czech Republic	4 916	2 325	539	360	23 071	16 435	5 045	3 409	1 260
Denmark	32 088	2 862	356	50 518	664 696	535 105	256 891	32 343	3 884
Dominican Republic	..	..	..	..	..	..	..	..	..
Ecuador	852	257	120	445	2 191	359	0	652	40
Egypt	1 497	230	518	660	9 780	4 079	..	2 913	442
El Salvador	473	250	114	139	994	227	..	409	19
Estonia	578	205	..	..	2 547	1 577	898	420	39
Finland	7 704	1 404	158	207	97 672	86 366	..	8 659	1 171
France	310 472	65 685	..	65 471	3 446 584	2 713 903	552 569	226 675	14 132
Germany	209 249	48 405	28 706	-52 595	2 422 173	1 894 110	211 298	362 558	2 919
Greece	2 898	1 294	..	..	23 189	17 045	4 011	4 605	..
Guatemala	686	323	177	0	1 645	814	..	575	119
Honduras	317	175	..	-246	849	254	..	..	42
Hong Kong, China	43 245	742	1 036	157	..	..	..	..	..
Hungary	2 339	1 045	645	89	10 437	8 464	4 789	1 194	272
Iceland	433	124	..	..	1 620	836	71	638	242
India	..	..	..	..	..	..	..	..	..
Indonesia	13 639	2 551	2 796	208	59 250	39 149	17 583	12 753	1 775
Ireland	34 873	1 279	3 509	..	529 679	462 459	348 495	37 212	..
Israel	16 613	2 469	2 423	1 865	238 717	209 256	153 487	11 565	2 298
Italy	119 759	17 382	13 682	-15	1 158 369	1 007 399	239 168	86 983	7 915
Japan	330 929	73 389	13 356	20 773	3 687 653	2 767 371	..	133 291	24 031
Korea	120 503	28 158	..	..	1 131 220	774 264	9 261	110 431	6 804
Latvia	640	156	70	4	1 732	1 241	555	351	43
Lithuania	506	216	12	24	1 978	1 346	422	449	53
Luxembourg	25 492	5 846	3 681	642	328 462	298 519	193 167	12 973	1 145
Malaysia	9 687	2 903	1 587	328	93 421	71 833	18 636	9 479	1 441
Mexico	17 490	1 837	4 294	5 916	96 327	76 366	..	12 396	1 873
Montenegro	..	..	..	..	..	..	..	..	..
Morocco	3 369	620	448	407	27 143	19 659	267	4 446	437
Netherlands	560 212	50 161	23 605	-15 580	136 740	471 389	116 820	71 472	..
New Zealand	..	..	..	..	..	..	..	..	..
Nicaragua	75	78	20	30	416	156	..	186	21
Norway	17 553	2 757	644	234	268 054	227 277	..	31 272	5 084
Panama	772	..	..	..	..	..	..	..	..
Paraguay	191	181	47	5	664	251	..	287	36
Peru	2 696	1 264	678	126	16 840	12 713	..	2 120	106
Poland	11 490	4 944	3 582	132	48 553	26 978	9 900	16 666	1 473
Portugal	13 488	2 228	1 064	385	61 281	34 670	18 115	6 943	764
Puerto Rico	..	..	..	..	..	..	..	..	..
Singapore	22 832	2 163	2 913	..	271 817	222 681	36 983	23 962	2 050
Slovak Republic	807	942	111	51	9 501	6 458	1 428	300	38
Slovenia	1 863	610	149	-18	9 173	6 462	1 801	2 060	249
South Africa	47 522	5 631	2 600	..	242 663	196 405	..	28 639	4 257
Spain	57 454	12 165	7 363	395	385 975	265 788	28 829	53 879	5 382
Sri Lanka	..	..	..	..	..	..	..	..	..
Sweden	..	..	..	33 802	763 718	231 807	..	205 865	69 147
Switzerland	57 508	5 538	6 300	1 702	522 791	378 334	25 243	58 200	6 336
Chinese Taipei	61 122	5 574	5 688	0	1 220 571	990 489	0	104 124	13 596
Thailand	..	..	..	..	..	..	..	..	..
Tunisia	..	..	..	..	..	..	..	..	..
Türkiye	5 340	2 096	1 707	1 010	32 271	11 528	..	3 256	1 353
United Kingdom	416 443	51 508	..	1 923	3 686 329	3 063 536	2 000 444	232 505	..
United States	1 666 320	429 664	154 584	171 843	7 810 604	1 404 486	..	1 773 752	133 172
Uruguay	520	296	197	480	6 247	..	..	769	186

.. Not available

Note: Detailed metadata at: *http://metalinks.oecd.org/ins/20230516/00cd*.

Source: *Balance sheet and income, OECD Insurance Statistics (database)*

Table 2. Balance sheet and income, direct insurance (Life insurance companies)

2021

Million US dollars

	Gross claims payments	Gross operating expenses	Commissions	Outstanding claims provision (changes)	Total assets	Gross technical provisions	Gross technical provisions unit-linked	Shareholders' equity	Net income
Argentina	215	123	14	-2	2 904	2 358	..	471	97
Australia	14 615	3 837	1 217	..	75 768	52 336	9 227	13 578	796
Austria	1 118	..	..	..	..	..	..	..	..
Belgium	517	58	25	27	16 282	9 082	348	755	60
Bermuda	..	..	..	..	..	..	..	..	..
Bolivia	286	113	23	..	746	402	..	186	-12
Brazil	863	1 213	197	22	112 256	107 788	99 615	3 358	48
Bulgaria	1	4	4	1	11	5	0	7	0
Canada	..	..	..	..	..	..	..	..	..
Chile	7 720	984	353	-808	60 963	51 818	6 242	5 476	1 229
Colombia	2 981	1 559	289	-326	15 814	12 445	..	2 272	158
Costa Rica	..	..	..	..	..	..	..	..	..
Cuba	..	..	..	..	..	..	..	..	..
Czech Republic	286	147	5	7	2 345	2 065	1 126	119	30
Denmark	24 292	900	56	49 917	631 084	519 718	256 891	23 044	2 087
Dominican Republic	..	..	..	..	..	..	..	..	..
Ecuador	4	3	0	10	176	96	0	47	-2
Egypt	856	101	225	96	5 685	2 663	..	1 161	208
El Salvador	265	108	49	95	394	106	..	118	-2
Estonia	.. c	.. c	..	..	.. c	.. c	.. c	..	..
Finland	4 604	466	158	111	80 037	75 037	..	3 400	523
France	30 973	26 934	..	64 300	532 720	465 672	105 424	42 260	1 787
Germany	89 185	12 604	9 281	-49 387	1 595 747	1 340 606	211 233	167 575	427
Greece	441	68	..	..	4 691	3 979	751	628	..
Guatemala	..	..	..	..	..	..	..	..	..
Honduras	..	..	..	..	..	..	..	..	-9
Hong Kong, China	33 878	..	..	..	..	..	..	..	..
Hungary	442	38	26	50	1 427	1 225	265	139	15
Iceland	19	13	..	..	170	84	71	46	25
India	..	..	..	..	..	..	..	..	..
Indonesia	11 443	1 550	1 574	-4	44 270	32 819	17 583	6 455	1 321
Ireland	28 730	558	1 760	..	445 395	410 068	348 495	18 205	..
Israel	..	..	..	..	..	..	..	..	..
Italy	20 737	1 034	652	-65	292 634	277 058	118 434	10 479	763
Japan	285 221	42 262	..	19 082	3 428 894	2 767 371	..	100 640	17 830
Korea	86 693	12 838	..	..	836 343	564 188	9 261	73 725	3 257
Latvia	..	0	..	..	0	0	..	..	..
Lithuania	42	22	0	1	474	431	363	37	15
Luxembourg	17 436	1 378	534	-5	272 777	261 559	193 167	3 827	289
Malaysia	7 473	1 775	1 271	..	80 919	66 152	18 636	4 380	840
Mexico	1 333	129	106	126	23 254	21 121	..	1 763	257
Montenegro	..	..	..	..	..	..	..	..	..
Morocco	567	28	20	48	3 249	2 789	120	111	15
Netherlands	141 664	10 143	1 493	-16 936	50 739	423 988	116 820	39 873	..
New Zealand	..	..	..	..	..	..	..	..	..
Nicaragua	..	..	..	..	..	..	..	..	..
Norway	7 934	1 050	131	..	229 254	208 490	..	14 431	1 877
Panama	131	..	..	..	..	..	..	..	..
Paraguay	0	0	0	..	..	..	..	..	..
Peru	445	168	83	-11	2 171	1 697	..	253	11
Poland	4 865	1 450	946	141	21 931	14 169	9 900	6 073	423
Portugal	5 862	397	180	-4	32 860	17 382	15 847	1 908	231
Puerto Rico	..	..	..	..	..	..	..	..	..
Singapore	13 211	653	1 677	..	152 267	130 590	24 819	8 415	618
Slovak Republic	385	201	37	40	1 793	1 116	732	42	10
Slovenia	0	2	..	0	30	14	..	16	0
South Africa	41 800	3 871	1 461	..	227 918	190 891	..	22 510	2 690
Spain	2 913	528	348	27	28 030	20 774	4 029	2 738	312
Sri Lanka	..	..	..	..	..	..	..	..	..
Sweden	..	..	..	3 739	678 670	192 515	..	181 031	62 933
Switzerland	29 579	1 226	1 064	-1 558	335 646	290 939	25 224	13 757	1 310
Chinese Taipei	57 446	4 218	4 645	0	1 204 122	981 711	0	98 309	12 882
Thailand	..	..	..	..	..	..	..	..	..
Tunisia	..	..	..	..	..	..	..	..	..
Türkiye	729	724	574	61	22 636	2 322	..	1 084	632
United Kingdom	330 354	12 988	..	-7 199	3 085 520	2 705 918	1 907 547	128 084	..
United States	456 571	78 202	54 264	54 536	5 047 000	22 621	..	548 134	49 027
Uruguay	0	0	0	0	0	..	..	0	0

.. Not available; c Confidential data

Note: Detailed metadata at: *http://metalinks.oecd.org/ins/20230516/00cd.*

Source: *Balance sheet and income, OECD Insurance Statistics (database)*

Table 3. Balance sheet and income, direct insurance (Non-life insurance companies)

2021

Million US dollars

	Gross claims payments	Gross operating expenses	Commissions	Outstanding claims provision (changes)	Total assets	Gross technical provisions	Gross technical provisions unit-linked	Shareholders' equity	Net income
Argentina	2 618	697	332	188	5 612	225	..	1 484	-18
Australia	26 810	6 465	1 823	..	101 186	69 875	..	19 199	1 124
Austria	1 935	..	..	..	..	..	..	..	..
Belgium	3 081	468	1 132	1 081	38 112	25 338	..	5 173	192
Bermuda	..	..	..	..	..	..	..	..	..
Bolivia	178	129	28	..	473	97	..	157	17
Brazil	1 595	1 426	869	111	7 109	4 358	0	1 544	216
Bulgaria	640	510	315	82	2 579	1 502	0	284	137
Canada	..	..	..	..	..	..	..	..	..
Chile	2 028	787	534	93	7 890	5 815	..	1 455	103
Colombia	2 375	1 537	482	-148	9 024	5 956	..	1 538	74
Costa Rica	25	18	16	0	114	52	0	41	4
Cuba	..	..	..	..	..	..	..	..	..
Czech Republic	215	184	50	57	620	274	0	163	20
Denmark	7 796	1 962	301	601	33 612	15 387	0	9 300	1 797
Dominican Republic	..	..	..	..	..	..	..	..	..
Ecuador	84	49	25	80	344	35	0	99	-10
Egypt	642	129	292	564	4 096	1 416	..	1 752	234
El Salvador	77	66	26	19	280	49	..	147	12
Estonia	390	163	..	..	993	460	..	420	39
Finland	3 100	938	.. c	96	17 635	11 329	..	5 259	648
France	73 782	38 751	..	1 171	368 092	175 462	0	75 560	5 456
Germany	120 064	35 801	19 425	-3 208	826 426	553 504	66	194 982	2 491
Greece	286	309	..	..	2 189	1 010	0	915	..
Guatemala	15	18	8	0	161	32	..	92	16
Honduras	..	..	..	..	..	..	..	..	30
Hong Kong, China	2 948	742	1 036	157	..	..	..	..	..
Hungary	114	80	41	22	443	201	0	172	22
Iceland	414	110	..	..	1 450	752	0	593	217
India	..	..	..	..	..	..	..	..	..
Indonesia	2 196	1 002	1 222	212	14 980	6 330	..	6 298	453
Ireland	6 143	720	1 749	..	84 284	52 391	..	19 006	..
Israel	1 164	244	133	559	6 830	4 776	0	959	158
Italy	6 950	3 650	2 802	386	32 413	19 090	..	9 187	455
Japan	45 709	31 127	13 356	1 691	258 759	..	..	32 652	6 202
Korea	33 809	15 320	..	..	294 877	210 076	..	36 706	3 547
Latvia	442	134	60	5	779	453	..	196	24
Lithuania	379	172	12	17	1 112	615	0	331	32
Luxembourg	8 056	4 468	3 147	647	55 685	36 960	0	9 146	856
Malaysia	2 214	1 127	316	328	12 502	5 681	0	5 099	601
Mexico	1 734	451	667	1 346	8 697	4 667	..	2 424	361
Montenegro	..	..	..	..	..	..	..	..	..
Morocco	233	114	34	47	2 738	1 285	0	909	78
Netherlands	418 548	40 018	22 113	1 355	86 001	47 402	0	31 598	..
New Zealand	..	..	..	..	..	..	..	..	..
Nicaragua	..	..	..	..	..	..	..	..	..
Norway	9 619	1 707	514	234	38 800	18 788	..	16 841	3 207
Panama	..	..	..	..	..	..	..	..	..
Paraguay	0	0	0	..	..	..	..	..	..
Peru	367	268	121	23	1 328	575	..	333	53
Poland	6 625	3 494	2 635	-9	26 622	12 809	..	10 593	1 051
Portugal	1 813	675	364	84	4 327	2 534	0	1 177	163
Puerto Rico	..	..	..	..	..	..	..	..	..
Singapore	2 671	751	49	..	22 706	11 361	0	7 600	659
Slovak Republic	..	35	17	4	..	92	0	16	4
Slovenia	520	63	6	-1	470	201	..	221	22
South Africa	5 722	1 759	1 139	..	14 745	5 514	..	6 129	1 567
Spain	12 786	4 192	2 069	75	34 780	17 492	0	11 511	1 393
Sri Lanka	..	..	..	..	..	..	..	..	..
Sweden	..	..	..	30 063	85 048	39 292	..	24 834	6 214
Switzerland	27 928	4 313	5 236	3 260	187 145	87 395	19	44 443	5 026
Chinese Taipei	3 675	1 356	1 044	0	16 449	8 778	0	5 815	714
Thailand	..	..	..	..	..	..	..	..	..
Tunisia	..	..	..	..	..	..	..	..	..
Türkiye	4 611	1 372	1 133	949	9 635	9 205	..	2 172	721
United Kingdom	15 398	8 760	..	73	57 049	..	..	18 875	..
United States	1 209 749	351 462	100 320	117 307	2 763 604	1 381 865	..	1 225 618	84 145
Uruguay	14	14	7	3	68	..	..	27	2

.. Not available; c Confidential data

Note: Detailed metadata at: *http://metalinks.oecd.org/ins/20230516/00cd.*

Source: *Balance sheet and income, OECD Insurance Statistics (database)*

Table 4. Portfolio allocation, direct insurance (All insurance companies)

2021

Million US dollars

	Cash and deposits	Land and buildings	Equity	Bills and bonds	Loans	Collective investment schemes	Private equity funds	Hedge funds	Structured products	Assets for unit-linked contracts	Total investments
Argentina	353	740	1 431	8 287	70	4 882	0	0	0	0	16 608
Australia	6 738	3 213	8 073	61 702	1 613	9 477	..	..	..	15 252	106 613
Austria	..	..	..	..	..	..	..	..	..	..	..
Belgium	7 347	11 311	28 215	216 227	46 351	23 828	1 483	..	1 572	57 963	392 814
Bermuda	..	..	..	..	..	..	..	..	..	..	..
Bolivia	53	112	8	405	17	0	41	0	0	0	683
Brazil	455	227	477	21 284	81	14 230	3 589	469	0	179 165	219 985
Bulgaria	..	..	..	..	..	..	..	..	..	..	..
Canada	..	..	..	..	..	..	..	..	..	..	..
Chile	2 161	4 297	451	27 999	12 555	6 476	0	0	0	6 290	60 645
Colombia	705	195	1 271	14 339	16	720	753	..	48	..	18 371
Costa Rica	172	0	168	2 728	387	89	0	0	0	0	3 543
Cuba	..	..	..	..	..	..	..	..	..	..	..
Czech Republic	797	34	1 173	10 045	254	1 140	12	23	38	3 899	17 442
Denmark	18 339	1 664	171 115	120 317	6 513	22 298	..	..	..	274 838	664 696
Dominican Republic	..	..	..	..	..	..	..	..	..	..	..
Ecuador	92	165	22	550	34	0	253	0	0	0	1 121
Egypt	..	..	..	..	..	..	..	..	..	..	..
El Salvador	292	7	1	226	25	26	..	..	..	..	582
Estonia	..	..	..	..	..	..	..	..	..	..	..
Finland	6 007	2 053	5 375	14 611	1 679	7 639	..	..	..	56 306	94 937
France	..	..	..	..	..	..	..	..	..	..	..
Germany	21 250	33 574	213 056	857 144	129 384	782 193	13 781	11 345	19 238	194 959	2 277 016
Greece	1 442	805	253	12 762	155	1 698	0	0	13	4 173	21 807
Guatemala	323	50	21	620	7	..	..	..	..	..	1 077
Honduras	48	5	38	371	20	0	0	0	0	0	481
Hong Kong, China	..	..	..	..	..	..	..	..	..	..	..
Hungary	233	148	89	4 022	10	317	..	..	..	4 808	9 845
Iceland	42	15	383	653	13	211	..	..	..	71	1 388
India	..	..	..	..	..	..	..	..	..	..	..
Indonesia	4 751	1 202	13 221	12 568	12	13 307	..	..	..	1 628	46 736
Ireland	..	..	..	..	..	..	..	..	..	..	..
Israel	6 639	2 622	2 754	35 951	6 838	3 309	3 464	179	126	155 243	219 171
Italy	13 136	5 438	73 571	596 425	4 989	123 256	..	..	..	239 483	1 086 822
Japan	..	..	..	..	..	..	..	..	..	..	..
Korea	16 331	14 850	48 396	396 199	198 633	..	..	..	..	99 215	1 055 408
Latvia	126	20	29	630	37	199	0	0	0	565	1 613
Lithuania	63	7	17	962	19	87	0	0	1	446	1 644
Luxembourg	4 104	254	3 041	44 521	255	7 963	..	..	..	194 216	318 381
Malaysia	5 333	1 174	7 663	39 431	2 699	..	..	..	..	19 843	87 142
Mexico	634	971	965	56 733	1 367	13 319	0	..	..	..	78 840
Montenegro	..	..	..	..	..	..	..	..	..	..	..
Morocco	..	..	..	..	..	..	..	..	..	..	..
Netherlands	..	..	..	..	..	..	..	..	..	..	..
New Zealand	..	..	..	..	..	..	..	..	..	..	..
Nicaragua	13	12	3	260	15	..	..	..	..	..	324
Norway	1 481	19 174	15 336	80 426	16 938	42 454	..	..	..	64 993	243 934
Panama	..	..	..	..	..	..	..	..	..	..	..
Paraguay	54	18	10	259	0	0	0	0	0	0	341
Peru	1 018	1 082	611	9 830	6	837	11	0	0	0	14 232
Poland	721	93	6 377	21 667	799	4 063	149	18	56	10 735	33 815
Portugal	1 065	526	3 471	29 161	375	2 275	77	75	428	18 142	55 610
Puerto Rico	..	..	..	..	..	..	..	..	..	..	..
Singapore	..	..	..	..	..	..	..	..	..	..	..
Slovak Republic	333	202	214	4 244	164	1 532	..	0	66	..	6 668
Slovenia	181	299	807	4 647	32	634	..	..	38	1 986	8 628
South Africa	14 077	514	36 383	41 745	5 952	119 086	0	514	3 982	0	244 074
Spain	18 869	12 913	20 127	245 166	2 088	18 257	1 419	1 286	6 058	36 524	352 659
Sri Lanka	..	..	..	..	..	..	..	..	..	..	..
Sweden	14 748	12 497	234 895	149 947	14 321	100 730	..	..	..	214 359	756 402
Switzerland	18 738	52 896	19 791	206 158	61 501	24 803	4 540	1 581	244	25 038	483 975
Chinese Taipei	34 082	59 819	104 247	694 552	45 868	50 189	18 774	..	15 120	96 354	1 190 893
Thailand	..	..	..	..	..	..	..	..	..	..	..
Tunisia	..	..	..	..	..	..	..	..	..	..	..
Türkiye	4 199	108	474	4 381	74	82	..	..	..	1 197	10 516
United Kingdom	30 445	21 300	85 548	704 830	140 040	274 328	8 204	6 811	462	1 826 428	3 114 035
United States	..	..	..	..	..	..	..	..	..	..	..
Uruguay	541	20	0	4 789	0	0	0	0	0	0	5 759

.. Not available

Note: Detailed metadata at: *http://metalinks.oecd.org/ins/20230516/c0a8.*

Source: *Outstanding investment by direct insurance companies, OECD Insurance Statistics (database)*

Table 5. Portfolio allocation, direct insurance (Life insurance companies)

2021

Million US dollars

	Cash and deposits	Land and buildings	Equity	Bills and bonds	Loans	Collective investment schemes	Private equity funds	Hedge funds	Structured products	Assets for unit-linked contracts	Total investments
Argentina	17	61	65	1 765	0	829	0	0	0	0	2 830
Australia	2 573	3 126	7 256	26 165	270	..	..	..	..	15 252	54 842
Austria	..	..	..	..	..	..	..	..	..	..	..
Belgium	641	388	1 135	6 012	2 230	1 474	9	..	25	348	12 252
Bermuda	..	..	..	..	..	..	..	..	..	..	..
Bolivia	45	75	4	278	17	0	34	0	0	0	500
Brazil	73	26	60	4 942	52	5 600	117	211	0	98 884	109 968
Bulgaria	..	..	..	..	..	..	..	..	..	..	..
Canada	..	..	..	..	..	..	..	..	..	..	..
Chile	1 757	4 240	433	26 424	12 532	6 329	0	0	0	6 290	58 256
Colombia	393	76	777	11 132	12	567	693	..	39	..	13 971
Costa Rica	..	..	..	..	..	..	..	..	..	..	..
Cuba	..	..	..	..	..	..	..	..	..	..	..
Czech Republic	..	..	..	..	..	..	..	..	..	..	..
Denmark	9 813	1 284	166 197	106 399	5 976	18 898	..	..	..	274 838	631 084
Dominican Republic	..	..	..	..	..	..	..	..	..	..	..
Ecuador	5	6	1	101	0	0	26	0	0	0	143
Egypt	..	..	..	..	..	..	..	..	..	..	..
El Salvador	127	6	0	106	3	11	..	..	..	..	254
Estonia	.. c	.. c	.. c	.. c	.. c	.. c	.. c	.. c	.. c	.. c	.. c
Finland	3 653	1 066	2 376	10 624	641	3 391	..	..	..	56 306	78 411
France	..	..	..	..	..	..	..	..	..	..	..
Germany	9 684	22 365	104 985	540 548	104 045	530 094	7 819	8 202	13 417	194 883	1 536 885
Greece	478	4	128	2 833	44	276	0	0	0	782	4 665
Guatemala	..	..	..	..	..	..	..	..	..	..	..
Honduras	..	..	..	..	..	..	..	..	..	..	..
Hong Kong, China	..	..	..	..	..	..	..	..	..	..	..
Hungary	18	4	10	968	1	85	..	..	..	285	1 387
Iceland	4	0	0	68	0	5	..	..	..	71	149
India	..	..	..	..	..	..	..	..	..	..	..
Indonesia	2 771	1 135	11 684	10 202	8	11 487	..	..	..	1 628	38 916
Ireland	..	..	..	..	..	..	..	..	..	..	..
Israel	..	..	..	..	..	..	..	..	..	..	..
Italy	1 832	366	4 746	134 521	17	17 605	..	..	..	118 570	284 139
Japan	82 539	48 972	246 139	2 302 553	238 280	..	..	..	..	..	3 344 237
Korea	11 770	10 031	38 232	311 649	130 783	..	..	..	..	99 215	815 885
Latvia	..	..	..	..	..	..	..	..	..	..	..
Lithuania	16	0	0	78	0	1	0	0	0	368	465
Luxembourg	1 887	56	2 061	23 044	84	6 507	..	..	..	194 216	270 464
Malaysia	3 389	1 054	7 452	36 320	2 691	..	..	..	..	19 843	76 579
Mexico	8	21	6	21 532	288	18	0	..	..	..	22 783
Montenegro	..	..	..	..	..	..	..	..	..	..	..
Morocco	..	..	..	..	..	..	..	..	..	..	..
Netherlands	..	..	..	..	..	..	..	..	..	..	..
New Zealand	..	..	..	..	..	..	..	..	..	..	..
Nicaragua	..	..	..	..	..	..	..	..	..	..	..
Norway	854	18 397	13 681	71 711	16 455	37 987	..	..	..	64 993	226 723
Panama	..	..	..	..	..	..	..	..	..	..	..
Paraguay	..	..	..	..	..	..	..	..	..	..	..
Peru	131	154	70	1 360	3	66	0	0	0	0	1 807
Poland	350	30	557	7 930	368	1 526	0	0	49	10 735	10 810
Portugal	285	218	272	13 153	318	692	9	0	25	15 902	30 874
Puerto Rico	..	..	..	..	..	..	..	..	..	..	..
Singapore	..	..	..	..	..	..	..	..	..	..	..
Slovak Republic	36	4	49	205	..	631	..	0	..	..	925
Slovenia	14	..	1	13	..	1	..	..	..	..	30
South Africa	10 970	406	35 242	36 617	5 825	117 903	0	488	3 954	0	227 918
Spain	812	336	899	17 071	170	1 151	182	22	2 514	4 013	26 746
Sri Lanka	..	..	..	..	..	..	..	..	..	..	..
Sweden	11 717	9 528	210 352	128 831	12 815	85 033	..	..	..	210 674	681 115
Switzerland	6 089	44 632	13 161	157 385	45 574	12 177	2 747	774	152	25 019	323 639
Chinese Taipei	33 041	58 382	101 810	689 961	45 854	49 311	18 767	..	15 120	96 354	1 178 889
Thailand	..	..	..	..	..	..	..	..	..	..	..
Tunisia	..	..	..	..	..	..	..	..	..	..	..
Türkiye	1 041	41	32	1 634	74	19	..	..	..	1 197	4 038
United Kingdom	14 631	18 315	67 224	456 456	124 046	237 353	6 409	5 224	387	1 826 055	2 756 978
United States	136 207	22 770	201 855	3 364 464	738 316	..	..	34 609	4 104	..	4 822 012
Uruguay	..	..	..	..	..	..	..	..	..	..	..

.. Not available; c Confidential data

Note: Detailed metadata at: *http://metalinks.oecd.org/ins/20230516/c0a8.*

Source: *Outstanding investment by direct insurance companies, OECD Insurance Statistics (database)*

Table 6. Portfolio allocation, direct insurance (Non-life insurance companies)

2021

Million US dollars

	Cash and deposits	Land and buildings	Equity	Bills and bonds	Loans	Collective investment schemes	Private equity funds	Hedge funds	Structured products	Assets for unit-linked contracts	Total investments
Argentina	65	161	132	2 485	1	1 475	0	0	0	0	4 577
Australia	4 165	87	817	35 537	1 342	9 477	..	..	..	..	51 771
Austria	..	..	..	..	..	..	..	..	..	..	..
Belgium	1 809	473	7 942	13 789	523	2 155	2	..	44	0	26 733
Bermuda	..	..	..	..	..	..	..	..	..	..	..
Bolivia	8	36	5	127	0	0	7	0	0	0	183
Brazil	77	52	1	1 721	0	621	18	24	0	0	2 515
Bulgaria	..	..	..	..	..	..	..	..	..	..	..
Canada	..	..	..	..	..	..	..	..	..	..	..
Chile	404	57	19	1 576	23	147	0	0	0	0	2 389
Colombia	312	119	494	3 207	4	154	60	..	9	..	4 400
Costa Rica	12	0	0	61	15	0	0	0	0	0	89
Cuba	..	..	..	..	..	..	..	..	..	..	..
Czech Republic	106	20	25	103	8	5	0	0	0	0	269
Denmark	8 526	381	4 917	13 918	537	3 400	..	..	..	0	33 612
Dominican Republic	..	..	..	..	..	..	..	..	..	..	..
Ecuador	14	29	3	83	1	0	37	0	0	0	168
Egypt	..	..	..	..	..	..	..	..	..	..	..
El Salvador	60	0	0	40	1	6	..	..	..	..	110
Estonia	216	0	2	640	2	6	0	0	0	0	872
Finland	2 355	988	2 999	3 987	1 037	4 248	..	..	..	..	16 526
France	..	..	..	..	..	..	..	..	..	..	..
Germany	11 566	11 209	108 071	316 596	25 339	252 099	5 961	3 143	5 821	76	740 131
Greece	292	189	50	1 046	3	323	0	0	1	0	1 952
Guatemala	50	3	0	49	5	..	..	..	..	..	112
Honduras	..	..	..	..	..	..	..	..	..	..	..
Hong Kong, China	..	..	..	..	..	..	..	..	..	..	..
Hungary	38	7	0	324	0	8	..	..	..	0	394
Iceland	38	15	383	585	13	206	..	..	..	0	1 239
India	..	..	..	..	..	..	..	..	..	..	..
Indonesia	1 979	67	1 537	2 366	4	1 820	..	..	..	..	7 820
Ireland	..	..	..	..	..	..	..	..	..	..	..
Israel	505	109	202	1 779	251	1 199	226	8	6	0	4 366
Italy	1 188	617	2 120	15 918	51	3 004	..	..	..	0	22 930
Japan	18 941	6 736	56 396	52 200	11 690	..	..	..	..	..	232 508
Korea	4 561	4 820	10 164	84 550	67 851	..	..	..	..	..	239 523
Latvia	66	20	29	440	37	58	0	0	0	0	655
Lithuania	33	7	11	655	5	57	0	0	0	0	808
Luxembourg	2 217	198	981	21 477	171	1 457	..	..	..	0	47 917
Malaysia	1 944	120	211	3 111	8	..	..	..	..	..	10 564
Mexico	205	207	102	3 425	35	77	0	..	..	..	4 427
Montenegro	..	..	..	..	..	..	..	..	..	..	..
Morocco	..	..	..	..	..	..	..	..	..	..	..
Netherlands	..	..	..	..	..	..	..	..	..	..	..
New Zealand	..	..	..	..	..	..	..	..	..	..	..
Nicaragua	..	..	..	..	..	..	..	..	..	..	..
Norway	627	777	1 655	8 715	483	4 467	..	..	..	..	17 210
Panama	..	..	..	..	..	..	..	..	..	..	..
Paraguay	..	..	..	..	..	..	..	..	..	..	..
Peru	110	56	114	222	0	28	0	0	0	0	705
Poland	371	63	5 820	13 736	431	2 538	149	18	7	..	23 005
Portugal	270	95	62	2 327	20	213	13	1	20	0	3 020
Puerto Rico	..	..	..	..	..	..	..	..	..	..	..
Singapore	..	..	..	..	..	..	..	..	..	..	..
Slovak Republic	..	..	..	..	..	..	..	..	..	..	..
Slovenia	34	20	5	335	..	16	..	..	..	..	410
South Africa	2 919	103	1 130	4 316	127	1 182	0	26	28	0	13 754
Spain	3 377	2 063	3 205	10 021	602	5 622	217	138	137	0	25 451
Sri Lanka	..	..	..	..	..	..	..	..	..	..	..
Sweden	3 031	2 968	24 543	21 116	1 507	15 696	..	..	..	3 685	75 287
Switzerland	12 649	8 263	6 630	48 773	15 927	12 626	1 794	807	92	19	160 336
Chinese Taipei	1 041	1 438	2 437	4 590	15	878	6	..	0	0	12 004
Thailand	..	..	..	..	..	..	..	..	..	..	..
Tunisia	..	..	..	..	..	..	..	..	..	..	..
Türkiye	3 159	68	441	2 747	..	63	..	..	..	0	6 478
United Kingdom	4 026	654	2 362	19 747	551	5 028	8	121	62	..	32 576
United States	210 402	18 854	692 059	1 367 675	25 343	..	..	-4	18	..	2 513 334
Uruguay	7	0	0	27	0	0	0	0	0	0	41

.. Not available

Note: Detailed metadata at: *http://metalinks.oecd.org/ins/20230516/c0a8.*

Source: *Outstanding investment by direct insurance companies, OECD Insurance Statistics (database)*

Table 7. Total gross premiums (Life and Non-life)

Million US dollars

	2014	2015	2016	2017	2018	2019	2020	2021
Argentina	18 622	19 376	19 749	18 519	20 137	12 574	12 387	13 242
Australia	97 011	78 796	74 145	72 339	69 991	61 277	57 397	66 723
Austria	25 102	21 091	20 647	20 485	21 880	21 090	..	..
Belgium	38 345	30 746	30 432	30 839	33 703	35 152	34 417	41 070
Bermuda	..	..	..	..	..	151 401	249 599	220 412
Bolivia	..	..	468	499	549	610	628	655
Brazil	69 867	55 519	58 914	66 431	61 462	62 990	48 672	52 302
Bulgaria	..	..	..	..	1 530	1 667	1 678	1 963
Canada	93 189	83 612	81 909	87 408	87 012	..	..	..
Chile	10 976	11 413	12 401	12 860	14 006	12 893	9 989	11 589
Colombia	9 693	8 003	8 047	8 977	9 409	9 389	8 421	9 638
Costa Rica	1 157	1 049	1 211	1 319	1 333	1 418	1 439	1 450
Cuba	..	..	..	..	..	..	..	..
Czech Republic	7 608	6 173	6 002	6 402	7 052	7 214	7 215	8 264
Denmark	37 098	31 997	33 498	37 549	40 976	38 589	40 999	46 770
Dominican Republic	..	..	..	..	1 222	..	..	..
Ecuador	..	2 316	2 135	..	..	1 797	..	1 724
Egypt	..	..	..	..	..	1 968	2 503	3 038
El Salvador	572	609	619	..	658	702	722	826
Estonia	839	764	815	924	1 092	1 102	1 070	1 186
Finland	14 125	11 917	10 012	10 084	5 156	6 744	4 611	6 051
France	294 033	250 873	314 251	314 319	338 708	332 471	302 729	362 503
Germany	338 764	293 086	294 660	311 208	335 669	344 268	365 897	396 718
Greece	5 056	3 964	3 908	4 213	4 485	4 538	4 690	5 330
Guatemala	749	804	856	953	964	1 006	1 048	1 170
Honduras	379	398	..	..	631	624	477	548
Hong Kong, China	43 121	47 901	59 301	64 310	69 089	..	..	80 559
Hungary	3 584	2 991	3 146	3 484	3 767	3 955	3 910	4 386
Iceland	444	420	487	611	652	612	545	634
India	..	70 878	..	100 841	..	107 818	..	..
Indonesia	14 325	14 629	17 290	19 483	18 967	19 763	18 098	19 724
Ireland	52 557	48 802	54 182	49 821	48 129	49 889	48 558	58 729
Israel	14 366	14 117	15 142	17 427	18 560	19 324	19 513	21 779
Italy	193 455	165 854	151 423	150 732	163 781	158 241	155 752	168 471
Japan	347 080	313 822	434 737	390 096	402 773	399 088	385 035	375 947
Korea	187 090	183 675	185 593	189 491	192 869	..	198 780	209 468
Latvia	687	589	589	730	893	960	911	1 005
Lithuania	798	716	786	895	1 037	1 059	1 091	1 231
Luxembourg	28 945	21 278	20 289	24 314	24 539	28 130	24 174	34 796
Malaysia	17 588	15 346	15 100	15 156	16 716	17 667	18 068	19 903
Mexico	27 349	24 929	24 150	26 569	28 250	31 346	28 301	33 084
Montenegro	..	..	..	..	..	..	..	..
Morocco	..	..	..	..	..	..	..	5 831
Netherlands	48 603	37 399	77 358	80 465	86 997	..	..	97 957
New Zealand	5 359	4 657	4 753	5 144	..	7 258	7 412	..
Nicaragua	178	191	204	..	224	..	201	220
Norway	26 461	20 647	20 210	20 407	21 993	22 064	21 331	27 534
Panama	..	..	..	..	..	1 707	1 670	1 798
Paraguay	..	428	368	390	..	438	..	404
Peru	3 602	3 709	3 354	3 500	3 938	4 263	4 051	4 588
Poland	17 412	14 539	14 213	16 495	17 211	16 627	16 266	17 922
Portugal	18 667	13 945	12 079	12 941	14 868	13 338	11 050	15 574
Puerto Rico	9 108	11 145	13 470	..	..	..	..	..
Singapore	30 379	30 331	33 160	36 830	..	44 929	51 049	60 341
Slovak Republic	2 986	2 400	..	5 047	..	2 823	2 791	2 731
Slovenia	2 783	2 386	2 416	2 596	2 863	2 963	3 123	3 401
South Africa	51 527	47 054	42 473	..	..	..	43 650	54 262
Spain	76 604	65 514	73 655	74 242	78 578	74 106	71 530	76 473
Sri Lanka	746	931	..	1 128	1 147	..	..	..
Sweden	49 890	40 254	39 107	44 382	49 044	48 704	55 220	73 097
Switzerland	74 480	70 367	67 483	67 772	69 456	69 986	69 040	70 929
Chinese Taipei	..	..	..	..	207 626	204 499	114 520	114 849
Thailand	..	..	..	..	..	..	..	..
Tunisia	..	..	864	909	..	..	..	..
Türkiye	12 314	11 775	13 718	13 074	11 333	12 126	12 215	12 425
United Kingdom	365 688	336 743	403 794	394 929	471 031	418 559	380 954	445 432
United States	2 431 323	2 621 083	2 703 793	2 836 293	2 632 284	2 773 916	2 934 829	3 242 715
Uruguay	1 303	1 277	..	1 576	..	1 554	1 463	1 600
OECD Total	4 961 922	4 852 388	5 215 041	5 346 884	5 311 380	5 031 218	5 225 023	..

.. Not available

Note: Detailed metadata at: *http://metalinks.oecd.org/ins/20230516/99ff*.

Source: *Insurance activity indicators, OECD Insurance Statistics (database)*

Table 8. Total gross premiums (Life)

Million US dollars

	2014	2015	2016	2017	2018	2019	2020	2021
Argentina	3 076	2 966	3 158	2 724	2 886	1 716	1 606	1 718
Australia	59 315	46 633	41 066	37 668	34 664	26 477	21 205	23 499
Austria	8 901	7 440	6 701	6 493	6 543	6 065	..	..
Belgium	21 664	17 045	16 560	16 547	18 437	18 181	16 819	18 472
Bermuda	..	..	..	..	..	80 400	172 566	126 792
Bolivia	..	..	157	202	238	274	296	309
Brazil	42 061	34 819	38 935	44 172	40 919	43 685	33 374	35 584
Bulgaria	..	..	..	..	216	212	209	311
Canada	26 712	24 001	23 795	25 754	26 213	..	..	..
Chile	7 224	7 795	8 726	8 930	9 633	8 641	5 956	6 655
Colombia	4 604	3 727	3 877	4 567	4 710	4 750	4 202	4 781
Costa Rica	142	133	186	194	215	227	215	238
Cuba	..	..	..	..	..	..	..	..
Czech Republic	3 429	2 537	2 435	2 451	2 583	2 314	2 229	2 408
Denmark	25 124	22 055	23 001	25 945	28 664	27 518	29 832	34 271
Dominican Republic	..	..	..	..	196	..	..	..
Ecuador	..	453	471	..	..	524	..	23
Egypt	..	..	..	..	..	860	1 157	1 538
El Salvador	147	156	153	..	165	180	196	489
Estonia	254	238	245	252	275	283	304	351
Finland	8 108	6 943	5 063	5 115	5 156	6 744	4 611	6 051
France	188 634	160 946	182 414	173 606	186 967	185 390	150 513	196 502
Germany	121 746	99 628	97 651	99 769	106 802	112 711	116 213	118 632
Greece	2 500	2 000	1 846	2 125	2 220	2 310	2 402	2 874
Guatemala	156	156	170	196	197	213	223	270
Honduras	134	145	..	..	210	201	163	190
Hong Kong, China	37 459	41 972	53 421	58 134	62 257	..	..	72 604
Hungary	1 965	1 529	1 559	1 679	1 742	1 751	1 722	1 988
Iceland	36	35	43	54	54	51	49	57
India	..	55 415	..	71 312	..	80 314	..	..
Indonesia	9 490	10 093	12 560	14 530	13 832	13 941	12 744	14 312
Ireland	43 221	38 853	37 127	39 617	36 272	35 902	34 495	46 968
Israel	7 426	7 568	7 986	9 368	10 016	10 615	10 546	11 595
Italy	148 645	129 077	114 779	112 984	122 310	118 872	115 896	125 497
Japan	347 080	313 822	328 210	293 005	302 966	292 247	276 258	270 596
Korea	106 200	104 820	104 530	102 221	102 538	..	101 326	103 896
Latvia	142	128	137	164	171	255	275	305
Lithuania	286	262	273	261	293	303	332	378
Luxembourg	27 166	19 641	18 568	22 318	22 523	25 512	21 362	30 494
Malaysia	10 594	9 306	9 317	9 603	10 709	11 628	11 912	12 977
Mexico	12 812	11 530	11 266	11 421	12 672	14 118	12 856	14 880
Montenegro	..	..	..	..	..	..	..	..
Morocco	..	..	..	..	..	..	..	2 581
Netherlands	23 202	16 307	15 198	14 654	14 136	..	..	21 155
New Zealand	..	..	..	..	..	1 714	1 689	..
Nicaragua	32	33	38	..	46	..	38	41
Norway	14 629	11 383	11 202	11 313	12 291	12 351	11 277	16 006
Panama	..	..	..	..	..	428	429	233
Paraguay	..	57	1	54	..	58	..	64
Peru	1 768	1 794	1 519	1 644	1 909	2 082	1 908	2 378
Poland	9 087	7 302	6 051	6 499	6 009	5 541	5 322	5 728
Portugal	13 617	9 411	7 200	7 581	9 188	7 567	4 901	8 785
Puerto Rico	570	542	1 279	..	..	..	..	..
Singapore	20 808	21 033	23 739	27 593	..	30 926	38 835	46 257
Slovak Republic	1 621	1 229	..	3 712	..	1 372	1 334	1 250
Slovenia	637	552	545	582	621	617	596	676
South Africa	41 476	37 576	33 870	..	..	..	33 634	42 999
Spain	33 612	28 532	34 695	33 262	34 263	30 780	26 559	28 209
Sri Lanka	265	395	..	467	474	..	..	..
Sweden	34 734	29 507	29 302	33 761	37 087	36 812	42 426	58 754
Switzerland	36 140	34 407	31 672	30 486	30 835	30 562	26 668	25 829
Chinese Taipei	..	..	..	..	201 388	197 955	107 233	106 351
Thailand	..	..	..	..	..	..	..	..
Tunisia	..	..	175	179	..	..	..	..
Türkiye	1 510	1 390	2 048	2 268	1 801	2 433	2 449	2 364
United Kingdom	268 267	246 702	277 703	272 461	339 319	304 010	268 648	313 983
United States	880 040	973 634	970 503	1 009 291	1 139 513	1 180 619	1 242 994	1 382 902
Uruguay	384	427	..	665	..	686	669	750
OECD Total	2 490 435	2 388 744	2 424 160	2 428 380	2 669 703	2 515 617	2 564 482	2 887 028

.. Not available

Note: Detailed metadata at: *http://metalinks.oecd.org/ins/20230516/99ff*.

Source: *Insurance activity indicators, OECD Insurance Statistics (database)*

Table 9. Total gross premiums (Non-life)

Million US dollars

	2014	2015	2016	2017	2018	2019	2020	2021
Argentina	15 546	16 410	16 591	15 795	17 251	10 859	10 781	11 525
Australia	37 695	32 163	33 079	34 671	35 328	34 800	36 192	43 224
Austria	16 201	13 651	13 946	13 992	15 337	15 025	..	..
Belgium	16 681	13 701	13 871	14 292	15 266	16 971	17 598	22 599
Bermuda	..	..	..	..	..	71 001	77 033	93 620
Bolivia	..	..	312	297	311	336	332	345
Brazil	27 806	20 699	19 979	22 258	20 543	19 305	15 297	16 719
Bulgaria	..	..	..	..	1 315	1 454	1 469	1 653
Canada	66 477	59 610	58 115	61 654	60 799	..	..	..
Chile	3 751	3 619	3 676	3 930	4 373	4 252	4 033	4 934
Colombia	5 089	4 276	4 170	4 411	4 699	4 639	4 218	4 857
Costa Rica	1 014	916	1 024	1 125	1 118	1 191	1 225	1 212
Cuba	..	..	..	..	..	..	..	..
Czech Republic	4 179	3 636	3 566	3 951	4 469	4 901	4 987	5 857
Denmark	11 974	9 943	10 497	11 604	12 312	11 071	11 166	12 500
Dominican Republic	..	..	..	..	1 026	..	..	..
Ecuador	..	1 864	1 665	..	..	1 274	..	1 701
Egypt	..	..	..	..	..	1 108	1 346	1 501
El Salvador	412	437	446	..	493	522	526	337
Estonia	584	526	570	672	817	818	766	835
Finland	6 017	4 974	4 949	4 968	..	..	..	..
France	105 399	89 928	131 837	140 713	151 741	147 082	152 216	166 001
Germany	217 018	193 459	197 010	211 439	228 866	231 557	249 684	278 086
Greece	2 556	1 964	2 063	2 088	2 265	2 227	2 287	2 455
Guatemala	593	648	685	757	767	792	825	900
Honduras	246	253	..	..	421	424	314	358
Hong Kong, China	5 661	5 929	5 880	6 177	6 832	..	..	7 955
Hungary	1 619	1 462	1 588	1 804	2 025	2 204	2 188	2 398
Iceland	408	384	444	556	598	561	496	577
India	..	15 463	..	29 529	..	27 504	..	..
Indonesia	4 835	4 537	4 730	4 954	5 136	5 823	5 354	5 412
Ireland	9 335	9 949	17 055	9 625	10 006	12 517	12 319	11 761
Israel	6 940	6 548	7 156	8 059	8 544	8 709	8 967	10 183
Italy	44 811	36 777	36 645	37 748	41 470	39 369	39 855	42 974
Japan	..	..	106 527	97 090	99 808	106 841	108 777	105 352
Korea	80 890	78 855	81 063	87 270	90 330	..	97 453	105 572
Latvia	546	462	452	566	721	704	636	699
Lithuania	513	454	513	634	744	756	759	854
Luxembourg	1 779	1 637	1 720	1 996	2 016	2 618	2 812	4 302
Malaysia	6 994	6 041	5 782	5 553	6 007	6 039	6 156	6 926
Mexico	14 536	13 399	12 884	15 148	15 578	17 228	15 446	18 204
Montenegro	..	..	..	..	..	..	..	..
Morocco	..	..	..	..	..	..	..	3 251
Netherlands	25 401	21 093	62 160	64 818	71 621	..	..	76 802
New Zealand	5 359	4 657	4 753	5 144	..	5 544	5 723	..
Nicaragua	146	158	166	..	178	..	162	179
Norway	11 833	9 264	9 008	9 094	9 702	9 713	10 054	11 527
Panama	..	..	..	..	..	1 279	1 242	1 564
Paraguay	..	371	367	335	..	380	..	340
Peru	1 834	1 916	1 835	1 856	2 029	2 181	2 143	2 209
Poland	8 325	7 237	8 162	9 996	11 202	11 086	10 944	12 195
Portugal	5 050	4 534	4 879	5 360	5 680	5 771	6 149	6 789
Puerto Rico	8 538	10 603	12 191	..	..	..	..	..
Singapore	9 571	9 298	9 421	9 238	..	14 003	12 215	14 083
Slovak Republic	1 366	1 171	..	1 335	..	1 451	1 457	1 481
Slovenia	2 146	1 833	1 871	2 014	2 242	2 346	2 526	2 725
South Africa	10 051	9 478	8 602	..	..	..	10 016	11 264
Spain	42 992	36 982	38 959	40 979	44 315	43 325	44 971	48 264
Sri Lanka	481	535	..	661	673	..	..	..
Sweden	15 156	10 746	9 805	10 621	11 957	11 892	12 793	14 343
Switzerland	38 340	35 959	35 811	37 287	38 621	39 424	42 372	45 100
Chinese Taipei	..	..	..	..	6 238	6 544	7 288	8 498
Thailand	..	..	..	..	..	..	..	..
Tunisia	..	..	689	730	..	..	..	..
Türkiye	10 804	10 386	11 670	10 806	9 532	9 693	9 765	10 061
United Kingdom	97 421	90 041	126 091	122 469	131 712	114 549	112 306	131 449
United States	1 551 283	1 647 449	1 733 290	1 827 002	1 492 771	1 593 297	1 691 835	1 859 813
Uruguay	918	850	..	911	..	868	794	850
OECD Total	2 471 487	2 463 645	2 790 882	2 916 932	2 638 586	2 514 130	2 724 976	3 065 983

.. Not available

Note: Detailed metadata at: *http://metalinks.oecd.org/ins/20230516/99ff*.

Source: *Insurance activity indicators, OECD Insurance Statistics (database)*

Table 10. Market share in OECD (Life and Non-life)

Per cent

	2014	2015	2016	2017	2018	2019	2020	2021
Australia	2.0	1.6	1.4	1.4	1.3	1.2	1.1	1.1
Austria	0.5	0.4	0.4	0.4	0.4	0.4	..	..
Belgium	0.8	0.6	0.6	0.6	0.6	0.7	0.7	0.7
Canada	1.9	1.7	1.6	1.6	1.6	..	..	..
Chile	0.2	0.2	0.2	0.2	0.3	0.3	0.2	0.2
Colombia	0.2	0.2	0.2	0.2	0.2	0.2	0.2	0.2
Costa Rica	0.0	0.0	0.0	0.0	0.0	0.0	0.0	0.0
Czech Republic	0.2	0.1	0.1	0.1	0.1	0.1	0.1	0.1
Denmark	0.7	0.7	0.6	0.7	0.8	0.8	0.8	0.8
Estonia	0.0	0.0	0.0	0.0	0.0	0.0	0.0	0.0
Finland	0.3	0.2	0.2	0.2	0.1	0.1	0.1	0.1
France	5.9	5.2	6.0	5.9	6.4	6.6	5.7	6.1
Germany	6.8	6.0	5.7	5.8	6.3	6.8	6.9	6.7
Greece	0.1	0.1	0.1	0.1	0.1	0.1	0.1	0.1
Hungary	0.1	0.1	0.1	0.1	0.1	0.1	0.1	0.1
Iceland	0.0	0.0	0.0	0.0	0.0	0.0	0.0	0.0
Ireland	1.1	1.0	1.0	0.9	0.9	1.0	0.9	1.0
Israel	0.3	0.3	0.3	0.3	0.3	0.4	0.4	0.4
Italy	3.9	3.4	2.9	2.8	3.1	3.1	2.9	2.8
Japan	7.0	6.5	8.3	7.3	7.6	7.9	7.3	6.3
Korea	3.8	3.8	3.6	3.5	3.6	..	3.8	3.5
Latvia	0.0	0.0	0.0	0.0	0.0	0.0	0.0	0.0
Lithuania	0.0	0.0	0.0	0.0	0.0	0.0	0.0	0.0
Luxembourg	0.6	0.4	0.4	0.5	0.5	0.6	0.5	0.6
Mexico	0.6	0.5	0.5	0.5	0.5	0.6	0.5	0.6
Netherlands	1.0	0.8	1.5	1.5	1.6	..	..	1.6
New Zealand	0.1	0.1	0.1	0.1	..	0.1	0.1	..
Norway	0.5	0.4	0.4	0.4	0.4	0.4	0.4	0.5
Poland	0.4	0.3	0.3	0.3	0.3	0.3	0.3	0.3
Portugal	0.4	0.3	0.2	0.2	0.3	0.3	0.2	0.3
Slovak Republic	0.1	0.0	..	0.1	..	0.1	0.1	0.0
Slovenia	0.1	0.0	0.0	0.0	0.1	0.1	0.1	0.1
Spain	1.5	1.4	1.4	1.4	1.5	1.5	1.4	1.3
Sweden	1.0	0.8	0.8	0.8	0.9	1.0	1.0	1.2
Switzerland	1.5	1.5	1.3	1.3	1.3	1.4	1.3	1.2
Türkiye	0.2	0.2	0.3	0.2	0.2	0.2	0.2	0.2
United Kingdom	7.4	6.9	7.7	7.4	8.9	8.3	7.2	7.5
United States	49.0	54.0	51.8	53.0	49.6	55.1	55.5	54.5
OECD Total	100.0	100.0	100.0	100.0	100.0	100.0	100.0	100.0

.. Not available

Note: Detailed metadata at: *http://metalinks.oecd.org/ins/20230516/99ff.*

Source: *Insurance activity indicators, OECD Insurance Statistics (database)*

Table 11. Market share in OECD (Life)

Per cent

	2014	2015	2016	2017	2018	2019	2020	2021
Australia	2.4	2.0	1.7	1.6	1.3	1.1	0.8	0.8
Austria	0.4	0.3	0.3	0.3	0.2	0.2	..	..
Belgium	0.9	0.7	0.7	0.7	0.7	0.7	0.7	0.6
Canada	1.1	1.0	1.0	1.1	1.0	..	..	..
Chile	0.3	0.3	0.4	0.4	0.4	0.3	0.2	0.2
Colombia	0.2	0.2	0.2	0.2	0.2	0.2	0.2	0.2
Costa Rica	0.0	0.0	0.0	0.0	0.0	0.0	0.0	0.0
Czech Republic	0.1	0.1	0.1	0.1	0.1	0.1	0.1	0.1
Denmark	1.0	0.9	0.9	1.1	1.1	1.1	1.2	1.2
Estonia	0.0	0.0	0.0	0.0	0.0	0.0	0.0	0.0
Finland	0.3	0.3	0.2	0.2	0.2	0.3	0.2	0.2
France	7.6	6.7	7.5	7.1	7.0	7.4	5.9	6.8
Germany	4.9	4.2	4.0	4.1	4.0	4.5	4.5	4.1
Greece	0.1	0.1	0.1	0.1	0.1	0.1	0.1	0.1
Hungary	0.1	0.1	0.1	0.1	0.1	0.1	0.1	0.1
Iceland	0.0	0.0	0.0	0.0	0.0	0.0	0.0	0.0
Ireland	1.7	1.6	1.5	1.6	1.4	1.4	1.3	1.6
Israel	0.3	0.3	0.3	0.4	0.4	0.4	0.4	0.4
Italy	6.0	5.4	4.7	4.7	4.6	4.7	4.5	4.3
Japan	13.9	13.1	13.5	12.1	11.3	11.6	10.8	9.4
Korea	4.3	4.4	4.3	4.2	3.8	..	4.0	3.6
Latvia	0.0	0.0	0.0	0.0	0.0	0.0	0.0	0.0
Lithuania	0.0	0.0	0.0	0.0	0.0	0.0	0.0	0.0
Luxembourg	1.1	0.8	0.8	0.9	0.8	1.0	0.8	1.1
Mexico	0.5	0.5	0.5	0.5	0.5	0.6	0.5	0.5
Netherlands	0.9	0.7	0.6	0.6	0.5	..	..	0.7
New Zealand	..	..	..	..	..	0.1	0.1	..
Norway	0.6	0.5	0.5	0.5	0.5	0.5	0.4	0.6
Poland	0.4	0.3	0.3	0.3	0.2	0.2	0.2	0.2
Portugal	0.5	0.4	0.3	0.3	0.3	0.3	0.2	0.3
Slovak Republic	0.1	0.1	..	0.2	..	0.1	0.1	0.0
Slovenia	0.0	0.0	0.0	0.0	0.0	0.0	0.0	0.0
Spain	1.4	1.2	1.4	1.4	1.3	1.2	1.0	1.0
Sweden	1.4	1.2	1.2	1.4	1.4	1.5	1.7	2.0
Switzerland	1.5	1.4	1.3	1.3	1.2	1.2	1.0	0.9
Türkiye	0.1	0.1	0.1	0.1	0.1	0.1	0.1	0.1
United Kingdom	10.8	10.3	11.5	11.2	12.7	12.1	10.5	10.9
United States	35.3	40.8	40.0	41.6	42.7	46.9	48.5	47.9
OECD Total	100.0	100.0	100.0	100.0	100.0	100.0	100.0	100.0

.. Not available

Note: Detailed metadata at: *http://metalinks.oecd.org/ins/20230516/99ff.*

Source: *Insurance activity indicators, OECD Insurance Statistics (database)*

Table 12. Market share in OECD (Non-life)

Per cent

	2014	2015	2016	2017	2018	2019	2020	2021
Australia	1.5	1.3	1.2	1.2	1.3	1.4	1.3	1.4
Austria	0.7	0.6	0.5	0.5	0.6	0.6	..	..
Belgium	0.7	0.6	0.5	0.5	0.6	0.7	0.6	0.7
Canada	2.7	2.4	2.1	2.1	2.3	..	..	..
Chile	0.2	0.1	0.1	0.1	0.2	0.2	0.1	0.2
Colombia	0.2	0.2	0.1	0.2	0.2	0.2	0.2	0.2
Costa Rica	0.0	0.0	0.0	0.0	0.0	0.0	0.0	0.0
Czech Republic	0.2	0.1	0.1	0.1	0.2	0.2	0.2	0.2
Denmark	0.5	0.4	0.4	0.4	0.5	0.4	0.4	0.4
Estonia	0.0	0.0	0.0	0.0	0.0	0.0	0.0	0.0
Finland	0.2	0.2	0.2	0.2	..	..	..	..
France	4.3	3.7	4.7	4.8	5.8	5.9	5.6	5.4
Germany	8.8	7.9	7.1	7.2	8.7	9.2	9.2	9.1
Greece	0.1	0.1	0.1	0.1	0.1	0.1	0.1	0.1
Hungary	0.1	0.1	0.1	0.1	0.1	0.1	0.1	0.1
Iceland	0.0	0.0	0.0	0.0	0.0	0.0	0.0	0.0
Ireland	0.4	0.4	0.6	0.3	0.4	0.5	0.5	0.4
Israel	0.3	0.3	0.3	0.3	0.3	0.3	0.3	0.3
Italy	1.8	1.5	1.3	1.3	1.6	1.6	1.5	1.4
Japan	..	..	3.8	3.3	3.8	4.3	4.0	3.4
Korea	3.3	3.2	2.9	3.0	3.4	..	3.6	3.4
Latvia	0.0	0.0	0.0	0.0	0.0	0.0	0.0	0.0
Lithuania	0.0	0.0	0.0	0.0	0.0	0.0	0.0	0.0
Luxembourg	0.1	0.1	0.1	0.1	0.1	0.1	0.1	0.1
Mexico	0.6	0.5	0.5	0.5	0.6	0.7	0.6	0.6
Netherlands	1.0	0.9	2.2	2.2	2.7	..	..	2.5
New Zealand	0.2	0.2	0.2	0.2	..	0.2	0.2	..
Norway	0.5	0.4	0.3	0.3	0.4	0.4	0.4	0.4
Poland	0.3	0.3	0.3	0.3	0.4	0.4	0.4	0.4
Portugal	0.2	0.2	0.2	0.2	0.2	0.2	0.2	0.2
Slovak Republic	0.1	0.0	..	0.0	..	0.1	0.1	0.0
Slovenia	0.1	0.1	0.1	0.1	0.1	0.1	0.1	0.1
Spain	1.7	1.5	1.4	1.4	1.7	1.7	1.7	1.6
Sweden	0.6	0.4	0.4	0.4	0.5	0.5	0.5	0.5
Switzerland	1.6	1.5	1.3	1.3	1.5	1.6	1.6	1.5
Türkiye	0.4	0.4	0.4	0.4	0.4	0.4	0.4	0.3
United Kingdom	3.9	3.7	4.5	4.2	5.0	4.6	4.1	4.3
United States	62.8	66.9	62.1	62.6	56.6	63.4	62.1	60.7
OECD Total	100.0	100.0	100.0	100.0	100.0	100.0	100.0	100.0

.. Not available

Note: Detailed metadata at: *http://metalinks.oecd.org/ins/20230516/99ff.*

Source: *Insurance activity indicators, OECD Insurance Statistics (database)*

Table 13. Density (Life and Non-life)

US dollar per inhabitant

	2014	2015	2016	2017	2018	2019	2020	2021
Argentina	405	418	422	393	428	264	258	274
Australia	3 688	2 926	2 660	2 540	2 383	2 011	1 839	2 124
Austria	2 657	2 227	2 143	2 176	2 284	2 219	2 285	2 433
Belgium	3 308	2 653	2 613	2 653	2 903	2 853	2 744	3 233
Bermuda	..	..	..	..	..	..	..	..
Bolivia	..	..	42	43	47	50	51	52
Brazil	346	273	287	321	295	300	230	246
Bulgaria	..	..	..	..	214	236	239	281
Canada	2 168	1 930	1 919	2 010	2 085	..	..	..
Chile	613	630	675	692	740	668	508	581
Colombia	207	169	169	186	191	186	164	185
Costa Rica	241	216	246	265	265	278	280	279
Cuba	..	..	..	..	..	..	..	..
Czech Republic	712	574	555	590	651	663	660	756
Denmark	6 543	5 610	5 699	6 315	6 842	6 486	6 911	7 854
Dominican Republic	..	..	..	..	119	..	..	..
Ecuador	..	139	127	98	100	103	..	97
Egypt	..	..	..	14	17	19	24	29
El Salvador	..	..	..	..	97	103	104	115
Estonia	638	581	619	702	826	830	805	892
Finland	2 556	2 150	1 797	1 803	935	1 221	835	1 093
France	4 110	3 554	4 108	4 246	4 560	4 453	4 052	4 812
Germany	3 131	2 597	2 602	2 838	3 049	3 090	3 233	3 421
Greece	457	361	359	388	414	419	434	496
Guatemala	46	48	50	55	54	55	56	62
Honduras	42	44	..	..	66	64	48	54
Hong Kong, China	5 658	6 259	7 651	8 264	8 801	..	10 284	10 200
Hungary	360	300	317	350	381	401	397	448
Iceland	1 329	1 245	1 436	1 783	1 840	1 684	1 495	1 714
India	..	54	62	71	..	78	82	..
Indonesia	55	56	66	73	71	72	65	71
Ireland	11 052	10 154	11 107	10 207	9 554	9 492	9 263	11 532
Israel	1 749	1 685	1 772	2 001	2 090	2 135	2 118	2 325
Italy	3 148	2 700	2 465	2 458	2 669	2 619	2 575	2 796
Japan	2 580	2 370	3 201	2 893	3 010	2 989	2 888	2 832
Korea	3 503	3 418	3 437	3 483	3 506	3 532	3 631	3 832
Latvia	343	297	299	374	461	500	477	531
Lithuania	272	246	274	317	370	379	390	441
Luxembourg	51 995	37 506	35 103	41 043	40 668	43 263	36 152	51 843
Malaysia	530	454	441	439	481	508	513	552
Mexico	224	202	194	210	222	243	216	250
Montenegro	..	..	..	..	..	170	171	..
Morocco	..	..	..	115	124	..	..	152
Netherlands	2 846	2 176	4 532	4 626	4 971	4 857	5 035	5 458
New Zealand	1 178	971	989	1 012	..	1 455	1 456	..
Nicaragua	29	30	32	34	35	31	31	34
Norway	5 132	3 967	3 972	3 858	4 131	4 119	3 961	5 085
Panama	..	..	..	..	..	372	355	371
Paraguay	..	63	53	56	61	61	59	55
Peru	116	118	106	109	122	128	120	135
Poland	453	372	361	420	436	418	409	451
Portugal	1 735	1 293	1 110	1 189	1 369	1 225	996	1 423
Puerto Rico	2 552	3 182	3 927	..	..	..	..	..
Singapore	4 489	4 400	4 631	5 411	..	5 764	6 537	8 304
Slovak Republic	544	434	..	927	..	518	510	498
Slovenia	1 198	1 012	1 028	1 105	1 223	1 250	1 287	1 393
South Africa	923	830	733	..	..	..	702	874
Spain	1 521	1 295	1 456	1 467	1 550	1 446	1 347	1 464
Sri Lanka	35	44	..	51	52	..	..	..
Sweden	4 908	3 961	3 796	4 248	4 646	4 572	5 163	6 811
Switzerland	7 892	7 456	7 025	6 904	6 962	6 879	6 646	6 682
Chinese Taipei	..	..	..	..	5 181	4 991	4 809	4 852
Thailand	..	..	..	..	..	..	..	..
Tunisia	..	..	75	75	72	70	76	83
Türkiye	151	145	162	152	126	131	131	134
United Kingdom	5 098	4 598	3 950	5 123	5 672	5 044	4 591	5 317
United States	5 970	6 305	6 500	6 718	7 089	7 498	7 902	8 565
Uruguay	377	368	..	451	425	442	414	452
OECD Total	3 177	3 042	3 192	3 298	3 494	3 559	3 600	..

.. Not available

Note: Detailed metadata at: *http://metalinks.oecd.org/ins/20230516/99ff*.

Source: *Insurance activity indicators, OECD Insurance Statistics (database)*

Table 14. Density (Life)

US dollar per inhabitant

	2014	2015	2016	2017	2018	2019	2020	2021
Argentina	70	67	70	60	63	37	34	36
Australia	2 321	1 781	1 521	1 335	1 180	847	639	708
Austria	1 039	860	765	735	735	683	683	707
Belgium	1 930	1 512	1 458	1 454	1 613	1 580	1 457	1 595
Bermuda	..	..	..	..	..	..	..	..
Bolivia	..	..	14	17	20	22	24	25
Brazil	209	171	190	214	196	208	158	167
Bulgaria	..	..	..	..	29	29	28	43
Canada	629	555	561	604	625	..	..	..
Chile	406	432	475	481	509	448	304	335
Colombia	100	80	83	96	98	96	83	94
Costa Rica	30	27	38	39	43	45	42	46
Cuba	..	..	..	..	..	..	..	..
Czech Republic	326	241	229	230	242	215	206	223
Denmark	4 443	3 878	4 006	4 495	4 939	4 719	5 098	5 833
Dominican Republic	..	..	..	..	19	..	..	..
Ecuador	..	28	28	27	30	30	..	1
Egypt	..	..	..	6	7	9	11	15
El Salvador	..	..	..	..	24	26	28	66
Estonia	193	181	186	191	208	213	229	264
Finland	1 485	1 268	923	929	935	1 221	835	1 093
France	2 684	2 344	2 391	2 449	2 636	2 576	2 111	2 752
Germany	1 456	1 180	1 148	1 197	1 282	1 350	1 383	1 420
Greece	228	184	171	197	207	215	224	269
Guatemala	10	9	10	11	11	12	12	15
Honduras	15	16	..	..	22	21	16	19
Hong Kong, China	5 082	5 644	7 040	7 640	8 147	..	9 513	9 399
Hungary	199	155	159	171	178	179	176	204
Iceland	111	107	128	161	155	142	134	155
India	..	42	47	53	..	59	62	..
Indonesia	38	39	49	56	52	52	47	53
Ireland	9 158	8 141	7 729	8 198	7 413	7 231	6 887	9 303
Israel	904	903	935	1 076	1 128	1 173	1 145	1 238
Italy	2 431	2 113	1 879	1 853	2 012	1 981	1 938	2 114
Japan	2 580	2 370	2 496	2 252	2 348	2 277	2 161	2 127
Korea	2 070	2 032	2 015	1 962	1 952	1 946	1 957	2 010
Latvia	71	64	70	84	89	133	144	161
Lithuania	97	90	95	92	105	108	119	135
Luxembourg	48 768	34 604	32 123	37 673	37 331	39 401	32 104	45 860
Malaysia	340	294	290	295	325	354	361	392
Mexico	106	95	91	92	101	111	100	115
Montenegro	..	..	..	..	..	31	36	..
Morocco	..	..	..	51	55	..	..	71
Netherlands	1 378	964	895	857	823	804	803	1 119
New Zealand	..	..	..	..	..	343	332	..
Nicaragua	5	5	6	7	7	6	6	6
Norway	2 837	2 187	2 133	2 139	2 309	2 306	2 094	2 956
Panama	..	..	..	..	..	96	93	45
Paraguay	..	8	0	8	9	8	9	9
Peru	57	57	48	52	59	63	57	70
Poland	239	192	159	171	158	146	140	151
Portugal	1 309	908	697	736	893	736	476	852
Puerto Rico	161	156	373	..	..	..	..	..
Singapore	3 392	3 404	3 611	4 374	..	4 537	5 356	6 932
Slovak Republic	299	227	..	683	..	252	243	228
Slovenia	309	268	264	282	300	297	285	320
South Africa	760	678	602	..	..	..	564	715
Spain	712	606	736	705	722	643	519	582
Sri Lanka	13	19	..	22	22	..	..	..
Sweden	3 562	2 994	2 931	3 335	3 625	3 564	4 087	5 621
Switzerland	4 378	4 113	3 739	3 573	3 592	3 533	3 055	2 925
Chinese Taipei	..	..	..	..	4 948	4 749	4 539	4 536
Thailand	..	..	..	..	..	..	..	..
Tunisia	..	..	15	15	16	16	18	21
Türkiye	19	17	25	27	21	28	28	27
United Kingdom	3 781	3 411	2 508	3 696	4 155	3 828	3 386	3 959
United States	2 475	2 576	2 587	2 641	2 782	2 947	3 123	3 349
Uruguay	111	123	..	190	169	195	189	212
OECD Total	1 758	1 639	1 593	1 646	1 744	1 767	1 734	1 915

.. Not available

Note: Detailed metadata at: *http://metalinks.oecd.org/ins/20230516/99ff.*

Source: *Insurance activity indicators, OECD Insurance Statistics (database)*

Table 15. Density (Non-life)

US dollar per inhabitant

	2014	2015	2016	2017	2018	2019	2020	2021
Argentina	335	351	352	333	365	227	224	238
Australia	1 367	1 145	1 139	1 206	1 203	1 164	1 200	1 416
Austria	1 617	1 367	1 377	1 441	1 550	1 536	1 602	1 726
Belgium	1 378	1 142	1 156	1 200	1 290	1 273	1 286	1 638
Bermuda	..	..	..	..	..	..	..	..
Bolivia	..	..	28	26	27	28	27	27
Brazil	138	102	97	108	99	92	72	79
Bulgaria	..	..	..	..	184	207	210	238
Canada	1 539	1 375	1 358	1 407	1 460	..	..	..
Chile	208	198	200	211	231	220	204	247
Colombia	107	89	86	90	94	90	81	91
Costa Rica	211	188	208	226	222	234	238	233
Cuba	..	..	..	..	..	..	..	..
Czech Republic	386	333	325	360	409	447	454	534
Denmark	2 101	1 732	1 692	1 820	1 903	1 767	1 813	2 020
Dominican Republic	..	..	..	..	100	..	..	..
Ecuador	..	112	98	71	71	73	..	95
Egypt	..	..	..	8	10	10	13	14
El Salvador	..	..	..	..	73	76	76	49
Estonia	444	400	433	510	618	617	577	628
Finland	1 071	882	875	873	..	..	..	..
France	1 427	1 209	1 717	1 797	1 924	1 877	1 941	2 060
Germany	1 674	1 417	1 454	1 641	1 767	1 740	1 850	2 001
Greece	229	177	188	190	207	204	210	226
Guatemala	36	39	40	43	43	44	44	47
Honduras	27	28	..	..	44	43	32	35
Hong Kong, China	577	615	611	624	654	..	770	801
Hungary	161	145	158	179	203	222	221	244
Iceland	1 217	1 138	1 308	1 621	1 685	1 542	1 361	1 560
India	..	11	15	18	..	20	20	..
Indonesia	18	17	17	18	18	20	17	19
Ireland	1 894	2 013	3 378	1 890	1 915	2 116	2 254	2 229
Israel	845	782	838	925	962	962	973	1 087
Italy	717	587	586	605	657	638	637	682
Japan	..	..	705	641	662	712	727	705
Korea	1 433	1 386	1 421	1 521	1 554	1 586	1 674	1 821
Latvia	273	232	230	290	373	366	333	369
Lithuania	175	156	179	224	265	271	271	306
Luxembourg	3 227	2 902	2 980	3 370	3 337	3 862	4 048	5 984
Malaysia	190	160	150	144	156	155	152	159
Mexico	118	107	102	119	121	132	116	136
Montenegro	..	..	..	..	..	140	135	..
Morocco	..	..	..	64	69	..	..	81
Netherlands	1 467	1 212	3 637	3 768	4 148	4 053	4 233	4 338
New Zealand	1 178	971	989	1 012	..	1 111	1 125	..
Nicaragua	24	25	26	28	28	25	25	27
Norway	2 295	1 780	1 840	1 719	1 822	1 813	1 867	2 129
Panama	..	..	..	..	..	275	262	326
Paraguay	..	54	53	48	53	53	50	46
Peru	59	61	58	58	62	65	63	65
Poland	214	180	202	249	278	272	268	299
Portugal	426	385	413	454	476	490	521	571
Puerto Rico	2 391	3 026	3 554	..	..	..	..	..
Singapore	1 098	996	1 021	1 037	..	1 227	1 181	1 372
Slovak Republic	244	207	..	244	..	266	267	270
Slovenia	889	744	765	823	923	953	1 002	1 072
South Africa	163	152	131	..	..	..	138	159
Spain	809	690	721	763	828	804	828	881
Sri Lanka	22	25	..	30	30	..	..	..
Sweden	1 346	967	865	913	1 021	1 008	1 076	1 190
Switzerland	3 514	3 343	3 286	3 331	3 370	3 346	3 591	3 757
Chinese Taipei	..	..	..	..	233	243	270	317
Thailand	..	..	..	..	..	..	..	..
Tunisia	..	..	60	59	56	54	58	62
Türkiye	131	128	137	125	105	103	103	108
United Kingdom	1 317	1 188	1 441	1 427	1 517	1 216	1 205	1 358
United States	3 495	3 729	3 913	4 077	4 308	4 551	4 779	5 216
Uruguay	266	245	..	261	256	247	225	240
OECD Total	1 419	1 403	1 598	1 652	1 750	1 792	1 870	2 032

.. Not available

Note: Detailed metadata at: *http://metalinks.oecd.org/ins/20230516/99ff*.

Source: *Insurance activity indicators, OECD Insurance Statistics (database)*

Table 16. Penetration (Life and Non-life)

Per cent

	2014	2015	2016	2017	2018	2019	2020	2021
Argentina	2.4	2.6	2.6	2.6	2.3	2.1	2.5	2.2
Australia	6.0	5.7	5.1	4.6	4.2	3.7	3.5	3.3
Austria	5.1	5.0	4.7	4.6	4.5	4.4	4.7	4.6
Belgium	6.9	6.4	6.2	6.0	6.1	6.1	6.1	6.2
Bermuda	..	..	..	..	..	..	..	..
Bolivia	..	..	1.4	1.3	1.3	1.4	1.6	1.6
Brazil	2.8	3.1	3.3	3.2	3.2	3.4	3.4	3.3
Bulgaria	..	..	..	..	2.3	2.4	2.4	2.4
Canada	4.2	4.4	4.5	4.4	4.5	..	..	..
Chile	4.2	4.7	4.9	4.6	4.7	4.6	3.9	3.6
Colombia	2.5	2.7	2.8	2.8	2.8	2.9	3.1	3.0
Costa Rica	2.2	1.9	2.1	2.2	2.1	2.2	2.3	2.2
Cuba	..	..	..	..	..	..	..	..
Czech Republic	3.6	3.2	3.0	2.9	2.8	2.8	2.9	2.9
Denmark	10.4	10.5	10.4	10.9	11.1	10.9	11.3	11.5
Dominican Republic	..	..	..	..	1.4	..	..	..
Ecuador	..	2.3	2.1	1.6	1.6	1.7	..	1.6
Egypt	..	..	..	0.7	0.7	0.6	0.7	0.7
El Salvador	..	..	..	..	2.4	2.5	2.7	2.7
Estonia	3.1	3.3	3.4	3.4	3.6	3.5	3.5	3.3
Finland	5.1	5.0	4.1	3.9	1.9	2.5	1.7	2.0
France	9.2	9.4	10.7	10.6	10.6	10.6	10.0	10.6
Germany	6.5	6.3	6.2	6.4	6.4	6.6	6.9	6.7
Greece	2.1	2.0	2.0	2.1	2.1	2.2	2.5	2.4
Guatemala	1.3	1.3	1.3	1.3	1.3	1.3	1.3	1.3
Honduras	1.9	1.9	..	..	2.6	2.5	2.0	1.9
Hong Kong, China	14.1	14.8	17.6	18.0	18.2	..	22.1	20.5
Hungary	2.5	2.4	2.4	2.4	2.3	2.4	2.5	2.4
Iceland	2.4	2.3	2.3	2.4	2.4	2.4	2.5	2.5
India	..	3.4	3.6	3.6	..	3.8	4.2	..
Indonesia	1.6	1.7	1.8	1.9	1.8	1.7	1.6	1.6
Ireland	19.9	16.4	17.7	14.6	12.1	11.8	10.9	11.5
Israel	4.6	4.7	4.7	4.9	5.0	4.9	4.8	4.5
Italy	8.8	8.9	7.9	7.5	7.6	7.8	8.1	7.9
Japan	6.7	6.7	7.6	7.3	7.7	7.3	7.1	7.1
Korea	12.0	11.9	11.7	11.0	10.5	11.1	11.5	11.0
Latvia	2.2	2.2	2.1	2.4	2.6	2.8	2.7	2.6
Lithuania	1.6	1.7	1.8	1.9	1.9	1.9	1.9	1.9
Luxembourg	41.6	35.2	32.5	36.9	34.3	37.8	30.9	38.0
Malaysia	4.7	4.7	4.6	4.4	4.3	4.5	5.0	4.8
Mexico	2.0	2.1	2.2	2.3	2.3	2.4	2.5	2.5
Montenegro	..	..	..	..	..	1.9	2.2	..
Morocco	..	..	..	3.6	3.7	..	..	4.2
Netherlands	5.4	4.8	9.8	9.5	9.3	9.2	9.6	9.4
New Zealand	2.7	2.6	2.5	2.4	..	3.4	3.5	..
Nicaragua	1.5	1.5	1.5	1.6	1.7	1.6	1.6	1.5
Norway	5.3	5.4	5.7	5.1	5.0	5.4	5.9	5.7
Panama	..	..	..	..	..	2.3	2.8	2.5
Paraguay	..	1.0	1.0	1.0	1.1	1.1	1.2	1.1
Peru	1.8	1.9	1.7	1.6	1.7	1.8	2.0	2.0
Poland	3.2	3.0	2.9	3.0	2.8	2.7	2.6	2.5
Portugal	7.8	6.7	5.6	5.5	5.8	5.3	4.5	5.9
Puerto Rico	8.8	10.7	12.8	..	..	..	..	..
Singapore	7.8	7.9	8.1	8.8	..	8.8	10.8	11.4
Slovak Republic	2.9	2.7	..	5.3	..	2.7	2.6	2.4
Slovenia	4.9	4.8	4.7	4.7	4.7	4.8	5.0	4.8
South Africa	13.2	13.3	12.7	..	..	..	12.5	12.6
Spain	5.2	5.0	5.5	5.2	5.1	4.9	5.0	4.9
Sri Lanka	0.9	1.1	..	1.3	1.3	..	..	..
Sweden	8.2	7.7	7.4	7.9	8.6	8.8	9.8	11.2
Switzerland	8.7	8.7	8.4	8.3	8.0	8.0	7.6	7.1
Chinese Taipei	..	..	..	..	20.1	19.3	16.9	14.4
Thailand	..	..	..	..	..	..	..	..
Tunisia	..	..	1.9	2.0	2.0	2.0	2.1	2.1
Türkiye	1.2	1.3	1.5	1.4	1.3	1.4	1.5	1.4
United Kingdom	10.7	10.1	9.5	12.5	13.0	11.7	11.2	11.3
United States	10.8	11.1	11.2	11.2	11.3	11.5	12.5	12.4
Uruguay	2.1	2.2	..	2.5	2.3	2.5	2.7	2.7
OECD Total	8.3	8.5	8.7	8.8	8.9	9.0	9.4	9.4

.. Not available

Note: Detailed metadata at: *http://metalinks.oecd.org/ins/20230516/99ff.*

Source: *Insurance activity indicators, OECD Insurance Statistics (database)*

Table 17. Penetration (Life)

Per cent

	2014	2015	2016	2017	2018	2019	2020	2021
Argentina	0.4	0.4	0.4	0.4	0.3	0.3	0.3	0.3
Australia	3.8	3.5	2.9	2.4	2.1	1.6	1.2	1.1
Austria	2.0	1.9	1.7	1.6	1.4	1.4	1.4	1.3
Belgium	4.0	3.7	3.5	3.3	3.4	3.4	3.2	3.1
Bermuda	..	..	..	..	..	..	..	..
Bolivia	..	..	0.5	0.5	0.6	0.6	0.8	0.7
Brazil	1.7	1.9	2.2	2.1	2.1	2.3	2.3	2.2
Bulgaria	..	..	..	..	0.3	0.3	0.3	0.4
Canada	1.2	1.3	1.3	1.3	1.3	..	..	..
Chile	2.8	3.2	3.5	3.2	3.2	3.1	2.3	2.1
Colombia	1.2	1.3	1.4	1.5	1.4	1.5	1.6	1.5
Costa Rica	0.3	0.2	0.3	0.3	0.3	0.4	0.3	0.4
Cuba	..	..	..	..	..	..	..	..
Czech Republic	1.6	1.3	1.2	1.1	1.0	0.9	0.9	0.8
Denmark	7.1	7.3	7.3	7.8	8.0	7.9	8.4	8.6
Dominican Republic	..	..	..	..	0.2	..	..	..
Ecuador	..	0.5	0.5	0.4	0.5	0.5	..	0.0
Egypt	..	..	..	0.3	0.3	0.3	0.3	0.4
El Salvador	..	..	..	..	0.6	0.6	0.7	1.5
Estonia	1.0	1.0	1.0	0.9	0.9	0.9	1.0	1.0
Finland	2.9	3.0	2.1	2.0	1.9	2.5	1.7	2.0
France	6.0	6.2	6.2	6.1	6.1	6.1	5.2	6.1
Germany	3.0	2.9	2.7	2.7	2.7	2.9	3.0	2.8
Greece	1.1	1.0	1.0	1.1	1.0	1.1	1.3	1.3
Guatemala	0.3	0.2	0.3	0.3	0.3	0.3	0.3	0.3
Honduras	0.7	0.7	..	..	0.9	0.8	0.7	0.7
Hong Kong, China	12.6	13.3	16.2	16.6	16.9	..	20.5	18.9
Hungary	1.4	1.2	1.2	1.2	1.1	1.1	1.1	1.1
Iceland	0.2	0.2	0.2	0.2	0.2	0.2	0.2	0.2
India	..	2.7	2.7	2.7	..	2.9	3.2	..
Indonesia	1.1	1.2	1.3	1.4	1.3	1.2	1.2	1.2
Ireland	16.5	13.2	12.3	11.8	9.4	9.0	8.1	9.3
Israel	2.4	2.5	2.5	2.6	2.7	2.7	2.6	2.4
Italy	6.8	6.9	6.0	5.7	5.8	5.9	6.1	6.0
Japan	6.7	6.7	5.9	5.7	6.0	5.5	5.3	5.3
Korea	7.1	7.1	6.9	6.2	5.8	6.1	6.2	5.8
Latvia	0.5	0.5	0.5	0.5	0.5	0.7	0.8	0.8
Lithuania	0.6	0.6	0.6	0.5	0.5	0.6	0.6	0.6
Luxembourg	39.0	32.4	29.7	33.9	31.5	34.5	27.4	33.6
Malaysia	3.0	3.0	3.0	3.0	2.9	3.1	3.5	3.4
Mexico	1.0	1.0	1.0	1.0	1.0	1.1	1.2	1.1
Montenegro	..	..	..	..	..	0.3	0.5	..
Morocco	..	..	..	1.6	1.6	..	..	1.9
Netherlands	2.6	2.1	1.9	1.8	1.5	1.5	1.5	1.9
New Zealand	..	..	..	..	..	0.8	0.8	..
Nicaragua	0.3	0.3	0.3	0.3	0.4	0.3	0.3	0.3
Norway	2.9	3.0	3.0	2.8	2.8	3.1	3.1	3.3
Panama	..	..	..	..	..	0.6	0.7	0.3
Paraguay	..	0.1	0.0	0.1	0.2	0.1	0.2	0.2
Peru	0.9	0.9	0.8	0.8	0.8	0.9	0.9	1.1
Poland	1.7	1.5	1.3	1.2	1.0	0.9	0.9	0.8
Portugal	5.9	4.7	3.5	3.4	3.8	3.2	2.1	3.5
Puerto Rico	0.6	0.5	1.2	..	..	..	..	..
Singapore	5.9	6.1	6.4	7.2	..	6.9	8.8	9.5
Slovak Republic	1.6	1.4	..	3.9	..	1.3	1.3	1.1
Slovenia	1.3	1.3	1.2	1.2	1.1	1.1	1.1	1.1
South Africa	10.9	10.8	10.5	..	..	..	10.0	10.3
Spain	2.4	2.4	2.8	2.5	2.4	2.2	1.9	1.9
Sri Lanka	0.3	0.5	..	0.5	0.5	..	..	..
Sweden	6.0	5.8	5.7	6.2	6.7	6.9	7.8	9.2
Switzerland	4.9	4.8	4.5	4.3	4.1	4.1	3.5	3.1
Chinese Taipei	..	..	..	..	19.2	18.3	16.0	13.4
Thailand	..	..	..	..	..	..	..	..
Tunisia	..	..	0.4	0.4	0.4	0.5	0.5	0.5
Türkiye	0.2	0.2	0.2	0.3	0.2	0.3	0.3	0.3
United Kingdom	7.9	7.5	6.0	9.0	9.5	8.9	8.2	8.4
United States	4.5	4.5	4.5	4.4	4.4	4.5	5.0	4.8
Uruguay	0.6	0.7	..	1.0	0.9	1.1	1.2	1.3
OECD Total	4.6	4.6	4.4	4.4	4.4	4.5	4.5	4.6

.. Not available

Note: Detailed metadata at: *http://metalinks.oecd.org/ins/20230516/99ff*.

Source: *Insurance activity indicators, OECD Insurance Statistics (database)*

Table 18. Penetration (Non-life)

Per cent

	2014	2015	2016	2017	2018	2019	2020	2021
Argentina	2.0	2.2	2.1	2.2	1.9	1.8	2.2	1.9
Australia	2.2	2.2	2.2	2.2	2.1	2.1	2.3	2.2
Austria	3.1	3.1	3.0	3.0	3.0	3.1	3.3	3.2
Belgium	2.9	2.8	2.7	2.7	2.7	2.7	2.8	3.2
Bermuda	..	..	..	..	..	..	..	..
Bolivia	..	..	0.9	0.8	0.8	0.8	0.8	0.8
Brazil	1.1	1.1	1.1	1.1	1.1	1.0	1.1	1.0
Bulgaria	..	..	..	..	1.9	2.1	2.1	2.0
Canada	3.0	3.2	3.2	3.1	3.1	..	..	..
Chile	1.4	1.5	1.5	1.4	1.5	1.5	1.6	1.5
Colombia	1.3	1.4	1.4	1.4	1.4	1.4	1.5	1.5
Costa Rica	1.9	1.6	1.7	1.9	1.8	1.8	2.0	1.9
Cuba	..	..	..	..	..	..	..	..
Czech Republic	1.9	1.9	1.8	1.7	1.7	1.9	2.0	2.0
Denmark	3.3	3.2	3.1	3.2	3.1	3.0	3.0	3.0
Dominican Republic	..	..	..	..	1.2	..	..	..
Ecuador	..	1.8	1.6	1.1	1.1	1.2	..	1.6
Egypt	..	..	..	0.4	0.4	0.3	0.3	0.3
El Salvador	..	..	..	..	1.8	1.8	2.0	1.1
Estonia	2.2	2.3	2.4	2.5	2.7	2.6	2.5	2.3
Finland	2.1	2.1	2.0	1.9	..	..	..	..
France	3.2	3.2	4.5	4.5	4.5	4.5	4.8	4.6
Germany	3.5	3.4	3.5	3.7	3.7	3.7	4.0	3.9
Greece	1.1	1.0	1.0	1.0	1.1	1.1	1.2	1.1
Guatemala	1.0	1.0	1.0	1.0	1.0	1.0	1.0	1.0
Honduras	1.2	1.2	..	..	1.7	1.7	1.3	1.2
Hong Kong, China	1.4	1.5	1.4	1.4	1.4	..	1.7	1.6
Hungary	1.1	1.1	1.2	1.2	1.2	1.3	1.4	1.3
Iceland	2.2	2.1	2.1	2.2	2.2	2.2	2.3	2.3
India	..	0.7	0.9	0.9	..	1.0	1.0	..
Indonesia	0.5	0.5	0.5	0.5	0.5	0.5	0.4	0.4
Ireland	3.4	3.3	5.4	2.7	2.4	2.6	2.6	2.2
Israel	2.2	2.2	2.2	2.3	2.3	2.2	2.2	2.1
Italy	2.0	1.9	1.9	1.9	1.9	1.9	2.0	1.9
Japan	..	..	1.7	1.6	1.7	1.7	1.8	1.8
Korea	4.9	4.8	4.9	4.8	4.6	5.0	5.3	5.2
Latvia	1.7	1.7	1.6	1.9	2.1	2.1	1.9	1.8
Lithuania	1.1	1.1	1.2	1.3	1.4	1.4	1.3	1.3
Luxembourg	2.6	2.7	2.8	3.0	2.8	3.4	3.5	4.4
Malaysia	1.7	1.7	1.6	1.4	1.4	1.4	1.5	1.4
Mexico	1.1	1.1	1.2	1.3	1.2	1.3	1.4	1.4
Montenegro	..	..	..	..	..	1.6	1.8	..
Morocco	..	..	..	2.0	2.1	..	..	2.2
Netherlands	2.8	2.7	7.9	7.7	7.8	7.7	8.1	7.5
New Zealand	2.7	2.6	2.5	2.4	..	2.6	2.7	..
Nicaragua	1.2	1.2	1.3	1.3	1.4	1.3	1.3	1.3
Norway	2.4	2.4	2.6	2.3	2.2	2.4	2.8	2.4
Panama	..	..	..	..	..	1.7	2.1	2.2
Paraguay	..	0.9	1.0	0.9	0.9	0.9	1.0	0.9
Peru	0.9	1.0	0.9	0.9	0.9	0.9	1.0	1.0
Poland	1.5	1.4	1.6	1.8	1.8	1.7	1.7	1.7
Portugal	1.9	2.0	2.1	2.1	2.0	2.1	2.3	2.4
Puerto Rico	8.3	10.2	11.6	..	..	..	..	..
Singapore	1.9	1.8	1.8	1.7	..	1.9	1.9	1.9
Slovak Republic	1.3	1.3	..	1.4	..	1.4	1.4	1.3
Slovenia	3.7	3.6	3.5	3.5	3.5	3.7	3.9	3.7
South Africa	2.3	2.4	2.3	..	..	..	2.5	2.3
Spain	2.7	2.7	2.7	2.7	2.7	2.7	3.1	2.9
Sri Lanka	0.6	0.6	..	0.7	0.7	..	..	..
Sweden	2.3	1.9	1.7	1.7	1.9	2.0	2.0	2.0
Switzerland	3.9	3.9	3.9	4.0	3.9	3.9	4.1	4.0
Chinese Taipei	..	..	..	..	0.9	0.9	1.0	0.9
Thailand	..	..	..	..	..	..	..	..
Tunisia	..	..	1.5	1.6	1.5	1.5	1.6	1.6
Türkiye	1.1	1.2	1.3	1.2	1.1	1.1	1.2	1.1
United Kingdom	2.8	2.6	3.5	3.5	3.5	2.8	2.9	2.9
United States	6.3	6.6	6.8	6.8	6.9	7.0	7.6	7.5
Uruguay	1.5	1.5	..	1.4	1.4	1.4	1.5	1.4
OECD Total	4.1	4.3	4.4	4.4	4.5	4.6	4.9	4.9

.. Not available

Note: Detailed metadata at: *http://metalinks.oecd.org/ins/20230516/99ff.*

Source: *Insurance activity indicators, OECD Insurance Statistics (database)*

Table 19. Life insurance share

Percentage of total insurance

Per cent

	2014	2015	2016	2017	2018	2019	2020	2021
Argentina	16.5	15.3	16.0	14.7	14.3	13.6	13.0	13.0
Australia	61.1	59.2	55.4	52.1	49.5	43.2	36.9	35.2
Austria	35.5	35.3	32.5	31.7	29.9	28.8	..	..
Belgium	56.5	55.4	54.4	53.7	54.7	51.7	48.9	45.0
Bermuda	..	..	..	..	..	53.1	69.1	57.5
Bolivia	..	..	33.5	40.4	43.3	44.9	47.2	47.3
Brazil	60.2	62.7	66.1	66.5	66.6	69.4	68.6	68.0
Bulgaria	..	..	..	..	14.1	12.7	12.5	15.8
Canada	28.7	28.7	29.1	29.5	30.1	..	..	..
Chile	65.8	68.3	70.4	69.4	68.8	67.0	59.6	57.4
Colombia	47.5	46.6	48.2	50.9	50.1	50.6	49.9	49.6
Costa Rica	12.3	12.7	15.4	14.7	16.1	16.0	14.9	16.4
Cuba	..	..	..	..	..	..	..	..
Czech Republic	45.1	41.1	40.6	38.3	36.6	32.1	30.9	29.1
Denmark	67.7	68.9	68.7	69.1	70.0	71.3	72.8	73.3
Dominican Republic	..	..	..	..	16.1	..	..	..
Ecuador	..	19.5	22.0	..	..	29.1	..	1.4
Egypt	..	..	..	..	..	43.7	46.2	50.6
El Salvador	25.7	25.6	24.7	..	25.1	25.6	27.1	59.2
Estonia	30.3	31.2	30.0	27.3	25.2	25.7	28.4	29.6
Finland	57.4	58.3	50.6	50.7	100.0	100.0	100.0	100.0
France	64.2	64.2	58.0	55.2	55.2	55.8	49.7	54.2
Germany	35.9	34.0	33.1	32.1	31.8	32.7	31.8	29.9
Greece	49.5	50.5	47.2	50.4	49.5	50.9	51.2	53.9
Guatemala	20.8	19.4	19.9	20.5	20.5	21.2	21.3	23.1
Honduras	35.3	36.4	..	..	33.3	32.2	34.1	34.6
Hong Kong, China	86.9	87.6	90.1	90.4	90.1	..	..	90.1
Hungary	54.8	51.1	49.5	48.2	46.2	44.3	44.0	45.3
Iceland	8.2	8.4	8.8	8.9	8.3	8.3	9.0	9.0
India	..	78.2	..	70.7	..	74.5	..	..
Indonesia	66.2	69.0	72.6	74.6	72.9	70.5	70.4	72.6
Ireland	82.2	79.6	68.5	79.5	75.4	72.0	71.0	80.0
Israel	51.7	53.6	52.7	53.8	54.0	54.9	54.0	53.2
Italy	76.8	77.8	75.8	75.0	74.7	75.1	74.4	74.5
Japan	100.0	100.0	75.5	75.1	75.2	73.2	71.7	72.0
Korea	56.8	57.1	56.3	53.9	53.2	..	51.0	49.6
Latvia	20.6	21.6	23.2	22.5	19.2	26.6	30.2	30.4
Lithuania	35.8	36.6	34.7	29.2	28.3	28.6	30.4	30.7
Luxembourg	93.9	92.3	91.5	91.8	91.8	90.7	88.4	87.6
Malaysia	60.2	60.6	61.7	63.4	64.1	65.8	65.9	65.2
Mexico	46.8	46.3	46.7	43.0	44.9	45.0	45.4	45.0
Montenegro	..	..	..	..	..	..	..	..
Morocco	..	..	..	..	..	..	..	44.3
Netherlands	47.7	43.6	19.6	18.2	16.2	..	..	21.6
New Zealand	..	..	..	..	..	23.6	22.8	..
Nicaragua	17.8	17.4	18.6	..	20.4	..	19.2	18.7
Norway	55.3	55.1	55.4	55.4	55.9	56.0	52.9	58.1
Panama	..	..	..	..	..	25.1	25.7	13.0
Paraguay	..	13.3	0.2	13.9	..	13.3	..	15.8
Peru	49.1	48.4	45.3	47.0	48.5	48.8	47.1	51.8
Poland	52.2	50.2	42.6	39.4	34.9	33.3	32.7	32.0
Portugal	72.9	67.5	59.6	58.6	61.8	56.7	44.4	56.4
Puerto Rico	6.3	4.9	9.5	..	..	..	..	..
Singapore	68.5	69.3	71.6	74.9	..	68.8	76.1	76.7
Slovak Republic	54.3	51.2	..	73.6	..	48.6	47.8	45.8
Slovenia	22.9	23.1	22.5	22.4	21.7	20.8	19.1	19.9
South Africa	80.5	79.9	79.7	..	..	..	77.1	79.2
Spain	43.9	43.6	47.1	44.8	43.6	41.5	37.1	36.9
Sri Lanka	35.5	42.5	..	41.4	41.3	..	..	..
Sweden	69.6	73.3	74.9	76.1	75.6	75.6	76.8	80.4
Switzerland	48.5	48.9	46.9	45.0	44.4	43.7	38.6	36.4
Chinese Taipei	..	..	..	..	97.0	96.8	93.6	92.6
Thailand	..	..	..	..	..	..	..	..
Tunisia	..	..	20.3	19.7	..	..	..	..
Türkiye	12.3	11.8	14.9	17.3	15.9	20.1	20.1	19.0
United Kingdom	73.4	73.3	68.8	69.0	72.0	72.6	70.5	70.5
United States	36.2	37.1	35.9	35.6	43.3	42.6	42.4	42.6
Uruguay	29.5	33.4	..	42.2	..	44.1	45.7	46.9
OECD Total	50.2	49.2	46.5	45.4	50.3	50.0	49.1	..

.. Not available

Note: Detailed metadata at: *http://metalinks.oecd.org/ins/20230516/99ff*.

Source: *Insurance activity indicators, OECD Insurance Statistics (database)*

Table 20. Direct total gross premiums per insurance company employee

US dollars

	2014	2015	2016	2017	2018	2019	2020	2021
Argentina	296 157	290 581	..	264 715	291 050	165 282	159 867	166 494
Australia	..	..	..	..	..	..	..	..
Austria	816 717	688 586	660 884	676 184	729 985	704 559	..	..
Belgium	..	..	..	..	..	..	..	..
Bermuda	..	..	..	..	..	..	..	..
Bolivia	..	..	112 942	99 464	101 913	106 567	152 952	138 058
Brazil	..	..	..	..	..	..	..	..
Bulgaria	..	..	..	..	..	..	..	..
Canada	..	..	..	..	..	..	..	..
Chile	454 677	495 261	510 666	519 672	558 276	512 932	466 063	519 550
Colombia	502 922	375 965	347 426	..	..	..	..	..
Costa Rica	..	..	..	..	..	..	..	422 644
Cuba	..	..	..	..	..	..	..	..
Czech Republic	..	..	..	..	..	..	..	181 323
Denmark	2 158 639	1 927 585	2 018 459	2 661 767	3 419 049	2 616 680	2 374 364	..
Dominican Republic	..	..	..	..	..	..	..	..
Ecuador	..	2 202 989	292 344	..	..	..	..	398 713
Egypt	..	..	..	..	..	40 536	..	..
El Salvador	..	..	..	..	195 773	..	206 498	..
Estonia	221 998	200 416	..	..	..	..	..	..
Finland	1 514 861	1 311 479	1 088 453	1 237 491	633 977	965 645	465 480	591 717
France	..	..	..	..	..	..	..	..
Germany	1 649 160	1 371 091	1 367 654	1 520 578	1 653 171	1 701 918	1 785 624	2 139 968
Greece	..	..	..	..	..	..	..	..
Guatemala	159 900	..	181 604	186 479	185 720	189 576	196 976	218 604
Honduras	183 148	217 165	..	..	1 497 747	1 768 927	207 995	213 737
Hong Kong, China	..	..	..	617 084	632 451	..	..	..
Hungary	161 509	147 122	169 626	168 073	197 023	177 672	208 722	260 413
Iceland	731 603	703 782	..	..	..	..	..	..
India	..	..	..	32 479	..	246 628	..	..
Indonesia	..	..	..	..	..	..	2 601 013	2 898 196
Ireland	..	..	..	..	..	..	..	..
Israel	..	..	..	..	..	..	..	..
Italy	729 106	622 717	585 098	..	..	..	..	..
Japan	130 139	144 659	..	1 060 963	..	..	..	..
Korea	580 368	591 071	610 886	638 233	628 010	..	734 315	872 897
Latvia	237 445	301 825	..	..	..	..	..	..
Lithuania	136 520	120 842	130 040	147 705	172 038	179 804	206 601	233 165
Luxembourg	4 328 321	2 997 287	2 886 004	3 019 973	2 823 429	2 443 072	1 649 515	2 406 785
Malaysia	650 745	461 454	465 847	435 343	475 776	492 833	505 221	549 754
Mexico	403 458	330 532	410 335	423 179	..	..	..	..
Montenegro	..	..	..	..	..	..	..	..
Morocco	..	..	..	..	..	..	..	348 507
Netherlands	..	..	..	..	..	..	..	..
New Zealand	..	..	..	..	..	..	..	..
Nicaragua	119 312	2 050 664	..	..	..	..	107 031	116 099
Norway	..	..	..	..	..	..	..	..
Panama	..	..	..	..	..	243 877	234 721	249 947
Paraguay	..	124 344	..	..	..	..	..	..
Peru	301 442	290 594	..	..	295 065	306 299	310 374	354 977
Poland	183 458	167 678	..	..	..	375 376	360 924	..
Portugal	551 505	416 277	371 983	413 352	506 932	493 481	420 557	705 887
Puerto Rico	704 962	856 812	1 042 984	..	..	..	..	..
Singapore	..	..	..	..	..	..	..	..
Slovak Republic	403 610	..	..	..	..	..	..	..
Slovenia	..	..	..	..	..	..	..	..
South Africa	..	..	..	..	..	..	..	..
Spain	403 450	..	..	..	..	..	..	..
Sri Lanka	24 436	26 631	..	17 383	17 439	..	..	..
Sweden	2 042 276	1 771 433	..	1 686 900	1 927 908	2 031 531	..	..
Switzerland	..	..	..	..	..	..	..	..
Chinese Taipei	..	..	..	..	183 841	198 719	187 023	189 304
Thailand	..	..	..	..	..	..	..	..
Tunisia	..	..	173 680	..	..	..	..	..
Türkiye	335 385	298 749	233 812	204 510	261 141	201 229	..	554 245
United Kingdom	..	..	..	..	..	..	..	..
United States	..	..	..	..	..	..	..	..
Uruguay	..	..	..	..	..	..	..	..
OECD Total	333 914	333 824	710 680	919 678	960 372	1 104 147	1 009 523	1 110 323

.. Not available

Note: Detailed metadata at: *http://metalinks.oecd.org/ins/20230516/99ff*.

Source: *Insurance activity indicators, OECD Insurance Statistics (database)*

Table 21. Retention ratio (Life and Non-life)

Per cent

	2014	2015	2016	2017	2018	2019	2020	2021
Argentina	86.5	87.5	88.4	88.7	89.3	87.3	86.3	85.0
Australia	86.0	83.8	80.4	77.1	77.9	74.1	69.4	68.8
Austria	83.6	84.2	81.1	82.7	87.2	86.4	..	..
Belgium	88.7	88.5	87.2	87.5	87.2	76.2	82.7	75.5
Bermuda	..	..	..	..	..	84.6	67.5	74.8
Bolivia	..	..	49.8	51.5	54.9	53.9	55.7	53.0
Brazil	95.2	95.4	95.8	95.7	95.6	95.5	94.3	93.4
Bulgaria	..	..	..	..	73.2	70.6	71.1	71.7
Canada	73.5	71.4	74.0	72.4	79.1	..	..	..
Chile	84.0	84.8	84.4	83.4	84.1	82.8	76.8	78.4
Colombia	82.5	81.5	80.1	81.6	81.1	80.4	78.2	76.8
Costa Rica	80.2	77.9	78.9	79.4	77.5	78.3	78.3	78.4
Cuba	..	..	..	..	..	..	..	..
Czech Republic	80.3	79.3	78.9	78.7	79.0	79.4	79.2	78.2
Denmark	97.2	97.1	96.9	96.7	97.2	97.8	98.4	98.4
Dominican Republic	..	..	..	..	69.1	..	..	..
Ecuador	..	72.4	72.3	..	..	67.0	..	67.1
Egypt	..	..	..	..	..	62.0	58.1	60.7
El Salvador	66.6	66.5	64.2	..	63.7	63.0	61.0	63.1
Estonia	..	..	..	..	..	..	..	..
Finland	97.6	97.7	97.3	97.4	99.5	99.5	99.2	99.4
France	91.0	88.6	84.8	88.0	87.7	87.0	84.9	85.7
Germany	89.0	87.7	87.9	87.5	86.1	86.4	85.7	84.0
Greece	87.6	87.2	88.8	89.2	88.7	89.6	89.8	89.9
Guatemala	64.2	64.9	67.8	67.2	65.2	65.6	64.7	64.4
Honduras	54.4	53.0	..	..	58.7	31.3	48.9	47.4
Hong Kong, China	87.7	88.3	90.4	90.4	90.7	..	..	85.9
Hungary	86.1	86.1	86.7	87.4	87.6	87.9	88.0	88.1
Iceland	94.4	94.8	95.4	96.0	95.9	96.3	95.9	96.0
India	..	95.2	..	91.8	..	91.0	..	..
Indonesia	83.8	84.8	86.0	87.3	86.8	85.6	85.0	86.8
Ireland	89.2	88.0	79.6	..	..	..	..	..
Israel	88.5	88.4	84.9	86.5	85.8	85.3	84.1	83.5
Italy	97.1	97.2	96.4	96.3	96.2	96.5	96.3	96.0
Japan	94.3	94.6	89.5	89.8	88.8	85.1	85.5	83.1
Korea	94.7	94.7	94.7	94.3	94.0	..	93.5	93.3
Latvia	96.3	95.9	95.3	93.2	89.8	90.3	91.6	92.0
Lithuania	95.2	95.1	95.0	91.5	90.4	90.9	92.8	92.8
Luxembourg	71.8	84.1	82.2	85.8	76.8	73.0	80.9	82.4
Malaysia	87.8	87.9	88.3	88.6	89.2	89.9	89.4	89.1
Mexico	83.9	83.0	84.4	81.4	83.2	81.3	82.0	81.9
Montenegro	..	..	..	..	..	..	..	..
Morocco	..	..	..	..	..	..	..	90.8
Netherlands	89.4	91.7	98.3	97.6	98.0	..	..	95.1
New Zealand	111.2	112.7	107.0	106.8	..	70.3	67.4	..
Nicaragua	63.3	65.7	66.7	..	60.9	..	56.1	52.0
Norway	93.1	92.2	92.7	93.0	93.3	93.7	93.0	93.8
Panama	..	..	..	..	..	63.4	63.6	65.5
Paraguay	..	79.6	78.0	77.4	..	74.2	..	72.5
Peru	75.5	74.5	73.3	75.0	76.3	77.0	74.1	73.5
Poland	92.4	90.5	87.9	88.4	88.4	87.6	86.9	85.4
Portugal	92.0	90.5	88.9	88.6	89.4	86.3	81.7	84.9
Puerto Rico	98.6	92.9	93.9	..	..	..	..	..
Singapore	86.8	79.2	77.6	77.0	..	74.2	85.8	81.8
Slovak Republic	85.3	84.5	..	92.2	..	85.5	85.7	85.5
Slovenia	86.9	88.1	87.7	86.5	86.8	85.8	87.7	84.8
South Africa	88.2	89.7	88.9	..	..	..	88.2	87.9
Spain	91.3	91.3	91.0	90.6	91.0	89.6	83.8	88.3
Sri Lanka	87.0	86.6	..	85.6	87.9	..	..	..
Sweden	95.6	97.0	97.3	97.2	97.4	96.9	..	97.1
Switzerland	92.9	93.1	93.7	92.6	92.6	92.3	92.1	91.6
Chinese Taipei	..	..	..	..	98.9	98.8	98.2	97.2
Thailand	..	..	..	..	..	..	..	..
Tunisia	..	..	80.9	100.0	..	..	..	..
Türkiye	75.0	74.8	76.1	72.0	70.9	71.5	70.9	69.7
United Kingdom	84.8	89.0	77.0	87.9	80.6	80.5	80.6	80.9
United States	74.9	72.8	72.5	71.4	83.7	84.4	83.1	81.3
Uruguay	90.8	91.5	..	92.9	..	91.9	91.1	92.2
OECD Total	82.5	80.7	79.4	79.6	85.6	85.0	84.3	83.4

.. Not available

Note: Detailed metadata at: *http://metalinks.oecd.org/ins/20230516/99ff*.

Source: *Insurance activity indicators, OECD Insurance Statistics (database)*

Table 22. Retention ratio (Life)

Per cent

	2014	2015	2016	2017	2018	2019	2020	2021
Argentina	97.1	97.2	96.7	96.8	96.8	95.7	94.1	93.0
Australia	92.5	91.3	89.3	82.5	84.2	76.5	67.1	66.5
Austria	97.4	97.6	97.4	97.8	97.8	97.8	..	..
Belgium	97.6	97.9	96.7	98.0	97.7	96.9	95.9	97.9
Bermuda	..	..	..	..	..	90.5	69.1	73.3
Bolivia	..	..	64.6	63.7	71.9	68.2	69.2	63.3
Brazil	99.6	99.5	99.6	99.5	99.6	99.6	99.6	99.6
Bulgaria	..	..	..	..	98.4	98.5	98.1	98.5
Canada	69.5	67.6	72.1	72.9	75.4	..	..	..
Chile	97.7	97.5	95.0	92.6	93.3	93.1	92.4	96.9
Colombia	94.2	94.7	93.9	92.8	92.0	91.2	90.9	90.9
Costa Rica	87.4	81.4	82.8	81.4	79.0	80.6	82.2	85.6
Cuba	..	..	..	..	..	..	..	..
Czech Republic	93.0	92.4	92.3	91.7	91.4	95.3	94.9	95.4
Denmark	99.8	99.8	99.8	99.8	99.9	99.9	99.9	99.9
Dominican Republic	..	..	..	..	76.5	..	..	..
Ecuador	..	81.6	99.2	..	..	99.0	..	89.6
Egypt	..	..	..	..	..	64.7	62.0	64.4
El Salvador	87.3	81.6	80.8	..	78.2	76.6	69.7	70.8
Estonia	..	..	..	..	..	..	..	..
Finland	99.5	99.5	99.3	99.4	99.5	99.5	99.2	99.4
France	94.1	90.7	86.5	93.2	93.9	93.1	92.6	93.3
Germany	97.0	97.0	96.6	97.0	96.2	97.3	97.2	95.7
Greece	95.6	95.9	96.2	95.0	95.1	95.7	96.4	96.7
Guatemala	76.6	76.9	80.9	79.9	78.1	79.2	78.7	80.3
Honduras	45.4	56.1	..	..	56.0	28.6	51.4	47.4
Hong Kong, China	90.5	91.0	92.8	92.7	93.4	..	..	87.9
Hungary	96.3	96.8	97.3	98.7	99.1	99.1	99.1	99.0
Iceland	82.3	83.7	85.2	85.9	85.0	85.6	86.1	85.9
India	..	99.6	..	99.5	..	99.4	..	..
Indonesia	96.7	96.8	97.3	97.4	97.1	96.8	96.6	97.0
Ireland	94.0	94.1	94.9	..	..	..	..	..
Israel	95.2	95.5	95.1	95.2	95.4	95.8	95.4	95.1
Italy	99.0	99.1	99.1	99.1	99.1	99.5	99.6	99.6
Japan	94.3	94.6	93.1	93.6	92.7	88.2	88.7	85.3
Korea	98.8	98.7	98.6	98.4	98.4	..	98.2	98.2
Latvia	99.8	99.8	99.8	99.8	99.8	99.2	99.2	99.2
Lithuania	98.5	98.0	98.5	98.3	97.8	98.5	98.4	98.4
Luxembourg	72.1	85.3	83.6	87.4	77.4	73.5	81.9	84.6
Malaysia	96.9	96.7	96.6	95.9	96.0	95.8	95.0	95.3
Mexico	96.6	96.4	96.2	95.4	95.4	95.5	95.8	96.3
Montenegro	..	..	..	..	..	..	..	..
Morocco	..	..	..	..	..	..	..	99.2
Netherlands	89.6	94.0	97.2	96.4	97.7	..	..	86.6
New Zealand	..	..	..	..	..	60.6	50.6	..
Nicaragua	55.3	59.2	58.2	..	62.4	..	62.2	50.4
Norway	98.9	98.7	98.9	98.9	99.1	99.3	99.3	99.4
Panama	..	..	..	..	..	49.0	0.0	0.0
Paraguay	..	81.7	41.0	83.0	..	80.0	..	79.3
Peru	84.4	84.7	82.4	83.7	85.0	86.9	86.4	84.0
Poland	98.5	98.2	98.3	99.4	98.7	98.5	98.0	97.8
Portugal	97.7	97.2	96.5	96.5	96.9	96.5	95.0	96.9
Puerto Rico	100.0	56.0	78.0	..	..	..	..	..
Singapore	96.1	88.4	84.3	82.3	..	79.0	93.3	89.1
Slovak Republic	98.2	97.9	..	99.0	..	95.5	94.9	94.2
Slovenia	96.9	96.7	96.3	96.4	96.4	96.3	94.5	98.7
South Africa	93.2	95.2	94.6	..	..	..	95.7	94.1
Spain	96.4	96.8	97.3	96.2	97.1	97.0	83.4	96.6
Sri Lanka	96.3	96.3	..	96.0	99.5	..	..	..
Sweden	99.6	99.8	99.9	99.7	99.8	99.7	..	99.8
Switzerland	99.4	99.4	99.3	99.3	98.8	99.4	99.4	99.2
Chinese Taipei	..	..	..	..	99.7	99.6	99.9	99.2
Thailand	..	..	..	..	..	..	..	..
Tunisia	..	..	90.4	100.0	..	..	..	..
Türkiye	94.8	95.1	95.8	96.2	95.5	96.0	96.2	95.7
United Kingdom	85.4	91.2	80.3	95.2	84.6	84.3	85.3	86.4
United States	88.3	80.4	80.0	77.8	75.2	78.6	75.2	71.8
Uruguay	97.6	97.6	..	97.4	..	97.5	97.4	97.9
OECD Total	91.6	88.6	86.7	87.6	84.9	85.1	83.3	81.9

.. Not available

Note: Detailed metadata at: *http://metalinks.oecd.org/ins/20230516/99ff*.

Source: *Insurance activity indicators, OECD Insurance Statistics (database)*

Table 23. Retention ratio (Non-life)

Per cent

	2014	2015	2016	2017	2018	2019	2020	2021
Argentina	84.4	85.7	86.8	87.3	88.0	86.0	85.1	83.8
Australia	75.7	73.0	69.3	71.3	71.8	72.3	70.8	70.1
Austria	76.0	77.0	73.3	75.8	82.7	81.7	..	..
Belgium	77.2	76.8	75.8	75.4	74.5	54.0	70.1	57.1
Bermuda	..	..	..	..	..	77.9	63.8	76.8
Bolivia	..	..	42.4	43.1	41.9	42.3	43.6	43.8
Brazil	88.5	88.5	88.4	88.3	87.7	86.4	82.7	80.2
Bulgaria	..	..	..	..	69.0	66.5	67.2	66.6
Canada	75.2	72.9	74.7	72.2	80.6	..	..	..
Chile	57.7	57.4	59.1	62.7	63.8	61.8	53.8	53.5
Colombia	72.0	69.9	67.3	70.1	70.2	69.3	65.6	63.0
Costa Rica	79.2	77.3	78.2	79.0	77.2	77.9	77.6	77.0
Cuba	..	..	..	..	..	..	..	..
Czech Republic	69.8	70.2	69.8	70.6	71.9	72.0	72.2	71.1
Denmark	91.7	91.1	90.6	89.9	91.1	92.5	94.3	94.3
Dominican Republic	..	..	..	..	67.7	..	..	..
Ecuador	..	70.1	64.7	..	..	53.8	..	66.8
Egypt	..	..	..	..	..	59.8	54.8	56.9
El Salvador	58.4	60.1	57.1	..	58.8	58.4	57.8	51.9
Estonia	..	..	..	..	..	..	..	..
Finland	95.0	95.2	95.3	95.4	..	..	..	..
France	85.3	84.8	82.4	81.7	80.1	79.2	77.3	76.7
Germany	84.6	82.9	83.7	83.0	81.3	81.1	80.4	79.0
Greece	79.8	78.3	82.2	83.3	82.5	83.2	83.0	82.0
Guatemala	61.0	62.0	64.5	63.9	61.8	62.0	60.9	59.6
Honduras	59.3	51.3	..	..	60.1	32.5	47.6	47.4
Hong Kong, China	69.0	69.8	68.9	68.7	65.8	..	..	67.1
Hungary	73.6	75.0	76.2	76.9	77.7	79.0	79.3	79.2
Iceland	95.5	95.8	96.3	97.0	96.9	97.2	96.9	97.0
India	..	79.5	..	73.1	..	66.4	..	..
Indonesia	58.4	58.3	55.7	57.6	58.9	58.8	57.5	60.0
Ireland	67.1	64.1	46.3	..	..	..	..	..
Israel	81.2	80.2	73.6	76.4	74.6	72.6	70.7	70.2
Italy	90.5	90.6	87.9	87.8	87.6	87.3	86.8	85.6
Japan	..	..	78.4	78.2	76.9	76.6	77.4	77.6
Korea	89.5	89.4	89.8	89.5	88.9	..	88.7	88.5
Latvia	95.4	94.8	93.9	91.3	87.4	87.1	88.2	88.8
Lithuania	93.3	93.4	93.0	88.6	87.5	87.9	90.4	90.3
Luxembourg	65.9	68.9	66.7	67.7	69.2	68.3	72.8	67.2
Malaysia	74.0	74.4	74.9	76.0	77.0	78.4	78.6	77.3
Mexico	72.8	71.5	74.0	70.8	73.2	69.7	70.6	70.0
Montenegro	..	..	..	..	..	..	..	..
Morocco	..	..	..	..	..	..	..	84.1
Netherlands	89.2	89.9	98.5	98.1	98.3	..	..	97.5
New Zealand	80.0	80.5	73.8	74.4	..	73.4	72.4	..
Nicaragua	65.0	67.0	68.7	..	60.5	..	54.6	52.4
Norway	85.9	84.3	85.0	85.5	86.0	86.5	86.0	86.1
Panama	..	..	..	..	..	68.2	0.0	0.0
Paraguay	..	79.3	78.0	76.5	..	73.3	..	71.2
Peru	67.0	65.0	65.7	67.3	68.1	67.4	63.3	62.3
Poland	85.8	82.8	80.2	81.3	82.8	82.1	81.4	79.5
Portugal	76.8	76.6	77.7	77.4	77.1	72.8	71.1	69.3
Puerto Rico	98.5	94.8	95.5	..	..	..	..	..
Singapore	66.5	58.4	60.9	61.0	..	63.5	62.2	57.9
Slovak Republic	69.9	70.4	..	73.3	..	76.1	77.3	78.2
Slovenia	84.0	85.5	85.2	83.6	84.2	83.0	86.1	81.4
South Africa	67.7	68.0	66.8	..	..	..	62.8	64.2
Spain	87.3	87.0	85.3	86.0	86.2	84.3	83.9	83.4
Sri Lanka	81.9	79.4	..	78.3	79.8	..	..	..
Sweden	86.5	89.3	89.5	89.1	89.9	88.2	..	86.0
Switzerland	86.7	87.0	88.8	87.1	87.5	86.7	87.5	87.3
Chinese Taipei	..	..	..	..	72.7	73.0	72.6	72.5
Thailand	..	..	..	..	..	..	..	..
Tunisia	..	..	78.6	100.0	..	..	..	..
Türkiye	72.2	72.1	72.7	66.9	66.2	65.3	64.6	63.6
United Kingdom	83.2	82.8	69.5	71.6	70.3	70.3	69.1	67.7
United States	67.3	68.2	68.3	67.9	90.1	88.8	88.9	88.4
Uruguay	87.9	88.4	..	89.7	..	87.4	85.7	87.2
OECD Total	73.4	73.0	73.0	72.9	86.3	85.0	85.2	84.8

.. Not available

Note: Detailed metadata at: *http://metalinks.oecd.org/ins/20230516/99ff.*

Source: *Insurance activity indicators, OECD Insurance Statistics (database)*

Table 24. Ratio of reinsurance accepted (Life and Non-life)

Per cent

	2014	2015	2016	2017	2018	2019	2020	2021
Argentina	7.2	7.0	6.7	6.6	5.5	5.5	5.4	5.3
Australia	10.1	10.9	12.5	13.0	14.3	16.1	17.7	18.2
Austria	9.6	8.9	9.3	6.4	7.2	6.8	..	..
Belgium	3.5	3.0	2.9	2.3	1.8	7.0	8.1	8.9
Bermuda	..	..	..	..	..	61.3	48.0	63.2
Bolivia	..	..	1.0	3.9	3.3	6.1	6.2	6.4
Brazil	0.0	0.0	0.0	0.0	0.0	0.0	0.0	0.0
Bulgaria	..	..	..	..	2.3	1.8	1.6	1.6
Canada	17.7	17.6	15.6	16.1	11.3	..	..	..
Chile	0.6	0.8	1.1	0.9	0.9	1.0	1.0	1.1
Colombia	1.9	2.0	1.8	1.9	2.0	2.0	1.9	2.0
Costa Rica	0.3	0.3	0.3	0.3	0.3	0.4	0.4	0.4
Cuba	..	..	..	..	..	..	..	..
Czech Republic	1.6	2.0	2.4	2.5	2.1	2.2	2.2	2.1
Denmark	0.8	0.8	2.9	3.3	3.5	2.4	1.8	1.9
Dominican Republic	..	..	..	..	..	..	..	..
Ecuador	..	2.0	1.7	..	..	0.6	..	0.6
Egypt	..	..	..	..	..	4.9	3.4	3.3
El Salvador	..	..	..	..	5.1	5.5	7.0	9.1
Estonia	..	..	..	..	0.0	0.0	..	..
Finland	1.4	1.3	1.5	1.6	0.0	0.1	0.0	0.0
France	10.5	8.9	15.7	12.7	12.7	12.8	12.6	13.1
Germany	22.4	24.6	24.5	24.6	24.7	25.4	26.5	28.3
Greece	1.2	1.1	1.0	0.9	0.9	0.9	0.7	0.7
Guatemala	2.7	3.1	2.9	2.9	3.4	2.8	3.1	2.7
Honduras	0.0	0.0	..	..	..	0.0	..	..
Hong Kong, China	4.8	4.5	4.8	4.7	4.6	..	..	6.3
Hungary	0.9	1.0	1.0	1.5	1.1	1.0	0.7	0.6
Iceland	2.5	2.4	1.7	1.4	1.7	1.7	0.1	0.2
India	..	0.7	..	5.8	..	0.5	..	..
Indonesia	2.5	2.1	2.0	1.8	1.8	2.2	3.6	1.4
Ireland	1.9	1.9	2.2	1.2	3.0	5.8	4.8	1.1
Israel	..	..	0.0	..	..	..	..	..
Italy	1.8	1.8	2.1	2.1	2.3	1.0	1.4	1.7
Japan	5.5	4.1	6.5	6.0	5.5	5.5	5.6	5.4
Korea	5.0	5.1	5.2	5.6	6.2	..	5.4	5.5
Latvia	0.0	0.0	0.0	0.0	0.0	0.1	0.0	0.0
Lithuania	0.0	0.0	0.0	0.0	0.0	0.0	0.0	0.0
Luxembourg	1.2	0.8	0.3	0.2	0.2	5.6	6.4	5.4
Malaysia	7.5	7.7	7.7	7.2	6.7	6.5	7.4	9.4
Mexico	1.8	1.7	1.6	1.7	1.7	1.8	2.3	2.4
Montenegro	..	..	..	..	..	..	..	..
Morocco	..	..	..	..	..	..	..	5.4
Netherlands	1.5	1.7	0.5	1.8	1.8	..	..	2.6
New Zealand	0.6	3.8	1.8	5.3	..	0.1	0.1	..
Nicaragua	..	..	..	..	..	..	..	..
Norway	..	..	..	..	..	..	..	..
Panama	..	..	..	..	..	8.2	9.0	10.4
Paraguay	..	1.1	1.0	0.7	..	0.4	..	0.4
Peru	0.7	0.6	0.6	0.7	0.6	0.8	1.0	0.6
Poland	1.0	2.7	3.5	3.2	3.7	4.5	4.6	4.8
Portugal	3.3	3.9	5.1	5.3	5.3	5.5	7.1	5.8
Puerto Rico	0.9	0.8	0.6	..	..	..	..	..
Singapore	19.2	19.7	21.7	17.6	..	26.8	27.2	24.9
Slovak Republic	1.4	2.0	..	0.2	..	0.0	0.2	0.5
Slovenia	11.3	12.5	12.1	12.1	11.7	12.2	13.6	13.6
South Africa	2.3	2.2	2.9	..	..	..	4.1	3.2
Spain	7.8	8.2	8.2	8.1	7.8	8.1	10.8	9.3
Sri Lanka	2.2	1.5	..	2.4	2.2	..	..	..
Sweden	4.1	3.1	3.0	3.1	3.1	3.0	3.0	2.6
Switzerland	13.8	12.7	13.3	14.2	15.0	16.0	17.2	18.3
Chinese Taipei	..	..	..	..	41.1	42.4	1.1	1.2
Thailand	..	..	..	..	..	..	..	..
Tunisia	..	..	1.2	5.3	..	..	..	..
Türkiye	5.0	3.1	5.9	6.0	8.5	10.0	8.5	8.5
United Kingdom	9.9	11.1	35.8	14.3	20.0	19.5	19.2	19.4
United States	21.8	22.8	22.3	23.0	11.9	11.2	10.8	12.3
Uruguay	0.0	0.0	..	0.0	..	0.0	0.0	0.0
OECD Total	15.4	16.6	18.4	17.2	11.8	11.8	11.5	12.3

.. Not available

Note: Detailed metadata at: *http://metalinks.oecd.org/ins/20230516/99ff.*

Source: *Insurance activity indicators, OECD Insurance Statistics (database)*

Table 25. Ratio of reinsurance accepted (Life)

Per cent

	2014	2015	2016	2017	2018	2019	2020	2021
Argentina	3.0	2.3	3.0	2.9	2.8	3.1	3.6	3.8
Australia	7.5	8.4	9.7	12.2	14.3	18.2	22.6	22.5
Austria	0.2	0.2	0.2	0.2	0.2	0.3	..	..
Belgium	0.4	0.3	0.4	0.3	0.3	0.5	0.2	0.1
Bermuda	..	..	..	..	..	38.3	38.4	46.3
Bolivia	..	..	0.0	3.3	4.8	6.1	5.5	5.2
Brazil	0.0	0.0	0.0	0.0	0.0	0.0	0.0	0.0
Bulgaria	..	..	..	..	5.0	5.8	6.1	4.1
Canada	16.6	17.5	15.0	14.4	11.8	..	..	..
Chile	0.1	0.4	1.0	0.8	0.8	0.9	0.8	0.8
Colombia	0.1	0.1	0.1	0.0	0.0	0.0	0.0	0.0
Costa Rica	0.0	0.0	0.0	0.0	0.0	0.0	0.0	0.0
Cuba	..	..	..	..	..	..	..	..
Czech Republic	0.0	0.0	0.6	0.6	0.7	0.9	1.0	1.1
Denmark	0.5	0.5	0.6	0.4	0.4	0.4	0.5	0.6
Dominican Republic	..	..	..	..	..	..	..	..
Ecuador	..	0.6	0.0	..	..	0.0	..	0.0
Egypt	..	..	..	..	..	0.3	0.3	0.3
El Salvador	..	..	..	..	5.0	5.1	7.5	11.4
Estonia	..	..	..	..	0.0	0.0	..	..
Finland	0.2	0.0	0.0	0.0	0.0	0.1	0.0	0.0
France	8.9	6.3	15.5	8.8	8.6	9.6	8.4	8.4
Germany	0.6	0.6	0.6	0.8	0.5	0.5	1.1	0.4
Greece	0.2	0.2	0.1	0.0	0.0	0.0	0.0	0.0
Guatemala	1.6	1.7	1.9	1.4	1.5	0.9	1.2	0.8
Honduras	0.0	0.0	..	..	..	0.0	..	..
Hong Kong, China	1.6	1.7	2.8	2.5	2.0	..	..	4.2
Hungary	0.0	0.0	0.0	0.0	0.0	0.0	0.0	0.0
Iceland	0.0	0.1	..	0.0	..	..	..	..
India	..	0.0	..	0.2	..	0.0	..	..
Indonesia	..	..	..	..	..	..	..	..
Ireland	1.1	1.2	0.7	0.2	0.1	0.3	0.3	0.2
Israel	..	..	0.0	..	..	..	..	..
Italy	1.3	1.3	1.5	1.5	1.4	0.3	0.3	0.2
Japan	5.5	4.1	3.4	2.6	2.0	1.7	1.5	1.3
Korea	1.1	1.1	1.3	1.4	1.7	..	0.0	0.0
Latvia	0.0	0.0	0.0	0.0	0.0	0.0	0.0	0.0
Lithuania	0.0	0.0	0.0	0.0	0.0	0.0	0.0	0.0
Luxembourg	1.3	0.8	0.4	0.2	0.2	5.2	5.9	4.5
Malaysia	1.4	1.4	1.4	1.6	1.7	1.1	1.1	1.1
Mexico	0.7	0.4	0.5	0.6	0.4	0.6	0.7	0.5
Montenegro	..	..	..	..	..	..	..	..
Morocco	..	..	..	..	..	..	..	0.7
Netherlands	0.0	0.0	0.0	0.1	0.0	..	..	7.5
New Zealand	..	..	..	..	..	0.2	0.2	..
Nicaragua	..	..	..	..	..	..	..	..
Norway	..	..	..	..	..	..	..	..
Panama	..	..	..	..	..	5.2	7.0	15.8
Paraguay	..	0.7	0.0	0.2	..	0.0	..	0.0
Peru	0.6	0.5	0.3	0.1	0.0	0.2	0.2	0.1
Poland	0.1	0.1	0.1	0.1	0.0	0.0	0.0	0.0
Portugal	0.0	0.0	0.0	0.0	0.0	0.0	0.0	0.0
Puerto Rico	0.0	0.0	0.5	..	..	..	..	..
Singapore	10.8	10.4	14.7	11.0	..	16.3	21.6	18.3
Slovak Republic	0.0	0.0	..	0.0	..	0.0	0.5	0.6
Slovenia	..	..	..	..	..	..	..	..
South Africa	0.0	0.0	0.0	..	..	..	0.0	0.0
Spain	1.6	1.5	1.5	1.4	1.5	1.7	7.5	2.1
Sri Lanka	..	0.0	..	0.6	..	..	..	..
Sweden	0.0	0.0	0.0	0.0	0.0	0.0	0.0	0.0
Switzerland	1.4	1.5	1.7	1.3	1.2	1.2	1.4	1.8
Chinese Taipei	..	..	..	..	42.0	43.4	0.3	0.3
Thailand	..	..	..	..	..	..	..	..
Tunisia	..	..	1.5	1.5	..	..	..	..
Türkiye	1.5	1.6	4.3	3.6	3.9	3.3	3.1	4.9
United Kingdom	9.0	10.0	40.7	10.4	18.7	15.9	15.5	14.9
United States	10.4	15.1	13.8	14.9	20.2	18.0	16.8	19.5
Uruguay	0.0	0.0	..	0.0	..	0.0	0.0	0.0
OECD Total	6.7	8.8	12.4	8.9	12.4	11.7	10.9	12.2

.. Not available

Note: Detailed metadata at: *http://metalinks.oecd.org/ins/20230516/99ff.*

Source: *Insurance activity indicators, OECD Insurance Statistics (database)*

Table 26. Ratio of reinsurance accepted (Non-life)

Per cent

	2014	2015	2016	2017	2018	2019	2020	2021
Argentina	8.0	7.8	7.5	7.2	6.0	5.9	5.6	5.5
Australia	14.3	14.7	16.0	13.9	14.3	14.5	14.9	15.8
Austria	14.7	13.6	13.7	9.2	10.2	9.4	..	..
Belgium	7.6	6.4	5.8	4.7	3.7	14.0	15.8	16.2
Bermuda	..	..	..	..	..	87.4	69.6	86.1
Bolivia	..	..	1.4	4.2	2.1	6.1	6.8	7.4
Brazil	0.1	0.0	0.0	0.0	0.0	0.0	0.0	0.0
Bulgaria	..	..	..	..	1.9	1.2	0.9	1.2
Canada	18.1	17.7	15.8	16.7	11.1	..	..	..
Chile	1.5	1.6	1.3	1.1	1.1	1.2	1.4	1.5
Colombia	3.5	3.7	3.5	3.8	3.9	4.0	3.7	4.0
Costa Rica	0.3	0.4	0.3	0.3	0.4	0.4	0.5	0.5
Cuba	..	..	..	..	..	..	..	..
Czech Republic	2.9	3.4	3.7	3.7	2.9	2.8	2.7	2.5
Denmark	1.3	1.4	8.0	9.8	10.7	7.3	5.4	5.6
Dominican Republic	..	..	..	..	..	..	..	..
Ecuador	..	2.4	2.2	..	..	0.9	..	0.6
Egypt	..	..	..	..	..	8.5	6.0	6.3
El Salvador	..	..	..	..	5.2	5.7	6.8	5.8
Estonia	..	..	..	..	0.0	0.0	..	..
Finland	3.0	3.0	3.0	3.3	..	..	..	..
France	13.3	13.5	16.1	17.4	17.8	16.9	16.7	18.8
Germany	34.7	37.0	36.4	35.9	36.0	37.6	38.4	40.1
Greece	2.2	1.9	1.8	1.8	1.7	1.7	1.5	1.5
Guatemala	3.0	3.4	3.2	3.3	3.9	3.3	3.6	3.3
Honduras	0.0	0.0	..	..	..	0.0	..	..
Hong Kong, China	26.1	24.2	23.3	25.1	28.3	..	..	25.4
Hungary	1.9	2.1	2.0	2.9	2.0	1.7	1.2	1.1
Iceland	2.7	2.6	1.9	1.5	1.9	1.8	0.1	0.2
India	..	3.0	..	19.4	..	2.0	..	..
Indonesia	7.3	6.8	7.5	7.2	6.6	7.3	12.1	5.1
Ireland	5.3	4.6	5.5	5.3	6.5	16.3	8.6	4.5
Israel	..	..	0.0	..	..	..	..	..
Italy	3.4	3.8	3.9	3.7	5.1	3.1	4.7	6.0
Japan	..	..	16.0	16.3	16.1	15.9	15.9	16.0
Korea	10.1	10.3	10.2	10.5	11.2	..	11.0	10.8
Latvia	0.0	0.0	0.0	0.0	0.0	0.1	0.1	0.0
Lithuania	0.0	0.0	0.0	0.0	0.0	0.0	0.0	0.1
Luxembourg	0.2	0.2	0.2	0.2	0.4	9.4	9.9	11.7
Malaysia	16.7	17.3	17.8	16.8	15.8	16.8	19.6	24.7
Mexico	2.7	2.7	2.6	2.6	2.7	2.8	3.7	3.9
Montenegro	..	..	..	..	..	..	..	..
Morocco	..	..	..	..	..	..	..	9.1
Netherlands	2.8	2.9	0.6	0.7	0.5	..	..	1.3
New Zealand	0.6	3.8	1.8	5.3	..	0.0	0.0	..
Nicaragua	..	..	..	..	..	..	..	..
Norway	..	..	..	..	..	..	..	..
Panama	..	..	..	..	..	9.2	9.7	9.5
Paraguay	..	1.2	1.0	0.8	..	0.5	..	0.5
Peru	0.8	0.7	0.8	1.3	1.1	1.4	1.6	1.1
Poland	2.1	5.3	6.1	5.2	5.7	6.8	6.9	7.1
Portugal	12.3	12.1	12.6	12.9	13.8	12.7	12.8	13.4
Puerto Rico	1.0	0.9	0.6	..	..	..	..	..
Singapore	37.3	40.7	39.2	37.0	..	50.0	45.0	46.9
Slovak Republic	3.1	4.0	..	0.8	..	0.0	0.0	0.5
Slovenia	14.6	16.3	15.7	15.5	14.9	15.5	16.8	17.0
South Africa	11.6	11.1	14.2	..	..	..	17.9	15.3
Spain	12.6	13.5	14.1	13.4	12.7	12.6	12.8	13.5
Sri Lanka	3.5	2.6	..	3.7	3.7	..	..	..
Sweden	13.5	11.4	11.8	13.0	12.6	12.4	12.7	13.3
Switzerland	25.4	23.4	23.6	24.8	26.0	27.5	27.1	27.8
Chinese Taipei	..	..	..	..	11.9	12.4	12.7	12.9
Thailand	..	..	..	..	..	..	..	..
Tunisia	..	..	1.1	6.2	..	..	..	..
Türkiye	5.4	3.3	6.1	6.5	9.3	11.7	9.9	9.4
United Kingdom	12.6	14.1	25.0	23.1	23.5	29.1	28.0	30.3
United States	28.2	27.4	27.0	27.4	5.6	6.2	6.4	6.8
Uruguay	0.0	0.0	..	0.0	..	0.0	0.0	0.0
OECD Total	24.1	24.2	23.6	24.0	11.0	11.8	12.0	12.5

.. Not available

Note: Detailed metadata at: *http://metalinks.oecd.org/ins/20230516/99ff*.

Source: *Insurance activity indicators, OECD Insurance Statistics (database)*

Table 27. Market share of foreign companies in the domestic market (Life)

Per cent

	2014	2015	2016	2017	2018	2019	2020	2021
Argentina	31.4	30.8	30.4	30.0	27.9	29.0	27.5	24.3
Australia	15.5	17.7	20.8	25.5	29.8	37.5	76.7	78.3
Austria	39.2	37.7	39.3	39.7	39.7	39.1	..	..
Belgium	..	..	..	..	..	..	..	..
Bermuda	..	..	..	..	..	..	..	..
Bolivia	..	..	29.9	20.8	27.8	28.0	27.4	28.9
Brazil	18.6	18.3	17.2	21.3	26.5	29.5	19.2	17.4
Bulgaria	..	..	..	..	97.2	97.2	96.7	96.7
Canada	26.0	21.0	18.7	18.1	15.2	..	..	..
Chile	45.0	41.8	41.6	44.5	43.0	45.0	42.4	45.2
Colombia	21.6	20.9	18.1	18.6	18.8	17.2	17.3	16.6
Costa Rica	17.0	23.0	25.0	33.9	37.2	37.3	36.5	36.4
Cuba	..	..	..	..	..	..	..	..
Czech Republic	96.7	96.3	96.8	96.4	95.9	97.1	96.5	99.0
Denmark	19.5	18.6	18.8	19.9	19.8	13.8	84.8	84.6
Dominican Republic	..	..	..	..	46.5	..	..	..
Ecuador	..	..	11.7	..	..	0.0	..	0.0
Egypt	..	..	..	..	..	..	..	..
El Salvador	9.6	9.4	9.6	..	10.3	9.9	8.1	6.2
Estonia	100.0	100.0	100.0	100.0	100.0	100.0	100.0	100.0
Finland	43.0	38.5	..	..	..	..	..	..
France	..	..	..	..	..	..	..	..
Germany	26.0	26.7	25.3	24.6	24.9	23.4	23.8	24.1
Greece	48.0	55.7	76.9	74.0	73.2	66.8	69.9	71.6
Guatemala	..	..	..	..	..	..	0.0	..
Honduras	59.6	62.2	..	..	62.7	59.6	58.2	57.9
Hong Kong, China	..	..	..	..	..	..	..	97.5
Hungary	96.2	95.8	96.9	96.6	96.3	96.4	96.2	95.9
Iceland	5.0	5.8	..	..	..	..	..	..
India	..	0.0	..	0.1	..	..	..	..
Indonesia	..	..	..	..	..	..	..	..
Ireland	4.5	4.7	..	5.3	2.5	1.3	0.1	..
Israel	0.4	0.4	0.4	0.4	0.4	17.7	16.8	18.7
Italy	31.3	30.5	33.1	32.1	37.1	37.0	35.8	35.6
Japan	20.1	20.6	21.8	22.7	22.5	22.5	23.0	23.6
Korea	13.2	12.4	14.7	16.1	14.3	..	21.0	20.6
Latvia	91.0	89.8	90.8	91.3	91.6	91.8	90.0	89.8
Lithuania	97.4	97.4	97.5	97.1	97.3	97.2	97.2	97.1
Luxembourg	96.4	92.5	77.2	90.6	92.2	93.1	75.6	74.3
Malaysia	68.8	69.6	69.7	71.8	70.4	72.5	72.4	70.4
Mexico	74.0	72.3	70.6	68.0	68.8	68.5	65.6	61.5
Montenegro	..	..	..	..	..	..	..	..
Morocco	..	..	..	..	..	..	..	23.6
Netherlands	4.6	18.5	19.2	23.3	19.9	..	..	14.6
New Zealand	..	..	..	..	..	77.7	75.8	..
Nicaragua	26.6	26.4	18.0	..	25.8	..	27.3	32.7
Norway	13.3	15.1	0.7	0.7	0.5	0.4	0.3	0.3
Panama	..	..	..	..	..	39.9	42.8	96.1
Paraguay	..	0.0	0.0	5.5	..	5.6	..	16.3
Peru	30.7	56.8	28.1	27.6	23.4	35.0	36.3	38.7
Poland	50.0	50.7	54.3	45.2	44.0	44.6	46.7	20.0
Portugal	54.0	64.2	77.5	93.8	90.8	85.2	91.2	91.4
Puerto Rico	7.8	0.0	38.0	..	..	..	..	..
Singapore	71.3	70.6	70.0	53.3	..	53.3	54.0	51.2
Slovak Republic	90.0	89.0	..	5.6	..	87.8	91.0	91.6
Slovenia	17.2	17.0	17.1	15.7	15.4	25.3	27.0	24.4
South Africa	35.2	33.3	34.6	..	..	..	13.0	13.0
Spain	12.8	12.3	..	..	..	..	..	..
Sri Lanka	2.4	1.7	..	..	..	..	..	..
Sweden	7.9	8.8	11.2	12.2	13.2	12.3	..	15.5
Switzerland	27.9	26.9	25.6	25.3	26.1	10.6	8.3	7.5
Chinese Taipei	..	..	..	..	46.7	47.7	7.4	9.4
Thailand	..	..	..	..	..	..	..	..
Tunisia	..	..	..	..	..	..	..	..
Türkiye	47.9	59.7	54.2	56.4	59.2	52.7	54.0	57.5
United Kingdom	16.0	16.9	..	..	..	..	..	..
United States	21.0	17.4	22.5	21.7	23.0	19.8	20.0	20.7
Uruguay	33.4	30.1	..	21.3	..	21.3	20.5	19.0

.. Not available

Note: Detailed metadata at: *http://metalinks.oecd.org/ins/20230516/99ff*.

Source: *Insurance activity indicators, OECD Insurance Statistics (database)*

Table 28. Market share of foreign undertakings in total domestic business (Life)

Branches or agencies

Per cent

	2014	2015	2016	2017	2018	2019	2020	2021
Argentina	3.9	3.2	3.4	3.5	3.7	5.0	5.3	6.2
Australia	..	..	..	..	..	..	..	..
Austria	0.0	0.0	0.0	0.0	0.0	0.0	..	..
Belgium	..	..	..	..	..	..	..	..
Bermuda	..	..	..	..	..	..	..	..
Bolivia	..	..	..	..	..	..	..	..
Brazil	..	0.0	0.0	0.0	0.0	0.0	0.0	0.0
Bulgaria	..	..	..	..	..	..	..	..
Canada	15.5	15.8	13.2	12.7	9.0	..	..	..
Chile	..	..	..	..	..	..	..	..
Colombia	0.0	..	..	..	..	..	..	..
Costa Rica	0.6	1.1	1.0	1.3	1.6	1.4	3.4	3.6
Cuba	..	..	..	..	..	..	..	..
Czech Republic	7.2	10.8	10.9	11.4	11.5	14.6	15.0	16.0
Denmark	..	..	..	..	..	..	..	..
Dominican Republic	..	..	..	..	..	..	..	..
Ecuador	..	..	..	..	..	0.0	..	0.0
Egypt	..	..	..	..	..	..	..	..
El Salvador	9.6	9.4	9.6	..	10.3	9.9	8.1	6.2
Estonia	2.7	2.8	2.2	3.1	5.2	8.3	10.9	9.8
Finland	..	..	..	..	..	..	..	..
France	..	..	..	..	..	..	..	..
Germany	3.9	4.0	3.9	4.0	3.8	3.7	4.4	3.7
Greece	0.0	0.0	0.0	0.0	0.0	0.0	0.0	0.0
Guatemala	..	..	..	..	..	..	0.0	..
Honduras	25.6	23.1	..	..	62.7	59.6	58.2	57.9
Hong Kong, China	..	..	..	..	..	..	..	66.6
Hungary	..	..	..	..	..	..	..	..
Iceland	..	..	..	..	..	..	..	..
India	..	0.0	..	0.1	..	..	..	..
Indonesia	..	..	..	..	..	..	..	..
Ireland	4.5	4.7	..	5.3	2.5	1.3	0.1	..
Israel	..	..	..	..	..	..	..	..
Italy	0.0	0.0	0.0	0.0	..	..	..	0.0
Japan	4.2	4.1	4.3	4.5	0.1	0.1	0.2	..
Korea	2.4	0.2	2.0	2.1	2.3	..	..	..
Latvia	58.5	59.3	61.4	63.1	65.5	44.8	47.3	52.5
Lithuania	43.1	41.8	40.8	41.4	43.3	62.2	62.7	63.1
Luxembourg	0.1	0.1	0.1	0.1	0.1	5.1	5.8	9.0
Malaysia	0.5	0.5	0.5	0.6	0.7	..	..	..
Mexico	..	..	..	..	..	..	..	..
Montenegro	..	..	..	..	..	..	..	..
Morocco	..	..	..	..	..	..	..	0.0
Netherlands	0.0	0.0	..	..	..	..	..	14.6
New Zealand	..	..	..	..	..	20.8	14.6	..
Nicaragua	..	..	..	..	..	..	..	..
Norway	1.4	0.7	0.7	0.7	0.5	0.4	0.3	0.3
Panama	..	..	..	..	..	39.3	..	0.0
Paraguay	..	0.0	0.0	..	..	0.0	..	0.0
Peru	..	..	..	..	..	..	..	..
Poland	..	..	..	..	..	..	..	..
Portugal	0.0	0.0	0.0	0.0	0.0	0.0	0.0	0.0
Puerto Rico	..	..	..	..	..	..	..	..
Singapore	32.6	30.7	32.3	8.7	..	15.2	19.8	16.0
Slovak Republic	4.4	4.8	..	5.6	..	15.3	17.8	23.2
Slovenia	..	..	..	..	..	..	..	..
South Africa	..	..	..	..	..	..	0.0	0.0
Spain	0.0	0.0	..	..	..	..	..	..
Sri Lanka	..	0.0	..	..	..	..	..	..
Sweden	0.7	..	..	..	..	..	..	..
Switzerland	0.0	0.0	0.0	0.0	0.0	0.1	0.1	0.1
Chinese Taipei	..	..	..	..	43.9	45.3	3.0	4.8
Thailand	..	..	..	..	..	..	..	..
Tunisia	..	..	..	..	..	..	..	..
Türkiye	..	..	0.0	0.0	0.0	..	0.0	..
United Kingdom	0.0	0.0	..	..	..	..	..	..
United States	..	..	0.0	0.0	0.0	0.0	0.0	0.0
Uruguay	0.0	0.0	..	0.0	..	0.0	0.0	0.0

.. Not available

Note: Detailed metadata at: *http://metalinks.oecd.org/ins/20230516/99ff*.

Source: *Insurance activity indicators, OECD Insurance Statistics (database)*

Table 29. Market share of foreign companies in the domestic market (Non-life)

Per cent

	2014	2015	2016	2017	2018	2019	2020	2021
Argentina	21.1	22.0	23.4	30.5	30.0	29.6	18.6	16.0
Australia	28.7	28.2	28.7	29.5	34.8	37.3	38.5	39.5
Austria	37.5	36.9	36.6	33.2	32.9	33.1	..	..
Belgium	..	..	..	..	..	..	..	..
Bermuda	..	..	..	..	..	..	..	..
Bolivia	..	..	27.9	29.1	25.5	25.1	25.8	24.9
Brazil	51.3	32.4	35.7	39.4	53.9	43.9	60.5	58.1
Bulgaria	..	..	..	..	47.2	44.7	42.5	42.2
Canada	44.8	41.6	40.9	41.3	37.5	..	..	..
Chile	63.5	62.7	79.0	75.6	73.8	73.5	72.0	84.2
Colombia	55.4	52.7	50.8	47.7	45.8	45.8	44.8	46.1
Costa Rica	14.2	17.5	20.5	22.8	25.4	25.4	27.1	31.6
Cuba	..	..	..	..	..	..	..	..
Czech Republic	89.4	90.0	89.1	88.6	87.8	86.9	86.6	94.8
Denmark	27.5	27.9	28.3	25.3	23.1	21.9	78.8	79.1
Dominican Republic	..	..	..	..	28.4	..	..	..
Ecuador	..	..	0.4	..	..	0.0	..	0.0
Egypt	..	..	..	..	..	..	..	..
El Salvador	0.0	0.0	0.0	..	4.5	4.2	3.8	..
Estonia	95.1	95.2	94.8	100.0	95.4	95.6	95.8	94.6
Finland	23.7	100.0	..	..	..	..	..	..
France	0.1	0.1	..	..	..	..	..	..
Germany	14.5	14.3	13.3	13.6	14.4	13.6	13.5	13.9
Greece	41.2	43.0	57.3	57.3	56.4	55.7	55.7	56.2
Guatemala	..	..	..	..	..	..	0.0	..
Honduras	40.3	42.8	..	..	49.3	47.3	44.0	44.6
Hong Kong, China	..	..	..	..	..	..	..	83.4
Hungary	94.7	92.8	91.7	91.4	91.4	91.4	92.5	93.3
Iceland	10.9	11.3	..	..	..	..	..	..
India	..	..	..	2.9	..	..	..	..
Indonesia	..	..	..	..	..	..	..	..
Ireland	24.3	22.2	..	17.1	16.6	22.8	14.4	..
Israel	3.4	4.0	3.8	3.8	3.8	18.9	18.0	18.3
Italy	28.9	32.2	31.8	31.1	30.0	31.4	30.0	28.6
Japan	..	..	9.4	7.5	9.4	8.7	9.2	9.3
Korea	3.7	3.7	3.7	3.8	4.1	..	4.3	4.5
Latvia	48.7	57.1	79.0	77.2	79.5	83.5	86.7	89.2
Lithuania	99.0	99.0	99.3	99.5	99.5	99.6	99.6	99.6
Luxembourg	53.3	52.8	51.7	51.1	50.2	63.7	64.0	69.3
Malaysia	46.6	47.8	48.5	51.9	52.9	53.4	53.5	55.4
Mexico	48.7	52.2	48.5	50.3	48.1	49.5	46.8	48.8
Montenegro	..	..	..	..	..	..	..	..
Morocco	..	..	..	..	..	..	..	34.4
Netherlands	11.6	16.3	2.6	2.3	1.7	..	..	0.2
New Zealand	..	..	..	..	..	74.7	74.2	..
Nicaragua	24.7	25.7	26.0	..	29.4	..	30.8	31.8
Norway	41.1	40.2	40.3	37.8	37.3	37.3	36.2	37.3
Panama	..	..	..	..	..	43.4	45.4	38.8
Paraguay	..	0.0	22.8	24.7	..	27.5	..	31.4
Peru	20.6	45.9	24.8	25.7	25.0	40.1	40.1	39.7
Poland	61.3	61.8	59.1	58.4	59.1	60.2	60.2	46.8
Portugal	84.2	84.3	91.0	91.6	91.0	91.1	90.8	90.9
Puerto Rico	51.8	41.0	55.6	..	..	..	..	..
Singapore	89.0	89.2	90.2	80.0	..	79.0	78.6	83.9
Slovak Republic	93.6	93.2	..	8.3	..	96.8	98.5	93.7
Slovenia	5.2	5.3	5.7	5.9	5.8	18.3	17.8	18.4
South Africa	39.5	34.6	37.4	..	..	..	14.5	10.9
Spain	28.8	23.6	..	..	..	..	..	..
Sri Lanka	4.7	4.8	..	16.0	10.6	..	..	..
Sweden	55.4	44.8	46.7	48.0	52.6	52.3	..	50.2
Switzerland	19.6	20.3	20.1	18.7	17.4	16.9	16.0	15.8
Chinese Taipei	..	..	..	..	9.9	9.7	9.7	9.1
Thailand	..	..	..	..	..	..	..	..
Tunisia	..	..	..	..	..	..	..	..
Türkiye	59.3	66.7	63.7	57.1	54.2	52.9	48.9	47.1
United Kingdom	57.8	57.5	0.3	0.5	0.5	0.7	0.5	1.0
United States	9.4	9.5	10.2	10.0	0.8	5.5	11.7	9.9
Uruguay	32.2	33.6	..	34.7	..	34.6	36.4	38.5

.. Not available

Note: Detailed metadata at: *http://metalinks.oecd.org/ins/20230516/99ff*.

Source: *Insurance activity indicators, OECD Insurance Statistics (database)*

Table 30. Market share of foreign undertakings in total domestic business (Non-life)

Branches or agencies

Per cent

	2014	2015	2016	2017	2018	2019	2020	2021
Argentina	3.2	2.5	2.4	2.6	2.1	2.2	2.2	2.2
Australia	10.1	9.1	9.9	9.6	11.9	13.2	15.1	16.7
Austria	0.1	0.0	0.0	0.1	0.1	0.1	..	..
Belgium	..	..	..	..	..	..	..	..
Bermuda	..	..	..	..	..	..	..	..
Bolivia	..	..	..	..	..	..	..	..
Brazil	..	0.0	0.0	0.0	0.0	0.0	0.0	0.0
Bulgaria	..	..	..	..	..	..	..	..
Canada	23.2	21.0	19.4	19.0	15.1	..	..	..
Chile	..	..	..	..	..	..	..	..
Colombia	0.0	..	..	..	..	..	..	..
Costa Rica	0.4	0.8	1.3	1.5	1.7	1.7	2.1	2.7
Cuba	..	..	..	..	..	..	..	..
Czech Republic	4.7	4.9	5.3	5.4	4.4	4.8	4.4	5.2
Denmark	..	..	..	..	..	..	..	..
Dominican Republic	..	..	..	..	..	..	..	..
Ecuador	..	..	..	..	..	0.0	..	0.0
Egypt	..	..	..	..	..	..	..	..
El Salvador	0.0	0.0	0.0	..	4.5	4.2	3.8	..
Estonia	14.8	13.5	15.0	15.1	15.3	15.9	21.8	21.2
Finland	..	..	..	..	..	..	..	..
France	0.1	0.1	..	..	..	..	..	..
Germany	3.2	3.5	3.1	3.8	4.0	3.6	3.8	4.5
Greece	0.0	0.0	0.0	0.0	0.0	0.0	0.0	0.0
Guatemala	..	..	..	..	..	..	0.0	..
Honduras	4.4	3.6	..	..	49.3	47.3	44.0	44.6
Hong Kong, China	..	..	..	..	..	..	..	28.0
Hungary	..	..	..	..	..	..	..	..
Iceland	..	..	..	..	..	..	..	..
India	..	..	..	2.9	..	..	..	..
Indonesia	..	..	..	..	..	..	..	..
Ireland	24.3	22.2	..	17.1	16.6	22.8	14.4	..
Israel	..	..	..	..	..	..	..	..
Italy	1.1	1.4	1.6	1.5	1.6	1.7	1.7	1.7
Japan	..	..	2.3	2.5	2.8	2.3	3.3	3.6
Korea	2.3	2.3	2.3	2.4	2.8	..	3.0	3.2
Latvia	20.4	20.2	22.6	27.0	28.1	29.6	30.0	32.6
Lithuania	53.1	53.9	46.8	48.4	51.4	51.5	50.8	49.2
Luxembourg	3.6	3.6	3.5	3.3	3.6	11.7	10.9	8.0
Malaysia	7.3	8.4	9.6	8.9	8.8	10.0	12.6	17.4
Mexico	..	..	..	..	..	..	..	..
Montenegro	..	..	..	..	..	..	..	..
Morocco	..	..	..	..	..	..	..	0.0
Netherlands	0.3	0.0	..	..	..	..	..	0.2
New Zealand	..	..	..	..	..	13.0	12.7	..
Nicaragua	..	..	..	..	..	..	..	..
Norway	41.1	40.2	40.3	37.8	37.3	37.3	36.2	37.3
Panama	..	..	..	..	..	41.4	..	0.0
Paraguay	..	0.0	0.0	..	..	0.0	..	0.0
Peru	..	..	..	..	..	..	..	..
Poland	..	..	..	..	..	..	..	..
Portugal	0.0	0.0	0.0	0.0	0.0	0.0	0.0	0.0
Puerto Rico	..	..	..	..	..	..	..	..
Singapore	39.6	38.2	37.4	36.5	..	31.7	40.0	35.6
Slovak Republic	8.7	8.5	..	8.3	..	7.7	5.8	17.9
Slovenia	..	..	..	..	..	..	..	..
South Africa	..	..	..	..	..	..	0.0	0.0
Spain	0.0	0.0	..	..	..	..	..	..
Sri Lanka	..	0.0	..	..	..	..	..	..
Sweden	8.2	..	..	..	..	..	..	..
Switzerland	5.5	6.0	7.1	7.5	5.8	5.2	4.5	4.5
Chinese Taipei	..	..	..	..	3.3	3.4	3.3	3.0
Thailand	..	..	..	..	..	..	..	..
Tunisia	..	..	..	..	..	..	..	..
Türkiye	0.3	0.4	0.4	0.5	0.7	1.0	1.2	1.1
United Kingdom	4.1	4.6	0.3	0.5	0.5	0.7	0.5	1.0
United States	0.0	0.1	0.1	0.1	0.1	0.0	0.0	0.0
Uruguay	0.0	0.0	..	0.0	..	0.0	0.0	0.0

.. Not available

Note: Detailed metadata at: *http://metalinks.oecd.org/ins/20230516/99ff*.

Source: *Insurance activity indicators, OECD Insurance Statistics (database)*

Country tables

AUSTRALIA

Table 1. Selected aggregates

Million AUD

	2014	2015	2016	2017	2018	2019	2020	2021
1.1 Insurance business written in the reporting country								
1.1.1 Insurance business, by ownership								
Gross premiums								
Domestic undertakings	103 414	100 992	95 348	90 032	88 064	81 517	75 436	79 212
Foreign controlled undertakings	17 983	19 150	19 836	21 498	24 659	26 308	35 921	37 610
Foreign companies (branches)	4 206	3 893	4 393	4 353	5 613	6 630	7 967	9 612
All undertakings	107 620	104 885	99 741	94 385	93 677	88 147	83 403	88 824
Premiums ceded								
Domestic undertakings	13 268	15 209	17 826	19 711	18 794	20 650	22 714	24 360
Foreign controlled undertakings	5 483	5 986	6 268	8 647	8 223	8 676	12 208	13 361
Foreign companies (branches)	1 842	1 739	1 759	1 873	1 875	2 155	2 770	3 336
All undertakings	15 110	16 948	19 585	21 584	20 669	22 805	25 484	27 696
Net written premiums								
Domestic undertakings	90 147	85 783	77 522	70 321	69 270	60 869	52 722	54 852
Foreign controlled undertakings	12 500	13 164	13 568	12 851	16 436	17 632	23 713	24 249
Foreign companies (branches)	2 365	2 154	2 634	2 480	3 738	4 475	5 197	6 276
All undertakings	92 511	87 937	80 156	72 801	73 008	65 344	57 919	61 128
1.1.2 Insurance business on foreign risks, gross premiums								
Life	686	701	711	706	880	1 176	1 156	1 134
Non-life	..	..	..	..	..	..	..	..
Composite total	..	..	..	..	..	..	..	..
Total	686	701	711	706	880	1 176	1 156	1 134
1.1.3 Life insurance payments, by class, gross premiums								
Annuities	..	..	..	..	..	..	..	..
Unit linked	..	..	..	..	..	..	..	..
Other life insurance	..	..	..	..	..	..	..	..
Total life insurance	60 881	56 868	49 890	43 141	39 741	31 149	23 860	24 231
***of which:** Pension contracts*	..	..	..	..	..	..	..	..
1.1.4 Non-life insurance payments, by class, gross premiums								
Motor vehicle insurance	13 467	13 749	14 512	15 447	15 789	16 471	16 885	17 819
Marine, aviation and other transport insurance	1 598	1 673	1 648	1 739	1 871	1 899	1 319	1 105
Freight insurance	..	..	..	..	..	..	..	..
Fire and other property damage insurance	11 836	12 031	12 297	12 713	13 428	14 391	15 736	17 340
Pecuniary loss insurance	1 454	1 493	1 443	1 352	1 230	1 169	1 076	1 097
General liability insurance	5 418	5 435	5 348	5 491	5 893	6 391	7 164	8 419
Accident and health	1 124	1 130	1 064	1 021	1 006	1 022	1 046	1 104
***of which:** Health*	..	..	..	..	..	..	..	..
Other non-life insurance	951	1 029	1 071	1 205	1 325	1 444	1 543	1 579
Treaty reinsurance	5 970	6 271	7 115	6 269	6 742	7 273	7 819	9 076
Total non-life insurance	41 818	42 811	44 498	45 237	47 283	50 060	52 588	57 539
1.2 Gross claims payments								
Life								
Domestic undertakings	64 828	56 547	59 350	47 307	46 989	43 814	94 607	23 756
Foreign controlled undertakings	5 876	6 681	7 133	9 207	8 564	9 141	80 540	19 477
Foreign companies (branches)	..	..	..	..	..	..	..	..
All undertakings	64 828	56 547	59 350	47 307	46 989	43 814	94 607	23 756
Non-life								
Domestic undertakings	26 293	29 311	28 026	29 946	30 252	33 037	40 491	33 439
Foreign controlled undertakings	5 446	6 183	5 534	6 453	8 199	8 425	11 044	8 663
Foreign companies (branches)	3 318	2 585	3 217	3 124	3 853	5 088	6 947	5 101
All undertakings	29 611	31 896	31 243	33 070	34 105	38 125	47 438	38 540
Composite, all undertakings	..	..	..	..	..	..	..	..
Total								
Domestic undertakings	91 121	85 858	87 376	77 253	77 241	76 851	135 098	57 195
Foreign controlled undertakings	11 322	12 864	12 667	15 660	16 763	17 566	91 584	28 140
Foreign companies (branches)	3 318	2 585	3 217	3 124	3 853	5 088	6 947	5 101
All undertakings	94 439	88 443	90 593	80 377	81 094	81 939	142 045	62 296
1.3 Commissions								
Life								
Domestic undertakings	3 118	3 087	3 129	2 514	2 402	2 052	1 740	1 620
Foreign controlled undertakings	451	460	464	494	483	470	1 347	1 445
Foreign companies (branches)	..	..	..	..	..	..	..	..
All undertakings	3 118	3 087	3 129	2 514	2 402	2 052	1 740	1 620
Non-life								
Domestic undertakings	566	816	1 038	1 070	1 310	1 338	1 418	1 644
Foreign controlled undertakings	270	276	308	341	418	452	534	569
Foreign companies (branches)	287	301	327	324	250	280	373	470
All undertakings	853	1 117	1 364	1 394	1 560	1 618	1 791	2 114
Composite, all undertakings	..	..	..	..	..	..	..	..
Total								
Domestic undertakings	3 684	3 903	4 167	3 584	3 712	3 390	3 158	3 264
Foreign controlled undertakings	721	736	772	835	901	923	1 881	2 014
Foreign companies (branches)	287	301	327	324	250	280	373	470
All undertakings	3 971	4 204	4 493	3 908	3 962	3 671	3 531	3 734

AUSTRALIA

Table 1. Selected aggregates *(cont.)*

Million AUD

	2014	2015	2016	2017	2018	2019	2020	2021
1.4 Gross operating expenses								
Life								
Domestic undertakings	8 128	8 041	8 666	8 457	9 370	8 045	6 999	6 773
Foreign controlled undertakings	2 393	2 487	3 038	3 239	4 439	3 546	5 724	6 304
Foreign companies (branches)	..	..	..	..	..	..	..	..
All undertakings	8 128	8 041	8 666	8 457	9 370	8 045	6 999	6 773
Non-life								
Domestic undertakings	7 502	7 497	7 368	7 475	7 517	7 979	8 354	8 455
Foreign controlled undertakings	1 704	1 850	1 829	1 975	2 378	2 710	2 782	2 694
Foreign companies (branches)	629	660	618	563	790	1 003	1 109	1 229
All undertakings	8 131	8 157	7 987	8 038	8 307	8 982	9 463	9 684
Composite, all undertakings	..	..	..	..	..	..	..	..
Total								
Domestic undertakings	15 630	15 538	16 034	15 932	16 887	16 024	15 353	15 228
Foreign controlled undertakings	4 097	4 337	4 867	5 214	6 817	6 256	8 505	8 998
Foreign companies (branches)	629	660	618	563	790	1 003	1 109	1 229
All undertakings	16 259	16 198	16 653	16 495	17 677	17 027	16 462	16 457
1.5 Insurance business written abroad by branches, gross premiums								
Life								
Branches and agencies	..	..	..	..	..	..	..	..
Subsidaries	..	..	..	..	..	..	..	..
Total	..	..	..	..	..	..	..	..
Non-life								
Branches and agencies	..	..	..	..	..	..	..	..
Subsidaries	..	..	..	..	..	..	..	..
Total	..	..	..	..	..	..	..	..
Composite total	..	..	..	..	..	..	..	..
Total								
Branches and agencies	..	..	..	..	..	..	..	..
Subsidaries	..	..	..	..	..	..	..	..
Total	..	..	..	..	..	..	..	..

.. Not available

Note: Detailed metadata at: *http://metalinks.oecd.org/ins/20230516/381d.*

Source: *OECD Insurance Statistics (database)*

AUSTRALIA

Table 2. Number of companies and employees

	2014	2015	2016	2017	2018	2019	2020	2021
2.1 Number of companies								
Life								
Domestic undertakings	28	28	29	29	29	28	28	27
Foreign controlled undertakings	14	13	13	13	14	13	21	22
Foreign companies (branches)	..	..	..	..	..	..	..	..
All undertakings	28	28	29	29	29	28	28	27
Non-life								
Domestic undertakings	74	70	68	58	58	58	58	58
Foreign controlled undertakings	19	19	17	15	17	16	16	15
Foreign companies (branches)	29	29	31	28	28	27	27	25
All undertakings	103	99	99	86	86	85	85	83
Composite, all undertakings	..	0	..	..	..	..	..	..
Reinsurance								
Domestic undertakings	3	2	2	2	2	2	2	2
Foreign controlled undertakings	1	1	1	1	1	2	2	2
Foreign companies (branches)	9	9	8	8	8	9	9	8
All undertakings	12	11	10	10	10	11	11	10
Total								
Domestic undertakings	105	100	99	89	89	88	88	87
Foreign controlled undertakings	34	33	31	29	32	31	39	39
Foreign companies (branches)	38	38	39	36	36	36	36	33
All undertakings	143	138	138	125	125	124	124	120
2.2 Number of employees								
Insurance undertakings	..	..	..	..	..	..	..	..
Intermediaries	..	..	..	..	..	..	..	..
Total	..	..	..	..	..	..	..	..

.. Not available

Note: Detailed metadata at: *http://metalinks.oecd.org/ins/20230516/381d*.

Source: *OECD Insurance Statistics (database)*

AUSTRIA

Table 1. Selected aggregates

Million EUR

	2014	2015	2016	2017	2018	2019	2020	2021
1.1 Insurance business written in the reporting country								
1.1.1 Insurance business, by ownership								
Gross premiums								
Domestic undertakings	18 889	19 003	18 647	18 126	18 520	18 831	..	..
Foreign controlled undertakings	7 196	7 060	6 979	6 390	6 467	6 549	..	..
Foreign companies (branches)	6	6	6	7	8	8	..	..
All undertakings	18 895	19 009	18 653	18 134	18 527	18 839	..	..
Premiums ceded								
Domestic undertakings	3 102	2 996	3 521	3 130	2 376	2 570	..	..
Foreign controlled undertakings	1 171	1 113	1 636	1 280	475	549	..	..
Foreign companies (branches)	0	0	0	0	0	0	..	..
All undertakings	3 102	2 996	3 522	3 131	2 376	2 571	..	..
Net written premiums								
Domestic undertakings	15 787	16 007	15 126	14 996	16 144	16 261	..	..
Foreign controlled undertakings	6 024	5 948	5 343	5 110	5 991	6 000	..	..
Foreign companies (branches)	6	6	6	7	7	8	..	..
All undertakings	15 793	16 013	15 131	15 003	16 151	16 268	..	..
1.1.2 Insurance business on foreign risks, gross premiums								
Life	22	20	14	3	4	23	..	..
Non-life	726	702	753	777	931	858	..	..
Composite	489	391	371	363	358	387	..	..
of which:								
Life	158	111	95	89	82	80	..	..
Non-life	331	280	276	274	276	306	..	..
Total	1 237	1 114	1 138	1 143	1 293	1 268	..	..
1.1.3 Life insurance payments, by class, gross premiums								
Annuities	1 822	1 946	1 531	1 434	1 367	1 361	..	..
Unit linked	1 011	933	864	812	972	1 013	..	..
Other life insurance	3 852	3 812	3 646	3 488	3 188	3 029	..	..
Total life insurance	6 685	6 692	6 041	5 735	5 527	5 403	..	..
***of which:** Pension contracts*	1 116	1 031	940	964	923	831	..	..
1.1.4 Non-life insurance payments, by class, gross premiums								
Motor vehicle insurance	1 447	3 920	4 043	3 980	4 207	4 292	..	..
Marine, aviation and other transport insurance	138	11	9	10	9	6	..	..
Freight insurance	..	155	148	137	165	164	..	..
Fire and other property damage insurance	1 058	3 153	3 178	3 013	3 030	3 170	..	..
Pecuniary loss insurance	183	178	176	166	169	168	..	..
General liability insurance	886	889	905	868	903	932	..	..
Accident and health	3 143	3 257	3 391	3 473	3 627	3 780	..	..
***of which:** Health*	1 905	2 007	2 096	2 167	2 264	2 374	..	..
Other non-life insurance	5 340	742	749	739	877	910	..	..
Treaty reinsurance	..	..	..	..	..	..	..	..
Total non-life insurance	12 195	12 303	12 599	12 386	12 987	13 421	..	..
1.2 Gross claims payments								
Life								
Domestic undertakings	1 110	1 254	947	977	933	956	..	..
Foreign controlled undertakings	714	837	920	959	914	938	..	..
Foreign companies (branches)	0	0	0	0	0	0	..	..
All undertakings	1 110	1 254	947	977	933	956	..	..
Non-life								
Domestic undertakings	1 632	2 072	2 203	1 939	1 936	1 995	..	..
Foreign controlled undertakings	873	1 288	2 620	1 893	1 862	1 936	..	..
Foreign companies (branches)	3	2	3	3	3	4	..	..
All undertakings	1 636	2 075	2 206	1 942	1 939	2 000	..	..
Composite								
Domestic undertakings	11 289	12 780	12 440	12 173	11 700	12 554	..	..
Foreign controlled undertakings	3 026	3 760	10 479	9 813	9 865	11 072	..	..
Foreign companies (branches)	0	0	0	0	0	0	..	..
All undertakings	11 289	12 780	12 440	12 173	11 700	12 554	..	..
of which:								
Life	5 955	7 193	6 817	6 194	5 688	6 294	..	..
Domestic undertakings	5 955	7 193	6 817	6 194	5 688	6 294	..	..
Foreign controlled undertakings	1 630	2 235	3 500	3 281	3 307	3 710	..	..
Foreign companies (branches)	0	0	0	0	0	0	..	..
All undertakings	5 955	7 193	6 817	6 194	5 688	6 294	..	..
Non-life	5 335	5 588	5 623	5 980	6 012	6 261	..	..
Domestic undertakings	5 335	5 588	5 623	5 980	6 012	6 261	..	..
Foreign controlled undertakings	1 396	1 525	6 979	6 532	6 558	7 362	..	..
Foreign companies (branches)	0	0	0	0	0	0	..	..
All undertakings	5 335	5 588	5 623	5 980	6 012	6 261	..	..
Total								
Domestic undertakings	14 032	16 107	15 590	15 089	14 568	15 506	..	..
Foreign controlled undertakings	4 613	5 885	14 018	12 665	12 641	13 945	..	..
Foreign companies (branches)	3	2	3	3	3	4	..	..
All undertakings	14 036	16 109	15 593	15 092	14 572	15 510	..	..

AUSTRIA

Table 1. Selected aggregates *(cont.)*

Million EUR

	2014	2015	2016	2017	2018	2019	2020	2021
1.3 Commissions								
Life								
Domestic undertakings	98	98	80	73	73	73	..	..
Foreign controlled undertakings	70	70	79	72	72	72	..	..
Foreign companies (branches)	0	0	0	0	0	0	..	..
All undertakings	98	98	80	73	73	73	..	..
Non-life								
Domestic undertakings	398	386	399	408	411	416	..	..
Foreign controlled undertakings	329	341	348	352	350	350	..	..
Foreign companies (branches)	1	1	1	2	2	2	..	..
All undertakings	399	387	400	410	413	418	..	..
Composite								
Domestic undertakings	2 279	2 354	2 392	2 365	2 335	2 402	..	..
Foreign controlled undertakings	666	739	734	725	706	747	..	..
Foreign companies (branches)	0	0	0	0	0	0	..	..
All undertakings	2 279	2 354	2 392	2 365	2 335	2 402	..	..
of which:								
Life	624	623	579	538	454	463	..	..
Domestic undertakings	624	623	579	538	454	463	..	..
Foreign controlled undertakings	163	188	163	149	106	112	..	..
Foreign companies (branches)	0	0	0	0	0	0	..	..
All undertakings	624	623	579	538	454	463	..	..
Non-life	1 655	1 731	1 812	1 827	1 881	1 939	..	..
Domestic undertakings	1 655	1 731	1 812	1 827	1 881	1 939	..	..
Foreign controlled undertakings	503	551	571	576	600	635	..	..
Foreign companies (branches)	0	0	0	0	0	0	..	..
All undertakings	1 655	1 731	1 812	1 827	1 881	1 939	..	..
Total								
Domestic undertakings	2 775	2 839	2 871	2 846	2 819	2 891	..	..
Foreign controlled undertakings	1 065	1 150	1 161	1 149	1 128	1 170	..	..
Foreign companies (branches)	1	1	1	2	2	2	..	..
All undertakings	2 776	2 840	2 872	2 848	2 821	2 893	..	..
1.4 Gross operating expenses								
Life								
Domestic undertakings	43	40	37	42	37	34	..	..
Foreign controlled undertakings	30	30	36	41	37	33	..	..
Foreign companies (branches)	0	0	0	0	0	0	..	..
All undertakings	43	40	37	42	37	34	..	..
Non-life								
Domestic undertakings	153	143	192	191	210	218	..	..
Foreign controlled undertakings	116	92	111	105	103	99	..	..
Foreign companies (branches)	1	1	1	1	1	1	..	..
All undertakings	154	144	193	192	210	219	..	..
Composite								
Domestic undertakings	623	678	702	696	741	777	..	..
Foreign controlled undertakings	167	185	177	181	178	183	..	..
Foreign companies (branches)	0	0	0	0	0	0	..	..
All undertakings	623	678	702	696	741	777	..	..
of which:								
Life	194	202	223	224	236	238	..	..
Domestic undertakings	194	202	223	224	236	238	..	..
Foreign controlled undertakings	61	68	63	58	60	63	..	..
Foreign companies (branches)	0	0	0	0	0	0	..	..
All undertakings	194	202	223	224	236	238	..	..
Non-life	428	476	479	472	505	539	..	..
Domestic undertakings	428	476	479	472	505	539	..	..
Foreign controlled undertakings	106	117	114	123	118	120	..	..
Foreign companies (branches)	0	0	0	0	0	0	..	..
All undertakings	428	476	479	472	505	539	..	..
Total								
Domestic undertakings	819	861	930	929	988	1 028	..	..
Foreign controlled undertakings	313	308	324	328	318	315	..	..
Foreign companies (branches)	1	1	1	1	1	1	..	..
All undertakings	820	862	931	930	989	1 029	..	..

Table 1. Selected aggregates *(cont.)*

Million EUR

	2014	2015	2016	2017	2018	2019	2020	2021
1.5 Insurance business written abroad by branches, gross premiums								
Life								
Branches and agencies	22	19	13	11	10	29	..	..
Subsidaries	..	..	..	..	..	..	..	..
Total	22	19	13	11	10	29	..	..
Non-life								
Branches and agencies	198	204	217	215	220	245	..	..
Subsidaries	..	..	..	..	..	..	..	..
Total	198	204	217	215	220	245	..	..
Composite								
Branches and agencies	368	284	251	275	279	261	..	..
Subsidaries	..	..	..	..	..	..	..	..
Total	368	284	251	275	279	261	..	..
of which:								
Life	103	78	83	78	73	71	..	..
Branches and agencies	103	78	83	78	73	71	..	..
Subsidaries	..	..	..	..	..	..	..	..
Total	103	78	83	78	73	71	..	..
Non-life	266	206	168	198	206	190	..	..
Branches and agencies	266	206	168	198	206	190	..	..
Subsidaries	..	..	..	..	..	..	..	..
Total	266	206	168	198	206	190	..	..
Total								
Branches and agencies	587	507	481	501	510	535	..	..
Subsidaries	..	..	..	..	..	..	..	..
Total	587	507	481	501	510	535	..	..

.. Not available

Note: Detailed metadata at: *http://metalinks.oecd.org/ins/20230516/ebb7.*

Source: *OECD Insurance Statistics (database)*

AUSTRIA

Table 2. Number of companies and employees

	2014	2015	2016	2017	2018	2019	2020	2021
2.1 Number of companies								
Life								
Domestic undertakings	7	7	6	6	6	6	..	..
Foreign controlled undertakings	3	3	4	4	4	4	..	..
Foreign companies (branches)	0	0	0	0	0	0	..	..
All undertakings	7	7	6	6	6	6	..	..
Non-life								
Domestic undertakings	12	12	12	12	12	12	..	..
Foreign controlled undertakings	8	8	8	8	7	7	..	..
Foreign companies (branches)	1	1	1	1	1	1	..	..
All undertakings	13	13	13	13	13	13	..	..
Composite								
Domestic undertakings	21	20	17	17	16	16	..	..
Foreign controlled undertakings	6	5	4	4	4	4	..	..
Foreign companies (branches)	0	0	0	0	0	0	..	..
All undertakings	21	20	17	17	16	16	..	..
Reinsurance								
Domestic undertakings	3	2	3	2	1	1	..	..
Foreign controlled undertakings	2	1	1	0	0	0	..	..
Foreign companies (branches)	0	0	0	0	0	0	..	..
All undertakings	3	2	3	2	1	1	..	..
Total								
Domestic undertakings	43	41	38	37	35	35	..	..
Foreign controlled undertakings	19	17	17	16	15	15	..	..
Foreign companies (branches)	1	1	1	1	1	1	..	..
All undertakings	44	42	39	38	36	36	..	..
2.2 Number of employees								
Insurance undertakings	27 791	27 911	28 336	28 367	27 804	27 903	..	..
Intermediaries	..	..	..	..	..	..	..	..
Total	27 791	27 911	28 336	28 367	27 804	27 903	..	..

.. Not available

Note: Detailed metadata at: *http://metalinks.oecd.org/ins/20230516/ebb7.*

Source: *OECD Insurance Statistics (database)*

BELGIUM

Table 1. Selected aggregates

Million EUR

	2014	2015	2016	2017	2018	2019	2020	2021
1.1 Insurance business written in the reporting country								
1.1.1 Insurance business, by ownership								
Gross premiums								
Domestic undertakings	28 863	27 712	27 493	27 299	28 539	31 400	30 132	34 725
Foreign controlled undertakings	..	..	..	..	..	..	..	..
Foreign companies (branches)	..	..	..	..	..	..	..	..
All undertakings	28 863	27 712	27 493	27 299	28 539	31 400	30 132	34 725
Premiums ceded								
Domestic undertakings	3 251	3 183	3 520	3 412	3 656	7 478	5 223	8 523
Foreign controlled undertakings	..	..	..	..	..	..	..	..
Foreign companies (branches)	..	..	..	..	..	..	..	..
All undertakings	3 251	3 183	3 520	3 412	3 656	7 478	5 223	8 523
Net written premiums								
Domestic undertakings	25 612	24 529	23 973	23 887	24 882	23 923	24 910	26 202
Foreign controlled undertakings	..	..	..	..	..	..	..	..
Foreign companies (branches)	..	..	..	..	..	..	..	..
All undertakings	25 612	24 529	23 973	23 887	24 882	23 923	24 910	26 202
1.1.2 Insurance business on foreign risks, gross premiums								
Life	15	24	20	17	6	15	0	0
Non-life	563	436	515	553	611	453	458	2 704
Composite	223	321	331	331	378	580	543	630
of which:								
Life	39	38	23	17	14	15	18	14
Non-life	184	282	308	313	364	565	524	616
Total	801	781	866	901	995	1 048	1 001	3 335
1.1.3 Life insurance payments, by class, gross premiums								
Annuities	..	..	..	..	..	..	..	..
Unit linked	2 524	3 008	2 221	3 182	3 520	3 341	3 352	4 094
Other life insurance	13 723	12 302	12 674	11 424	12 051	12 826	11 351	11 503
Total life insurance	16 247	15 310	14 895	14 606	15 571	16 167	14 703	15 597
***of which:** Pension contracts*	..	..	..	..	..	..	..	..
1.1.4 Non-life insurance payments, by class, gross premiums								
Motor vehicle insurance	3 542	3 585	..	..	..	..	..	..
Marine, aviation and other transport insurance	69	81	..	..	..	..	..	..
Freight insurance	100	73	..	..	..	..	..	..
Fire and other property damage insurance	2 755	2 708	..	..	..	..	..	..
Pecuniary loss insurance	725	598	..	..	..	..	..	..
General liability insurance	785	762	..	..	..	..	..	..
Accident and health	3 695	3 653	..	..	..	..	..	..
***of which:** Health*	1 708	1 849	..	..	..	..	..	..
Other non-life insurance	885	888	..	..	..	..	..	..
Treaty reinsurance	..	..	..	..	..	..	..	..
Total non-life insurance	12 556	12 349	12 532	12 652	12 926	15 159	15 407	19 107
1.2 Gross claims payments								
Life								
Domestic undertakings	626	469	642	521	731	694	300	437
Foreign controlled undertakings	..	..	..	..	..	..	..	..
Foreign companies (branches)	..	..	..	..	..	..	..	..
All undertakings	626	469	642	521	731	694	300	437
Non-life								
Domestic undertakings	2 272	2 363	2 539	2 316	1 489	1 989	2 397	3 332
Foreign controlled undertakings	..	..	..	..	..	..	..	..
Foreign companies (branches)	..	..	..	..	..	..	..	..
All undertakings	2 272	2 363	2 539	2 316	1 489	1 989	2 397	3 332
Composite								
Domestic undertakings	24 323	25 926	25 229	24 184	22 308	22 683	23 407	23 598
Foreign controlled undertakings	..	..	..	..	..	..	..	..
Foreign companies (branches)	..	..	..	..	..	..	..	..
All undertakings	24 323	25 926	25 229	24 184	22 308	22 683	23 407	23 598
of which:								
Life	17 418	19 244	18 328	17 466	16 063	15 914	17 108	16 478
Domestic undertakings	17 418	19 244	18 328	17 466	16 063	15 914	17 108	16 478
Foreign controlled undertakings	..	..	..	..	..	..	..	..
Foreign companies (branches)	..	..	..	..	..	..	..	..
All undertakings	17 418	19 244	18 328	17 466	16 063	15 914	17 108	16 478
Non-life	6 905	6 682	6 901	6 717	6 244	6 770	6 299	7 120
Domestic undertakings	6 905	6 682	6 901	6 717	6 244	6 770	6 299	7 120
Foreign controlled undertakings	..	..	..	..	..	..	..	..
Foreign companies (branches)	..	..	..	..	..	..	..	..
All undertakings	6 905	6 682	6 901	6 717	6 244	6 770	6 299	7 120
Total								
Domestic undertakings	27 222	28 758	28 410	27 020	24 527	25 366	26 104	27 367
Foreign controlled undertakings	..	..	..	..	..	..	..	..
Foreign companies (branches)	..	..	..	..	..	..	..	..
All undertakings	27 222	28 758	28 410	27 020	24 527	25 366	26 104	27 367

Table 1. Selected aggregates *(cont.)*

Million EUR

	2014	2015	2016	2017	2018	2019	2020	2021
1.3 Commissions								
Life								
Domestic undertakings	45	47	55	56	64	67	15	21
Foreign controlled undertakings	..	..	..	..	..	..	..	..
Foreign companies (branches)	..	..	..	..	..	..	..	..
All undertakings	45	47	55	56	64	67	15	21
Non-life								
Domestic undertakings	450	550	616	607	303	287	265	764
Foreign controlled undertakings	..	..	..	..	..	..	..	..
Foreign companies (branches)	..	..	..	..	..	..	..	..
All undertakings	450	550	616	607	303	287	265	764
Composite								
Domestic undertakings	2 478	2 493	2 484	2 536	2 161	2 442	2 514	2 695
Foreign controlled undertakings	..	..	..	..	..	..	..	..
Foreign companies (branches)	..	..	..	..	..	..	..	..
All undertakings	2 478	2 493	2 484	2 536	2 161	2 442	2 514	2 695
of which:								
Life	852	833	765	756	730	735	757	802
Domestic undertakings	852	833	765	756	730	735	757	802
Foreign controlled undertakings	..	..	..	..	..	..	..	..
Foreign companies (branches)	..	..	..	..	..	..	..	..
All undertakings	852	833	765	756	730	735	757	802
Non-life	1 626	1 660	1 719	1 779	1 431	1 707	1 758	1 893
Domestic undertakings	1 626	1 660	1 719	1 779	1 431	1 707	1 758	1 893
Foreign controlled undertakings	..	..	..	..	..	..	..	..
Foreign companies (branches)	..	..	..	..	..	..	..	..
All undertakings	1 626	1 660	1 719	1 779	1 431	1 707	1 758	1 893
Total								
Domestic undertakings	2 973	3 090	3 155	3 198	2 529	2 797	2 793	3 479
Foreign controlled undertakings	..	..	..	..	..	..	..	..
Foreign companies (branches)	..	..	..	..	..	..	..	..
All undertakings	2 973	3 090	3 155	3 198	2 529	2 797	2 793	3 479
1.4 Gross operating expenses								
Life								
Domestic undertakings	41	45	47	51	61	60	25	49
Foreign controlled undertakings	..	..	..	..	..	..	..	..
Foreign companies (branches)	..	..	..	..	..	..	..	..
All undertakings	41	45	47	51	61	60	25	49
Non-life								
Domestic undertakings	643	618	641	678	382	363	426	396
Foreign controlled undertakings	..	..	..	..	..	..	..	..
Foreign companies (branches)	..	..	..	..	..	..	..	..
All undertakings	643	618	641	678	382	363	426	396
Composite								
Domestic undertakings	2 197	2 205	2 320	2 402	2 306	2 425	2 480	2 507
Foreign controlled undertakings	..	..	..	..	..	..	..	..
Foreign companies (branches)	..	..	..	..	..	..	..	..
All undertakings	2 197	2 205	2 320	2 402	2 306	2 425	2 480	2 507
of which:								
Life	833	824	859	869	883	895	922	945
Domestic undertakings	833	824	859	869	883	895	922	945
Foreign controlled undertakings	..	..	..	..	..	..	..	..
Foreign companies (branches)	..	..	..	..	..	..	..	..
All undertakings	833	824	859	869	883	895	922	945
Non-life	1 364	1 382	1 461	1 533	1 423	1 529	1 557	1 562
Domestic undertakings	1 364	1 382	1 461	1 533	1 423	1 529	1 557	1 562
Foreign controlled undertakings	..	..	..	..	..	..	..	..
Foreign companies (branches)	..	..	..	..	..	..	..	..
All undertakings	1 364	1 382	1 461	1 533	1 423	1 529	1 557	1 562
Total								
Domestic undertakings	2 881	2 868	3 008	3 130	2 749	2 847	2 931	2 951
Foreign controlled undertakings	..	..	..	..	..	..	..	..
Foreign companies (branches)	..	..	..	..	..	..	..	..
All undertakings	2 881	2 868	3 008	3 130	2 749	2 847	2 931	2 951

Table 1. Selected aggregates *(cont.)*

Million EUR

	2014	2015	2016	2017	2018	2019	2020	2021
1.5 Insurance business written abroad by branches, gross premiums								
Life								
Branches and agencies	2	0	0	0	0	0	0	0
Subsidaries	..	..	..	..	..	..	..	..
Total	2	..	0	0	0	0	0	0
Non-life								
Branches and agencies	1 572	1 931	1 854	1 843	1 912	991	3 544	4 015
Subsidaries	..	..	..	..	..	..	..	..
Total	1 572	1 931	1 854	1 843	1 912	991	3 544	4 015
Composite								
Branches and agencies	1 121	1 156	1 197	1 337	1 246	2 622	2 049	2 649
Subsidaries	..	..	..	..	..	..	..	..
Total	1 121	1 156	1 197	1 337	1 246	2 622	2 049	2 649
of which:								
Life	16	16	14	61	57	559	683	796
Branches and agencies	16	16	14	61	57	559	683	796
Subsidaries	..	..	..	..	..	..	..	..
Total	16	16	14	61	57	559	683	796
Non-life	1 105	1 141	1 183	1 276	1 189	2 063	1 366	1 853
Branches and agencies	1 105	1 141	1 183	1 276	1 189	2 063	1 366	1 853
Subsidaries	..	..	..	..	..	..	..	..
Total	1 105	1 141	1 183	1 276	1 189	2 063	1 366	1 853
Total								
Branches and agencies	2 696	3 087	3 051	3 181	3 158	3 614	5 592	6 664
Subsidaries	..	..	..	..	..	..	..	..
Total	2 696	3 087	3 051	3 181	3 158	3 614	5 592	6 664

.. Not available

Note: Detailed metadata at: *http://metalinks.oecd.org/ins/20230516/4126.*

Source: *OECD Insurance Statistics (database)*

Table 2. Number of companies and employees

	2014	2015	2016	2017	2018	2019	2020	2021
2.1 Number of companies								
Life								
Domestic undertakings	15	15	12	10	9	9	8	6
Foreign controlled undertakings	..	..	..	..	..	..	..	..
Foreign companies (branches)	8	8	10	10	7	7	6	6
All undertakings	23	23	22	20	16	16	14	12
Non-life								
Domestic undertakings	42	41	38	34	36	35	35	36
Foreign controlled undertakings	..	..	..	..	..	..	..	..
Foreign companies (branches)	36	32	32	33	36	36	29	26
All undertakings	78	73	70	67	72	71	64	62
Composite								
Domestic undertakings	23	23	22	23	22	22	21	20
Foreign controlled undertakings	..	..	..	..	..	..	..	..
Foreign companies (branches)	2	2	2	2	2	2	2	1
All undertakings	25	25	24	25	24	24	23	21
Reinsurance								
Domestic undertakings	1	1	1	1	2	2	2	2
Foreign controlled undertakings	..	..	..	..	..	..	..	..
Foreign companies (branches)	1	1	1	1	1	0	0	1
All undertakings	2	2	2	2	3	2	2	3
Total								
Domestic undertakings	81	80	73	68	69	68	66	64
Foreign controlled undertakings	..	..	..	..	..	..	..	..
Foreign companies (branches)	47	43	45	46	46	45	37	34
All undertakings	128	123	118	114	115	113	103	98
2.2 Number of employees								
Insurance undertakings	..	..	..	..	..	..	..	..
Intermediaries	..	..	..	..	..	..	..	..
Total	..	..	..	..	..	..	..	..

.. Not available

Note: Detailed metadata at: *http://metalinks.oecd.org/ins/20230516/4126.*

Source: *OECD Insurance Statistics (database)*

CANADA

Table 1. Selected aggregates

Million CAD

	2014	2015	2016	2017	2018	2019	2020	2021
1.1 Insurance business written in the reporting country								
1.1.1 Insurance business, by ownership								
Gross premiums								
Domestic undertakings	81 347	86 082	89 439	93 962	97 815	..	..	..
Foreign controlled undertakings	18 957	17 321	18 250	19 658	19 804	..	..	..
Foreign companies (branches)	21 604	20 840	19 141	19 488	14 937	..	..	..
All undertakings	102 951	106 922	108 580	113 450	112 752	..	..	..
Premiums ceded								
Domestic undertakings	22 771	25 855	23 885	26 759	19 135	..	..	..
Foreign controlled undertakings	5 070	4 912	5 107	7 154	6 751	..	..	..
Foreign companies (branches)	4 469	4 735	4 370	4 568	4 467	..	..	..
All undertakings	27 240	30 590	28 255	31 327	23 602	..	..	..
Net written premiums								
Domestic undertakings	58 576	60 227	65 554	67 204	78 680	..	..	..
Foreign controlled undertakings	13 888	12 410	13 142	12 504	13 053	..	..	..
Foreign companies (branches)	17 135	16 104	14 771	14 920	10 470	..	..	..
All undertakings	75 710	76 331	80 325	82 123	89 150	..	..	..
1.1.2 Insurance business on foreign risks, gross premiums								
Life	..	..	..	..	..	..	..	..
Non-life	..	..	..	..	..	..	..	..
Composite	..	..	..	..	..	..	..	..
of which:								
Life	..	..	..	..	..	..	..	..
Non-life	..	..	..	..	..	..	..	..
Total	..	..	..	..	..	..	..	..
1.1.3 Life insurance payments, by class, gross premiums								
Annuities	5 562	5 539	5 966	6 558	7 390	..	..	..
Unit linked	..	..	..	..	..	..	..	..
Other life insurance	..	..	..	..	..	..	..	..
Total life insurance	..	..	..	..	..	..	..	..
***of which:** Pension contracts*	..	..	..	..	..	..	..	..
1.1.4 Non-life insurance payments, by class, gross premiums								
Motor vehicle insurance	21 007	21 426	21 938	23 234	24 519	..	..	..
Marine, aviation and other transport insurance	773	716	769	700	1 143	..	..	..
Freight insurance	..	..	..	..	..	..	..	..
Fire and other property damage insurance	18 994	19 992	20 599	21 593	28 429	..	..	..
Pecuniary loss insurance	2 271	2 613	2 659	2 708	2 559	..	..	..
General liability insurance	5 830	6 289	6 339	6 398	10 463	..	..	..
Accident and health	25 708	26 370	25 944	26 471	24 315	..	..	..
***of which:** Health*	..	..	..	..	..	..	..	..
Other non-life insurance	138	275	368	440	170	..	..	..
Treaty reinsurance	..	..	..	..	..	..	..	..
Total non-life insurance	74 721	77 682	78 616	81 545	91 598	..	..	..
1.2 Gross claims payments								
Life								
Domestic undertakings	0	0	3	..	3	..	..	..
Foreign controlled undertakings	0	0	0	..	0	..	..	..
Foreign companies (branches)	41	13	3	3	3	..	..	..
All undertakings	41	13	6	3	6	..	..	..
Non-life								
Domestic undertakings	25 194	25 500	30 110	29 433	30 596	..	..	..
Foreign controlled undertakings	8 332	8 552	11 171	11 043	11 435	..	..	..
Foreign companies (branches)	5 901	4 694	6 748	4 566	6 479	..	..	..
All undertakings	31 095	30 193	36 858	33 999	37 075	..	..	..
Composite								
Domestic undertakings	9 477	10 030	11 984	12 753	18 600	..	..	..
Foreign controlled undertakings	881	303	336	396	435	..	..	..
Foreign companies (branches)	7 182	7 161	5 671	5 797	1 025	..	..	..
All undertakings	16 659	17 190	17 654	18 549	19 626	..	..	..
of which:								
Life	5 480	5 747	5 919	6 342	6 699	..	..	..
Domestic undertakings	3 858	4 186	4 581	4 981	6 073	..	..	..
Foreign controlled undertakings	344	188	210	256	301	..	..	..
Foreign companies (branches)	1 622	1 561	1 339	1 361	626	..	..	..
All undertakings	5 480	5 747	5 919	6 342	6 699	..	..	..
Non-life	11 179	11 444	11 735	12 207	12 927	..	..	..
Domestic undertakings	5 620	5 844	7 403	7 772	12 528	..	..	..
Foreign controlled undertakings	537	115	127	139	134	..	..	..
Foreign companies (branches)	5 560	5 600	4 332	4 435	399	..	..	..
All undertakings	11 179	11 444	11 735	12 207	12 927	..	..	..
Total								
Domestic undertakings	34 671	35 529	42 097	42 186	49 199	..	..	..
Foreign controlled undertakings	9 213	8 854	11 508	11 439	11 870	..	..	..
Foreign companies (branches)	13 124	11 867	12 422	10 366	7 507	..	..	..
All undertakings	47 795	47 396	54 518	52 552	56 706	..	..	..

Table 1. Selected aggregates *(cont.)*

Million CAD

	2014	2015	2016	2017	2018	2019	2020	2021
1.3 Commissions								
Life								
Domestic undertakings	..	0	0	0	..	..	..	..
Foreign controlled undertakings	..	..	..	..	..	..	..	..
Foreign companies (branches)	..	0	0	0	..	..	..	..
All undertakings	..	0	0	0	..	..	..	..
Non-life								
Domestic undertakings	..	5 441	5 666	5 434	6 103	..	..	..
Foreign controlled undertakings	..	1 882	1 938	2 087	2 182	..	..	..
Foreign companies (branches)	..	1 104	1 177	1 299	1 492	..	..	..
All undertakings	..	6 545	6 843	6 733	7 595	..	..	..
Composite								
Domestic undertakings	..	4 787	5 363	5 218	5 127	..	..	..
Foreign controlled undertakings	..	97	94	97	150	..	..	..
Foreign companies (branches)	..	193	156	197	174	..	..	..
All undertakings	..	4 980	5 519	5 416	5 301	..	..	..
of which:								
Life	..	3 572	4 059	3 893	3 812	..	..	..
Domestic undertakings	..	3 457	3 982	3 801	3 734	..	..	..
Foreign controlled undertakings	..	65	72	75	93	..	..	..
Foreign companies (branches)	..	115	77	93	78	..	..	..
All undertakings	..	3 572	4 059	3 893	3 812	..	..	..
Non-life	..	1 408	1 460	1 522	1 489	..	..	..
Domestic undertakings	..	1 330	1 381	1 418	1 393	..	..	..
Foreign controlled undertakings	..	32	22	22	57	..	..	..
Foreign companies (branches)	..	78	79	105	97	..	..	..
All undertakings	..	1 408	1 460	1 522	1 489	..	..	..
Total								
Domestic undertakings	..	10 228	11 029	10 653	11 230	..	..	..
Foreign controlled undertakings	..	1 979	2 032	2 184	2 332	..	..	..
Foreign companies (branches)	..	1 298	1 333	1 496	1 666	..	..	..
All undertakings	..	11 526	12 362	12 149	12 896	..	..	..
1.4 Gross operating expenses								
Life								
Domestic undertakings	24	22	30	29	25	..	..	..
Foreign controlled undertakings	0	0	0	0	0	..	..	..
Foreign companies (branches)	28	15	10	9	10	..	..	..
All undertakings	52	37	40	38	36	..	..	..
Non-life								
Domestic undertakings	4 032	4 493	4 725	4 694	4 658	..	..	..
Foreign controlled undertakings	1 385	1 488	1 756	1 635	1 548	..	..	..
Foreign companies (branches)	855	689	673	672	704	..	..	..
All undertakings	4 887	5 182	5 398	5 366	5 362	..	..	..
Composite								
Domestic undertakings	12 612	14 400	17 159	17 966	19 399	..	..	..
Foreign controlled undertakings	736	187	194	248	251	..	..	..
Foreign companies (branches)	206	272	518	713	259	..	..	..
All undertakings	12 818	14 672	17 677	18 679	19 658	..	..	..
of which:								
Life	..	..	..	..	..	..	..	..
Domestic undertakings	..	..	..	..	..	..	..	..
Foreign controlled undertakings	..	..	..	..	..	..	..	..
Foreign companies (branches)	..	..	..	..	..	..	..	..
All undertakings	..	..	..	..	..	..	..	..
Non-life	..	..	..	..	..	..	..	..
Domestic undertakings	..	..	..	..	..	..	..	..
Foreign controlled undertakings	..	..	..	..	..	..	..	..
Foreign companies (branches)	..	..	..	..	..	..	..	..
All undertakings	..	..	..	..	..	..	..	..
Total								
Domestic undertakings	16 668	18 915	21 914	22 689	24 082	..	..	..
Foreign controlled undertakings	2 121	1 675	1 950	1 883	1 799	..	..	..
Foreign companies (branches)	1 089	976	1 201	1 394	973	..	..	..
All undertakings	17 757	19 891	23 115	24 083	25 055	..	..	..

Table 1. Selected aggregates *(cont.)*

Million CAD

	2014	2015	2016	2017	2018	2019	2020	2021
1.5 Insurance business written abroad by branches, gross premiums								
Life								
Branches and agencies	..	..	..	..	..	..	..	..
Subsidaries	..	..	..	..	..	..	..	..
Total	0	0	0	0	0	..	..	..
Non-life								
Branches and agencies	..	..	..	..	..	..	..	..
Subsidaries	..	..	..	..	..	..	..	..
Total	1 320	1 500	1 502	1 522	2 658	..	..	..
Composite								
Branches and agencies	..	..	..	..	..	..	..	..
Subsidaries	..	..	..	..	..	..	..	..
Total	31 162	40 235	50 713	54 040	57 636	..	..	..
of which:								
Life	27 224	..	..	..	..	..	..	..
Branches and agencies	..	..	..	..	..	..	..	..
Subsidaries	..	..	..	..	..	..	..	..
Total	27 224	..	..	..	..	..	..	..
Non-life	3 939	..	..	..	..	..	..	..
Branches and agencies	..	..	..	..	..	..	..	..
Subsidaries	..	..	..	..	..	..	..	..
Total	3 939	..	..	..	..	..	..	..
Total								
Branches and agencies	..	..	..	..	..	..	..	..
Subsidaries	..	..	..	..	..	..	..	..
Total	32 482	41 736	52 215	55 562	60 294	..	..	..

.. Not available

Note: Detailed metadata at: *http://metalinks.oecd.org/ins/20230516/4e54.*

Source: *OECD Insurance Statistics (database)*

CANADA

Table 2. Number of companies and employees

	2014	2015	2016	2017	2018	2019	2020	2021
2.1 Number of companies								
Life								
Domestic undertakings	1	1	3	3	3	..	..	..
Foreign controlled undertakings	0	0	0	0	0	..	..	..
Foreign companies (branches)	5	5	2	2	2	..	..	..
All undertakings	6	6	5	5	5	..	..	..
Non-life								
Domestic undertakings	66	66	63	61	57	..	..	..
Foreign controlled undertakings	28	28	27	27	25	..	..	..
Foreign companies (branches)	60	58	54	54	54	..	..	..
All undertakings	126	124	117	115	111	..	..	..
Composite								
Domestic undertakings	34	33	31	31	29	..	..	..
Foreign controlled undertakings	9	7	7	8	7	..	..	..
Foreign companies (branches)	23	22	20	20	20	..	..	..
All undertakings	57	55	51	51	49	..	..	..
Reinsurance								
Domestic undertakings	5	5	5	5	5	..	..	..
Foreign controlled undertakings	5	5	5	5	5	..	..	..
Foreign companies (branches)	25	26	28	28	28	..	..	..
All undertakings	30	31	33	33	33	..	..	..
Total								
Domestic undertakings	106	105	102	100	94	..	..	..
Foreign controlled undertakings	42	40	39	40	37	..	..	..
Foreign companies (branches)	113	111	104	104	104	..	..	..
All undertakings	219	216	206	204	198	..	..	..
2.2 Number of employees								
Insurance undertakings	..	..	..	..	..	..	..	..
Intermediaries	..	..	..	..	..	..	..	..
Total	..	..	..	..	..	..	..	..

.. Not available

Note: Detailed metadata at: *http://metalinks.oecd.org/ins/20230516/4e54.*

Source: *OECD Insurance Statistics (database)*

CHILE

Table 1. Selected aggregates

Million CLP

	2014	2015	2016	2017	2018	2019	2020	2021
1.1 Insurance business written in the reporting country								
1.1.1 Insurance business, by ownership								
Gross premiums								
Domestic undertakings	6 260 019	7 465 743	8 394 971	8 344 320	8 981 504	9 062 220	7 918 466	8 795 472
Foreign controlled undertakings	3 211 682	3 614 011	4 422 880	4 504 671	4 722 316	4 929 006	4 303 271	5 435 970
Foreign companies (branches)	..	..	..	..	..	..	..	..
All undertakings	6 260 019	7 465 743	8 394 971	8 344 320	8 981 504	9 062 220	7 918 466	8 795 472
Premiums ceded								
Domestic undertakings	998 507	1 135 872	1 310 392	1 382 346	1 428 339	1 561 858	1 835 991	1 900 073
Foreign controlled undertakings	676 439	749 522	953 240	901 373	921 260	1 052 698	1 243 020	1 422 315
Foreign companies (branches)	..	..	..	..	..	..	..	..
All undertakings	998 507	1 135 872	1 310 392	1 382 346	1 428 339	1 561 858	1 835 991	1 900 073
Net written premiums								
Domestic undertakings	5 261 513	6 329 871	7 084 578	6 961 974	7 553 165	7 500 362	6 082 475	6 895 399
Foreign controlled undertakings	2 535 243	2 864 489	3 469 640	3 603 299	3 801 056	3 876 308	3 060 251	4 013 655
Foreign companies (branches)	..	..	..	..	..	..	..	..
All undertakings	5 261 513	6 329 871	7 084 578	6 961 974	7 553 165	7 500 362	6 082 475	6 895 399
1.1.2 Insurance business on foreign risks, gross premiums								
Life	..	..	..	..	..	..	..	..
Non-life	..	..	..	..	..	..	..	..
Composite total	..	..	..	..	..	..	..	..
Total	..	..	..	..	..	..	..	..
1.1.3 Life insurance payments, by class, gross premiums								
Annuities	1 692 693	2 343 736	2 759 473	2 456 649	2 767 820	2 455 785	1 142 205	1 258 861
Unit linked	475 508	613 110	712 539	728 441	582 074	547 256	593 921	727 952
Other life insurance	1 948 628	2 123 123	2 373 130	2 560 094	2 775 274	3 016 938	2 945 626	3 023 191
Total life insurance	4 116 829	5 079 969	5 845 142	5 745 185	6 125 167	6 019 980	4 681 752	5 010 004
***of which:** Pension contracts*	..	..	..	..	..	..	..	..
1.1.4 Non-life insurance payments, by class, gross premiums								
Motor vehicle insurance	509 632	554 020	607 928	658 852	741 818	776 970	736 081	840 149
Marine, aviation and other transport insurance	129 698	148 074	132 318	134 870	152 066	172 407	201 879	187 488
Freight insurance	0	0	0	0	0	0	0	0
Fire and other property damage insurance	788 536	901 636	926 988	899 548	999 817	1 123 188	1 409 387	1 590 708
Pecuniary loss insurance	62 708	73 291	81 763	83 750	89 411	93 093	87 538	178 730
General liability insurance	56 828	41 342	34 468	30 188	41 483	46 072	52 866	326 373
Accident and health	30 296	46 180	53 105	66 796	74 322	78 869	80 419	152 446
***of which:** Health*	6 186	2 268	8 145	7 442	15 661	4 707	5 386	3 942
Other non-life insurance	561 863	602 569	651 596	675 973	705 464	697 812	628 887	468 988
Treaty reinsurance	0	0	0	0	0	0	0	0
Total non-life insurance	2 139 562	2 367 113	2 488 165	2 549 976	2 804 382	2 988 410	3 197 056	3 744 881
1.2 Gross claims payments								
Life								
Domestic undertakings	4 027 828	2 853 170	3 342 724	3 838 076	4 106 073	4 387 098	4 479 889	5 865 572
Foreign controlled undertakings	1 580 430	1 020 903	1 219 666	1 524 203	1 999 198	1 833 862	1 756 966	2 153 103
Foreign companies (branches)	..	..	..	..	..	..	..	..
All undertakings	4 027 828	2 853 170	3 342 724	3 838 076	4 106 073	4 387 098	4 479 889	5 865 572
Non-life								
Domestic undertakings	260 092	1 421 296	1 491 740	1 515 015	1 432 942	1 475 444	1 677 063	1 539 085
Foreign controlled undertakings	157 970	889 183	1 193 951	1 168 469	1 032 572	1 053 771	1 214 440	1 292 350
Foreign companies (branches)	..	..	..	..	..	..	..	..
All undertakings	260 092	1 421 296	1 491 740	1 515 015	1 432 942	1 475 444	1 677 063	1 539 085
Composite, all undertakings	..	..	..	..	..	..	..	..
Total								
Domestic undertakings	4 287 920	4 274 466	4 834 464	5 353 090	5 539 015	5 862 542	6 156 953	7 404 657
Foreign controlled undertakings	1 738 400	1 910 087	2 413 617	2 692 672	3 031 770	2 887 633	2 971 406	3 445 453
Foreign companies (branches)	..	..	..	..	..	..	..	..
All undertakings	4 287 920	4 274 466	4 834 464	5 353 090	5 539 015	5 862 542	6 156 953	7 404 657
1.3 Commissions								
Life								
Domestic undertakings	263 060	301 418	318 445	330 472	360 325	349 461	284 087	267 772
Foreign controlled undertakings	139 650	164 172	159 299	171 055	186 888	181 279	151 525	180 232
Foreign companies (branches)	..	..	..	..	..	..	..	..
All undertakings	263 060	301 418	318 445	330 472	360 325	349 461	284 087	267 772
Non-life								
Domestic undertakings	260 092	287 918	312 001	322 793	360 936	368 082	247 360	405 187
Foreign controlled undertakings	157 970	171 469	242 835	238 778	261 147	261 710	242 482	347 895
Foreign companies (branches)	..	..	..	..	..	..	..	..
All undertakings	260 092	287 918	312 001	322 793	360 936	368 082	247 360	405 187
Composite, all undertakings	..	..	..	..	..	..	..	..
Total								
Domestic undertakings	523 153	589 336	630 445	653 265	721 261	717 542	531 447	672 959
Foreign controlled undertakings	297 621	335 641	402 134	409 832	448 035	442 989	394 006	528 126
Foreign companies (branches)	..	..	..	..	..	..	..	..
All undertakings	523 153	589 336	630 445	653 265	721 261	717 542	531 447	672 959

CHILE

Table 1. Selected aggregates *(cont.)*

Million CLP

	2014	2015	2016	2017	2018	2019	2020	2021
1.4 Gross operating expenses								
Life								
Domestic undertakings	583 313	612 178	664 997	732 176	776 679	883 091	772 695	747 517
Foreign controlled undertakings	284 692	308 320	316 103	364 993	390 610	413 417	351 006	457 351
Foreign companies (branches)	..	..	..	..	..	..	..	..
All undertakings	583 313	612 178	664 997	732 176	776 679	883 091	772 695	747 517
Non-life								
Domestic undertakings	382 886	412 676	457 861	501 804	533 252	569 035	575 211	597 301
Foreign controlled undertakings	266 721	288 658	367 114	406 682	414 288	431 095	421 765	523 632
Foreign companies (branches)	..	..	..	..	..	..	..	..
All undertakings	382 886	412 676	457 861	501 804	533 252	569 035	575 211	597 301
Composite, all undertakings	..	..	..	..	..	..	..	..
Total								
Domestic undertakings	966 199	1 024 854	1 122 857	1 233 980	1 309 931	1 452 126	1 347 906	1 344 818
Foreign controlled undertakings	551 413	596 978	683 216	771 674	804 898	844 512	772 772	980 982
Foreign companies (branches)	..	..	..	..	..	..	..	..
All undertakings	966 199	1 024 854	1 122 857	1 233 980	1 309 931	1 452 126	1 347 906	1 344 818
1.5 Insurance business written abroad by branches, gross premiums								
Life								
Branches and agencies	..	..	..	..	..	..	..	..
Subsidaries	..	..	..	..	..	..	..	..
Total	..	..	..	..	..	..	..	..
Non-life								
Branches and agencies	..	..	..	..	..	..	..	..
Subsidaries	..	..	..	..	..	..	..	..
Total	..	..	..	..	..	..	..	..
Composite total	..	..	..	..	..	..	..	..
Total								
Branches and agencies	..	..	..	..	..	..	..	..
Subsidaries	..	..	..	..	..	..	..	..
Total	..	..	..	..	..	..	..	..

.. Not available

Note: Detailed metadata at: *http://metalinks.oecd.org/ins/20230516/b694.*

Source: *OECD Insurance Statistics (database)*

Table 2. Number of companies and employees

	2014	2015	2016	2017	2018	2019	2020	2021
2.1 Number of companies								
Life								
Domestic undertakings	34	36	36	36	37	37	35	32
Foreign controlled undertakings	12	13	13	15	16	13	13	14
Foreign companies (branches)	..	..	0	..	..	..	..	..
All undertakings	34	36	36	36	37	37	35	32
Non-life								
Domestic undertakings	29	30	30	32	32	34	34	33
Foreign controlled undertakings	17	18	11	19	17	18	18	20
Foreign companies (branches)	..	..	0	..	..	..	..	..
All undertakings	29	30	30	32	32	34	34	33
Composite, all undertakings	**0**	**0**	**0**	..	..	..	..	..
Reinsurance								
Domestic undertakings	1	1	1	1	1	1	1	1
Foreign controlled undertakings	1	..	1	1	1	1	1	..
Foreign companies (branches)	..	..	0	..	..	..	..	..
All undertakings	1	1	1	1	1	1	1	1
Total								
Domestic undertakings	64	67	67	69	70	72	70	66
Foreign controlled undertakings	30	31	25	35	33	32	32	34
Foreign companies (branches)	..	..	0	..	..	..	..	..
All undertakings	64	67	67	69	70	72	70	66
2.2 Number of employees								
Insurance undertakings	17 039	15 368	16 414	16 859	16 908	16 891	15 049	15 103
Intermediaries	6 959	7 499	7 599	7 663	7 945	7 997	6 159	6 961
Total	23 998	22 867	24 013	24 522	24 853	24 888	21 208	22 064

.. Not available

Note: Detailed metadata at: *http://metalinks.oecd.org/ins/20230516/b694.*

Source: *OECD Insurance Statistics (database)*

COLOMBIA

Table 1. Selected aggregates

Million COP

	2014	2015	2016	2017	2018	2019	2020	2021
1.1 Insurance business written in the reporting country								
1.1.1 Insurance business, by ownership								
Gross premiums								
Domestic undertakings	19 396 882	21 943 459	24 585 330	26 496 734	27 809 761	30 812 229	31 099 908	36 086 976
Foreign controlled undertakings	7 635 672	8 309 246	8 622 786	8 718 250	8 981 678	9 654 677	9 654 677	11 346 570
Foreign companies (branches)	0	..	..	..	..	..	..	..
All undertakings	19 396 882	21 943 459	24 585 330	26 496 734	27 809 761	30 812 229	31 099 908	36 086 976
Premiums ceded								
Domestic undertakings	3 392 593	4 062 439	4 883 531	4 863 385	5 257 745	6 045 450	6 767 555	8 360 958
Foreign controlled undertakings	1 762 391	1 871 332	2 075 143	1 676 354	1 762 454	2 052 794	2 052 794	3 032 693
Foreign companies (branches)	0	..	..	..	..	..	..	..
All undertakings	3 392 593	4 062 439	4 883 531	4 863 385	5 257 745	6 045 450	6 767 555	8 360 958
Net written premiums								
Domestic undertakings	16 004 289	17 881 020	19 701 798	21 633 350	22 552 017	24 766 779	24 332 353	27 726 018
Foreign controlled undertakings	5 873 280	6 437 914	6 547 643	7 041 896	7 219 224	7 601 883	7 601 883	8 313 877
Foreign companies (branches)	0	..	..	..	..	..	..	..
All undertakings	16 004 289	17 881 020	19 701 798	21 633 350	22 552 017	24 766 779	24 332 353	27 726 018
1.1.2 Insurance business on foreign risks, gross premiums								
Life	..	..	..	..	..	..	..	..
Non-life	..	..	..	..	..	..	..	..
Composite	..	..	..	..	..	..	..	..
of which:								
Life	..	..	..	..	..	..	..	..
Non-life	..	..	..	..	..	..	..	..
Total	..	..	..	..	..	..	..	..
1.1.3 Life insurance payments, by class, gross premiums								
Annuities	814 432	1 096 967	1 759 549	2 019 643	2 204 084	2 452 253	2 120 094	2 786 794
Unit linked	..	..	..	..	..	..	..	..
Other life insurance	8 389 995	9 114 695	10 077 271	11 453 593	11 714 575	13 136 500	13 400 560	15 113 894
Total life insurance	9 204 427	10 211 663	11 836 820	13 473 236	13 918 659	15 588 754	15 520 655	17 900 689
of which: *Pension contracts*	642 645	904 089	1 559 392	1 854 412	2 031 168	2 264 302	1 977 198	2 625 043
1.1.4 Non-life insurance payments, by class, gross premiums								
Motor vehicle insurance	2 389 604	2 628 864	2 982 278	3 365 337	3 491 141	3 668 192	3 441 435	3 869 692
Marine, aviation and other transport insurance	96 118	134 015	140 118	142 304	135 408	183 512	201 882	246 221
Freight insurance	264 282	285 223	301 591	290 964	293 469	315 021	316 943	359 905
Fire and other property damage insurance	1 984 995	2 388 974	2 596 551	2 592 128	2 787 985	2 992 325	3 320 280	3 802 709
Pecuniary loss insurance	1 876 165	2 171 112	2 173 155	2 035 235	2 188 222	2 421 701	2 555 692	3 248 953
General liability insurance	782 424	834 365	913 075	922 751	1 073 809	1 273 279	1 444 796	1 805 649
Accident and health	431 508	480 854	588 263	543 225	482 136	610 901	538 817	633 905
of which: *Health*	55 613	59 071	60 349	60 216	62 250	63 711	64 807	59 268
Other non-life insurance	2 359 305	2 800 552	3 044 763	3 126 668	3 436 491	3 758 816	3 759 407	4 219 253
Treaty reinsurance	..	..	..	..	..	..	..	..
Total non-life insurance	10 184 400	11 723 960	12 739 794	13 018 612	13 888 659	15 223 747	15 579 253	18 186 288
1.2 Gross claims payments								
Life								
Domestic undertakings	4 732 708	5 219 437	5 850 532	6 614 108	7 506 898	7 797 284	7 860 957	11 160 628
Foreign controlled undertakings	1 102 287	1 246 232	1 223 887	1 289 528	1 379 180	1 393 943	1 249 680	1 626 894
Foreign companies (branches)	..	..	..	..	..	..	..	..
All undertakings	4 732 708	5 219 437	5 850 532	6 614 108	7 506 898	7 797 284	7 860 957	11 160 628
Non-life								
Domestic undertakings	4 266 391	5 013 568	6 555 550	6 355 609	6 662 371	8 175 580	7 443 559	8 890 746
Foreign controlled undertakings	2 261 082	2 565 529	3 043 646	2 668 837	2 829 971	3 777 045	3 156 618	3 739 398
Foreign companies (branches)	..	..	..	..	..	..	..	..
All undertakings	4 266 391	5 013 568	6 555 550	6 355 609	6 662 371	8 175 580	7 443 559	8 890 746
Composite								
Domestic undertakings	..	..	..	..	..	..	..	..
Foreign controlled undertakings	..	..	..	..	..	..	..	..
Foreign companies (branches)	..	..	..	..	..	..	..	..
All undertakings	..	..	..	..	..	..	..	..
of which:								
Life	..	..	..	..	..	..	..	..
Domestic undertakings	..	..	..	..	..	..	..	..
Foreign controlled undertakings	..	..	..	..	..	..	..	..
Foreign companies (branches)	..	..	..	..	..	..	..	..
All undertakings	..	..	..	..	..	..	..	..
Non-life	..	..	..	..	..	..	..	..
Domestic undertakings	..	..	..	..	..	..	..	..
Foreign controlled undertakings	..	..	..	..	..	..	..	..
Foreign companies (branches)	..	..	..	..	..	..	..	..
All undertakings	..	..	..	..	..	..	..	..
Total								
Domestic undertakings	8 999 099	10 233 005	12 406 082	12 969 717	14 169 269	15 972 864	15 304 517	20 051 374
Foreign controlled undertakings	3 363 369	3 811 761	4 267 533	3 958 365	4 209 152	5 170 989	4 406 298	5 366 292
Foreign companies (branches)	..	..	..	..	..	..	..	..
All undertakings	8 999 099	10 233 005	12 406 082	12 969 717	14 169 269	15 972 864	15 304 517	20 051 374

COLOMBIA

Table 1. Selected aggregates *(cont.)*

Million COP

	2014	2015	2016	2017	2018	2019	2020	2021
1.3 Commissions								
Life								
Domestic undertakings	..	..	..	..	..	..	..	..
Foreign controlled undertakings	..	..	..	..	..	..	..	..
Foreign companies (branches)	..	..	..	..	..	..	..	..
All undertakings	..	..	..	..	..	..	..	..
Non-life								
Domestic undertakings	..	..	..	..	..	..	..	..
Foreign controlled undertakings	..	..	..	..	..	..	..	..
Foreign companies (branches)	..	..	..	..	..	..	..	..
All undertakings	..	..	..	..	..	..	..	..
Composite								
Domestic undertakings	..	..	..	..	..	..	..	..
Foreign controlled undertakings	..	..	..	..	..	..	..	..
Foreign companies (branches)	..	..	..	..	..	..	..	..
All undertakings	..	..	..	..	..	..	..	..
of which:								
Life	..	..	..	..	..	..	..	..
Domestic undertakings	..	..	..	..	..	..	..	..
Foreign controlled undertakings	..	..	..	..	..	..	..	..
Foreign companies (branches)	..	..	..	..	..	..	..	..
All undertakings	..	..	..	..	..	..	..	..
Non-life	..	..	..	..	..	..	..	..
Domestic undertakings	..	..	..	..	..	..	..	..
Foreign controlled undertakings	..	..	..	..	..	..	..	..
Foreign companies (branches)	..	..	..	..	..	..	..	..
All undertakings	..	..	..	..	..	..	..	..
Total								
Domestic undertakings	..	..	..	..	..	..	..	..
Foreign controlled undertakings	..	..	..	..	..	..	..	..
Foreign companies (branches)	..	..	..	..	..	..	..	..
All undertakings	..	..	..	..	..	..	..	..
1.4 Gross operating expenses								
Life								
Domestic undertakings	3 306 113	3 596 035	3 847 673	4 227 762	4 582 318	5 170 933	5 550 438	5 836 194
Foreign controlled undertakings	708 464	1 077 766	1 100 785	1 280 372	1 383 239	1 421 144	1 366 545	1 361 100
Foreign companies (branches)	..	..	..	..	..	..	..	..
All undertakings	3 306 113	3 596 035	3 847 673	4 227 762	4 582 318	5 170 933	5 550 438	5 836 194
Non-life								
Domestic undertakings	3 907 054	4 067 473	4 555 295	4 738 383	4 996 774	5 709 898	5 708 230	5 756 649
Foreign controlled undertakings	2 331 832	2 418 659	2 624 752	2 729 921	2 665 162	3 071 224	2 886 040	3 159 787
Foreign companies (branches)	..	..	..	..	..	..	..	..
All undertakings	3 907 054	4 067 473	4 555 295	4 738 383	4 996 774	5 709 898	5 708 230	5 756 649
Composite								
Domestic undertakings	..	..	..	..	..	..	..	..
Foreign controlled undertakings	..	..	..	..	..	..	..	..
Foreign companies (branches)	..	..	..	..	..	..	..	..
All undertakings	..	..	..	..	..	..	..	..
of which:								
Life	..	..	..	..	..	..	..	..
Domestic undertakings	..	..	..	..	..	..	..	..
Foreign controlled undertakings	..	..	..	..	..	..	..	..
Foreign companies (branches)	..	..	..	..	..	..	..	..
All undertakings	..	..	..	..	..	..	..	..
Non-life	..	..	..	..	..	..	..	..
Domestic undertakings	..	..	..	..	..	..	..	..
Foreign controlled undertakings	..	..	..	..	..	..	..	..
Foreign companies (branches)	..	..	..	..	..	..	..	..
All undertakings	..	..	..	..	..	..	..	..
Total								
Domestic undertakings	7 213 167	7 663 508	8 402 968	8 966 145	9 579 092	10 880 831	11 258 668	11 592 843
Foreign controlled undertakings	3 040 295	3 496 425	3 725 536	4 010 293	4 048 401	4 492 368	4 252 585	4 520 886
Foreign companies (branches)	..	..	..	..	..	..	..	..
All undertakings	7 213 167	7 663 508	8 402 968	8 966 145	9 579 092	10 880 831	11 258 668	11 592 843

COLOMBIA

Table 1. Selected aggregates *(cont.)*

Million COP

	2014	2015	2016	2017	2018	2019	2020	2021
1.5 Insurance business written abroad by branches, gross premiums								
Life								
Branches and agencies	..	..	..	..	..	..	..	..
Subsidaries	..	..	..	..	..	..	..	..
Total	..	..	..	..	..	..	..	..
Non-life								
Branches and agencies	..	..	..	..	..	..	..	..
Subsidaries	..	..	..	..	..	..	..	..
Total	..	..	..	..	..	..	..	..
Composite								
Branches and agencies	..	..	..	..	..	..	..	..
Subsidaries	..	..	..	..	..	..	..	..
Total	..	..	..	..	..	..	..	..
of which:								
Life	..	..	..	..	..	..	..	..
Branches and agencies	..	..	..	..	..	..	..	..
Subsidaries	..	..	..	..	..	..	..	..
Total	..	..	..	..	..	..	..	..
Non-life	..	..	..	..	..	..	..	..
Branches and agencies	..	..	..	..	..	..	..	..
Subsidaries	..	..	..	..	..	..	..	..
Total	..	..	..	..	..	..	..	..
Total								
Branches and agencies	..	..	..	..	..	..	..	..
Subsidaries	..	..	..	..	..	..	..	..
Total	..	..	..	..	..	..	..	..

.. Not available

Note: Detailed metadata at: *http://metalinks.oecd.org/ins/20230516/c11e.*

Source: *OECD Insurance Statistics (database)*

Table 2. Number of companies and employees

	2014	2015	2016	2017	2018	2019	2020	2021
2.1 Number of companies								
Life								
Domestic undertakings	19	19	19	20	20	18	18	19
Foreign controlled undertakings	9	9	9	10	10	9	9	9
Foreign companies (branches)	0	0	0	0	0	0	0	0
All undertakings	19	19	19	20	20	18	18	19
Non-life								
Domestic undertakings	26	28	26	26	26	26	25	25
Foreign controlled undertakings	18	19	17	17	17	17	16	16
Foreign companies (branches)	0	0	0	0	0	0	0	0
All undertakings	26	28	26	26	26	26	25	25
Composite								
Domestic undertakings	..	..	..	..	..	..	0	..
Foreign controlled undertakings	..	..	..	..	..	..	0	..
Foreign companies (branches)	..	..	..	..	..	..	0	..
All undertakings	..	..	..	..	..	..	0	..
Reinsurance								
Domestic undertakings	0	0	0	..	..	0	0	..
Foreign controlled undertakings	0	0	0	..	..	0	0	..
Foreign companies (branches)	..	..	0	..	..	..	0	..
All undertakings	0	0	0	..	..	0	0	..
Total								
Domestic undertakings	45	47	45	46	46	44	43	44
Foreign controlled undertakings	27	28	26	27	27	26	25	25
Foreign companies (branches)	0	0	0	0	0	0	0	..
All undertakings	45	47	45	46	46	44	43	44
2.2 Number of employees								
Insurance undertakings	18 913	20 862	22 734	24 073	28 043	27 322	24 697	24 263
Intermediaries	..	..	..	..	..	..	..	..
Total	18 913	20 862	22 734	..	..	..	..	..

.. Not available

Note: Detailed metadata at: *http://metalinks.oecd.org/ins/20230516/c11e.*

Source: *OECD Insurance Statistics (database)*

COSTA RICA

Table 1. Selected aggregates

Million CRC

	2014	2015	2016	2017	2018	2019	2020	2021
1.1 Insurance business written in the reporting country								
1.1.1 Insurance business, by ownership								
Gross premiums								
Domestic undertakings	620 043	556 143	651 302	737 832	756 535	819 389	822 288	874 554
Foreign controlled undertakings	87 914	97 325	131 352	172 203	197 174	214 166	220 614	265 706
Foreign companies (branches)	2 549	4 820	8 124	10 859	12 731	13 588	19 582	25 655
All undertakings	622 592	560 964	659 425	748 691	769 266	832 977	841 870	900 209
Premiums ceded								
Domestic undertakings	123 137	123 797	138 584	153 940	172 213	180 275	181 144	191 900
Foreign controlled undertakings	51 318	51 490	67 548	86 837	102 855	109 389	107 388	113 739
Foreign companies (branches)	287	378	571	624	606	436	1 559	2 265
All undertakings	123 423	124 175	139 155	154 564	172 819	180 711	182 703	194 165
Net written premiums								
Domestic undertakings	496 907	432 347	512 718	583 892	584 322	639 113	641 143	682 655
Foreign controlled undertakings	36 596	45 835	63 804	85 366	94 320	104 777	113 226	151 967
Foreign companies (branches)	2 262	4 442	7 553	10 235	12 125	13 152	18 023	23 390
All undertakings	499 169	436 789	520 270	594 126	596 447	652 266	659 166	706 045
1.1.2 Insurance business on foreign risks, gross premiums								
Life	..	..	..	..	..	..	..	..
Non-life	..	..	..	..	..	..	..	..
Composite	..	..	..	..	..	..	..	..
of which:								
Life	..	..	..	..	..	..	..	..
Non-life	..	..	..	..	..	..	..	..
Total	..	..	..	..	..	..	..	..
1.1.3 Life insurance payments, by class, gross premiums								
Annuities	0	0	0	0	0	..	..	..
Unit linked	0	0	0	0	0	..	..	..
Other life insurance	76 618	71 125	101 364	110 272	124 136	133 588	125 495	147 809
Total life insurance	76 618	71 125	101 364	110 272	124 136	133 588	125 495	147 809
***of which:** Pension contracts*	..	0	0	0	0	..	..	..
1.1.4 Non-life insurance payments, by class, gross premiums								
Motor vehicle insurance	139 654	146 734	163 204	170 987	169 973	176 027	166 349	171 550
Marine, aviation and other transport insurance	1 723	1 801	1 874	2 111	2 437	3 065	2 307	3 380
Freight insurance	8 495	7 413	7 330	7 999	8 314	8 004	8 155	9 334
Fire and other property damage insurance	97 862	100 909	107 910	121 283	116 697	118 241	128 285	140 860
Pecuniary loss insurance	16 284	15 253	28 143	33 154	26 704	30 597	46 252	32 099
General liability insurance	10 040	10 506	10 270	14 075	15 981	17 967	19 109	21 104
Accident and health	271 915	207 219	239 328	288 806	305 020	345 483	345 917	374 072
***of which:** Health*	..	55 740	69 536	81 856	91 160	159 361	141 194	143 218
Other non-life insurance	0	0	0	0	0	0	0	0
Treaty reinsurance	0	0	0	..	..	..	..	..
Total non-life insurance	545 972	489 835	558 059	638 416	645 127	699 385	716 375	752 400
1.2 Gross claims payments								
Life								
Domestic undertakings	0	0	0	..	..	..	..	..
Foreign controlled undertakings	0	0	0	..	..	..	..	..
Foreign companies (branches)	0	0	0	..	..	..	..	..
All undertakings	0	0	0	..	..	..	..	..
Non-life								
Domestic undertakings	4 619	6 862	13 836	25 561	17 809	14 783	11 791	15 696
Foreign controlled undertakings	4 619	6 862	13 836	25 561	17 809	14 783	11 791	15 696
Foreign companies (branches)	0	0	0	0	0	..	..	0
All undertakings	4 619	6 862	13 836	25 561	17 809	14 783	11 791	15 696
Composite								
Domestic undertakings	310 662	334 327	342 248	329 870	366 280	381 042	346 144	422 589
Foreign controlled undertakings	21 033	33 023	30 239	39 000	52 410	57 067	57 646	71 720
Foreign companies (branches)	588	1 521	2 265	4 799	5 787	7 104	8 630	13 064
All undertakings	311 250	335 848	344 513	334 668	372 067	388 145	354 774	435 654
of which:								
Life	34 501	34 008	43 740	50 670	56 210	68 489	67 465	108 401
Domestic undertakings	34 501	34 008	43 740	50 664	56 070	68 315	67 232	107 262
Foreign controlled undertakings	1 651	2 244	4 374	8 530	12 043	15 707	13 375	22 171
Foreign companies (branches)	0	0	0	6	141	174	233	1 138
All undertakings	34 501	34 008	43 740	50 670	56 210	68 489	67 465	108 401
Non-life	276 749	301 840	300 773	283 999	315 857	319 657	287 309	327 253
Domestic undertakings	276 161	300 318	298 508	279 206	310 211	312 727	278 912	315 327
Foreign controlled undertakings	19 382	30 779	25 866	30 471	40 367	41 360	44 271	49 549
Foreign companies (branches)	588	1 521	2 265	4 793	5 646	6 930	8 397	11 926
All undertakings	276 749	301 840	300 773	283 999	315 857	319 657	287 309	327 253
Total								
Domestic undertakings	315 281	341 189	356 084	355 430	384 089	395 825	357 935	438 285
Foreign controlled undertakings	25 652	39 885	44 075	64 561	70 219	71 851	69 437	87 416
Foreign companies (branches)	588	1 521	2 265	4 799	5 787	7 104	8 630	13 064
All undertakings	315 869	342 710	358 349	360 229	389 876	402 928	366 565	451 350

COSTA RICA

Table 1. Selected aggregates *(cont.)*

Million CRC

	2014	2015	2016	2017	2018	2019	2020	2021
1.3 Commissions								
Life								
Domestic undertakings	0	..	..	..	..	..	..	..
Foreign controlled undertakings	0	..	..	..	..	..	..	..
Foreign companies (branches)	0	..	..	..	..	..	..	..
All undertakings	0	..	..	..	..	..	..	..
Non-life								
Domestic undertakings	785	..	..	..	..	..	..	..
Foreign controlled undertakings	785	..	..	..	..	..	..	..
Foreign companies (branches)	0	..	..	0	0	..	..	..
All undertakings	785	..	..	..	..	..	..	..
Composite								
Domestic undertakings	42 598	..	..	..	..	..	..	..
Foreign controlled undertakings	5 657	..	..	..	..	..	..	..
Foreign companies (branches)	437	..	..	..	..	..	..	..
All undertakings	43 035	..	..	..	..	..	..	..
of which:								
Life	..	..	..	..	..	..	..	..
Domestic undertakings	..	..	..	..	..	..	..	..
Foreign controlled undertakings	..	..	..	..	..	..	..	..
Foreign companies (branches)	..	..	..	..	..	..	..	..
All undertakings	..	..	..	..	..	..	..	..
Non-life	..	..	..	..	..	..	..	..
Domestic undertakings	..	..	..	..	..	..	..	..
Foreign controlled undertakings	..	..	..	..	..	..	..	..
Foreign companies (branches)	..	..	..	..	..	..	..	..
All undertakings	..	..	..	..	..	..	..	..
Total								
Domestic undertakings	43 383	..	..	..	..	..	..	..
Foreign controlled undertakings	6 443	..	..	..	..	..	..	..
Foreign companies (branches)	437	..	..	0	0	..	..	..
All undertakings	43 820	..	..	..	..	..	..	..
1.4 Gross operating expenses								
Life								
Domestic undertakings	0	0	0	..	..	..	..	..
Foreign controlled undertakings	0	0	0	..	..	..	..	..
Foreign companies (branches)	0	0	0	..	..	..	..	..
All undertakings	0	0	0	..	..	..	..	..
Non-life								
Domestic undertakings	3 618	3 133	5 210	6 934	7 901	8 241	9 307	11 199
Foreign controlled undertakings	3 618	3 133	5 210	6 934	7 901	8 241	9 307	11 199
Foreign companies (branches)	0	0	0	0	0	0	..	..
All undertakings	3 618	3 133	5 210	6 934	7 901	8 241	9 307	11 199
Composite								
Domestic undertakings	209 755	122 357	117 143	136 707	151 705	173 182	168 577	170 076
Foreign controlled undertakings	18 563	17 025	23 243	26 834	29 811	35 093	38 454	45 190
Foreign companies (branches)	1 566	2 196	3 395	3 987	4 818	5 298	6 565	7 823
All undertakings	211 320	124 553	120 538	140 694	156 522	178 480	175 142	177 900
of which:								
Life	..	19 351	23 644	28 303	31 698	36 077	36 125	38 360
Domestic undertakings	..	18 985	23 091	27 759	30 943	35 083	34 350	36 536
Foreign controlled undertakings	..	4 411	5 270	8 141	9 285	10 528	10 638	13 306
Foreign companies (branches)	..	367	553	544	755	993	1 775	1 824
All undertakings	..	19 351	23 644	28 303	31 698	36 077	36 125	38 360
Non-life	..	105 202	96 894	112 391	124 824	142 403	139 017	139 540
Domestic undertakings	..	103 372	94 052	108 948	120 762	138 099	134 227	133 540
Foreign controlled undertakings	..	12 614	17 973	18 693	20 526	24 565	27 816	31 884
Foreign companies (branches)	..	1 830	2 842	3 443	4 062	4 304	4 790	6 000
All undertakings	..	105 202	96 894	112 391	124 824	142 403	139 017	139 540
Total								
Domestic undertakings	213 373	125 490	122 353	143 640	159 606	181 423	177 885	181 275
Foreign controlled undertakings	22 180	20 158	28 453	33 768	37 712	43 334	47 761	56 389
Foreign companies (branches)	1 566	2 196	3 395	3 987	4 818	5 298	6 565	7 823
All undertakings	214 938	127 686	125 748	147 628	164 423	186 721	184 450	189 099

Table 1. Selected aggregates *(cont.)*

Million CRC

	2014	2015	2016	2017	2018	2019	2020	2021
1.5 Insurance business written abroad by branches, gross premiums								
Life								
Branches and agencies	..	..	..	..	..	..	..	..
Subsidaries	..	..	..	..	..	..	..	..
Total	..	..	..	..	..	..	..	..
Non-life								
Branches and agencies	..	..	..	..	..	..	..	..
Subsidaries	..	..	..	..	..	..	..	..
Total	..	..	..	..	..	..	..	..
Composite								
Branches and agencies	..	..	..	..	..	..	..	..
Subsidaries	..	..	..	..	..	..	..	..
Total	..	..	..	..	..	..	..	..
of which:								
Life	..	..	..	..	..	..	..	..
Branches and agencies	..	..	..	..	..	..	..	..
Subsidaries	..	..	..	..	..	..	..	..
Total	..	..	..	..	..	..	..	..
Non-life	..	..	..	..	..	..	..	..
Branches and agencies	..	..	..	..	..	..	..	..
Subsidaries	..	..	..	..	..	..	..	..
Total	..	..	..	..	..	..	..	..
Total								
Branches and agencies	..	..	..	..	..	..	..	..
Subsidaries	..	..	..	..	..	..	..	..
Total	..	..	..	..	..	..	..	..

.. Not available

Note: Detailed metadata at: *http://metalinks.oecd.org/ins/20230516/db60*.

Source: *OECD Insurance Statistics (database)*

COSTA RICA

Table 2. Number of companies and employees

	2014	2015	2016	2017	2018	2019	2020	2021
2.1 Number of companies								
Life								
Domestic undertakings	0	0	0	..	..	..	..	..
Foreign controlled undertakings	0	0	0	..	..	..	..	..
Foreign companies (branches)	0	0	0	..	..	..	..	..
All undertakings	0	0	0	..	..	..	..	..
Non-life								
Domestic undertakings	3	3	3	3	3	3	3	3
Foreign controlled undertakings	3	3	3	3	3	3	3	3
Foreign companies (branches)	0	0	0	0	0	0	0	0
All undertakings	3	3	3	3	3	3	3	3
Composite								
Domestic undertakings	8	8	8	8	8	8	8	8
Foreign controlled undertakings	6	6	6	6	6	6	6	6
Foreign companies (branches)	2	2	2	2	2	2	2	2
All undertakings	10	10	10	10	10	10	10	10
Reinsurance								
Domestic undertakings	0	0	0	0	0	0	0	0
Foreign controlled undertakings	0	0	0	0	0	0	0	0
Foreign companies (branches)	0	0	0	0	0	0	0	0
All undertakings	0	0	0	0	0	0	0	0
Total								
Domestic undertakings	11	11	11	11	11	11	11	11
Foreign controlled undertakings	9	9	9	9	9	9	9	9
Foreign companies (branches)	2	2	2	2	2	2	2	2
All undertakings	13	13	13	13	13	13	13	13
2.2 Number of employees								
Insurance undertakings	..	..	..	..	2	1 965	3 330	3 416
Intermediaries	..	..	..	..	..	..	..	..
Total	..	..	..	..	..	..	..	3 416

.. Not available

Note: Detailed metadata at: *http://metalinks.oecd.org/ins/20230516/db60.*

Source: *OECD Insurance Statistics (database)*

CZECH REPUBLIC

Table 1. Selected aggregates

Million CZK

	2014	2015	2016	2017	2018	2019	2020	2021
1.1 Insurance business written in the reporting country								
1.1.1 Insurance business, by ownership								
Gross premiums								
Domestic undertakings	148 755	140 688	135 581	138 186	142 473	152 231	154 641	164 178
Foreign controlled undertakings	137 200	129 432	124 165	125 585	128 377	136 031	137 284	157 040
Foreign companies (branches)	9 164	11 159	11 102	11 459	10 768	13 208	12 830	14 972
All undertakings	157 919	151 846	146 683	149 645	153 241	165 439	167 470	179 150
Premiums ceded								
Domestic undertakings	29 915	29 857	28 913	30 449	31 057	32 569	33 265	36 095
Foreign controlled undertakings	26 601	26 578	25 450	26 230	26 704	27 639	27 948	33 536
Foreign companies (branches)	1 250	1 561	1 993	1 484	1 048	1 450	1 562	2 956
All undertakings	31 165	31 418	30 905	31 933	32 105	34 018	34 827	39 051
Net written premiums								
Domestic undertakings	118 839	110 831	106 669	107 737	111 416	119 662	121 376	128 084
Foreign controlled undertakings	110 598	102 854	98 714	99 356	101 673	108 393	109 336	123 504
Foreign companies (branches)	7 914	9 598	9 109	9 976	9 720	11 758	11 268	12 016
All undertakings	126 754	120 429	115 778	117 713	121 136	131 421	132 644	140 100
1.1.2 Insurance business on foreign risks, gross premiums								
Life	0	0	0	0	0	0	0	..
Non-life	993	524	274	738	874	1 906	1 329	..
Composite	2 121	1 867	1 843	2 777	3 561	3 503	3 708	..
of which:								
Life	360	4	0	1 805	1 897	2 099	2 216	..
Non-life	1 761	1 863	1 843	972	1 664	1 404	1 492	..
Total	3 113	2 390	2 117	3 515	4 435	5 408	5 037	..
1.1.3 Life insurance payments, by class, gross premiums								
Annuities	1 505	1 413	..	..	..	..	..	0
Unit linked	37 632	35 125	26 131	25 608	25 199	19 296	17 682	17 362
Other life insurance	32 042	25 876	33 110	31 425	30 653	33 652	33 535	33 787
Total life insurance	71 179	62 414	59 240	57 033	55 852	52 948	51 217	51 149
***of which:** Pension contracts*	..	..	..	0	0	0	.. c	426
1.1.4 Non-life insurance payments, by class, gross premiums								
Motor vehicle insurance	37 855	39 633	38 212	40 533	44 078	48 204	51 677	57 185
Marine, aviation and other transport insurance	294	331	912	1 073	1 072	1 056	933	975
Freight insurance	461	466	0	..	..	..	..	..
Fire and other property damage insurance	21 687	22 655	23 042	24 244	24 997	26 621	27 852	30 038
Pecuniary loss insurance	4 933	3 770	3 959	4 030	3 309	3 805	3 166	3 840
General liability insurance	13 164	13 810	13 609	14 559	15 207	16 661	17 283	18 432
Accident and health	5 342	5 393	5 136	5 460	5 802	13 242	12 739	14 541
***of which:** Health*	0	0	0	2 474	2 575	3 260	2 460	3 225
Other non-life insurance	3 002	3 374	2 223	2 364	2 489	2 432	2 088	2 425
Treaty reinsurance	0	0	0	..	..	..	..	..
Total non-life insurance	86 738	89 431	87 092	92 263	96 954	112 021	115 738	127 436
1.2 Gross claims payments								
Life								
Domestic undertakings	1 307	702	.. c	.. c	.. c	.. c	.. c	.. c
Foreign controlled undertakings	1 307	702	.. c	.. c	.. c	.. c	0	0
Foreign companies (branches)	6 044	6 376	6 094	6 249	5 572	6 169	5 967	6 138
All undertakings	7 352	7 077	6 456	6 567	5 875	6 176	6 004	6 203
Non-life								
Domestic undertakings	6 045	2 285	2 103	2 172	2 681	3 159	3 595	3 115
Foreign controlled undertakings	1 734	1 288	1 072	1 070	1 349	1 507	1 577	263
Foreign companies (branches)	1 353	1 216	1 674	1 764	1 344	1 778	1 837	1 540
All undertakings	7 398	3 501	3 777	3 936	4 025	4 937	5 432	4 655
Composite								
Domestic undertakings	90 284	84 909	81 024	80 221	80 773	87 779	80 849	95 714
Foreign controlled undertakings	84 712	79 681	75 835	75 301	75 653	82 528	74 838	95 081
Foreign companies (branches)	0	0	0	0	0	..	0	0
All undertakings	90 284	84 909	81 024	80 221	80 773	87 779	80 849	95 714
of which:								
Life	50 972	44 105	37 676	36 087	37 421	37 517	31 915	34 321
Domestic undertakings	50 972	44 105	37 676	36 087	37 421	37 517	31 915	34 321
Foreign controlled undertakings	49 092	42 631	36 570	35 018	36 422	37 483	31 018	34 291
Foreign companies (branches)	0	0	0	0	0	..	0	0
All undertakings	50 972	44 105	37 676	36 087	37 421	37 517	31 915	34 321
Non-life	39 312	40 805	43 348	44 134	43 352	50 263	48 934	61 393
Domestic undertakings	39 312	40 805	43 348	44 134	43 352	50 263	48 934	61 393
Foreign controlled undertakings	35 620	37 050	39 265	40 283	39 231	45 044	43 820	60 790
Foreign companies (branches)	0	0	0	0	0	..	0	0
All undertakings	39 312	40 805	43 348	44 134	43 352	50 263	48 934	61 393
Total								
Domestic undertakings	97 636	87 896	83 490	82 712	83 757	90 945	84 480	98 894
Foreign controlled undertakings	87 754	81 671	77 269	76 690	77 305	84 035	76 415	95 344
Foreign companies (branches)	7 397	7 592	7 767	8 012	6 916	7 947	7 804	7 678
All undertakings	105 033	95 488	91 257	90 724	90 673	98 892	92 285	106 572

Table 1. Selected aggregates *(cont.)*

Million CZK

	2014	2015	2016	2017	2018	2019	2020	2021
1.3 Commissions								
Life								
Domestic undertakings	..	..	..	..	..	..	..	..
Foreign controlled undertakings	..	..	..	..	..	..	..	..
Foreign companies (branches)	..	..	..	..	..	..	..	..
All undertakings	..	..	..	..	..	..	..	..
Non-life								
Domestic undertakings	..	..	..	..	..	..	..	..
Foreign controlled undertakings	..	..	..	..	..	..	..	..
Foreign companies (branches)	..	..	..	..	..	..	..	..
All undertakings	..	..	..	..	..	..	..	..
Composite								
Domestic undertakings	..	..	..	..	..	..	..	..
Foreign controlled undertakings	..	..	..	..	..	..	..	..
Foreign companies (branches)	..	..	..	..	..	..	..	..
All undertakings	..	..	..	..	..	..	..	..
of which:								
Life	..	..	..	..	..	..	..	..
Domestic undertakings	..	..	..	..	..	..	..	..
Foreign controlled undertakings	..	..	..	..	..	..	..	..
Foreign companies (branches)	..	..	..	..	..	..	..	..
All undertakings	..	..	..	..	..	..	..	..
Non-life	..	..	..	..	..	..	..	..
Domestic undertakings	..	..	..	..	..	..	..	..
Foreign controlled undertakings	..	..	..	..	..	..	..	..
Foreign companies (branches)	..	..	..	..	..	..	..	..
All undertakings	..	..	..	..	..	..	..	..
Total								
Domestic undertakings	..	..	..	..	..	..	..	..
Foreign controlled undertakings	..	..	..	..	..	..	..	..
Foreign companies (branches)	..	..	..	..	..	..	..	..
All undertakings	..	..	..	..	..	..	..	..
1.4 Gross operating expenses								
Life								
Domestic undertakings	759	739	.. c	.. c	.. c	.. c	.. c	.. c
Foreign controlled undertakings	759	739	.. c	.. c	.. c	.. c	0	0
Foreign companies (branches)	1 459	2 036	2 015	1 894	1 905	2 451	2 581	2 985
All undertakings	2 219	2 775	2 520	2 251	2 232	2 485	2 694	3 177
Non-life								
Domestic undertakings	1 805	1 571	1 203	2 170	2 988	2 902	3 313	2 106
Foreign controlled undertakings	937	883	622	979	1 044	1 424	1 509	450
Foreign companies (branches)	841	1 203	1 224	1 412	1 401	1 767	370	1 873
All undertakings	2 646	2 773	2 427	3 582	4 389	4 669	3 683	3 979
Composite								
Domestic undertakings	22 207	20 341	21 319	36 095	41 260	40 228	42 178	43 247
Foreign controlled undertakings	21 233	19 120	19 893	32 685	36 930	36 082	37 560	42 722
Foreign companies (branches)	0	0	0	0	0	..	0	..
All undertakings	22 207	20 341	21 319	36 095	41 260	40 228	42 178	43 247
of which:								
Life	11 475	9 613	9 217	11 707	12 405	10 887	11 607	11 127
Domestic undertakings	11 475	9 613	9 217	11 707	12 405	10 887	11 607	11 127
Foreign controlled undertakings	11 050	9 059	8 637	10 795	11 445	10 249	10 933	11 063
Foreign companies (branches)	0	0	0	0	0	..	0	..
All undertakings	11 475	9 613	9 217	11 707	12 405	10 887	11 607	11 127
Non-life	10 733	10 728	12 102	24 388	28 855	29 341	30 571	32 120
Domestic undertakings	10 733	10 728	12 102	24 388	28 855	29 341	30 571	32 120
Foreign controlled undertakings	10 184	10 061	11 256	21 890	25 485	25 833	26 627	31 659
Foreign companies (branches)	0	0	0	0	0	..	0	..
All undertakings	10 733	10 728	12 102	24 388	28 855	29 341	30 571	32 120
Total								
Domestic undertakings	24 772	22 650	23 027	38 621	44 574	43 164	45 605	45 545
Foreign controlled undertakings	22 929	20 742	21 020	34 020	38 301	37 505	39 069	43 171
Foreign companies (branches)	2 301	3 239	3 239	3 307	3 307	4 218	2 950	4 858
All undertakings	27 072	25 889	26 266	41 928	47 881	47 382	48 555	50 403

Table 1. Selected aggregates *(cont.)*

Million CZK

	2014	2015	2016	2017	2018	2019	2020	2021
1.5 Insurance business written abroad by branches, gross premiums								
Life								
Branches and agencies	0	0	0	0	0	0	0	0
Subsidaries	..	..	..	..	..	..	..	..
Total	0	0	..	0	0	0	0	0
Non-life								
Branches and agencies	313	351	377	596	804	1 076	1 290	207
Subsidaries	..	..	..	..	..	..	..	..
Total	313	351	377	596	804	1 076	1 290	207
Composite								
Branches and agencies	4 528	5 164	1 697	1 805	1 897	2 099	2 216	6 825
Subsidaries	..	..	..	..	..	..	..	..
Total	4 528	5 164	1 697	1 805	1 897	2 099	2 216	6 825
of which:								
Life	1 434	1 460	1 697	1 805	1 897	2 099	2 216	2 726
Branches and agencies	1 434	1 460	1 697	1 805	1 897	2 099	2 216	2 726
Subsidaries	..	..	..	..	..	..	..	..
Total	1 434	1 460	1 697	1 805	1 897	2 099	2 216	2 726
Non-life	3 095	3 704	..	0	0	0	0	4 099
Branches and agencies	3 095	3 704	0	0	0	0	0	4 099
Subsidaries	..	..	..	..	..	..	..	..
Total	3 095	3 704	..	0	0	0	0	4 099
Total								
Branches and agencies	4 841	5 516	2 074	2 401	2 700	3 175	3 507	7 032
Subsidaries	..	..	..	..	..	..	..	..
Total	4 841	5 516	2 074	2 401	2 700	3 175	3 507	7 032

.. Not available; c Confidential data

Note: Detailed metadata at: *http://metalinks.oecd.org/ins/20230516/737e.*

Source: *OECD Insurance Statistics (database)*

Table 2. Number of companies and employees

	2014	2015	2016	2017	2018	2019	2020	2021
2.1 Number of companies								
Life								
Domestic undertakings	2	2	1	1	1	1	1	1
Foreign controlled undertakings	2	2	1	1	1	0	0	0
Foreign companies (branches)	4	5	5	5	6	6	4	4
All undertakings	6	7	6	6	7	7	5	5
Non-life								
Domestic undertakings	15	15	13	11	11	11	11	9
Foreign controlled undertakings	7	5	4	3	3	3	3	2
Foreign companies (branches)	16	18	19	17	14	13	13	14
All undertakings	31	33	32	28	25	24	24	23
Composite								
Domestic undertakings	15	14	14	14	14	13	13	11
Foreign controlled undertakings	12	11	11	11	11	10	10	9
Foreign companies (branches)	0	0	0	0	0	1	0	0
All undertakings	15	14	14	14	14	14	13	11
Reinsurance								
Domestic undertakings	1	1	1	1	1	1	1	1
Foreign controlled undertakings	1	1	1	1	1	1	1	1
Foreign companies (branches)	..	..	..	0	0	0	0	0
All undertakings	1	1	1	1	1	1	1	1
Total								
Domestic undertakings	33	32	29	27	27	26	26	22
Foreign controlled undertakings	22	19	17	16	16	14	14	12
Foreign companies (branches)	20	23	24	22	20	20	17	18
All undertakings	53	55	53	49	47	46	43	40
2.2 Number of employees								
Insurance undertakings	..	..	..	..	..	11 545	11 403	2 225
Intermediaries	..	..	..	..	..	..	..	42 408
Total	..	..	..	..	..	..	..	44 632

.. Not available

Note: Detailed metadata at: *http://metalinks.oecd.org/ins/20230516/737e.*

Source: *OECD Insurance Statistics (database)*

DENMARK

Table 1. Selected aggregates

Million DKK

	2014	2015	2016	2017	2018	2019	2020	2021
1.1 Insurance business written in the reporting country								
1.1.1 Insurance business, by ownership								
Gross premiums								
Domestic undertakings	208 213	215 276	225 500	247 934	258 749	257 368	268 220	294 050
Foreign controlled undertakings	46 022	46 192	49 042	53 373	53 706	41 503	222 991	244 522
Foreign companies (branches)	..	..	..	..	..	..	..	..
All undertakings	208 213	215 276	225 500	247 934	258 749	257 368	268 220	294 050
Premiums ceded								
Domestic undertakings	5 875	6 309	6 943	8 079	7 160	5 780	4 388	4 775
Foreign controlled undertakings	2 080	2 462	2 355	2 024	1 666	794	3 568	3 951
Foreign companies (branches)	..	..	..	..	..	..	..	..
All undertakings	5 875	6 309	6 943	8 079	7 160	5 780	4 388	4 775
Net written premiums								
Domestic undertakings	202 338	208 966	218 557	239 855	251 589	251 588	263 831	289 274
Foreign controlled undertakings	43 942	43 730	46 687	51 349	52 040	40 709	219 423	240 572
Foreign companies (branches)	..	..	..	..	..	..	..	..
All undertakings	202 338	208 966	218 557	239 855	251 589	251 588	263 831	289 274
1.1.2 Insurance business on foreign risks, gross premiums								
Life	631	631	..	..	..	..	..	..
Non-life	23 099	22 611	..	..	..	..	..	..
Composite total	..	..	..	..	..	..	..	..
Total	23 730	23 242	..	..	..	..	..	..
1.1.3 Life insurance payments, by class, gross premiums								
Annuities	..	..	..	..	..	..	..	..
Unit linked	..	..	..	..	..	..	..	..
Other life insurance	..	..	..	..	..	..	..	..
Total life insurance	140 314	147 662	153 907	170 623	180 289	182 733	194 220	214 182
***of which:** Pension contracts*	..	..	..	..	..	..	..	..
1.1.4 Non-life insurance payments, by class, gross premiums								
Motor vehicle insurance	19 310	19 146	21 247	23 487	25 929	21 607	19 813	..
Marine, aviation and other transport insurance	1 174	1 105	1 857	1 844	1 769	1 763	1 575	..
Freight insurance	..	0	..	..	..	..	0	..
Fire and other property damage insurance	22 855	22 642	25 107	26 732	26 184	26 145	26 724	..
Pecuniary loss insurance	402	417	1 113	2 045	1 921	2 086	2 334	..
General liability insurance	2 377	2 314	3 203	3 411	3 494	3 659	3 845	..
Accident and health	15 063	15 282	15 965	16 727	16 051	16 759	17 015	..
***of which:** Health*	1 265	1 337	4 498	4 657	4 129	4 641	4 703	..
Other non-life insurance	5 156	5 052	1 635	1 759	1 710	1 808	1 790	..
Treaty reinsurance	867	937	538	616	687	11	11	..
Total non-life insurance	67 204	66 895	70 665	76 621	77 745	73 838	73 052	78 587
1.2 Gross claims payments								
Life								
Domestic undertakings	124 323	98 376	115 270	112 996	128 844	128 044	140 781	152 725
Foreign controlled undertakings	24 385	20 765	23 573	22 740	25 299	19 923	23 259	15 903
Foreign companies (branches)	..	..	..	..	..	..	..	..
All undertakings	124 323	98 376	115 270	112 996	128 844	128 044	140 781	152 725
Non-life								
Domestic undertakings	46 601	47 833	44 773	45 620	46 939	47 270	47 399	49 017
Foreign controlled undertakings	13 007	13 316	11 816	11 605	11 136	10 436	10 585	9 987
Foreign companies (branches)	..	..	..	..	..	..	..	..
All undertakings	46 601	47 833	44 773	45 620	46 939	47 270	47 399	49 017
Composite, all undertakings	..	..	..	..	..	..	..	..
Total								
Domestic undertakings	170 924	146 209	160 043	158 616	175 783	175 314	188 180	201 742
Foreign controlled undertakings	37 392	34 081	35 389	34 345	36 435	30 359	33 844	25 890
Foreign companies (branches)	..	..	..	..	..	..	..	..
All undertakings	170 924	146 209	160 043	158 616	175 783	175 314	188 180	201 742
1.3 Commissions								
Life								
Domestic undertakings	195	199	175	207	246	209	269	259
Foreign controlled undertakings	60	36	34	26	30	0	..	..
Foreign companies (branches)	..	..	..	..	..	..	..	..
All undertakings	195	199	175	207	246	209	269	259
Non-life								
Domestic undertakings	1 613	1 879	1 361	1 320	1 262	1 350	1 329	1 481
Foreign controlled undertakings	579	891	494	463	446	465	417	483
Foreign companies (branches)	..	..	..	..	..	..	..	..
All undertakings	1 613	1 879	1 361	1 320	1 262	1 350	1 329	1 481
Composite, all undertakings	..	..	..	..	..	..	..	..
Total								
Domestic undertakings	1 808	2 079	1 536	1 527	1 508	1 559	1 598	1 740
Foreign controlled undertakings	639	927	528	489	476	465	417	483
Foreign companies (branches)	..	..	..	..	..	..	..	..
All undertakings	1 808	2 079	1 536	1 527	1 508	1 559	1 598	1 740

DENMARK

Table 1. Selected aggregates *(cont.)*

Million DKK

	2014	2015	2016	2017	2018	2019	2020	2021
1.4 Gross operating expenses								
Life								
Domestic undertakings	4 887	4 570	4 788	4 971	5 138	5 428	5 278	5 658
Foreign controlled undertakings	1 377	1 284	1 268	1 386	1 349	1 133	923	891
Foreign companies (branches)	..	..	..	..	..	..	..	..
All undertakings	4 887	4 570	4 788	4 971	5 138	5 428	6 201	5 658
Non-life								
Domestic undertakings	11 564	11 856	12 050	12 003	11 298	11 258	11 154	12 338
Foreign controlled undertakings	3 867	4 065	3 780	3 542	2 778	2 666	2 597	2 596
Foreign companies (branches)	..	..	..	..	..	..	..	..
All undertakings	11 564	11 856	12 050	12 003	11 322	11 258	13 751	12 338
Composite, all undertakings	..	..	..	..	..	..	..	..
Total								
Domestic undertakings	16 451	16 426	16 838	16 974	16 436	16 686	16 432	17 996
Foreign controlled undertakings	5 244	5 349	5 048	4 928	4 127	3 799	3 520	3 487
Foreign companies (branches)	..	..	..	..	..	..	..	..
All undertakings	16 451	16 426	16 838	16 974	16 460	16 686	19 952	17 996
1.5 Insurance business written abroad by branches, gross premiums								
Life								
Branches and agencies	..	..	..	..	..	..	..	..
Subsidaries	..	..	..	..	..	..	..	..
Total	..	..	..	..	..	..	..	..
Non-life								
Branches and agencies	9 286	8 607	19 043	19 072	18 499	18 804	18 699	20 905
Subsidaries	..	..	..	..	..	..	..	..
Total	9 286	8 607	19 043	19 072	18 499	18 804	18 699	20 905
Composite total	..	..	..	..	..	..	..	..
Total								
Branches and agencies	9 286	8 607	19 043	19 072	18 499	18 804	18 699	20 905
Subsidaries	..	..	..	..	..	..	..	..
Total	9 286	8 607	19 043	19 072	18 499	18 804	18 699	20 905

.. Not available

Note: Detailed metadata at: *http://metalinks.oecd.org/ins/20230516/01ed.*

Source: *OECD Insurance Statistics (database)*

DENMARK

Table 2. Number of companies and employees

	2014	2015	2016	2017	2018	2019	2020	2021
2.1 Number of companies								
Life								
Domestic undertakings	37	33	33	33	31	29	28	28
Foreign controlled undertakings	4	4	4	4	4	3	3	3
Foreign companies (branches)	1	1	1	2	2	3	6	4
All undertakings	38	34	34	35	33	32	34	35
Non-life								
Domestic undertakings	63	63	63	59	55	52	53	53
Foreign controlled undertakings	6	6	6	6	5	4	4	4
Foreign companies (branches)	49	49	53	56	67	58	35	47
All undertakings	112	112	116	115	122	110	88	104
Composite, all undertakings	**0**	**0**	**0**	..	..	..	..	..
Reinsurance								
Domestic undertakings	7	7	5	6	5	5	3	3
Foreign controlled undertakings	..	..	0	..	..	..	..	..
Foreign companies (branches)	..	..	..	..	..	..	3	3
All undertakings	7	7	5	6	5	5	6	6
Total								
Domestic undertakings	107	103	101	98	91	86	84	84
Foreign controlled undertakings	10	10	10	10	9	7	7	7
Foreign companies (branches)	50	50	54	58	69	61	44	54
All undertakings	157	153	155	156	160	147	128	145
2.2 Number of employees								
Insurance undertakings	17 057	16 472	16 112	13 640	11 568	14 391	16 950	17 895
Intermediaries	..	..	..	..	..	..	..	..
Total	17 057	16 472	16 112	13 640	11 568	14 391	16 950	..

.. Not available

Note: Detailed metadata at: *http://metalinks.oecd.org/ins/20230516/01ed.*

Source: *OECD Insurance Statistics (database)*

ESTONIA

Table 1. Selected aggregates

Million EUR

	2014	2015	2016	2017	2018	2019	2020	2021
1.1 Insurance business written in the reporting country								
1.1.1 Insurance business, by ownership								
Gross premiums								
Domestic undertakings	561	619	654	721	807	847	762	824
Foreign controlled undertakings	539	596	627	721	775	815	734	786
Foreign companies (branches)	70	70	82	97	118	137	175	179
All undertakings	631	689	736	818	925	984	937	1 003
Premiums ceded								
Domestic undertakings	28	29	31	31	45	48	44	41
Foreign controlled undertakings	2	20	22	22	34	38	35	34
Foreign companies (branches)	..	..	..	..	..	..	..	..
All undertakings	..	..	..	..	..	..	..	..
Net written premiums								
Domestic undertakings	534	590	624	690	762	799	718	783
Foreign controlled undertakings	217	576	605	670	741	777	699	752
Foreign companies (branches)	..	..	..	..	..	..	..	..
All undertakings	..	..	..	..	..	..	..	..
1.1.2 Insurance business on foreign risks, gross premiums								
Life	..	..	..	..	..	..	..	..
Non-life	..	..	..	..	..	..	..	..
Composite	..	..	..	..	..	..	..	..
of which:								
Life	..	..	..	..	..	..	..	..
Non-life	..	..	..	..	..	..	..	..
Total	..	..	..	..	..	..	..	..
1.1.3 Life insurance payments, by class, gross premiums								
Annuities	19	24	27	27	..	..	..	..
Unit linked	109	118	116	116	120	137	141	170
Other life insurance	63	72	80	80	113	116	125	127
Total life insurance	191	215	221	223	233	253	266	297
***of which:** Pension contracts*	37	36	40	39	39	..	..	..
1.1.4 Non-life insurance payments, by class, gross premiums								
Motor vehicle insurance	244	259	292	345	404	409	362	366
Marine, aviation and other transport insurance	2	2	6	6	6	8	13	17
Freight insurance	4	4	..	..	..	..	..	..
Fire and other property damage insurance	107	115	127	140	159	174	172	180
Pecuniary loss insurance	9	9	12	17	21	27	26	28
General liability insurance	16	19	21	22	26	27	27	30
Accident and health	42	42	54	43	70	81	67	80
***of which:** Health*	..	..	..	..	20	25	25	30
Other non-life insurance	16	23	4	7	6	5	4	5
Treaty reinsurance	..	..	..	..	..	0	0	..
Total non-life insurance	440	474	515	580	692	731	671	706
1.2 Gross claims payments								
Life								
Domestic undertakings	..	97	87	.. c	.. c	.. c	.. c	.. c
Foreign controlled undertakings	..	97	87	.. c	.. c	.. c	.. c	.. c
Foreign companies (branches)	..	..	0	2	12	6	5	..
All undertakings	..	97	87	93	80	78	..	..
Non-life								
Domestic undertakings	..	230	243	270	315	343	289	330
Foreign controlled undertakings	..	217	228	253	297	323	274	310
Foreign companies (branches)	..	40	43	49	55	67	80	85
All undertakings	246	271	287	319	370	410	369	415
Composite								
Domestic undertakings	..	..	38	36	48	53	46	78
Foreign controlled undertakings	..	..	38	36	48	53	46	78
Foreign companies (branches)	..	..	3	4	4	8	18	..
All undertakings	..	..	42	40	52	61	..	..
of which:								
Life	..	..	34	40	39	46	..	..
Domestic undertakings	..	..	31	36	35	38	31	60
Foreign controlled undertakings	..	..	31	36	35	38	31	60
Foreign companies (branches)	..	..	3	4	4	8	17	..
All undertakings	..	..	34	40	39	46	..	..
Non-life	..	..	8	0	13	15	..	..
Domestic undertakings	..	..	8	0	13	15	15	18
Foreign controlled undertakings	..	..	8	0	13	15	15	18
Foreign companies (branches)	..	..	0	0	0	0	1	..
All undertakings	..	..	8	0	13	15	..	..
Total								
Domestic undertakings	..	328	369	397	431	468	412	489
Foreign controlled undertakings	..	314	354	380	413	448	397	469
Foreign companies (branches)	..	40	47	55	71	81	103	85
All undertakings	246	368	416	452	502	549	369	415

ESTONIA

Table 1. Selected aggregates *(cont.)*

Million EUR

	2014	2015	2016	2017	2018	2019	2020	2021
1.3 Commissions								
Life								
Domestic undertakings	21	23	..	..	..	..	..	..
Foreign controlled undertakings	21	23	..	..	..	..	..	..
Foreign companies (branches)	..	..	..	..	..	..	..	..
All undertakings	..	23	..	..	..	..	..	..
Non-life								
Domestic undertakings	73	78	..	..	..	..	..	..
Foreign controlled undertakings	69	73	..	..	..	..	..	..
Foreign companies (branches)	..	..	..	..	..	..	..	..
All undertakings	..	78	..	..	..	..	..	..
Composite								
Domestic undertakings	..	..	..	..	..	..	..	..
Foreign controlled undertakings	..	..	..	..	..	..	..	..
Foreign companies (branches)	..	..	..	..	..	..	..	..
All undertakings	..	..	..	..	..	..	..	..
of which:								
Life	..	..	..	..	..	..	..	..
Domestic undertakings	..	..	..	..	..	..	..	..
Foreign controlled undertakings	..	..	..	..	..	..	..	..
Foreign companies (branches)	..	..	..	..	..	..	..	..
All undertakings	..	..	..	..	..	..	..	..
Non-life	..	..	..	..	..	..	..	..
Domestic undertakings	..	..	..	..	..	..	..	..
Foreign controlled undertakings	..	..	..	..	..	..	..	..
Foreign companies (branches)	..	..	..	..	..	..	..	..
All undertakings	..	..	..	..	..	..	..	..
Total								
Domestic undertakings	94	101	..	..	..	..	..	..
Foreign controlled undertakings	89	95	..	..	..	..	..	..
Foreign companies (branches)	..	..	..	..	..	..	..	..
All undertakings	..	101	..	..	..	..	..	..
1.4 Gross operating expenses								
Life								
Domestic undertakings	9	11	..	..	.. c	.. c	.. c	.. c
Foreign controlled undertakings	9	11	..	..	.. c	.. c	.. c	.. c
Foreign companies (branches)	..	..	..	..	..	..	..	..
All undertakings	..	11	..	..	..	..	10	11
Non-life								
Domestic undertakings	30	27	115	137	153	157	131	138
Foreign controlled undertakings	29	26	..	..	142	148	123	129
Foreign companies (branches)	..	..	..	..	..	..	..	..
All undertakings	..	27	..	..	..	..	131	138
Composite								
Domestic undertakings	..	..	..	..	25	25	21	24
Foreign controlled undertakings	..	..	..	..	25	25	21	24
Foreign companies (branches)	..	..	..	..	..	..	..	..
All undertakings	..	..	..	..	..	..	21	24
of which:								
Life	..	..	..	..	..	..	18	21
Domestic undertakings	..	..	..	..	21	21	18	21
Foreign controlled undertakings	..	..	..	..	21	21	18	21
Foreign companies (branches)	..	..	..	..	..	..	..	..
All undertakings	..	..	..	..	..	..	18	21
Non-life	..	..	..	..	..	..	3	3
Domestic undertakings	..	..	..	..	4	4	3	3
Foreign controlled undertakings	..	..	..	..	4	4	3	3
Foreign companies (branches)	..	..	..	..	..	..	..	..
All undertakings	..	..	..	..	..	..	3	3
Total								
Domestic undertakings	40	38	115	137	188	191	162	173
Foreign controlled undertakings	38	36	..	..	177	182	154	164
Foreign companies (branches)	..	..	..	..	..	..	..	..
All undertakings	..	38	..	..	..	..	162	173

Table 1. Selected aggregates *(cont.)*

Million EUR

	2014	2015	2016	2017	2018	2019	2020	2021
1.5 Insurance business written abroad by branches, gross premiums								
Life								
Branches and agencies	114	130	96	..	84	94	97	109
Subsidaries	..	..	..	..	..	..	..	..
Total	114	130	96	..	..	94	..	..
Non-life								
Branches and agencies	174	190	201	243	289	307	266	279
Subsidaries	..	..	..	..	..	..	..	..
Total	174	190	201	243	289	307	266	279
Composite								
Branches and agencies	..	..	52	..	73	88	107	131
Subsidaries	..	..	..	..	..	..	..	..
Total	..	..	52	..	..	88	..	..
of which:								
Life	..	..	42	..	..	67	..	..
Branches and agencies	..	..	42	..	56	67	86	106
Subsidaries	..	..	..	..	..	..	..	..
Total	..	..	42	..	..	67	..	..
Non-life	..	..	10	..	..	21	..	..
Branches and agencies	..	..	10	..	17	21	21	25
Subsidaries	..	..	..	..	..	..	..	..
Total	..	..	10	..	..	21	..	..
Total								
Branches and agencies	288	320	349	243	446	489	471	519
Subsidaries	..	..	..	..	..	..	..	..
Total	288	320	349	243	289	489	266	279

.. Not available; c Confidential data
Note: Detailed metadata at: *http://metalinks.oecd.org/ins/20230516/488b.*
Source: *OECD Insurance Statistics (database)*

ESTONIA

Table 2. Number of companies and employees

	2014	2015	2016	2017	2018	2019	2020	2021
2.1 Number of companies								
Life								
Domestic undertakings	4	4	2	1	1	1	1	1
Foreign controlled undertakings	4	4	2	1	1	1	1	1
Foreign companies (branches)	1	1	0	1	1	1	1	1
All undertakings	5	5	2	2	2	2	2	2
Non-life								
Domestic undertakings	8	8	8	7	7	7	6	7
Foreign controlled undertakings	5	5	5	4	4	4	3	3
Foreign companies (branches)	4	3	4	4	6	6	6	6
All undertakings	12	11	12	11	13	13	12	13
Composite								
Domestic undertakings	0	0	2	2	2	1	1	1
Foreign controlled undertakings	0	0	2	2	2	1	1	1
Foreign companies (branches)	0	0	1	1	1	2	2	2
All undertakings	0	0	3	3	3	3	3	3
Reinsurance								
Domestic undertakings	0	0	0	0	0	0	..	..
Foreign controlled undertakings	0	0	0	..	0	0	..	..
Foreign companies (branches)	..	0	0	..	0	0	..	..
All undertakings	..	0	0	..	0	0	..	..
Total								
Domestic undertakings	12	12	12	10	10	9	8	..
Foreign controlled undertakings	9	9	9	7	7	6	5	..
Foreign companies (branches)	5	4	5	6	8	9	9	..
All undertakings	17	16	17	16	18	18	17	..
2.2 Number of employees								
Insurance undertakings	2 561	2 581	..	..	..	..	..	..
Intermediaries	1 217	1 232	..	..	..	..	..	..
Total	3 778	3 813	..	..	..	..	..	..

.. Not available

Note: Detailed metadata at: *http://metalinks.oecd.org/ins/20230516/488b*.

Source: *OECD Insurance Statistics (database)*

FINLAND

Table 1. Selected aggregates

Million EUR

	2014	2015	2016	2017	2018	2019	2020	2021
1.1 Insurance business written in the reporting country								
1.1.1 Insurance business, by ownership								
Gross premiums								
Domestic undertakings	10 632	10 741	9 045	8 926	7 922	9 620	7 865	9 078
Foreign controlled undertakings	3 698	6 892	..	..	..	..	..	..
Foreign companies (branches)	..	..	..	..	..	..	..	..
All undertakings	10 632	10 741	9 045	8 926	4 366	6 024	4 037	5 116
Premiums ceded								
Domestic undertakings	259	246	241	230	-251	341	264	217
Foreign controlled undertakings	15	217	..	..	..	..	..	..
Foreign companies (branches)	..	..	..	..	..	..	..	..
All undertakings	259	246	241	230	-24	24	31	29
Net written premiums								
Domestic undertakings	10 373	10 495	8 804	8 696	7 671	9 271	7 601	8 861
Foreign controlled undertakings	3 683	6 675	..	..	..	..	..	..
Foreign companies (branches)	..	..	..	..	..	..	..	..
All undertakings	10 373	10 495	8 804	8 696	4 342	5 992	4 006	5 087
1.1.2 Insurance business on foreign risks, gross premiums								
Life	..	..	..	..	..	..	..	..
Non-life	..	..	..	..	..	..	..	..
Composite total	..	..	..	..	..	..	..	..
Total	..	..	..	..	..	..	..	..
1.1.3 Life insurance payments, by class, gross premiums								
Annuities	2 544	2 287	694	621	608	2 235	592	538
Unit linked	2 929	3 224	2 446	2 265	1 757	2 230	1 457	1 779
Other life insurance	619	745	1 433	1 641	2 000	1 554	1 988	2 799
Total life insurance	6 092	6 256	4 573	4 527	4 365	6 020	4 037	5 116
***of which:** Pension contracts*	756	597	675	2 265	593	638	581	569
1.1.4 Non-life insurance payments, by class, gross premiums								
Motor vehicle insurance	1 591	1 639	1 639	1 586	1 213	1 228	1 267	1 322
Marine, aviation and other transport insurance	70	68	73	69	69	84	95	100
Freight insurance	56	52	57	55	43	45	44	47
Fire and other property damage insurance	985	1 030	1 028	972	790	800	832	836
Pecuniary loss insurance	30	28	22	20	19	19	21	25
General liability insurance	392	385	234	218	193	79	175	216
Accident and health	1 060	1 058	1 119	1 183	957	1 029	1 034	1 084
***of which:** Health*	299	290	368	395	343	387	415	442
Other non-life insurance	152	88	163	151	124	129	138	148
Treaty reinsurance	135	135	136	144	148	150	173	139
Total non-life insurance	4 471	4 483	4 471	4 398	3 556	3 563	3 779	3 917
1.2 Gross claims payments								
Life								
Domestic undertakings	3 871	3 957	4 324	4 233	4 632	7 239	4 183	3 893
Foreign controlled undertakings	1 160	1 124	.. c	.. c	.. c	.. c	.. c	.. c
Foreign companies (branches)	..	..	..	..	..	..	..	..
All undertakings	3 871	3 957	4 324	4 233	4 632	7 239	4 183	3 893
Non-life								
Domestic undertakings	2 939	2 872	3 103	3 179	2 538	2 625	2 634	2 621
Foreign controlled undertakings	724	2 872	.. c	.. c	.. c	.. c	.. c	.. c
Foreign companies (branches)	..	..	..	..	.. c	.. c	.. c	.. c
All undertakings	2 939	2 872	3 103	3 179	.. c	.. c	.. c	.. c
Composite, all undertakings	..	..	..	..	..	..	..	..
Total								
Domestic undertakings	6 810	6 829	7 427	7 412	7 170	9 864	6 817	6 514
Foreign controlled undertakings	1 884	3 996	..	..	..	..	..	..
Foreign companies (branches)	..	..	..	..	..	..	..	..
All undertakings	6 810	6 829	7 427	7 412	4 632	7 239	4 183	3 893
1.3 Commissions								
Life								
Domestic undertakings	-83	101	126	121	116	113	79	134
Foreign controlled undertakings	-10	15	.. c	.. c	.. c	.. c	.. c	..
Foreign companies (branches)	..	..	..	..	..	..	..	..
All undertakings	-83	101	126	121	..	..	..	134
Non-life								
Domestic undertakings	-142	113	166	160	131	142	140	135
Foreign controlled undertakings	-18	23	.. c	.. c	.. c	.. c	.. c	.. c
Foreign companies (branches)	..	..	..	..	..	..	..	..
All undertakings	-142	113	166	160	..	..	..	.. c
Composite, all undertakings	..	..	..	..	..	..	..	..
Total								
Domestic undertakings	-225	214	292	281	247	255	219	269
Foreign controlled undertakings	-28	38	..	..	..	..	..	..
Foreign companies (branches)	..	..	..	..	..	..	..	..
All undertakings	-225	214	292	281	..	..	..	134

FINLAND

Table 1. Selected aggregates *(cont.)*

Million EUR

	2014	2015	2016	2017	2018	2019	2020	2021
1.4 Gross operating expenses								
Life								
Domestic undertakings	317	316	341	355	359	385	368	394
Foreign controlled undertakings	36	34	.. c	.. c	.. c	.. c	.. c	.. c
Foreign companies (branches)	..	..	..	..	..	..	..	..
All undertakings	317	316	341	355	359	385	368	394
Non-life								
Domestic undertakings	844	847	876	884	746	832	774	793
Foreign controlled undertakings	158	847	.. c	.. c	.. c	.. c	.. c	.. c
Foreign companies (branches)	..	..	..	..	..	..	..	..
All undertakings	844	847	876	884	..	..	..	..
Composite, all undertakings	..	..	..	..	..	..	..	..
Total								
Domestic undertakings	1 161	1 163	1 217	1 239	1 105	1 217	1 142	1 187
Foreign controlled undertakings	194	881	..	..	..	..	..	..
Foreign companies (branches)	..	..	..	..	..	..	..	..
All undertakings	1 161	1 163	1 217	1 239	359	385	368	394
1.5 Insurance business written abroad by branches, gross premiums								
Life								
Branches and agencies	107	17	..	..	..	..	..	..
Subsidaries	..	..	..	..	..	..	..	..
Total	107	17	..	..	..	..	..	..
Non-life								
Branches and agencies	..	..	..	..	..	..	..	..
Subsidaries	..	..	..	..	..	..	..	..
Total	..	..	..	..	..	..	..	..
Composite total	..	..	..	..	..	..	..	..
Total								
Branches and agencies	107	17	..	..	..	..	..	..
Subsidaries	..	..	..	..	..	..	..	..
Total	107	17	..	..	..	..	..	..

.. Not available; c Confidential data

Note: Detailed metadata at: *http://metalinks.oecd.org/ins/20230516/0d29.*

Source: *OECD Insurance Statistics (database)*

FINLAND

Table 2. Number of companies and employees

	2014	2015	2016	2017	2018	2019	2020	2021
2.1 Number of companies								
Life								
Domestic undertakings	13	13	11	10	10	11	9	9
Foreign controlled undertakings	1	1	1	1	1	1	1	0
Foreign companies (branches)	..	..	..	..	10	10	11	11
All undertakings	13	13	11	10	20	21	20	19
Non-life								
Domestic undertakings	38	38	37	37	40	37	32	34
Foreign controlled undertakings	1	1	2	2	1	1	1	1
Foreign companies (branches)	..	..	..	..	8	8	8	8
All undertakings	38	38	37	37	48	46	40	42
Composite, all undertakings	..	..	..	..	0	..	..	..
Reinsurance								
Domestic undertakings	..	..	..	..	0	..	..	..
Foreign controlled undertakings	..	..	..	..	0	..	..	..
Foreign companies (branches)	..	..	..	..	0	..	..	..
All undertakings	..	..	..	..	0	..	..	..
Total								
Domestic undertakings	51	51	48	47	50	48	41	43
Foreign controlled undertakings	2	2	3	3	2	2	2	1
Foreign companies (branches)	..	..	..	..	18	18	19	19
All undertakings	51	51	48	47	68	67	60	61
2.2 Number of employees								
Insurance undertakings	8 980	8 750	8 815	7 751	7 866	6 893	9 813	10 143
Intermediaries	216	221	244	265	265	86	93	83
Total	9 196	8 971	9 059	8 016	8 131	6 979	9 906	10 226

.. Not available

Note: Detailed metadata at: *http://metalinks.oecd.org/ins/20230516/0d29.*

Source: *OECD Insurance Statistics (database)*

FRANCE

Table 1. Selected aggregates

Million EUR

	2014	2015	2016	2017	2018	2019	2020	2021
1.1 Insurance business written in the reporting country								
1.1.1 Insurance business, by ownership								
Gross premiums								
Domestic undertakings	221 223	226 000	..	..	286 809	296 989	265 041	306 494
Foreign controlled undertakings	..	..	..	..	..	..	..	..
Foreign companies (branches)	103	111	..	..	..	..	..	..
All undertakings	221 327	226 111	283 901	278 237	286 809	296 989	265 041	306 494
Premiums ceded								
Domestic undertakings	19 932	25 840	..	..	35 307	38 657	39 897	43 805
Foreign controlled undertakings	..	..	..	..	..	..	..	..
Foreign companies (branches)	22	21	..	..	..	..	..	..
All undertakings	19 954	25 861	43 153	33 277	35 307	38 657	39 897	43 805
Net written premiums								
Domestic undertakings	201 291	200 160	..	..	251 502	258 332	225 144	262 689
Foreign controlled undertakings	..	..	..	..	..	..	..	..
Foreign companies (branches)	82	90	..	..	..	..	..	..
All undertakings	201 373	200 250	240 747	244 960	251 502	258 332	225 144	262 689
1.1.2 Insurance business on foreign risks, gross premiums								
Life	73	60	..	..	..	..	..	..
Non-life	1 876	2 188	..	..	..	..	..	..
Composite	468	485	..	..	..	..	..	..
of which:								
Life	456	482	..	..	..	..	..	..
Non-life	12	3	..	..	..	..	..	..
Total	2 416	2 734	..	..	..	..	..	..
1.1.3 Life insurance payments, by class, gross premiums								
Annuities	..	..	..	..	..	..	..	..
Unit linked	..	..	28 208	38 135	38 569	39 657	39 333	54 944
Other life insurance	..	..	111 059	102 007	106 170	110 125	81 323	97 321
Total life insurance	..	..	139 267	140 142	144 740	149 781	120 656	152 265
of which: *Pension contracts*	..	..	..	..	..	..	..	..
1.1.4 Non-life insurance payments, by class, gross premiums								
Motor vehicle insurance	..	..	..	..	..	..	..	..
Marine, aviation and other transport insurance	..	..	..	..	..	..	..	..
Freight insurance	..	..	..	..	..	..	..	..
Fire and other property damage insurance	..	..	..	..	..	..	..	..
Pecuniary loss insurance	..	..	..	..	..	..	..	..
General liability insurance	..	..	..	..	..	..	..	..
Accident and health	..	..	..	..	..	..	..	..
of which: *Health*	..	..	..	..	..	..	..	..
Other non-life insurance	..	..	..	..	..	..	..	..
Treaty reinsurance	..	..	..	..	..	..	..	..
Total non-life insurance	..	..	119 104	124 560	128 064	131 451	133 266	140 353
1.2 Gross claims payments								
Life								
Domestic undertakings	26 144	26 794	..	..	21 986	23 357	23 635	26 187
Foreign controlled undertakings	..	..	..	..	..	..	..	..
Foreign companies (branches)	..	..	..	..	..	..	..	..
All undertakings	26 144	26 794	133 135	145 577	21 986	23 357	23 635	26 187
Non-life								
Domestic undertakings	61 895	63 029	..	..	56 407	60 336	61 799	62 382
Foreign controlled undertakings	..	..	..	..	..	..	..	..
Foreign companies (branches)	52	51	..	..	..	..	..	..
All undertakings	61 947	63 080	95 217	101 007	56 407	60 336	61 799	62 382
Composite								
Domestic undertakings	86 518	91 862	..	..	158 076	158 713	154 653	173 933
Foreign controlled undertakings	..	..	..	..	..	..	..	..
Foreign companies (branches)	..	..	..	..	..	..	..	..
All undertakings	86 518	91 862	..	..	158 076	158 713	154 653	173 933
of which:								
Life	..	..	..	..	111 830	112 716	103 838	119 384
Domestic undertakings	..	..	..	..	111 830	112 716	103 838	119 384
Foreign controlled undertakings	..	..	..	..	..	..	..	..
Foreign companies (branches)	..	..	..	..	..	..	..	..
All undertakings	..	..	..	..	111 830	112 716	103 838	119 384
Non-life	..	..	..	..	46 246	45 996	50 815	54 549
Domestic undertakings	..	..	..	..	46 246	45 996	50 815	54 549
Foreign controlled undertakings	..	..	..	..	..	..	..	..
Foreign companies (branches)	..	..	..	..	..	..	..	..
All undertakings	..	..	..	..	46 246	45 996	50 815	54 549
Total								
Domestic undertakings	174 557	181 685	..	..	236 469	242 406	240 087	262 503
Foreign controlled undertakings	..	..	..	..	..	..	..	..
Foreign companies (branches)	52	51	..	..	..	..	..	..
All undertakings	174 608	181 736	228 352	246 584	236 469	242 406	240 087	262 503

Table 1. Selected aggregates *(cont.)*

Million EUR

	2014	2015	2016	2017	2018	2019	2020	2021
1.3 Commissions								
Life								
Domestic undertakings	..	..	..	..	..	..	..	..
Foreign controlled undertakings	..	..	..	..	..	..	..	..
Foreign companies (branches)	..	..	..	..	..	..	..	..
All undertakings	..	..	..	..	..	..	..	..
Non-life								
Domestic undertakings	..	..	..	..	..	..	..	..
Foreign controlled undertakings	..	..	..	..	..	..	..	..
Foreign companies (branches)	..	..	..	..	..	..	..	..
All undertakings	..	..	..	..	..	..	..	..
Composite								
Domestic undertakings	..	..	..	..	..	..	..	..
Foreign controlled undertakings	..	..	..	..	..	..	..	..
Foreign companies (branches)	..	..	..	..	..	..	..	..
All undertakings	..	..	..	..	..	..	..	..
of which:								
Life	..	..	..	..	..	..	..	..
Domestic undertakings	..	..	..	..	..	..	..	..
Foreign controlled undertakings	..	..	..	..	..	..	..	..
Foreign companies (branches)	..	..	..	..	..	..	..	..
All undertakings	..	..	..	..	..	..	..	..
Non-life	..	..	..	..	..	..	..	..
Domestic undertakings	..	..	..	..	..	..	..	..
Foreign controlled undertakings	..	..	..	..	..	..	..	..
Foreign companies (branches)	..	..	..	..	..	..	..	..
All undertakings	..	..	..	..	..	..	..	..
Total								
Domestic undertakings	..	..	..	..	..	..	..	..
Foreign controlled undertakings	..	..	..	..	..	..	..	..
Foreign companies (branches)	..	..	..	..	..	..	..	..
All undertakings	..	..	..	..	..	..	..	..
1.4 Gross operating expenses								
Life								
Domestic undertakings	2 893	2 914	..	..	2 545	2 697	3 187	3 342
Foreign controlled undertakings	..	..	..	..	..	..	..	..
Foreign companies (branches)	..	..	..	..	..	..	..	..
All undertakings	2 893	2 914	15 848	16 123	2 545	2 697	3 187	3 342
Non-life								
Domestic undertakings	16 156	15 936	..	..	18 654	20 368	22 338	22 859
Foreign controlled undertakings	..	..	..	..	..	..	..	..
Foreign companies (branches)	8	..	..	..	..	..	..	..
All undertakings	16 164	15 936	27 415	27 948	18 654	20 368	22 338	22 859
Composite								
Domestic undertakings	13 439	14 727	..	..	24 734	25 749	28 970	29 335
Foreign controlled undertakings	..	..	..	..	..	..	..	..
Foreign companies (branches)	..	..	..	..	..	..	..	..
All undertakings	13 439	14 727	..	..	24 734	25 749	28 970	29 335
of which:								
Life	10 808	11 414	..	..	13 366	16 771	18 778	19 431
Domestic undertakings	..	..	..	..	13 366	16 771	18 778	19 431
Foreign controlled undertakings	..	..	..	..	..	..	..	..
Foreign companies (branches)	..	..	..	..	..	..	..	..
All undertakings	10 808	11 414	..	..	13 366	16 771	18 778	19 431
Non-life	2 631	3 313	..	..	11 368	8 979	10 192	9 905
Domestic undertakings	..	..	..	..	11 368	8 979	10 192	9 905
Foreign controlled undertakings	..	..	..	..	..	..	..	..
Foreign companies (branches)	..	..	..	..	..	..	..	..
All undertakings	2 631	3 313	..	..	11 368	8 979	10 192	9 905
Total								
Domestic undertakings	32 488	33 578	..	..	45 933	48 814	54 495	55 536
Foreign controlled undertakings	..	..	..	..	..	..	..	..
Foreign companies (branches)	8	..	..	..	..	..	..	..
All undertakings	32 497	33 578	43 263	44 071	45 933	48 814	54 495	55 536

Table 1. Selected aggregates *(cont.)*

Million EUR

	2014	2015	2016	2017	2018	2019	2020	2021
1.5 Insurance business written abroad by branches, gross premiums								
Life								
Branches and agencies	2 860	3 373	4 393	5 050	..	..	4 041	5 156
Subsidaries	..	..	..	..	..	..	..	..
Total	2 860	3 373	4 393	5 050	..	..	4 041	5 156
Non-life								
Branches and agencies	4 960	5 460	8 837	9 719	..	..	12 991	15 165
Subsidaries	..	..	..	..	..	..	..	..
Total	4 960	5 460	8 837	9 719	..	..	12 991	15 165
Composite								
Branches and agencies	..	..	..	..	..	..	..	..
Subsidaries	..	..	..	..	..	..	..	..
Total	..	..	..	..	..	..	..	..
of which:								
Life	..	..	..	..	..	..	..	..
Branches and agencies	..	..	..	..	..	..	..	..
Subsidaries	..	..	..	..	..	..	..	..
Total	..	..	..	..	..	..	..	..
Non-life	..	..	..	..	..	..	..	..
Branches and agencies	..	..	..	..	..	..	..	..
Subsidaries	..	..	..	..	..	..	..	..
Total	..	..	..	..	..	..	..	..
Total								
Branches and agencies	7 820	8 834	13 230	14 769	..	..	17 032	20 321
Subsidaries	..	..	..	..	..	..	..	..
Total	7 820	8 834	13 230	14 769	..	..	17 032	20 321

.. Not available

Note: Detailed metadata at: *http://metalinks.oecd.org/ins/20230516/d0e0.*

Source: *OECD Insurance Statistics (database)*

FRANCE

Table 2. Number of companies and employees

	2014	2015	2016	2017	2018	2019	2020	2021
2.1 Number of companies								
Life								
Domestic undertakings	55	51	..	..	..	..	..	..
Foreign controlled undertakings	..	..	..	..	..	..	..	..
Foreign companies (branches)	..	..	..	..	..	..	..	..
All undertakings	55	51	..	..	..	..	52	..
Non-life								
Domestic undertakings	206	191	..	..	..	..	..	..
Foreign controlled undertakings	..	..	..	..	..	..	..	..
Foreign companies (branches)	4	4	..	..	..	..	..	..
All undertakings	210	195	394	381	364	345	348	342
Composite								
Domestic undertakings	38	39	..	..	..	..	..	..
Foreign controlled undertakings	..	..	..	..	..	..	..	..
Foreign companies (branches)	..	..	..	..	..	..	..	..
All undertakings	38	39	239	236	239	243	177	230
Reinsurance								
Domestic undertakings	15	16	..	..	..	..	..	..
Foreign controlled undertakings	..	..	..	..	..	..	..	..
Foreign companies (branches)	..	..	..	..	..	..	..	..
All undertakings	15	16	14	14	12	10	12	14
Total								
Domestic undertakings	314	297	..	..	..	..	..	..
Foreign controlled undertakings	..	..	..	..	..	..	..	..
Foreign companies (branches)	4	4	..	..	..	..	..	..
All undertakings	318	301	647	631	615	598	589	586
2.2 Number of employees								
Insurance undertakings	..	..	..	..	..	..	..	..
Intermediaries	..	..	..	..	..	..	..	..
Total	..	..	..	..	..	..	..	..

.. Not available

Note: Detailed metadata at: *http://metalinks.oecd.org/ins/20230516/d0e0.*

Source: *OECD Insurance Statistics (database)*

GERMANY

Table 1. Selected aggregates

Million EUR

	2014	2015	2016	2017	2018	2019	2020	2021
1.1 Insurance business written in the reporting country								
1.1.1 Insurance business, by ownership								
Gross premiums								
Domestic undertakings	246 201	254 407	257 208	264 933	273 036	296 378	307 670	321 161
Foreign controlled undertakings	38 694	39 170	36 978	36 644	39 215	40 551	41 054	42 649
Foreign companies (branches)	8 796	9 751	8 994	10 550	11 199	11 148	12 674	14 262
All undertakings	254 997	264 158	266 203	275 483	284 235	307 527	320 345	335 423
Premiums ceded								
Domestic undertakings	27 853	32 499	31 990	34 336	39 483	41 736	45 657	53 555
Foreign controlled undertakings	4 615	4 593	4 041	4 046	4 482	4 167	4 276	4 947
Foreign companies (branches)	103	114	112	132	127	83	85	89
All undertakings	27 956	32 613	32 102	34 469	39 609	41 819	45 742	53 644
Net written premiums								
Domestic undertakings	218 348	221 907	225 218	230 596	233 553	254 643	262 014	267 606
Foreign controlled undertakings	34 078	34 577	32 937	32 598	34 732	36 383	36 779	37 702
Foreign companies (branches)	8 693	9 637	8 882	10 418	11 073	11 065	12 589	14 173
All undertakings	227 041	231 545	234 100	241 014	244 626	265 707	274 603	281 779
1.1.2 Insurance business on foreign risks, gross premiums								
Life	..	..	..	..	..	..	..	..
Non-life	..	..	..	..	..	..	..	..
Composite total	..	..	..	..	..	..	..	..
Total	..	..	..	..	..	..	..	..
1.1.3 Life insurance payments, by class, gross premiums								
Annuities	34 019	31 782	31 215	30 000	31 730	36 776	35 056	..
Unit linked	13 863	13 863	15 351	15 994	17 293	18 685	21 318	23 965
Other life insurance	40 891	41 214	38 845	41 612	40 959	44 755	44 288	75 927
Total life insurance	88 774	86 859	85 411	87 606	89 982	100 217	100 663	99 892
***of which:** Pension contracts*	..	..	..	..	..	..	..	37 331
1.1.4 Non-life insurance payments, by class, gross premiums								
Motor vehicle insurance	31 425	32 589	36 521	40 579	44 565	46 631	47 107	46 990
Marine, aviation and other transport insurance	4 379	5 116	4 749	4 933	5 050	5 786	6 340	7 173
Freight insurance	..	..	..	..	..	..	..	..
Fire and other property damage insurance	35 422	38 830	42 499	46 541	50 056	55 618	61 518	62 002
Pecuniary loss insurance	2 088	2 197	2 376	3 872	3 857	4 134	4 022	8 110
General liability insurance	14 213	15 425	16 126	17 517	18 440	20 008	21 756	25 977
Accident and health	48 811	49 176	49 721	52 572	52 301	54 040	56 357	62 706
***of which:** Health*	40 924	41 627	37 178	39 328	40 220	41 217	43 011	54 585
Other non-life insurance	4 865	31 030	25 991	21 153	19 528	20 628	21 500	22 162
Treaty reinsurance	..	..	..	..	..	..	..	..
Total non-life insurance	141 203	174 363	177 983	187 167	193 798	206 844	218 600	235 120
1.2 Gross claims payments								
Life								
Domestic undertakings	74 625	73 307	78 596	69 073	70 871	75 975	74 210	75 406
Foreign controlled undertakings	17 510	17 929	17 942	16 501	16 759	17 071	16 996	17 950
Foreign companies (branches)	..	..	..	..	..	..	..	.. c
All undertakings	74 625	73 307	78 596	69 073	70 871	75 975	74 210	75 406
Non-life								
Domestic undertakings	72 709	77 667	78 086	84 787	87 989	139 877	145 813	161 152
Foreign controlled undertakings	8 955	3 653	9 227	9 500	10 110	13 369	13 934	16 647
Foreign companies (branches)	..	..	..	..	..	..	..	.. c
All undertakings	72 709	77 667	78 086	84 787	87 989	139 877	145 813	161 152
Composite, all undertakings	..	..	..	..	..	..	..	..
Total								
Domestic undertakings	147 334	150 974	156 682	153 859	158 861	215 852	220 024	236 558
Foreign controlled undertakings	26 465	21 581	27 169	26 001	26 869	30 440	30 930	34 597
Foreign companies (branches)	..	..	..	..	..	..	..	..
All undertakings	147 334	150 974	156 682	153 859	158 861	215 852	220 024	236 558
1.3 Commissions								
Life								
Domestic undertakings	5 583	5 069	4 987	4 794	4 961	5 618	5 628	7 789
Foreign controlled undertakings	1 533	1 488	1 238	1 138	1 211	1 306	1 389	2 031
Foreign companies (branches)	..	..	..	..	..	..	..	.. c
All undertakings	5 583	5 069	4 987	4 794	4 961	5 618	5 628	7 789
Non-life								
Domestic undertakings	10 221	10 740	11 105	12 173	12 647	13 656	14 022	14 543
Foreign controlled undertakings	1 626	257	1 594	1 623	1 806	1 940	1 988	2 350
Foreign companies (branches)	..	..	..	..	..	..	..	.. c
All undertakings	10 221	10 740	11 105	12 173	12 647	13 656	14 022	14 543
Composite, all undertakings	..	..	..	..	..	..	..	..
Total								
Domestic undertakings	15 805	15 810	16 092	16 967	17 609	19 273	19 650	22 331
Foreign controlled undertakings	3 159	1 745	2 832	2 760	3 017	3 247	3 377	4 382
Foreign companies (branches)	..	..	..	..	..	..	..	..
All undertakings	15 805	15 810	16 092	16 967	17 609	19 273	19 650	22 331

Table 1. Selected aggregates *(cont.)*

Million EUR

	2014	2015	2016	2017	2018	2019	2020	2021
1.4 Gross operating expenses								
Life								
Domestic undertakings	3 963	4 008	3 902	3 907	3 901	3 769	3 774	10 657
Foreign controlled undertakings	894	1 036	938	952	1 001	974	949	2 635
Foreign companies (branches)	..	..	..	..	..	..	..	.. c
All undertakings	3 963	4 008	3 902	3 907	3 901	3 769	3 774	10 657
Non-life								
Domestic undertakings	10 296	10 627	10 807	11 161	11 390	13 638	13 299	50 319
Foreign controlled undertakings	1 187	324	1 183	1 210	1 297	1 448	1 427	4 970
Foreign companies (branches)	..	..	..	..	..	..	..	.. c
All undertakings	10 296	10 627	10 807	11 161	11 390	13 638	13 299	50 319
Composite, all undertakings	..	..	..	..	..	..	..	..
Total								
Domestic undertakings	14 259	14 635	14 709	15 068	15 291	17 406	17 072	60 976
Foreign controlled undertakings	2 081	1 361	2 121	2 163	2 297	2 421	2 377	7 604
Foreign companies (branches)	..	..	..	..	..	..	..	..
All undertakings	14 259	14 635	14 709	15 068	15 291	17 406	17 072	60 976
1.5 Insurance business written abroad by branches, gross premiums								
Life								
Branches and agencies	..	..	..	..	200	481	302	1 452
Subsidaries	..	..	..	..	..	..	..	..
Total	..	..	..	..	200	481	302	1 452
Non-life								
Branches and agencies	..	..	..	..	22 495	25 723	27 574	29 787
Subsidaries	..	..	..	..	..	..	..	..
Total	..	..	..	..	22 495	25 723	27 574	29 787
Composite total	..	..	..	..	..	..	..	..
Total								
Branches and agencies	..	..	..	..	22 695	26 203	27 876	31 238
Subsidaries	..	..	..	..	..	..	..	..
Total	..	..	..	..	22 695	26 203	27 876	31 238

.. Not available; c Confidential data
Note: Detailed metadata at: *http://metalinks.oecd.org/ins/20230516/12a6.*
Source: *OECD Insurance Statistics (database)*

GERMANY

Table 2. Number of companies and employees

	2014	2015	2016	2017	2018	2019	2020	2021
2.1 Number of companies								
Life								
Domestic undertakings	91	85	85	86	86	84	82	80
Foreign controlled undertakings	17	14	14	15	16	16	16	16
Foreign companies (branches)	2	2	2	1	1	1	1	1
All undertakings	93	87	87	87	87	85	83	81
Non-life								
Domestic undertakings	255	257	252	251	250	254	251	222
Foreign controlled undertakings	21	22	18	17	21	23	20	20
Foreign companies (branches)	3	3	2	2	1	1	1	1
All undertakings	258	260	254	253	251	255	252	223
Composite, all undertakings	0	0	0	..	..	..	..	..
Reinsurance								
Domestic undertakings	27	27	27	27	28	29	28	29
Foreign controlled undertakings	3	3	3	3	3	3	3	4
Foreign companies (branches)	1	1	1	1	1	1	0	0
All undertakings	28	28	28	28	29	30	28	29
Total								
Domestic undertakings	373	369	364	364	364	367	361	331
Foreign controlled undertakings	41	39	35	35	40	42	39	40
Foreign companies (branches)	6	6	5	4	3	3	2	2
All undertakings	379	375	369	368	367	370	363	333
2.2 Number of employees								
Insurance undertakings	126 755	128 784	..	..	..	..	..	..
Intermediaries	26 982	25 917	..	..	..	..	..	..
Total	153 737	154 701	156 675	154 262	152 888	150 886	150 547	132 996

.. Not available

Note: Detailed metadata at: *http://metalinks.oecd.org/ins/20230516/12a6.*

Source: *OECD Insurance Statistics (database)*

GREECE

Table 1. Selected aggregates

Million EUR

	2014	2015	2016	2017	2018	2019	2020	2021
1.1 Insurance business written in the reporting country								
1.1.1 Insurance business, by ownership								
Gross premiums								
Domestic undertakings	3 806	3 573	3 531	3 729	3 798	4 053	4 106	4 506
Foreign controlled undertakings	1 696	1 766	2 350	2 450	2 458	2 487	2 585	2 908
Foreign companies (branches)	0	0	0	0	0	0	0	0
All undertakings	3 806	3 573	3 531	3 729	3 798	4 053	4 106	4 506
Premiums ceded								
Domestic undertakings	471	459	396	402	429	423	418	454
Foreign controlled undertakings	206	201	244	260	274	270	262	287
Foreign companies (branches)	0	0	0	0	0	0	0	0
All undertakings	471	459	396	402	429	423	418	454
Net written premiums								
Domestic undertakings	3 334	3 114	3 135	3 328	3 369	3 631	3 688	4 052
Foreign controlled undertakings	1 490	1 565	2 106	2 190	2 183	2 218	2 322	2 621
Foreign companies (branches)	0	0	0	0	0	0	0	0
All undertakings	3 335	3 114	3 135	3 328	3 369	3 631	3 688	4 052
1.1.2 Insurance business on foreign risks, gross premiums								
Life	..	..	..	..	..	..	..	..
Non-life	..	..	..	..	..	..	..	..
Composite	..	..	..	..	..	..	..	..
of which:								
Life	..	..	..	..	..	..	..	..
Non-life	..	..	..	..	..	..	..	..
Total	..	..	..	..	..	..	..	..
1.1.3 Life insurance payments, by class, gross premiums								
Annuities	129	125	0	0	0	0	0	0
Unit linked	396	326	250	347	380	363	641	999
Other life insurance	1 353	1 348	1 416	1 533	1 499	1 700	1 462	1 431
Total life insurance	1 879	1 799	1 666	1 881	1 879	2 064	2 103	2 430
***of which:** Pension contracts*	151	156	..	..	..	..	..	..
1.1.4 Non-life insurance payments, by class, gross premiums								
Motor vehicle insurance	1 154	1 006	911	938	948	968	946	950
Marine, aviation and other transport insurance	19	20	32	34	38	38	39	44
Freight insurance	21	21	..	0	0	0	0	0
Fire and other property damage insurance	448	440	410	398	409	402	406	427
Pecuniary loss insurance	30	30	40	28	31	36	43	50
General liability insurance	67	68	65	63	75	83	89	106
Accident and health	57	57	300	242	263	298	318	333
***of which:** Health*	0	..	..	0	0	0	0	0
Other non-life insurance	128	129	137	146	153	165	162	166
Treaty reinsurance	0	..	..	0	0	0	0	0
Total non-life insurance	1 924	1 770	1 896	1 848	1 918	1 990	2 003	2 076
1.2 Gross claims payments								
Life								
Domestic undertakings	900	744	..	..	..	..	..	..
Foreign controlled undertakings	1	502	..	..	..	..	..	..
Foreign companies (branches)	0	0	..	..	..	..	..	..
All undertakings	900	744	..	..	..	..	..	..
Non-life								
Domestic undertakings	355	314	..	..	..	..	..	..
Foreign controlled undertakings	224	109	..	..	..	..	..	..
Foreign companies (branches)	1	0	..	..	..	..	..	..
All undertakings	356	314	..	..	..	..	..	..
Composite								
Domestic undertakings	1 018	931	..	..	..	..	..	..
Foreign controlled undertakings	412	347	..	..	..	..	..	..
Foreign companies (branches)	0	0	..	..	..	..	..	..
All undertakings	1 018	931	..	..	..	..	..	..
of which:								
Life	613	573	..	..	..	..	..	..
Domestic undertakings	613	573	..	..	..	..	..	..
Foreign controlled undertakings	7	220	..	..	..	..	..	..
Foreign companies (branches)	0	0	..	..	..	..	..	..
All undertakings	613	573	..	..	..	..	..	..
Non-life	405	358	..	..	..	..	..	..
Domestic undertakings	405	358	..	..	..	..	..	..
Foreign controlled undertakings	405	126	..	..	..	..	..	..
Foreign companies (branches)	0	0	..	..	..	..	..	..
All undertakings	405	358	..	..	..	..	..	..
Total								
Domestic undertakings	2 273	1 989	..	..	..	..	..	..
Foreign controlled undertakings	637	957	..	..	..	..	..	..
Foreign companies (branches)	1	0	..	..	..	..	..	..
All undertakings	2 274	1 989	..	..	..	..	..	..

GREECE

Table 1. Selected aggregates *(cont.)*

Million EUR

	2014	2015	2016	2017	2018	2019	2020	2021
1.3 Commissions								
Life								
Domestic undertakings	95	91	..	..	..	..	..	..
Foreign controlled undertakings	70	70	..	..	..	..	..	..
Foreign companies (branches)	0	0	..	..	..	..	..	..
All undertakings	95	91	..	..	..	..	..	..
Non-life								
Domestic undertakings	161	158	..	..	..	..	..	..
Foreign controlled undertakings	63	66	..	..	..	..	..	..
Foreign companies (branches)	0	0	..	..	..	..	..	..
All undertakings	162	158	..	..	..	..	..	..
Composite								
Domestic undertakings	276	709	..	..	..	..	..	..
Foreign controlled undertakings	115	115	..	..	..	..	..	..
Foreign companies (branches)	0	0	..	..	..	..	..	..
All undertakings	276	709	..	..	..	..	..	..
of which:								
Life	102	544	..	..	..	..	..	..
Domestic undertakings	102	544	..	..	..	..	..	..
Foreign controlled undertakings	39	40	..	..	..	..	..	..
Foreign companies (branches)	0	0	..	..	..	..	..	..
All undertakings	102	544	..	..	..	..	..	..
Non-life	174	164	..	..	..	..	..	..
Domestic undertakings	174	164	..	..	..	..	..	..
Foreign controlled undertakings	76	75	..	..	..	..	..	..
Foreign companies (branches)	0	0	..	..	..	..	..	..
All undertakings	174	164	..	..	..	..	..	..
Total								
Domestic undertakings	532	957	..	..	..	..	..	..
Foreign controlled undertakings	248	251	..	..	..	..	..	..
Foreign companies (branches)	0	0	..	..	..	..	..	..
All undertakings	532	957	..	..	..	..	..	..
1.4 Gross operating expenses								
Life								
Domestic undertakings	176	163	35	38	39	46	49	57
Foreign controlled undertakings	141	132	32	35	35	40	42	49
Foreign companies (branches)	0	..	0	0	0	0	0	0
All undertakings	176	163	35	38	39	46	49	57
Non-life								
Domestic undertakings	264	247	248	301	242	256	253	261
Foreign controlled undertakings	115	116	145	168	104	112	112	117
Foreign companies (branches)	0	0	0	0	0	0	0	0
All undertakings	264	247	248	301	242	256	253	261
Composite								
Domestic undertakings	404	371	700	701	811	774	759	775
Foreign controlled undertakings	154	150	448	438	550	495	489	500
Foreign companies (branches)	0	..	0	0	0	0	0	0
All undertakings	404	371	700	701	811	774	759	775
of which:								
Life	144	145	315	322	312	283	302	321
Domestic undertakings	144	145	315	322	312	283	302	321
Foreign controlled undertakings	53	52	231	223	219	216	209	222
Foreign companies (branches)	0	..	0	0	0	0	0	0
All undertakings	144	145	315	322	312	283	302	321
Non-life	260	226	385	379	499	492	458	454
Domestic undertakings	260	226	385	379	499	492	458	454
Foreign controlled undertakings	101	98	217	215	331	279	279	278
Foreign companies (branches)	0	..	0	0	0	0	0	0
All undertakings	260	226	385	379	499	492	458	454
Total								
Domestic undertakings	844	781	983	1 041	1 092	1 076	1 062	1 094
Foreign controlled undertakings	410	398	625	641	689	647	643	665
Foreign companies (branches)	0	0	0	0	0	0	0	0
All undertakings	844	781	983	1 041	1 092	1 076	1 062	1 094

Table 1. Selected aggregates *(cont.)*

Million EUR

	2014	2015	2016	2017	2018	2019	2020	2021
1.5 Insurance business written abroad by branches, gross premiums								
Life								
Branches and agencies	..	..	..	0	0	0	0	0
Subsidaries	..	..	..	0	0	0	0	0
Total	..	..	..	0	0	0	0	0
Non-life								
Branches and agencies	..	..	..	1	3	6	7	10
Subsidaries	..	..	..	0	0	0	0	0
Total	..	..	..	1	3	6	7	10
Composite								
Branches and agencies	..	..	..	0	18	4	5	7
Subsidaries	..	..	..	0	0	0	0	0
Total	..	..	..	0	18	4	5	7
of which:								
Life	..	..	..	0	0	0	0	0
Branches and agencies	..	..	..	0	0	0	0	0
Subsidaries	..	..	..	0	0	0	0	0
Total	..	..	..	0	0	0	0	0
Non-life	..	..	..	0	17	4	5	7
Branches and agencies	..	..	..	0	17	4	5	7
Subsidaries	..	..	..	0	0	0	0	0
Total	..	..	..	0	17	4	5	7
Total								
Branches and agencies	..	..	..	1	21	10	12	17
Subsidaries	..	..	..	0	0	0	0	0
Total	..	..	..	1	21	10	12	17

.. Not available

Note: Detailed metadata at: *http://metalinks.oecd.org/ins/20230516/b936.*

Source: *OECD Insurance Statistics (database)*

GREECE

Table 2. Number of companies and employees

	2014	2015	2016	2017	2018	2019	2020	2021
2.1 Number of companies								
Life								
Domestic undertakings	11	11	4	3	2	2	2	2
Foreign controlled undertakings	7	7	2	2	1	1	1	1
Foreign companies (branches)	0	0	0	0	0	0	0	0
All undertakings	11	11	4	3	2	2	2	2
Non-life								
Domestic undertakings	24	24	24	22	20	19	18	18
Foreign controlled undertakings	6	5	7	6	5	5	4	4
Foreign companies (branches)	2	2	0	0	0	0	0	0
All undertakings	26	26	24	22	20	19	18	18
Composite								
Domestic undertakings	11	11	17	17	17	17	17	16
Foreign controlled undertakings	4	4	10	10	10	10	10	9
Foreign companies (branches)	0	0	0	0	0	0	0	0
All undertakings	11	11	17	17	17	17	17	16
Reinsurance								
Domestic undertakings	0	0	0	0	0	0	0	0
Foreign controlled undertakings	0	0	0	0	0	0	0	0
Foreign companies (branches)	0	0	0	0	0	0	0	0
All undertakings	0	0	0	0	0	0	0	0
Total								
Domestic undertakings	46	46	45	42	39	38	37	36
Foreign controlled undertakings	17	16	19	18	16	16	15	14
Foreign companies (branches)	2	2	0	0	0	0	..	..
All undertakings	48	48	45	42	39	38	37	36
2.2 Number of employees								
Insurance undertakings	..	..	..	..	..	..	..	..
Intermediaries	..	..	..	..	..	..	..	..
Total	..	..	..	..	..	..	..	..

.. Not available

Note: Detailed metadata at: *http://metalinks.oecd.org/ins/20230516/b936*.

Source: *OECD Insurance Statistics (database)*

Table 1. Selected aggregates

Million HUF

	2014	2015	2016	2017	2018	2019	2020	2021
1.1 Insurance business written in the reporting country								
1.1.1 Insurance business, by ownership								
Gross premiums								
Domestic undertakings	833 664	835 428	885 781	956 006	1 017 779	1 149 523	1 204 157	1 329 544
Foreign controlled undertakings	796 332	788 248	835 272	897 699	953 320	1 075 690	1 133 759	1 255 974
Foreign companies (branches)	..	..	..	..	..	..	..	..
All undertakings	833 664	835 428	885 781	956 006	1 017 779	1 149 523	1 204 157	1 329 544
Premiums ceded								
Domestic undertakings	116 117	115 801	118 081	120 524	126 479	139 265	144 337	157 761
Foreign controlled undertakings	108 557	104 464	107 021	106 729	113 942	128 554	134 943	149 406
Foreign companies (branches)	..	..	..	..	..	..	..	..
All undertakings	116 117	115 801	118 081	120 524	126 479	139 265	144 337	157 761
Net written premiums								
Domestic undertakings	717 547	719 627	767 700	835 482	891 300	1 010 258	1 059 820	1 171 783
Foreign controlled undertakings	687 774	683 784	728 251	790 970	839 379	947 137	998 815	1 106 568
Foreign companies (branches)	..	..	..	..	..	..	..	..
All undertakings	717 547	719 627	767 700	835 482	891 300	1 010 258	1 059 820	1 171 783
1.1.2 Insurance business on foreign risks, gross premiums								
Life	3 533	4 234	4 317	4 630	5 116	5 343	5 895	156
Non-life	1 923	1 052	2 308	2 657	2 100	2 517	191	-3
Composite	2 829	4 368	8 142	9 004	8 816	7 724	8 213	12 621
of which:								
Life	228	216	177	172	199	808	1 063	4 513
Non-life	2 602	4 152	7 965	8 832	8 617	6 916	7 150	8 108
Total	8 285	9 654	14 767	16 291	16 033	15 584	14 299	12 773
1.1.3 Life insurance payments, by class, gross premiums								
Annuities	3 147	3 479	..	..	..	..	..	..
Unit linked	282 059	266 857	..	..	..	..	..	..
Other life insurance	171 738	156 617	..	..	..	..	..	..
Total life insurance	456 944	426 953	438 718	460 791	470 685	509 033	530 350	602 569
of which: *Pension contracts*	..	10	..	..	..	..	..	..
1.1.4 Non-life insurance payments, by class, gross premiums								
Motor vehicle insurance	152 283	175 045	203 396	232 622	263 731	332 134	356 761	375 196
Marine, aviation and other transport insurance	793	879	142	172	201	354	276	343
Freight insurance	2 856	3 165	5 733	6 143	6 313	6 159	6 542	6 813
Fire and other property damage insurance	158 219	161 160	168 736	179 697	188 516	203 660	219 757	243 301
Pecuniary loss insurance	3 672	4 822	5 430	5 027	6 051	6 737	5 066	4 818
General liability insurance	21 904	23 585	21 274	24 525	26 379	27 271	28 248	30 306
Accident and health	28 358	29 859	22 389	24 898	31 241	36 837	26 958	33 437
of which: *Health*	9 558	8 668	4 250	5 557	8 909	11 827	10 598	13 937
Other non-life insurance	8 557	9 909	19 916	22 112	24 662	27 338	30 138	32 602
Treaty reinsurance	..	..	..	..	..	..	..	..
Total non-life insurance	376 641	408 424	447 017	495 197	547 094	640 490	673 746	726 815
1.2 Gross claims payments								
Life								
Domestic undertakings	130 633	150 198	155 047	172 359	156 899	185 600	178 105	133 982
Foreign controlled undertakings	121 318	139 595	147 047	160 787	146 733	171 402	165 880	119 681
Foreign companies (branches)	..	..	..	..	..	..	..	..
All undertakings	130 633	150 198	155 047	172 359	156 899	185 600	178 105	133 982
Non-life								
Domestic undertakings	27 416	30 571	34 112	32 258	34 114	32 143	34 180	34 523
Foreign controlled undertakings	13 973	14 605	16 056	12 917	12 308	11 636	12 726	13 452
Foreign companies (branches)	..	..	..	..	..	..	..	..
All undertakings	27 416	30 571	34 112	32 258	34 114	32 143	34 180	34 523
Composite								
Domestic undertakings	379 879	356 926	361 448	389 622	413 120	463 620	454 559	540 608
Foreign controlled undertakings	379 879	356 926	361 448	389 622	413 120	463 620	454 559	540 608
Foreign companies (branches)	..	..	..	..	..	..	..	..
All undertakings	379 879	356 926	361 448	389 622	413 120	463 620	454 559	540 608
of which:								
Life	212 244	180 098	176 820	185 216	205 734	230 696	215 006	287 970
Domestic undertakings	212 244	180 098	176 820	185 216	205 734	230 696	215 006	287 970
Foreign controlled undertakings	212 244	180 098	176 820	185 216	205 734	230 696	215 006	287 970
Foreign companies (branches)	..	..	..	..	..	..	..	..
All undertakings	212 244	180 098	176 820	185 216	205 734	230 696	215 006	287 970
Non-life	167 635	176 829	184 628	204 406	207 386	232 924	239 553	252 638
Domestic undertakings	167 635	176 829	184 628	204 406	207 386	232 924	239 553	252 638
Foreign controlled undertakings	167 635	176 829	184 628	204 406	207 386	232 924	239 553	252 638
Foreign companies (branches)	..	..	..	..	..	..	..	..
All undertakings	167 635	176 829	184 628	204 406	207 386	232 924	239 553	252 638
Total								
Domestic undertakings	537 928	537 695	550 607	594 239	604 133	681 363	666 843	709 113
Foreign controlled undertakings	515 171	511 127	524 551	563 326	572 162	646 658	633 164	673 741
Foreign companies (branches)	..	..	..	..	..	..	..	..
All undertakings	537 928	537 695	550 607	594 239	604 133	681 363	666 843	709 113

Table 1. Selected aggregates *(cont.)*

Million HUF

	2014	2015	2016	2017	2018	2019	2020	2021
1.3 Commissions								
Life								
Domestic undertakings	14 024	13 526	16 531	17 513	15 243	16 536	17 362	7 876
Foreign controlled undertakings	11 559	11 089	14 360	15 017	12 599	13 254	14 687	5 214
Foreign companies (branches)	..	..	..	..	..	..	..	..
All undertakings	14 024	13 526	16 531	17 513	15 243	16 536	17 362	7 876
Non-life								
Domestic undertakings	7 243	9 161	10 325	13 383	14 338	15 392	12 260	11 989
Foreign controlled undertakings	4 948	5 986	5 650	6 550	6 809	7 114	5 650	5 993
Foreign companies (branches)	..	..	..	..	..	..	..	..
All undertakings	7 243	9 161	10 325	13 383	14 338	15 392	12 260	11 989
Composite								
Domestic undertakings	72 592	79 086	108 207	114 286	123 934	138 745	149 512	174 147
Foreign controlled undertakings	72 592	79 086	108 207	114 286	123 934	138 745	149 512	174 147
Foreign companies (branches)	..	..	..	..	..	..	..	..
All undertakings	72 592	79 086	108 207	114 286	123 934	138 745	149 512	174 147
of which:								
Life	30 235	29 116	39 083	38 017	36 194	39 422	42 535	57 394
Domestic undertakings	30 235	29 116	39 083	38 017	36 194	39 422	42 535	57 394
Foreign controlled undertakings	30 235	29 116	39 083	38 017	36 194	39 422	42 535	57 394
Foreign companies (branches)	..	..	..	..	..	..	..	..
All undertakings	30 235	29 116	39 083	38 017	36 194	39 422	42 535	57 394
Non-life	42 357	49 970	69 124	76 269	87 740	99 323	106 977	116 753
Domestic undertakings	42 357	49 970	69 124	76 269	87 740	99 323	106 977	116 753
Foreign controlled undertakings	42 357	49 970	69 124	76 269	87 740	99 323	106 977	116 753
Foreign companies (branches)	..	..	..	..	..	..	..	..
All undertakings	42 357	49 970	69 124	76 269	87 740	99 323	106 977	116 753
Total								
Domestic undertakings	93 859	101 773	135 063	145 182	153 515	170 673	179 134	194 012
Foreign controlled undertakings	89 099	96 162	128 218	135 853	143 341	159 113	169 848	185 353
Foreign companies (branches)	..	..	..	..	..	..	..	..
All undertakings	93 859	101 773	135 063	145 182	153 515	170 673	179 134	194 012
1.4 Gross operating expenses								
Life								
Domestic undertakings	35 399	32 897	34 946	34 955	32 702	34 429	33 133	11 532
Foreign controlled undertakings	30 053	29 279	31 818	30 865	28 684	31 147	30 457	8 869
Foreign companies (branches)	..	..	..	..	..	..	..	..
All undertakings	35 399	32 897	34 946	34 955	32 702	34 429	33 133	11 532
Non-life								
Domestic undertakings	17 638	20 337	21 977	21 528	19 122	24 892	22 813	24 370
Foreign controlled undertakings	11 890	14 690	13 298	10 965	11 520	12 934	12 482	14 275
Foreign companies (branches)	..	..	..	..	..	..	..	..
All undertakings	17 638	20 337	21 977	21 528	19 122	24 892	22 813	24 370
Composite								
Domestic undertakings	181 142	167 842	176 431	185 944	203 460	226 949	239 438	281 000
Foreign controlled undertakings	181 142	167 842	176 431	185 944	203 460	226 949	239 438	281 000
Foreign companies (branches)	..	..	..	..	..	..	..	..
All undertakings	181 142	167 842	176 431	185 944	203 460	226 949	239 438	281 000
of which:								
Life	70 675	55 349	56 859	50 779	55 001	63 365	63 028	94 450
Domestic undertakings	70 675	55 349	56 859	50 779	55 001	63 365	63 028	94 450
Foreign controlled undertakings	70 675	55 349	56 859	50 779	55 001	63 365	63 028	94 450
Foreign companies (branches)	..	..	..	..	..	..	..	..
All undertakings	70 675	55 349	56 859	50 779	55 001	63 365	63 028	94 450
Non-life	110 467	112 493	119 571	135 165	148 459	163 584	176 410	186 550
Domestic undertakings	110 467	112 493	119 571	135 165	148 459	163 584	176 410	186 550
Foreign controlled undertakings	110 467	112 493	119 571	135 165	148 459	163 584	176 410	186 550
Foreign companies (branches)	..	..	..	..	..	..	..	..
All undertakings	110 467	112 493	119 571	135 165	148 459	163 584	176 410	186 550
Total								
Domestic undertakings	234 179	221 076	233 354	242 427	255 284	286 269	295 384	316 903
Foreign controlled undertakings	223 085	211 811	221 547	227 774	243 664	271 030	282 377	304 144
Foreign companies (branches)	..	..	..	..	..	..	..	..
All undertakings	234 179	221 076	233 354	242 427	255 284	286 269	295 384	316 903

Table 1. Selected aggregates *(cont.)*

Million HUF

	2014	2015	2016	2017	2018	2019	2020	2021
1.5 Insurance business written abroad by branches, gross premiums								
Life								
Branches and agencies	..	..	..	..	..	..	..	..
Subsidaries	..	..	..	..	..	..	..	..
Total	..	..	..	..	..	..	..	..
Non-life								
Branches and agencies	..	..	..	..	..	..	..	..
Subsidaries	..	..	..	..	..	..	..	..
Total	..	..	..	..	..	..	..	..
Composite								
Branches and agencies	..	..	..	..	..	..	..	..
Subsidaries	..	..	..	..	..	..	..	..
Total	..	..	..	..	..	..	..	..
of which:								
Life	..	..	..	..	..	..	..	..
Branches and agencies	..	..	..	..	..	..	..	..
Subsidaries	..	..	..	..	..	..	..	..
Total	..	..	..	..	..	..	..	..
Non-life	..	..	..	..	..	..	..	..
Branches and agencies	..	..	..	..	..	..	..	..
Subsidaries	..	..	..	..	..	..	..	..
Total	..	..	..	..	..	..	..	..
Total								
Branches and agencies	..	..	..	..	..	..	..	..
Subsidaries	..	..	..	..	..	..	..	..
Total	..	..	..	..	..	..	..	..

.. Not available
Note: Detailed metadata at: *http://metalinks.oecd.org/ins/20230516/ba83*.
Source: *OECD Insurance Statistics (database)*

HUNGARY

Table 2. Number of companies and employees

	2014	2015	2016	2017	2018	2019	2020	2021
2.1 Number of companies								
Life								
Domestic undertakings	10	10	8	7	6	5	5	4
Foreign controlled undertakings	7	7	7	6	5	4	4	3
Foreign companies (branches)	..	0	0	0	0	0	0	0
All undertakings	10	10	8	7	6	5	5	4
Non-life								
Domestic undertakings	12	11	10	9	9	9	9	9
Foreign controlled undertakings	6	6	6	5	5	5	5	5
Foreign companies (branches)	14	13	14	13	12	11	12	13
All undertakings	26	24	24	22	21	20	21	22
Composite								
Domestic undertakings	10	9	9	9	8	8	8	9
Foreign controlled undertakings	10	9	9	9	8	8	8	9
Foreign companies (branches)	1	2	2	2	2	1	1	1
All undertakings	11	11	11	11	10	9	9	10
Reinsurance								
Domestic undertakings	..	..	..	..	..	..	..	..
Foreign controlled undertakings	..	..	..	..	..	..	..	..
Foreign companies (branches)	..	..	..	..	..	..	..	..
All undertakings	..	..	..	..	..	..	..	..
Total								
Domestic undertakings	32	30	27	25	23	22	22	22
Foreign controlled undertakings	23	22	22	20	18	17	17	17
Foreign companies (branches)	15	15	16	15	14	12	13	14
All undertakings	47	45	43	40	37	34	35	36
2.2 Number of employees								
Insurance undertakings	9 229	8 728	8 542	8 133	11 116	8 858	7 047	6 960
Intermediaries	12 768	11 392	9 822	12 287	7 791	13 186	11 553	9 776
Total	21 997	20 121	18 364	20 420	18 907	22 044	18 600	16 735

.. Not available

Note: Detailed metadata at: *http://metalinks.oecd.org/ins/20230516/ba83.*

Source: *OECD Insurance Statistics (database)*

ICELAND

Table 1. Selected aggregates

Million ISK

	2014	2015	2016	2017	2018	2019	2020	2021
1.1 Insurance business written in the reporting country								
1.1.1 Insurance business, by ownership								
Gross premiums								
Domestic undertakings	51 849	55 346	58 777	65 274	70 561	74 978	73 768	80 456
Foreign controlled undertakings	5 401	6 010	..	..	..	..	..	..
Foreign companies (branches)	..	..	..	..	..	..	..	..
All undertakings	51 849	55 346	58 777	65 274	70 561	74 978	73 768	80 456
Premiums ceded								
Domestic undertakings	2 918	2 882	2 725	2 613	2 869	2 802	3 009	3 229
Foreign controlled undertakings	310	272	..	..	..	..	..	..
Foreign companies (branches)	..	..	..	..	..	..	..	..
All undertakings	2 918	2 882	2 725	2 613	2 869	2 802	3 009	3 229
Net written premiums								
Domestic undertakings	48 931	52 465	56 052	62 662	67 693	72 176	70 759	77 227
Foreign controlled undertakings	5 091	5 737	..	..	..	..	..	..
Foreign companies (branches)	..	..	..	..	..	..	..	..
All undertakings	48 931	52 465	56 052	62 662	67 693	72 176	70 759	77 227
1.1.2 Insurance business on foreign risks, gross premiums								
Life	0	0	0	0	0	0	..	0
Non-life	2 563	3 018	1 010	1 737	3 444	1 735	..	120
Composite total	..	..	..	..	..	..	..	..
Total	2 563	3 018	1 010	1 737	3 444	1 735	..	120
1.1.3 Life insurance payments, by class, gross premiums								
Annuities	111	473	..	..	..	..	..	..
Unit linked	87	91	20	32	23	17	15	12
Other life insurance	4 042	4 087	5 141	5 789	5 815	6 199	6 587	7 230
Total life insurance	4 240	4 651	5 161	5 821	5 837	6 217	6 603	7 242
***of which:** Pension contracts*	0	0	0	0	0	0	0	0
1.1.4 Non-life insurance payments, by class, gross premiums								
Motor vehicle insurance	22 084	23 952	28 398	33 127	35 842	38 310	36 944	41 382
Marine, aviation and other transport insurance	3 419	3 690	3 631	3 139	3 251	3 130	2 680	2 978
Freight insurance	646	751	0	0	0	0	0	0
Fire and other property damage insurance	13 903	13 911	12 484	13 048	14 472	15 552	15 679	16 663
Pecuniary loss insurance	23	27	33	26	59	70	106	72
General liability insurance	2 565	2 672	3 078	3 561	3 974	4 163	4 222	4 599
Accident and health	4 947	5 646	5 960	6 509	7 093	7 507	7 507	7 501
***of which:** Health*	..	..	..	..	..	..	..	..
Other non-life insurance	22	42	32	42	33	29	28	18
Treaty reinsurance	0	0	0	0	0	0	0	0
Total non-life insurance	47 608	50 690	53 616	59 453	64 724	68 761	67 165	73 214
1.2 Gross claims payments								
Life								
Domestic undertakings	1 529	1 325	1 690	1 755	1 752	2 380	2 326	2 388
Foreign controlled undertakings	30	58	..	..	..	..	..	..
Foreign companies (branches)	..	..	..	..	..	..	..	..
All undertakings	1 529	1 325	1 690	1 755	1 752	2 380	2 326	2 388
Non-life								
Domestic undertakings	32 554	36 082	41 655	43 781	51 533	52 944	52 454	52 621
Foreign controlled undertakings	3 520	4 169	..	..	..	..	..	..
Foreign companies (branches)	..	..	..	..	..	..	..	..
All undertakings	32 554	36 082	41 655	43 781	51 533	52 944	52 454	52 621
Composite, all undertakings	..	..	..	..	..	..	..	..
Total								
Domestic undertakings	34 083	37 407	43 345	45 536	53 285	55 324	54 780	55 008
Foreign controlled undertakings	3 550	4 227	..	..	..	..	..	..
Foreign companies (branches)	..	..	..	..	..	..	..	..
All undertakings	34 083	37 407	43 345	45 536	53 285	55 324	54 780	55 008
1.3 Commissions								
Life								
Domestic undertakings	118	90	..	..	..	..	..	..
Foreign controlled undertakings	42	3	..	..	..	..	..	..
Foreign companies (branches)	..	..	..	..	..	..	..	..
All undertakings	118	90	..	..	..	..	..	..
Non-life								
Domestic undertakings	39	36	..	..	..	..	..	..
Foreign controlled undertakings	0	0	..	..	..	..	..	..
Foreign companies (branches)	..	..	..	..	..	..	..	..
All undertakings	39	36	..	..	..	..	..	..
Composite, all undertakings	..	..	..	..	..	..	..	..
Total								
Domestic undertakings	157	126	..	..	..	..	..	..
Foreign controlled undertakings	42	3	..	..	..	..	..	..
Foreign companies (branches)	..	..	..	..	..	..	..	..
All undertakings	157	126	..	..	..	..	..	..

ICELAND

Table 1. Selected aggregates *(cont.)*

Million ISK

	2014	2015	2016	2017	2018	2019	2020	2021
1.4 Gross operating expenses								
Life								
Domestic undertakings	1 098	1 498	1 231	1 528	1 394	1 411	1 472	1 695
Foreign controlled undertakings	18	161	..	..	..	..	..	..
Foreign companies (branches)	..	..	..	..	..	..	..	..
All undertakings	1 098	1 498	1 231	1 528	1 394	1 411	1 472	1 695
Non-life								
Domestic undertakings	9 680	4 314	6 931	7 422	11 994	12 605	12 414	14 022
Foreign controlled undertakings	1 086	1 225	..	..	..	..	..	..
Foreign companies (branches)	..	..	..	..	..	..	..	..
All undertakings	9 680	4 314	6 931	7 422	12 026	12 605	12 414	14 022
Composite, all undertakings	..	..	..	..	..	..	..	..
Total								
Domestic undertakings	10 778	5 812	8 162	8 950	13 389	14 016	13 886	15 716
Foreign controlled undertakings	1 104	1 387	..	..	..	..	..	..
Foreign companies (branches)	..	..	..	..	..	..	..	..
All undertakings	10 778	5 812	8 162	8 950	13 421	14 016	13 886	15 716
1.5 Insurance business written abroad by branches, gross premiums								
Life								
Branches and agencies	..	..	..	..	..	..	..	..
Subsidaries	..	..	..	..	..	..	..	..
Total	..	..	..	..	..	..	..	..
Non-life								
Branches and agencies	..	..	..	..	..	..	..	..
Subsidaries	..	..	..	..	..	..	..	..
Total	..	..	..	..	..	..	..	..
Composite total	..	..	..	..	..	..	..	..
Total								
Branches and agencies	..	..	..	..	..	..	..	..
Subsidaries	..	..	..	..	..	..	..	..
Total	..	..	..	..	..	..	..	..

.. Not available

Note: Detailed metadata at: *http://metalinks.oecd.org/ins/20230516/a944.*

Source: *OECD Insurance Statistics (database)*

ICELAND

Table 2. Number of companies and employees

	2014	2015	2016	2017	2018	2019	2020	2021
2.1 Number of companies								
Life								
Domestic undertakings	5	5	4	4	4	4	4	4
Foreign controlled undertakings	1	1	..	..	..	..	0	0
Foreign companies (branches)	1	1	..	..	..	..	0	0
All undertakings	6	6	4	4	4	4	4	4
Non-life								
Domestic undertakings	5	5	4	4	4	4	4	4
Foreign controlled undertakings	1	1	..	..	..	..	0	0
Foreign companies (branches)	1	1	..	..	..	..	0	0
All undertakings	6	6	4	4	4	4	4	4
Composite, all undertakings	**0**	**0**	**0**	**0**	**0**	**0**	**0**	**0**
Reinsurance								
Domestic undertakings	2	2	0	0	0	0	0	0
Foreign controlled undertakings	..	..	..	..	..	..	0	0
Foreign companies (branches)	..	..	..	..	..	..	0	0
All undertakings	2	2	0	0	0	0	0	0
Total								
Domestic undertakings	12	12	8	8	8	8	8	8
Foreign controlled undertakings	2	2	0	0	0	0	0	0
Foreign companies (branches)	2	2	0	0	0	0	0	0
All undertakings	14	14	8	8	8	8	8	8
2.2 Number of employees								
Insurance undertakings	..	582	..	..	..	..	..	..
Intermediaries	592	..	..	..	..	..	..	..
Total	592	582	..	..	..	..	..	..

.. Not available

Note: Detailed metadata at: *http://metalinks.oecd.org/ins/20230516/a944.*

Source: *OECD Insurance Statistics (database)*

IRELAND

Table 1. Selected aggregates

Million EUR

	2014	2015	2016	2017	2018	2019	2020	2021
1.1 Insurance business written in the reporting country								
1.1.1 Insurance business, by ownership								
Gross premiums								
Domestic undertakings	36 377	40 340	48 949	40 281	36 998	40 282	39 402	49 655
Foreign controlled undertakings	..	..	..	..	..	..	..	..
Foreign companies (branches)	3 184	3 645	..	3 821	3 756	4 283	3 111	..
All undertakings	39 561	43 985	48 949	44 102	40 754	44 565	42 513	49 655
Premiums ceded								
Domestic undertakings	3 891	4 933	9 985	..	..	..	..	..
Foreign controlled undertakings	..	..	..	..	..	..	..	..
Foreign companies (branches)	371	359	..	..	..	..	..	..
All undertakings	4 262	5 292	9 985	..	..	..	..	..
Net written premiums								
Domestic undertakings	32 486	35 407	38 964	..	..	..	..	..
Foreign controlled undertakings	..	..	..	..	..	..	..	..
Foreign companies (branches)	2 813	3 286	..	..	..	..	..	..
All undertakings	35 299	38 693	38 964	..	..	..	..	..
1.1.2 Insurance business on foreign risks, gross premiums								
Life	21 410	23 192	..	19 774	16 644	16 606	15 156	18 326
Non-life	3 960	4 263	..	2 277	2 671	3 032	3 381	3 066
Composite	..	..	..	6	191	180	149	..
of which:								
Life	..	..	..	..	..	..	..	..
Non-life	..	..	..	..	..	..	..	..
Total	25 370	27 455	..	22 057	19 506	19 818	18 686	21 392
1.1.3 Life insurance payments, by class, gross premiums								
Annuities	..	..	0	0	0	0	..	0
Unit linked	..	..	28 838	30 737	26 568	27 840	26 616	36 397
Other life insurance	..	..	4 477	4 279	4 102	4 135	3 489	3 237
Total life insurance	32 171	34 587	33 315	35 016	30 670	31 975	30 105	39 634
of which: *Pension contracts*	..	..	..	..	..	..	..	..
1.1.4 Non-life insurance payments, by class, gross premiums								
Motor vehicle insurance	1 599	1 795	3 905	2 086	2 067	2 900	2 374	2 098
Marine, aviation and other transport insurance	143	163	421	144	219	292	565	672
Freight insurance	..	..	0	0	..	0	..	0
Fire and other property damage insurance	1 758	1 768	4 023	1 401	1 503	2 156	2 148	1 866
Pecuniary loss insurance	124	92	332	830	848	1 152	1 098	842
General liability insurance	1 301	1 400	2 887	1 288	1 296	1 967	1 812	1 709
Accident and health	1 235	2 750	1 935	2 396	2 323	2 575	2 670	2 736
of which: *Health*	..	..	..	..	..	..	..	..
Other non-life insurance	494	585	1 159	158	217	139	118	22
Treaty reinsurance	373	414	746	217	..	0	0	0
Total non-life insurance	7 027	8 967	15 408	8 520	8 473	11 181	10 785	9 944
1.2 Gross claims payments								
Life								
Domestic undertakings	27 434	28 474	32 280	26 726	25 196	26 254	27 596	30 970
Foreign controlled undertakings	..	..	..	..	..	..	..	..
Foreign companies (branches)	1 114	1 356	..	2 435	2 052	836	267	..
All undertakings	28 548	29 830	32 280	29 161	27 248	27 090	27 863	30 970
Non-life								
Domestic undertakings	3 853	5 343	15 941	8 482	8 283	9 604	11 850	12 644
Foreign controlled undertakings	..	..	..	..	..	..	..	..
Foreign companies (branches)	1 177	1 179	..	725	871	1 714	978	..
All undertakings	5 030	6 522	15 941	9 207	9 154	11 318	12 828	12 644
Composite								
Domestic undertakings	..	..	..	..	..	..	..	..
Foreign controlled undertakings	..	..	..	..	..	..	..	..
Foreign companies (branches)	..	..	..	357	983	974	1 023	..
All undertakings	..	..	..	357	983	974	1 023	..
of which:								
Life	..	..	..	..	..	..	..	..
Domestic undertakings	..	..	..	..	..	..	..	..
Foreign controlled undertakings	..	..	..	..	..	..	..	..
Foreign companies (branches)	..	..	..	..	..	..	..	..
All undertakings	..	..	..	..	..	..	..	..
Non-life	..	..	..	..	..	..	..	..
Domestic undertakings	..	..	..	..	..	..	..	..
Foreign controlled undertakings	..	..	..	..	..	..	..	..
Foreign companies (branches)	..	..	..	..	..	..	..	..
All undertakings	..	..	..	..	..	..	..	..
Total								
Domestic undertakings	31 287	33 817	48 221	35 208	33 479	35 858	39 446	43 614
Foreign controlled undertakings	..	..	..	..	..	..	..	..
Foreign companies (branches)	2 291	2 535	..	3 517	3 906	3 524	2 268	..
All undertakings	33 578	36 352	48 221	38 725	37 385	39 382	41 714	43 614

Table 1. Selected aggregates *(cont.)*

Million EUR

	2014	2015	2016	2017	2018	2019	2020	2021
1.3 Commissions								
Life								
Domestic undertakings	2 051	2 281	2 198	1 517	1 625	1 497	1 526	1 482
Foreign controlled undertakings	..	..	..	..	..	..	..	..
Foreign companies (branches)	64	59	..	94	44	-10	1	..
All undertakings	2 115	2 340	2 198	1 611	1 669	1 487	1 527	1 482
Non-life								
Domestic undertakings	764	896	2 292	957	1 012	1 187	1 343	1 431
Foreign controlled undertakings	..	..	..	..	..	..	..	..
Foreign companies (branches)	248	299	..	194	221	227	247	..
All undertakings	1 012	1 195	2 292	1 511	1 233	1 414	1 590	1 431
Composite								
Domestic undertakings	..	..	..	..	..	..	..	..
Foreign controlled undertakings	..	..	..	..	..	..	..	..
Foreign companies (branches)	..	..	..	80	110	94	114	..
All undertakings	..	..	..	80	110	94	114	..
of which:								
Life	..	..	..	..	..	..	..	..
Domestic undertakings	..	..	..	..	..	..	..	..
Foreign controlled undertakings	..	..	..	..	..	..	..	..
Foreign companies (branches)	..	..	..	..	..	..	..	..
All undertakings	..	..	..	..	..	..	..	..
Non-life	..	..	..	..	..	..	..	..
Domestic undertakings	..	..	..	..	..	..	..	..
Foreign controlled undertakings	..	..	..	..	..	..	..	..
Foreign companies (branches)	..	..	..	..	..	..	..	..
All undertakings	..	..	..	..	..	..	..	..
Total								
Domestic undertakings	2 815	3 177	4 490	2 474	2 637	2 684	2 869	2 913
Foreign controlled undertakings	..	..	..	..	..	..	..	..
Foreign companies (branches)	312	358	..	368	375	311	362	..
All undertakings	3 127	3 535	4 490	3 202	3 012	2 995	3 231	2 913
1.4 Gross operating expenses								
Life								
Domestic undertakings	1 429	1 437	1 319	444	..	..	..	..
Foreign controlled undertakings	..	..	..	..	..	..	..	..
Foreign companies (branches)	657	158	..	..	..	..	..	..
All undertakings	2 086	1 595	1 319	444	..	..	..	..
Non-life								
Domestic undertakings	589	484	1 873	932	..	..	..	..
Foreign controlled undertakings	..	..	..	..	..	..	..	..
Foreign companies (branches)	223	224	..	..	..	..	..	..
All undertakings	812	708	1 873	932	..	..	..	..
Composite								
Domestic undertakings	..	..	..	..	..	..	..	..
Foreign controlled undertakings	..	..	..	..	..	..	..	..
Foreign companies (branches)	..	..	..	..	..	..	..	..
All undertakings	..	..	..	..	..	..	..	..
of which:								
Life	..	..	..	..	..	..	..	..
Domestic undertakings	..	..	..	..	..	..	..	..
Foreign controlled undertakings	..	..	..	..	..	..	..	..
Foreign companies (branches)	..	..	..	..	..	..	..	..
All undertakings	..	..	..	..	..	..	..	..
Non-life	..	..	..	..	..	..	..	..
Domestic undertakings	..	..	..	..	..	..	..	..
Foreign controlled undertakings	..	..	..	..	..	..	..	..
Foreign companies (branches)	..	..	..	..	..	..	..	..
All undertakings	..	..	..	..	..	..	..	..
Total								
Domestic undertakings	2 018	1 921	3 192	1 376	..	..	..	..
Foreign controlled undertakings	..	..	..	..	..	..	..	..
Foreign companies (branches)	880	382	..	..	..	..	..	..
All undertakings	2 898	2 303	3 192	1 376	..	..	..	..

Table 1. Selected aggregates *(cont.)*

Million EUR

	2014	2015	2016	2017	2018	2019	2020	2021
1.5 Insurance business written abroad by branches, gross premiums								
Life								
Branches and agencies	5 970	6 234	..	6 438	5 266	6 513	7 182	8 494
Subsidaries	..	..	..	..	..	..	..	..
Total	5 970	6 234	..	6 438	5 266	6 513	7 182	8 494
Non-life								
Branches and agencies	9 640	9 835	..	8 739	9 029	11 204	15 553	17 411
Subsidaries	..	..	..	..	..	..	..	..
Total	9 640	9 835	..	8 739	9 029	11 204	15 553	17 411
Composite								
Branches and agencies	..	..	..	..	..	..	..	..
Subsidaries	..	..	..	..	..	..	..	..
Total	..	..	..	..	..	..	..	..
of which:								
Life	..	..	..	..	..	..	..	..
Branches and agencies	..	..	..	..	..	..	..	..
Subsidaries	..	..	..	..	..	..	..	..
Total	..	..	..	..	..	..	..	..
Non-life	..	..	..	..	..	..	..	..
Branches and agencies	..	..	..	..	..	..	..	..
Subsidaries	..	..	..	..	..	..	..	..
Total	..	..	..	..	..	..	..	..
Total								
Branches and agencies	15 610	16 069	..	15 177	14 295	17 717	22 735	25 905
Subsidaries	..	..	..	..	..	..	..	..
Total	15 610	16 069	..	15 177	14 295	17 717	22 735	25 905

.. Not available

Note: Detailed metadata at: *http://metalinks.oecd.org/ins/20230516/07ea.*

Source: *OECD Insurance Statistics (database)*

Table 2. Number of companies and employees

	2014	2015	2016	2017	2018	2019	2020	2021
2.1 Number of companies								
Life								
Domestic undertakings	51	48	44	45	42	43	39	36
Foreign controlled undertakings	..	..	0	0	..	..	..	..
Foreign companies (branches)	8	11	11	12	13	15	4	8
All undertakings	59	59	55	57	55	58	43	44
Non-life								
Domestic undertakings	102	101	90	99	95	95	92	92
Foreign controlled undertakings	..	..	0	0	..	..	..	..
Foreign companies (branches)	30	32	31	30	38	33	33	27
All undertakings	132	133	121	129	133	128	125	119
Composite								
Domestic undertakings	0	0	0	1	0	..	..	..
Foreign controlled undertakings	0	0	0	0	..	..	..	..
Foreign companies (branches)	0	0	0	0	0	..	7	..
All undertakings	0	0	0	1	0	..	7	..
Reinsurance								
Domestic undertakings	75	67	61	64	63	59	58	60
Foreign controlled undertakings	..	..	0	0	..	..	..	..
Foreign companies (branches)	0	0	0	0	0	..	..	..
All undertakings	75	67	61	64	63	59	58	60
Total								
Domestic undertakings	228	216	196	209	200	197	189	188
Foreign controlled undertakings	..	..	0	0	..	..	..	..
Foreign companies (branches)	38	43	42	42	51	48	44	35
All undertakings	266	259	238	251	251	245	233	223
2.2 Number of employees								
Insurance undertakings	8 095	9 404	..	..	..	..	..	..
Intermediaries	..	..	..	..	..	..	..	..
Total	..	..	..	..	..	..	..	..

.. Not available

Note: Detailed metadata at: *http://metalinks.oecd.org/ins/20230516/07ea.*

Source: *OECD Insurance Statistics (database)*

ISRAEL

Table 1. Selected aggregates

Million ILS

	2014	2015	2016	2017	2018	2019	2020	2021
1.1 Insurance business written in the reporting country								
1.1.1 Insurance business, by ownership								
Gross premiums								
Domestic undertakings	51 400	54 869	58 153	62 730	66 640	68 881	67 171	70 349
Foreign controlled undertakings	953	1 135	1 165	1 234	1 296	12 576	11 659	13 025
Foreign companies (branches)	..	..	..	..	..	..	..	..
All undertakings	51 400	54 869	58 153	62 730	66 640	68 881	67 171	70 349
Premiums ceded								
Domestic undertakings	5 934	6 356	8 756	8 468	9 454	10 098	10 693	11 623
Foreign controlled undertakings	162	232	225	228	249	1 646	1 595	1 993
Foreign companies (branches)	..	..	..	..	..	..	..	..
All undertakings	5 934	6 356	8 756	8 468	9 454	10 098	10 693	11 623
Net written premiums								
Domestic undertakings	45 466	48 512	49 398	54 263	57 186	58 782	56 479	58 727
Foreign controlled undertakings	791	903	940	1 006	1 047	10 930	10 064	11 032
Foreign companies (branches)	..	..	..	..	..	..	..	..
All undertakings	45 466	48 512	49 398	54 263	57 186	58 782	56 479	58 727
1.1.2 Insurance business on foreign risks, gross premiums								
Life	..	..	..	..	..	..	..	..
Non-life	..	..	..	..	..	..	..	..
Composite	..	..	..	..	..	..	..	..
of which:								
Life	..	..	..	..	..	..	..	..
Non-life	..	..	..	..	..	..	..	..
Total	..	..	..	..	..	..	..	..
1.1.3 Life insurance payments, by class, gross premiums								
Annuities	1 194	1 084	1 273	1 125	1 118	1 108	891	766
Unit linked	18 236	20 266	20 897	23 867	25 433	26 378	24 759	25 305
Other life insurance	7 141	8 066	8 492	8 730	9 412	10 352	10 654	11 385
Total life insurance	26 571	29 416	30 662	33 722	35 963	37 838	36 304	37 455
***of which:** Pension contracts*	..	..	..	..	..	..	..	..
1.1.4 Non-life insurance payments, by class, gross premiums								
Motor vehicle insurance	11 439	11 775	13 053	13 396	14 129	13 976	13 708	14 312
Marine, aviation and other transport insurance	38	39	38	36	40	43	45	49
Freight insurance	170	174	176	187	174	173	174	181
Fire and other property damage insurance	4 292	4 238	4 375	4 481	4 549	4 720	4 914	5 196
Pecuniary loss insurance	278	307	335	348	480	359	390	425
General liability insurance	2 697	2 814	2 917	3 094	3 250	3 402	3 627	4 139
Accident and health	5 425	5 678	6 086	6 961	7 548	7 826	7 482	7 992
***of which:** Health*	4 189	4 203	4 448	5 144	5 614	5 908	5 587	6 063
Other non-life insurance	492	426	502	506	506	545	527	601
Treaty reinsurance	0	0	0	..	0	0	0	0
Total non-life insurance	24 830	25 452	27 483	29 009	30 676	31 043	30 867	32 894
1.2 Gross claims payments								
Life								
Domestic undertakings	3	6	8	.. c	..	..	..	..
Foreign controlled undertakings	..	..	0	..	..	..	..	..
Foreign companies (branches)	..	..	..	..	..	..	..	..
All undertakings	3	6	8	.. c	..	..	..	..
Non-life								
Domestic undertakings	2 470	2 589	2 180	2 124	2 189	2 368	2 835	3 759
Foreign controlled undertakings	..	39	72	22	30	36	60	159
Foreign companies (branches)	..	..	..	..	..	..	..	..
All undertakings	2 470	2 589	2 180	2 124	2 189	2 368	2 835	3 759
Composite								
Domestic undertakings	27 644	30 828	31 879	35 461	36 580	40 374	43 454	49 904
Foreign controlled undertakings	462	640	538	0	578	6 432	7 179	8 116
Foreign companies (branches)	..	..	..	..	..	..	..	..
All undertakings	27 644	30 828	31 879	35 461	36 580	40 374	43 454	49 904
of which:								
Life	13 825	15 363	16 243	18 411	19 489	23 113	26 215	31 942
Domestic undertakings	13 825	15 363	16 243	18 411	19 489	23 113	26 215	31 942
Foreign controlled undertakings	26	39	36	42	50	3 257	4 035	5 022
Foreign companies (branches)	..	..	..	..	..	..	..	..
All undertakings	13 825	15 363	16 243	18 411	19 489	23 113	26 215	31 942
Non-life	13 819	15 465	15 636	17 051	17 091	17 261	17 239	17 962
Domestic undertakings	13 819	15 465	15 636	17 051	17 091	17 261	17 239	17 962
Foreign controlled undertakings	436	600	502	575	528	3 175	3 144	3 094
Foreign companies (branches)	..	..	..	..	..	..	..	..
All undertakings	13 819	15 465	15 636	17 051	17 091	17 261	17 239	17 962
Total								
Domestic undertakings	30 117	33 422	34 067	37 598	38 769	42 742	46 289	53 664
Foreign controlled undertakings	462	679	609	22	608	6 469	7 239	8 275
Foreign companies (branches)	..	..	..	..	..	..	..	..
All undertakings	30 117	33 422	34 067	37 598	38 769	42 742	46 289	53 664

Table 1. Selected aggregates *(cont.)*

Million ILS

	2014	2015	2016	2017	2018	2019	2020	2021
1.3 Commissions								
Life								
Domestic undertakings	6	15	19	.. c	..	..	..	..
Foreign controlled undertakings	..	..	0	..	..	..	..	..
Foreign companies (branches)	..	..	..	..	..	..	..	..
All undertakings	6	15	19	.. c	..	..	..	..
Non-life								
Domestic undertakings	281	317	291	341	358	347	389	429
Foreign controlled undertakings	..	0	0	0	0	0	0	0
Foreign companies (branches)	..	..	..	..	..	..	..	..
All undertakings	281	317	291	341	358	347	389	429
Composite								
Domestic undertakings	5 940	6 296	6 709	7 109	7 592	7 630	7 109	7 399
Foreign controlled undertakings	..	42	40	..	38	1 429	1 211	1 276
Foreign companies (branches)	..	..	..	..	..	..	..	..
All undertakings	5 940	6 296	6 709	7 109	7 592	7 630	7 109	7 399
of which:								
Life	2 639	2 912	3 097	3 215	3 531	3 507	3 283	3 606
Domestic undertakings	2 639	2 912	3 097	3 215	3 531	3 507	3 283	3 606
Foreign controlled undertakings	1	1	1	1	1	461	429	552
Foreign companies (branches)	..	..	..	..	..	..	..	..
All undertakings	2 639	2 912	3 097	3 215	3 531	3 507	3 283	3 606
Non-life	3 300	3 384	3 612	3 893	4 061	4 123	3 826	3 793
Domestic undertakings	3 300	3 384	3 612	3 893	4 061	4 123	3 826	3 793
Foreign controlled undertakings	38	41	39	37	37	968	782	725
Foreign companies (branches)	..	..	..	..	..	..	..	..
All undertakings	3 300	3 384	3 612	3 893	4 061	4 123	3 826	3 793
Total								
Domestic undertakings	6 226	6 628	7 019	7 464	7 950	7 976	7 498	7 828
Foreign controlled undertakings	..	42	40	0	38	1 429	1 211	1 276
Foreign companies (branches)	..	..	..	..	..	..	..	..
All undertakings	6 226	6 628	7 019	7 464	7 950	7 976	7 498	7 828
1.4 Gross operating expenses								
Life								
Domestic undertakings	10	32	32	.. c	..	..	..	..
Foreign controlled undertakings	..	..	0	..	..	..	..	..
Foreign companies (branches)	..	..	..	..	..	..	..	..
All undertakings	10	32	32	.. c	..	..	..	..
Non-life								
Domestic undertakings	322	402	380	417	32	33	647	788
Foreign controlled undertakings	..	30	29	33	36	37	36	128
Foreign companies (branches)	..	..	..	..	..	..	..	..
All undertakings	322	402	380	417	32	33	647	788
Composite								
Domestic undertakings	5 169	5 719	6 033	6 504	13 992	6 773	6 816	7 186
Foreign controlled undertakings	276	282	275	278	289	1 365	1 443	1 507
Foreign companies (branches)	..	..	..	..	..	..	..	..
All undertakings	5 169	5 719	6 033	6 504	13 992	6 773	6 816	7 186
of which:								
Life	2 608	2 790	2 707	2 849	2 946	3 041	3 065	3 267
Domestic undertakings	2 608	2 790	2 707	2 849	2 946	3 041	3 065	3 267
Foreign controlled undertakings	56	54	55	51	51	641	629	684
Foreign companies (branches)	..	..	..	..	..	..	..	..
All undertakings	2 608	2 790	2 707	2 849	2 946	3 041	3 065	3 267
Non-life	2 561	2 721	2 785	3 002	3 185	3 297	3 314	3 384
Domestic undertakings	2 561	2 721	2 785	3 002	3 185	3 297	3 314	3 384
Foreign controlled undertakings	220	228	220	227	239	724	756	754
Foreign companies (branches)	..	..	..	..	..	..	..	..
All undertakings	2 561	2 721	2 785	3 002	3 185	3 297	3 314	3 384
Total								
Domestic undertakings	5 501	6 153	6 445	6 940	14 024	6 806	7 462	7 975
Foreign controlled undertakings	276	312	304	311	325	1 402	1 478	1 634
Foreign companies (branches)	..	..	..	..	..	..	..	..
All undertakings	5 501	6 153	6 445	6 940	14 024	6 806	7 462	7 975

Table 1. Selected aggregates *(cont.)*

Million ILS

	2014	2015	2016	2017	2018	2019	2020	2021
1.5 Insurance business written abroad by branches, gross premiums								
Life								
Branches and agencies	..	..	..	..	..	..	..	..
Subsidaries	..	..	..	..	..	..	..	..
Total	..	..	..	..	..	..	..	..
Non-life								
Branches and agencies	..	..	..	..	..	..	..	..
Subsidaries	..	..	..	..	..	..	..	..
Total	..	..	..	..	..	..	..	..
Composite								
Branches and agencies	..	..	..	..	..	..	..	..
Subsidaries	..	..	..	..	..	..	..	..
Total	..	..	..	..	..	..	..	..
of which:								
Life	..	..	..	..	..	..	..	..
Branches and agencies	..	..	..	..	..	..	..	..
Subsidaries	..	..	..	..	..	..	..	..
Total	..	..	..	..	..	..	..	..
Non-life	..	..	..	..	..	..	..	..
Branches and agencies	..	..	..	..	..	..	..	..
Subsidaries	..	..	..	..	..	..	..	..
Total	..	..	..	..	..	..	..	..
Total								
Branches and agencies	..	..	..	..	..	..	..	..
Subsidaries	..	..	..	..	..	..	..	..
Total	..	..	..	..	..	..	..	..

.. Not available; c Confidential data

Note: Detailed metadata at: *http://metalinks.oecd.org/ins/20230516/6b7e.*

The statistical data for Israel are supplied by and under the responsibility of the relevant Israeli authorities. The use of such data by the OECD is without prejudice to the status of the Golan Heights, East Jerusalem and Israeli settlements in the West Bank under the terms of international law.

Source: *OECD Insurance Statistics (database)*

ISRAEL

Table 2. Number of companies and employees

	2014	2015	2016	2017	2018	2019	2020	2021
2.1 Number of companies								
Life								
Domestic undertakings	1	2	2	1	0	0	..	..
Foreign controlled undertakings	..	0	..	..	0	0	..	..
Foreign companies (branches)	..	0	..	..	0	0	..	..
All undertakings	1	2	2	1	0	0	..	..
Non-life								
Domestic undertakings	12	10	10	10	12	12	14	14
Foreign controlled undertakings	..	1	1	1	1	1	1	2
Foreign companies (branches)	3	3	3	3	3	3	3	3
All undertakings	15	13	13	13	15	15	17	17
Composite								
Domestic undertakings	10	11	10	10	10	10	9	9
Foreign controlled undertakings	1	1	1	1	1	2	2	2
Foreign companies (branches)	..	0	..	..	0	0	..	..
All undertakings	10	11	10	10	10	10	9	9
Reinsurance								
Domestic undertakings	..	0	..	..	0	0	..	..
Foreign controlled undertakings	..	0	..	..	0	0	..	..
Foreign companies (branches)	..	0	..	..	0	0	..	..
All undertakings	0	0	0	..	0	0	..	..
Total								
Domestic undertakings	23	23	22	21	22	22	23	23
Foreign controlled undertakings	1	2	..	2	2	3	3	3
Foreign companies (branches)	3	3	3	3	3	3	..	..
All undertakings	26	26	25	24	25	25	26	26
2.2 Number of employees								
Insurance undertakings	..	..	..	..	..	..	..	..
Intermediaries	..	..	..	..	..	..	..	..
Total	..	..	..	..	..	..	..	..

.. Not available

Note: Detailed metadata at: *http://metalinks.oecd.org/ins/20230516/6b7e*.

The statistical data for Israel are supplied by and under the responsibility of the relevant Israeli authorities. The use of such data by the OECD is without prejudice to the status of the Golan Heights, East Jerusalem and Israeli settlements in the West Bank under the terms of international law.

Source: *OECD Insurance Statistics (database)*

ITALY

Table 1. Selected aggregates

Million EUR

	2014	2015	2016	2017	2018	2019	2020	2021
1.1 Insurance business written in the reporting country								
1.1.1 Insurance business, by ownership								
Gross premiums								
Domestic undertakings	145 244	149 011	136 278	132 924	138 120	140 752	135 774	141 820
Foreign controlled undertakings	44 419	45 694	44 287	41 990	48 367	49 764	46 241	47 587
Foreign companies (branches)	375	473	521	504	565	601	588	621
All undertakings	145 619	149 484	136 799	133 429	138 685	141 353	136 362	142 441
Premiums ceded								
Domestic undertakings	4 203	4 079	4 914	4 939	5 213	4 904	4 958	5 583
Foreign controlled undertakings	991	983	1 822	1 829	1 867	1 940	1 748	1 861
Foreign companies (branches)	58	53	62	57	67	74	75	88
All undertakings	4 262	4 132	4 976	4 996	5 281	4 979	5 033	5 671
Net written premiums								
Domestic undertakings	141 041	144 932	131 364	127 986	132 907	135 847	130 815	136 237
Foreign controlled undertakings	43 428	44 711	42 465	40 160	46 500	47 824	44 493	45 726
Foreign companies (branches)	317	420	459	447	497	527	513	533
All undertakings	141 358	145 352	131 823	128 433	133 404	136 374	131 328	136 770
1.1.2 Insurance business on foreign risks, gross premiums								
Life	1	1	1	1	3	10	4	12
Non-life	59	54	59	57	72	85	73	77
Composite	1 904	2 016	2 070	2 037	2 008	3 652	1 230	1 671
of which:								
Life	1 073	1 166	1 255	1 252	1 215	1 538	140	131
Non-life	831	849	814	784	792	2 114	1 090	1 540
Total	1 963	2 071	2 130	2 095	2 082	3 747	1 307	1 760
1.1.3 Life insurance payments, by class, gross premiums								
Annuities	956	737	710	716	701	705	683	579
Unit linked	21 829	31 884	23 848	31 305	29 887	27 928	29 609	39 811
Other life insurance	87 639	82 220	77 596	66 709	71 545	77 445	71 036	65 497
Total life insurance	110 424	114 842	102 154	98 730	102 133	106 077	101 329	105 887
***of which:** Pension contracts*	4 873	5 492	5 848	6 308	6 631	7 536	8 735	7 585
1.1.4 Non-life insurance payments, by class, gross premiums								
Motor vehicle insurance	17 468	16 590	16 260	16 097	16 262	16 393	15 621	15 344
Marine, aviation and other transport insurance	334	326	417	387	288	349	314	333
Freight insurance	212	204	198	202	209	226	174	183
Fire and other property damage insurance	5 611	5 544	5 863	5 851	6 116	6 373	5 847	6 215
Pecuniary loss insurance	1 018	1 034	1 119	1 204	1 203	1 309	1 079	1 176
General liability insurance	2 879	2 952	3 073	3 094	3 198	3 427	3 314	3 517
Accident and health	5 221	5 415	5 868	6 200	6 471	7 004	6 516	6 788
***of which:** Health*	2 149	2 323	2 655	2 909	3 142	3 534	3 290	3 462
Other non-life insurance	988	1 082	1 217	1 293	1 373	1 528	1 425	1 513
Treaty reinsurance	0	0	0	0	0	..	0	0
Total non-life insurance	33 730	33 147	34 015	34 326	35 121	36 607	34 289	35 069
1.2 Gross claims payments								
Life								
Domestic undertakings	22 852	22 955	21 169	21 166	21 382	22 878	21 687	17 478
Foreign controlled undertakings	10 413	12 229	10 866	10 142	10 653	12 066	11 516	8 301
Foreign companies (branches)	0	0	0	0	0	0	..	0
All undertakings	22 852	22 955	21 169	21 166	21 382	22 878	21 687	17 478
Non-life								
Domestic undertakings	5 016	4 931	4 776	5 209	5 170	5 458	4 744	5 773
Foreign controlled undertakings	1 853	2 005	2 008	2 021	1 920	1 994	1 699	1 987
Foreign companies (branches)	257	308	369	364	357	394	363	431
All undertakings	5 273	5 240	5 144	5 574	5 527	5 852	5 107	6 205
Composite								
Domestic undertakings	61 204	65 892	59 690	68 163	69 576	71 806	72 016	77 556
Foreign controlled undertakings	14 972	16 842	16 097	17 146	17 740	18 704	18 921	23 619
Foreign companies (branches)	0	0	0	0	0	0	..	0
All undertakings	61 204	65 892	59 690	68 163	69 576	71 806	72 016	77 556
of which:								
Life	43 279	48 546	43 755	52 096	53 576	55 052	56 549	59 969
Domestic undertakings	43 279	48 546	43 755	52 096	53 576	55 052	56 549	59 969
Foreign controlled undertakings	11 217	12 693	12 061	13 358	13 790	14 438	14 915	19 524
Foreign companies (branches)	0	0	0	0	0	0	..	0
All undertakings	43 279	48 546	43 755	52 096	53 576	55 052	56 549	59 969
Non-life	17 925	17 346	15 935	16 067	16 000	16 754	15 467	17 588
Domestic undertakings	17 925	17 346	15 935	16 067	16 000	16 754	15 467	17 588
Foreign controlled undertakings	3 754	4 149	4 037	3 788	3 950	4 266	4 006	4 095
Foreign companies (branches)	0	0	0	0	0	0	..	0
All undertakings	17 925	17 346	15 935	16 067	16 000	16 754	15 467	17 588
Total								
Domestic undertakings	89 071	93 778	85 635	94 539	96 128	100 143	98 447	100 808
Foreign controlled undertakings	27 238	31 075	28 972	29 309	30 313	32 763	32 135	33 906
Foreign companies (branches)	257	308	369	364	357	394	363	431
All undertakings	89 328	94 087	86 003	94 904	96 485	100 536	98 810	101 239

ITALY

Table 1. Selected aggregates *(cont.)*

Million EUR

	2014	2015	2016	2017	2018	2019	2020	2021
1.3 Commissions								
Life								
Domestic undertakings	650	641	626	620	590	669	592	552
Foreign controlled undertakings	430	436	449	434	432	465	405	319
Foreign companies (branches)	0	0	0	0	..	..	..	0
All undertakings	650	641	626	620	590	1 134	592	552
Non-life								
Domestic undertakings	1 656	1 706	1 748	1 829	1 915	2 087	1 946	2 145
Foreign controlled undertakings	608	734	767	752	777	828	741	690
Foreign companies (branches)	72	93	107	108	123	136	133	144
All undertakings	1 729	1 799	1 855	1 937	2 038	3 051	2 079	2 289
Composite								
Domestic undertakings	7 573	7 699	7 571	7 600	7 673	7 791	7 704	7 972
Foreign controlled undertakings	1 978	2 106	2 006	2 073	2 139	2 153	2 081	2 147
Foreign companies (branches)	0	0	0	0	..	..	..	0
All undertakings	7 573	7 699	7 571	7 600	7 673	9 944	7 704	7 972
of which:								
Life	2 273	2 447	2 306	2 317	2 300	2 804	2 187	2 365
Domestic undertakings	2 273	2 447	2 306	2 317	2 300	2 253	2 187	2 365
Foreign controlled undertakings	510	542	504	550	608	550	581	650
Foreign companies (branches)	0	0	0	0	..	..	..	0
All undertakings	2 273	2 447	2 306	2 317	2 300	2 804	2 187	2 365
Non-life	5 300	5 251	5 265	5 283	5 372	7 141	5 516	5 608
Domestic undertakings	5 300	5 251	5 265	5 283	5 372	5 538	5 516	5 608
Foreign controlled undertakings	1 468	1 564	1 502	1 523	1 531	1 603	1 499	1 497
Foreign companies (branches)	0	0	0	0	..	..	..	0
All undertakings	5 300	5 251	5 265	5 283	5 372	7 141	5 516	5 608
Total								
Domestic undertakings	9 879	10 046	9 945	10 049	10 177	10 546	10 242	10 669
Foreign controlled undertakings	3 015	3 277	3 222	3 259	3 349	3 446	3 227	3 157
Foreign companies (branches)	72	93	107	108	123	136	133	144
All undertakings	9 952	10 139	10 052	10 157	10 300	14 129	10 375	10 813
1.4 Gross operating expenses								
Life								
Domestic undertakings	953	948	963	970	925	1 008	957	874
Foreign controlled undertakings	622	634	673	658	649	681	643	521
Foreign companies (branches)	0	0	0	0	..	..	..	0
All undertakings	953	948	963	970	925	1 689	957	874
Non-life								
Domestic undertakings	2 252	2 332	2 390	2 501	2 634	2 869	2 675	2 880
Foreign controlled undertakings	818	968	1 012	992	1 022	1 106	1 016	951
Foreign companies (branches)	110	144	176	174	183	197	192	206
All undertakings	2 362	2 476	2 565	2 676	2 817	4 172	2 868	3 086
Composite								
Domestic undertakings	9 686	9 829	9 860	9 929	10 069	10 269	10 218	10 736
Foreign controlled undertakings	2 443	2 632	2 566	2 658	2 742	2 707	2 633	2 744
Foreign companies (branches)	0	0	0	0	..	..	..	0
All undertakings	9 686	9 829	9 860	9 929	10 069	12 976	10 218	10 736
of which:								
Life	3 109	3 292	3 196	3 223	3 244	3 991	3 101	3 395
Domestic undertakings	3 109	3 292	3 196	3 223	3 244	3 213	3 101	3 395
Foreign controlled undertakings	696	743	708	773	833	778	814	913
Foreign companies (branches)	0	0	0	0	..	..	..	0
All undertakings	3 109	3 292	3 196	3 223	3 244	3 991	3 101	3 395
Non-life	6 577	6 537	6 664	6 706	6 825	8 985	7 117	7 342
Domestic undertakings	6 577	6 537	6 664	6 706	6 825	7 056	7 117	7 342
Foreign controlled undertakings	1 747	1 889	1 858	1 885	1 909	1 929	1 819	1 832
Foreign companies (branches)	0	0	0	0	..	..	..	0
All undertakings	6 577	6 537	6 664	6 706	6 825	8 985	7 117	7 342
Total								
Domestic undertakings	12 891	13 109	13 213	13 400	13 629	14 146	13 850	14 490
Foreign controlled undertakings	3 883	4 234	4 251	4 307	4 413	4 494	4 291	4 216
Foreign companies (branches)	110	144	176	174	183	197	192	206
All undertakings	13 001	13 253	13 388	13 574	13 812	18 837	14 042	14 697

Table 1. Selected aggregates *(cont.)*

Million EUR

	2014	2015	2016	2017	2018	2019	2020	2021
1.5 Insurance business written abroad by branches, gross premiums								
Life								
Branches and agencies	1	1	3	1	2	0	0	0
Subsidaries	3 469	4 224	1 339	1 712	1 403	1 529	1 308	1 732
Total	3 469	4 226	1 342	1 713	1 404	1 529	1 308	1 732
Non-life								
Branches and agencies	12	9	10	13	7	15	9	10
Subsidaries	0	0	0	0	..	..	0	0
Total	12	9	10	13	7	15	9	10
Composite								
Branches and agencies	892	868	1 376	1 114	1 138	2 791	2 380	2 589
Subsidaries	54 902	58 541	57 863	60 367	56 485	56 132	54 047	62 420
Total	55 795	59 409	59 239	61 482	57 623	58 923	56 426	65 010
of which:								
Life	39 878	42 059	41 554	43 469	40 058	40 286	37 604	44 839
Branches and agencies	175	235	477	215	208	1 366	1 263	1 336
Subsidaries	39 703	41 824	41 077	43 254	39 850	38 920	36 341	43 503
Total	39 878	42 059	41 554	43 469	40 058	40 286	37 604	44 839
Non-life	15 917	17 350	17 685	18 012	17 565	18 637	18 823	20 171
Branches and agencies	718	633	899	899	930	1 425	1 116	1 254
Subsidaries	15 199	16 717	16 785	17 113	16 635	17 212	17 706	18 917
Total	15 917	17 350	17 685	18 012	17 565	18 637	18 823	20 171
Total								
Branches and agencies	905	878	1 390	1 128	1 147	2 806	2 389	2 599
Subsidaries	58 371	62 765	59 202	62 079	57 887	57 661	55 355	64 152
Total	59 276	63 643	60 592	63 207	59 034	60 467	57 743	66 751

.. Not available

Note: Detailed metadata at: *http://metalinks.oecd.org/ins/20230516/d0d1*.

Source: *OECD Insurance Statistics (database)*

Table 2. Number of companies and employees

	2014	2015	2016	2017	2018	2019	2020	2021
2.1 Number of companies								
Life								
Domestic undertakings	38	35	32	30	26	26	26	21
Foreign controlled undertakings	20	19	17	13	11	11	11	8
Foreign companies (branches)	19	20	22	19	20	20	20	19
All undertakings	57	55	54	49	46	46	46	40
Non-life								
Domestic undertakings	63	58	54	50	51	52	50	49
Foreign controlled undertakings	18	19	18	16	16	17	16	16
Foreign companies (branches)	60	65	65	73	81	77	74	67
All undertakings	123	123	119	123	132	129	124	116
Composite								
Domestic undertakings	21	21	21	20	20	20	20	20
Foreign controlled undertakings	8	9	10	9	9	9	9	9
Foreign companies (branches)	14	14	13	14	13	13	12	10
All undertakings	35	35	34	34	33	33	32	30
Reinsurance								
Domestic undertakings	0	0	0	0	..	..	..	0
Foreign controlled undertakings	0	0	0	0	..	..	..	0
Foreign companies (branches)	7	7	7	7	7	6	6	7
All undertakings	7	7	7	7	7	6	6	7
Total								
Domestic undertakings	122	114	107	100	97	98	96	90
Foreign controlled undertakings	46	47	45	38	36	37	36	33
Foreign companies (branches)	100	106	107	113	121	116	112	103
All undertakings	222	220	214	213	218	214	208	193
2.2 Number of employees								
Insurance undertakings	40 259	40 588	40 872	40 386	40 028	39 733	40 192	40 452
Intermediaries	220 288	220 850	212 596	..	..	..	..	..
Total	260 547	261 438	253 468	..	..	..	..	..

.. Not available

Note: Detailed metadata at: *http://metalinks.oecd.org/ins/20230516/d0d1*.

Source: *OECD Insurance Statistics (database)*

JAPAN

Table 1. Selected aggregates

Million JPY

	2014	2015	2016	2017	2018	2019	2020	2021
1.1 Insurance business written in the reporting country								
1.1.1 Insurance business, by ownership								
Gross premiums								
Domestic undertakings	46 031 579	46 908 456	42 615 488	41 452 663	44 740 881	42 580 813	40 267 595	41 022 789
Foreign controlled undertakings	6 724 592	7 046 820	6 617 836	6 432 494	8 315 056	7 768 028	7 364 989	7 723 416
Foreign companies (branches)	1 548 143	1 537 624	1 703 444	1 739 958	348 167	314 078	426 961	413 660
All undertakings	37 222 352	37 748 110	44 318 932	43 192 621	45 089 048	42 894 891	40 694 556	41 436 449
Premiums ceded								
Domestic undertakings	4 207 229	4 127 260	4 449 638	4 176 204	4 817 685	6 191 736	5 616 176	6 704 649
Foreign controlled undertakings	2 084 233	1 890 218	2 143 727	1 733 566	2 285 450	2 793 927	2 286 106	2 437 903
Foreign companies (branches)	47 768	75 917	214 477	239 041	223 967	206 605	293 419	285 116
All undertakings	2 129 106	2 022 086	4 664 115	4 415 245	5 041 652	6 398 341	5 909 595	6 989 765
Net written premiums								
Domestic undertakings	41 824 350	42 781 196	38 165 836	37 276 448	39 923 181	36 388 692	34 651 403	34 318 130
Foreign controlled undertakings	4 640 359	5 156 602	4 474 105	4 698 925	6 029 602	4 974 097	5 078 879	5 285 512
Foreign companies (branches)	1 500 375	1 461 707	1 488 976	1 499 865	124 190	107 464	133 553	128 536
All undertakings	35 093 246	35 726 024	39 654 812	38 776 313	40 047 371	36 496 156	34 784 956	34 446 666
1.1.2 Insurance business on foreign risks, gross premiums								
Life	..	..	..	..	..	..	..	..
Non-life	..	..	..	..	..	..	..	..
Composite total	..	..	..	..	..	..	..	..
Total	..	..	..	..	..	..	..	..
1.1.3 Life insurance payments, by class, gross premiums								
Annuities	5 154 122	4 729 892	4 340 846	3 607 407	3 875 104	3 300 278	3 087 609	3 288 591
Unit linked	..	..	..	..	..	..	..	..
Other life insurance	30 015 418	31 464 495	27 968 949	27 990 703	29 370 822	27 589 307	25 659 381	26 139 276
Total life insurance	35 169 540	36 194 387	32 309 795	31 598 110	33 245 926	30 889 585	28 746 990	29 427 867
***of which:** Pension contracts*	4 175 622	4 562 867	3 057 696	2 953 431	2 861 906	2 833 705	2 549 060	..
1.1.4 Non-life insurance payments, by class, gross premiums								
Motor vehicle insurance	5 786 949	5 916 489	6 026 253	5 814 388	5 905 312	5 988 484	5 781 766	5 699 643
Marine, aviation and other transport insurance	170 115	186 542	159 142	152 632	150 286	177 296	170 320	175 605
Freight insurance	248 817	242 488	230 397	239 546	253 139	250 516	243 978	284 832
Fire and other property damage insurance	2 104 111	2 228 178	..	..	..	..	..	..
Pecuniary loss insurance	299 082	342 570	..	..	..	..	..	..
General liability insurance	598 945	615 167	633 290	657 637	692 945	713 193	725 688	756 174
Accident and health	979 477	982 614	..	..	..	..	..	..
***of which:** Health*	214	-152	..	..	..	..	..	..
Other non-life insurance	169 874	183 922	..	..	..	..	..	..
Treaty reinsurance	..	..	..	..	..	..	..	..
Total non-life insurance	10 357 370	10 697 970	10 859 799	10 750 127	11 173 102	11 483 495	11 496 729	11 611 727
1.2 Gross claims payments								
Life								
Domestic undertakings	34 214 304	31 685 988	28 227 418	28 115 903	28 748 864	29 502 430	30 087 116	31 436 678
Foreign controlled undertakings	6 428 288	5 559 928	5 107 453	5 198 975	5 980 013	6 200 318	5 696 378	6 316 992
Foreign companies (branches)	738 243	768 206	786 644	827 193	37 839	45 369	51 496	..
All undertakings	34 952 547	32 454 194	29 014 062	28 943 096	28 786 703	29 547 799	30 138 612	31 436 678
Non-life								
Domestic undertakings	5 953 809	5 917 050	6 694 135	5 856 017	7 585 094	7 135 164	6 214 759	6 225 303
Foreign controlled undertakings	373 601	366 795	383 518	237 359	480 088	411 562	332 483	307 915
Foreign companies (branches)	..	..	104 648	98 935	222 146	200 874	291 564	150 564
All undertakings	..	..	6 798 783	5 954 952	7 807 240	7 336 038	6 506 323	6 375 867
Composite, all undertakings	..	..	..	..	..	..	..	..
Total								
Domestic undertakings	40 168 113	37 603 038	34 921 553	33 971 920	36 333 958	36 637 594	36 301 875	37 661 981
Foreign controlled undertakings	6 801 889	5 926 723	5 490 971	5 436 334	6 460 101	6 611 880	6 028 861	6 624 907
Foreign companies (branches)	738 243	768 206	891 292	926 128	259 985	246 243	343 060	150 564
All undertakings	34 952 547	32 454 194	35 812 845	34 898 048	36 593 943	36 883 837	36 644 935	37 812 545
1.3 Commissions								
Life								
Domestic undertakings	..	..	..	..	..	..	..	..
Foreign controlled undertakings	..	..	..	..	..	..	..	..
Foreign companies (branches)	..	..	..	..	..	..	..	..
All undertakings	..	..	..	..	..	..	..	..
Non-life								
Domestic undertakings	1 229 205	1 273 631	1 240 454	1 221 324	1 241 826	1 296 198	1 335 507	1 343 523
Foreign controlled undertakings	33 975	37 223	20 067	-15 311	-19 855	-27 941	-31 429	-39 911
Foreign companies (branches)	..	..	-19 897	-29 330	-33 799	-1 094	-43 029	-48 142
All undertakings	..	..	1 220 557	1 191 994	1 208 027	1 295 104	1 292 478	1 295 381
Composite, all undertakings	..	..	..	..	..	..	..	..
Total								
Domestic undertakings	1 229 205	1 273 631	1 240 454	1 221 324	1 241 826	1 296 198	1 335 507	1 343 523
Foreign controlled undertakings	33 975	37 223	20 067	-15 311	-19 855	-27 941	-31 429	-39 911
Foreign companies (branches)	..	..	-19 897	-29 330	-33 799	-1 094	-43 029	-48 142
All undertakings	..	..	1 220 557	1 191 994	1 208 027	1 295 104	1 292 478	1 295 381

Table 1. Selected aggregates *(cont.)*

Million JPY

	2014	2015	2016	2017	2018	2019	2020	2021
1.4 Gross operating expenses								
Life								
Domestic undertakings	4 178 568	4 356 425	4 369 595	4 385 030	4 856 591	4 691 017	4 580 593	4 658 084
Foreign controlled undertakings	893 811	945 921	948 132	965 055	1 353 249	1 282 164	1 237 324	1 261 003
Foreign companies (branches)	320 518	349 858	357 069	366 406	22 814	23 341	21 191	..
All undertakings	4 499 086	4 706 283	4 726 664	4 751 436	4 879 405	4 714 358	4 601 784	4 658 084
Non-life								
Domestic undertakings	3 189 416	3 275 358	3 247 478	3 206 606	3 318 518	3 389 286	3 429 411	3 529 524
Foreign controlled undertakings	238 092	249 835	207 689	125 459	185 822	158 127	136 824	131 345
Foreign companies (branches)	..	..	34 405	37 023	34 772	61 577	34 791	32 156
All undertakings	..	..	3 281 883	3 243 629	3 353 290	3 450 863	3 464 202	3 561 680
Composite, all undertakings	..	..	..	..	..	..	..	..
Total								
Domestic undertakings	7 367 984	7 631 783	7 617 073	7 591 636	8 175 109	8 080 303	8 010 004	8 187 608
Foreign controlled undertakings	1 131 903	1 195 756	1 155 821	1 090 514	1 539 071	1 440 291	1 374 148	1 392 348
Foreign companies (branches)	320 518	349 858	391 474	403 429	57 586	84 918	55 982	32 156
All undertakings	4 499 086	4 706 283	8 008 547	7 995 065	8 232 695	8 165 221	8 065 986	8 219 764
1.5 Insurance business written abroad by branches, gross premiums								
Life								
Branches and agencies	..	..	..	..	..	..	..	..
Subsidaries	..	..	..	..	..	..	..	..
Total	..	..	..	..	..	..	..	..
Non-life								
Branches and agencies	..	..	..	..	..	..	..	..
Subsidaries	..	..	..	..	..	..	..	..
Total	..	..	..	..	..	..	..	..
Composite total	..	..	..	..	..	..	..	..
Total								
Branches and agencies	..	..	..	..	..	..	..	..
Subsidaries	..	..	..	..	..	..	..	..
Total	..	..	..	..	..	..	..	..

.. Not available

Note: Detailed metadata at: *http://metalinks.oecd.org/ins/20230516/9a53.*

Source: *OECD Insurance Statistics (database)*

Table 2. Number of companies and employees

	2014	2015	2016	2017	2018	2019	2020	2021
2.1 Number of companies								
Life								
Domestic undertakings	39	38	38	38	40	41	41	42
Foreign controlled undertakings	13	13	13	13	14	14	12	13
Foreign companies (branches)	3	3	3	3	1	1	1	0
All undertakings	42	41	41	41	41	42	42	42
Non-life								
Domestic undertakings	30	30	30	29	30	32	32	33
Foreign controlled undertakings	7	7	7	6	7	7	7	7
Foreign companies (branches)	22	22	21	23	21	21	21	21
All undertakings	52	52	51	52	51	53	53	54
Composite, all undertakings	**0**	**0**	**0**	..	..	..	..	..
Reinsurance								
Domestic undertakings	..	..	..	..	..	..	..	..
Foreign controlled undertakings	..	..	..	..	..	..	..	..
Foreign companies (branches)	..	..	..	..	..	..	..	..
All undertakings	..	..	..	..	..	..	..	..
Total								
Domestic undertakings	..	68	68	67	70	..	73	75
Foreign controlled undertakings	..	20	20	19	21	..	19	20
Foreign companies (branches)	..	25	24	26	22	..	22	21
All undertakings	..	93	92	93	92	..	95	96
2.2 Number of employees								
Insurance undertakings	226 043	120 353	..	..	..	..	..	..
Intermediaries	2 293 863	2 059 743	..	..	..	..	..	..
Total	2 519 906	2 080 096	..	345 582	..	..	..	..

.. Not available

Note: Detailed metadata at: *http://metalinks.oecd.org/ins/20230516/9a53.*

Source: *OECD Insurance Statistics (database)*

KOREA

Table 1. Selected aggregates

Million KRW

	2014	2015	2016	2017	2018	2019	2020	2021
1.1 Insurance business written in the reporting country								
1.1.1 Insurance business, by ownership								
Gross premiums								
Domestic undertakings	192 380 611	205 460 047	210 800 275	209 464 937	206 866 894	..	231 158 909	235 735 392
Foreign controlled undertakings	13 324 532	15 765 302	16 670 208	17 513 911	14 930 441	..	26 652 331	26 029 553
Foreign companies (branches)	4 594 745	2 267 929	4 629 847	4 849 409	5 320 101	..	3 453 833	3 885 827
All undertakings	196 975 356	207 727 976	215 430 122	214 314 346	212 186 995	..	234 612 743	239 621 219
Premiums ceded								
Domestic undertakings	9 694 294	10 255 858	10 505 959	11 215 981	11 733 647	..	13 990 016	14 730 449
Foreign controlled undertakings	478 174	638 961	599 183	611 390	584 975	..	1 057 754	1 078 774
Foreign companies (branches)	651 726	732 347	817 712	990 510	1 035 820	..	1 183 597	1 326 959
All undertakings	10 346 020	10 988 205	11 323 671	12 206 491	12 769 467	..	15 173 613	16 057 408
Net written premiums								
Domestic undertakings	182 686 317	195 204 189	200 294 316	198 248 956	195 133 247	..	217 168 894	221 004 943
Foreign controlled undertakings	12 846 358	15 126 341	16 071 025	16 902 521	14 345 466	..	25 594 577	24 950 780
Foreign companies (branches)	3 943 019	1 535 582	3 812 135	3 858 899	4 284 281	..	2 270 236	2 558 868
All undertakings	186 629 336	196 739 771	204 106 451	202 107 855	199 417 528	..	219 439 130	223 563 811
1.1.2 Insurance business on foreign risks, gross premiums								
Life	..	..	..	..	..	..	..	..
Non-life	..	..	..	..	..	..	..	..
Composite total	..	..	..	..	..	..	..	..
Total	..	..	..	..	..	..	..	..
1.1.3 Life insurance payments, by class, gross premiums								
Annuities	23 905 884	24 586 649	21 347 503	19 558 128	17 605 227	..	17 041 847	17 111 318
Unit linked	20 670 949	20 643 073	19 406 180	19 623 687	18 834 528	..	17 224 130	17 935 071
Other life insurance	65 998 453	71 983 930	79 057 566	74 791 666	74 403 374	..	85 321 224	83 802 820
Total life insurance	110 575 286	117 213 652	119 811 249	113 973 481	110 843 129	..	119 587 220	118 849 210
***of which:** Pension contracts*	11 817 288	13 694 337	16 718 996	14 905 838	16 869 826	..	22 552 785	23 851 056
1.1.4 Non-life insurance payments, by class, gross premiums								
Motor vehicle insurance	14 188 378	15 635 198	16 975 333	17 426 917	17 276 192	..	20 157 896	20 934 403
Marine, aviation and other transport insurance	1 006 367	971 854	854 536	917 229	832 470	..	1 026 829	1 093 135
Freight insurance	0	..	..	..	..	..	..	..
Fire and other property damage insurance	484 799	472 624	471 017	428 560	373 175	..	374 725	435 129
Pecuniary loss insurance	1 601 517	1 672 799	1 693 861	1 858 689	2 133 544	..	2 322 178	2 313 282
General liability insurance	910 341	967 362	1 100 438	1 182 101	1 233 606	..	1 616 339	1 741 137
Accident and health	24 196 315	39 104 233	30 297 640	33 024 528	36 093 627	..	42 228 583	46 150 125
***of which:** Health*	10 090 810	11 740 294	13 406 917	14 799 985	16 444 106	..	20 528 740	22 199 900
Other non-life insurance	32 685 216	30 357 048	42 702 138	43 864 781	41 435 506	..	47 294 397	48 102 191
Treaty reinsurance	0	..	..	..	..	..	..	..
Total non-life insurance	85 163 744	89 181 118	94 094 963	98 702 805	99 378 120	..	115 020 946	120 769 403
1.2 Gross claims payments								
Life								
Domestic undertakings	61 070 702	65 751 692	77 155 805	78 055 802	77 155 805	..	95 341 531	99 173 054
Foreign controlled undertakings	69 035 817	6 945 034	9 505 582	10 803 105	9 505 582	..	18 268 575	19 572 299
Foreign companies (branches)	1 292 842	1 333 124	1 410 493	1 457 100	1 410 493	..	..	..
All undertakings	62 363 544	67 084 816	78 566 298	79 512 902	78 566 298	..	95 341 531	99 173 054
Non-life								
Domestic undertakings	30 233 735	30 895 053	32 747 964	35 060 020	40 091 995	..	48 381 362	43 673 793
Foreign controlled undertakings	844 722	843 763	802 729	767 651	824 571	..	910 807	670 623
Foreign companies (branches)	1 098 087	1 264 227	1 282 459	1 285 551	1 554 862	..	2 212 454	1 764 708
All undertakings	31 331 823	32 159 280	34 030 423	36 345 571	41 646 857	..	50 593 816	45 438 501
Composite, all undertakings	..	..	..	..	..	..	..	..
Total								
Domestic undertakings	91 304 438	96 646 745	109 903 769	113 115 822	117 247 800	..	143 722 893	142 846 847
Foreign controlled undertakings	69 880 539	7 788 797	10 308 311	11 570 756	10 330 153	..	19 179 382	20 242 922
Foreign companies (branches)	2 390 929	2 597 351	2 692 952	2 742 651	2 965 355	..	2 212 454	1 764 708
All undertakings	93 695 367	99 244 096	112 596 721	115 858 473	120 213 155	..	145 935 347	144 611 555
1.3 Commissions								
Life								
Domestic undertakings	..	..	..	..	..	..	..	..
Foreign controlled undertakings	..	..	..	..	..	..	..	..
Foreign companies (branches)	..	..	..	..	..	..	..	..
All undertakings	..	..	..	..	..	..	..	..
Non-life								
Domestic undertakings	..	..	..	..	..	..	..	..
Foreign controlled undertakings	..	..	..	..	..	..	..	..
Foreign companies (branches)	..	..	..	..	..	..	..	..
All undertakings	..	..	..	..	..	..	..	..
Composite, all undertakings	..	..	..	..	..	..	..	..
Total								
Domestic undertakings	..	..	..	..	..	..	..	..
Foreign controlled undertakings	..	..	..	..	..	..	..	..
Foreign companies (branches)	..	..	..	..	..	..	..	..
All undertakings	..	..	..	..	..	..	..	..

Table 1. Selected aggregates *(cont.)*

Million KRW

	2014	2015	2016	2017	2018	2019	2020	2021
1.4 Gross operating expenses								
Life								
Domestic undertakings	27 511 983	28 987 407	28 236 989	28 574 504	36 539 562	..	15 375 567	14 686 222
Foreign controlled undertakings	806 034	756 903	5 074 779	5 675 330	5 878 573	..	3 667 962	3 499 744
Foreign companies (branches)	4 595 483	5 009 714	760 976	619 584	790 806	..	..	..
All undertakings	32 107 466	33 997 121	28 997 965	29 194 088	37 330 368	..	15 375 567	14 686 222
Non-life								
Domestic undertakings	16 760 436	13 511 865	14 238 364	15 685 551	16 637 805	..	18 024 767	18 081 767
Foreign controlled undertakings	245 017	182 669	163 724	225 860	254 141	..	336 057	377 319
Foreign companies (branches)	1 116 586	405 386	411 714	434 676	510 688	..	566 518	605 418
All undertakings	17 877 022	13 917 251	14 650 078	16 120 227	17 148 493	..	18 591 285	18 687 185
Composite, all undertakings	..	..	..	..	..	..	..	..
Total								
Domestic undertakings	44 272 419	42 499 272	42 475 353	44 260 055	53 177 367	..	33 400 334	32 767 989
Foreign controlled undertakings	1 051 051	939 572	5 238 503	5 901 190	6 132 714	..	4 004 019	3 877 063
Foreign companies (branches)	5 712 069	5 415 100	1 172 690	1 054 260	1 301 494	..	566 518	605 418
All undertakings	49 984 488	47 914 372	43 648 043	45 314 315	54 478 861	..	33 966 852	33 373 407
1.5 Insurance business written abroad by branches, gross premiums								
Life								
Branches and agencies	..	..	..	..	..	..	..	..
Subsidaries	..	..	..	..	..	..	..	..
Total	..	..	..	..	..	..	..	..
Non-life								
Branches and agencies	..	..	..	..	..	..	..	..
Subsidaries	..	..	..	..	..	..	..	..
Total	..	..	..	..	..	..	..	..
Composite total	..	..	..	..	..	..	..	..
Total								
Branches and agencies	..	..	..	..	..	..	..	..
Subsidaries	..	..	..	..	..	..	..	..
Total	..	..	..	..	..	..	..	..

.. Not available

Note: Detailed metadata at: *http://metalinks.oecd.org/ins/20230516/3f06.*

Source: *OECD Insurance Statistics (database)*

Table 2. Number of companies and employees

	2014	2015	2016	2017	2018	2019	2020	2021
2.1 Number of companies								
Life								
Domestic undertakings	24	24	24	24	24	..	24	23
Foreign controlled undertakings	7	7	8	8	8	..	9	9
Foreign companies (branches)	1	1	1	1	1	..	0	..
All undertakings	25	25	25	25	25	..	24	23
Non-life								
Domestic undertakings	17	17	17	18	17	..	17	16
Foreign controlled undertakings	4	4	4	5	4	..	4	3
Foreign companies (branches)	5	5	5	6	5	..	4	4
All undertakings	22	22	22	24	22	..	21	20
Composite, all undertakings	**0**	**0**	**0**	..	..	..	..	..
Reinsurance								
Domestic undertakings	1	1	1	1	1	..	1	1
Foreign controlled undertakings	0	0	0	0	0	..	0	..
Foreign companies (branches)	8	8	9	9	9	..	9	9
All undertakings	9	9	10	10	10	..	10	10
Total								
Domestic undertakings	42	42	42	43	42	..	42	40
Foreign controlled undertakings	11	11	12	13	12	..	13	12
Foreign companies (branches)	14	14	15	16	15	..	13	13
All undertakings	56	56	57	59	57	..	55	53
2.2 Number of employees								
Insurance undertakings	61 158	59 685	58 833	57 854	58 833	..	58 617	56 625
Intermediaries	245 127	235 319	229 292	222 411	229 292	..	197 418	170 240
Total	306 285	295 004	288 125	280 265	288 125	..	256 035	226 865

.. Not available
Note: Detailed metadata at: *http://metalinks.oecd.org/ins/20230516/3f06.*
Source: *OECD Insurance Statistics (database)*

LATVIA

Table 1. Selected aggregates

Million EUR

	2014	2015	2016	2017	2018	2019	2020	2021
1.1 Insurance business written in the reporting country								
1.1.1 Insurance business, by ownership								
Gross premiums								
Domestic undertakings	371	379	364	419	489	569	517	521
Foreign controlled undertakings	151	188	267	293	352	446	419	431
Foreign companies (branches)	146	152	168	227	267	289	281	328
All undertakings	517	531	532	646	756	857	798	849
Premiums ceded								
Domestic undertakings	19	22	25	44	77	83	67	68
Foreign controlled undertakings	4	7	18	27	54	58	58	60
Foreign companies (branches)	..	..	..	..	..	..	..	..
All undertakings	19	22	25	44	77	83	67	68
Net written premiums								
Domestic undertakings	352	357	339	375	412	486	449	453
Foreign controlled undertakings	147	182	249	266	298	388	360	371
Foreign companies (branches)	146	152	168	227	267	289	281	328
All undertakings	498	509	507	602	679	774	731	781
1.1.2 Insurance business on foreign risks, gross premiums								
Life	..	..	0	0	..	..	..	..
Non-life	..	..	160	204	234	226	189	189
Composite	..	..	0	0	0	69	70	72
of which:								
Life	..	..	0	0	0	69	70	72
Non-life	..	..	..	0	..	..	..	..
Total	..	..	160	204	234	296	259	262
1.1.3 Life insurance payments, by class, gross premiums								
Annuities	0	0	11	18	25	41	59	58
Unit linked	34	43	45	57	55	102	97	114
Other life insurance	73	72	68	70	65	85	85	86
Total life insurance	107	115	124	145	145	228	241	258
of which: *Pension contracts*	0	0	..	..	..	..	37	25
1.1.4 Non-life insurance payments, by class, gross premiums								
Motor vehicle insurance	222	221	229	301	381	370	319	307
Marine, aviation and other transport insurance	2	2	2	5	4	4	3	2
Freight insurance	3	3	3	1	3	3	3	4
Fire and other property damage insurance	86	84	76	84	90	104	95	117
Pecuniary loss insurance	13	14	12	11	16	20	21	20
General liability insurance	21	21	19	19	21	23	21	26
Accident and health	52	58	55	63	78	85	84	100
of which: *Health*	42	48	45	54	64	71	71	85
Other non-life insurance	12	13	13	16	18	20	11	15
Treaty reinsurance	0	0	0	0	0	0	0	0
Total non-life insurance	411	416	409	501	611	629	557	591
1.2 Gross claims payments								
Life								
Domestic undertakings	26	29	0	0	..	..	..	0
Foreign controlled undertakings	24	27	0	0	0	..	..	0
Foreign companies (branches)	31	34	0	0	..	..	..	0
All undertakings	57	63	0	0	..	..	..	..
Non-life								
Domestic undertakings	184	198	180	193	229	303	245	247
Foreign controlled undertakings	77	92	139	126	170	231	186	198
Foreign companies (branches)	43	50	60	78	86	101	105	127
All undertakings	226	248	240	271	315	404	350	374
Composite								
Domestic undertakings	..	..	33	43	43	86	81	97
Foreign controlled undertakings	..	..	27	31	34	77	70	85
Foreign companies (branches)	..	..	40	47	48	59	71	70
All undertakings	..	..	72	90	91	145	152	167
of which:								
Life	..	..	72	90	91	145	152	167
Domestic undertakings	..	..	33	43	43	86	81	97
Foreign controlled undertakings	..	..	27	31	34	77	70	85
Foreign companies (branches)	..	..	40	47	48	59	71	70
All undertakings	..	..	72	90	91	145	152	167
Non-life	..	..	..	0	..	..	..	..
Domestic undertakings	..	..	..	0	..	..	..	..
Foreign controlled undertakings	..	..	..	0	..	..	..	..
Foreign companies (branches)	..	..	..	0	..	..	..	..
All undertakings	..	..	..	0	..	..	..	..
Total								
Domestic undertakings	209	227	213	236	272	388	325	344
Foreign controlled undertakings	102	119	166	158	203	308	256	284
Foreign companies (branches)	73	83	99	125	134	161	176	198
All undertakings	283	311	312	361	406	549	501	541

Table 1. Selected aggregates *(cont.)*

Million EUR

	2014	2015	2016	2017	2018	2019	2020	2021
1.3 Commissions								
Life								
Domestic undertakings	1	0	0	0	0	..	..	..
Foreign controlled undertakings	1	1	0	0	0	..	..	..
Foreign companies (branches)	5	6	..	..	..	..	..	..
All undertakings	6	6	0	0	0	..	..	..
Non-life								
Domestic undertakings	45	34	32	40	65	60	51	51
Foreign controlled undertakings	7	11	16	13	37	38	37	39
Foreign companies (branches)	12	13	..	..	..	..	..	..
All undertakings	58	47	32	40	65	60	51	51
Composite								
Domestic undertakings	..	..	0	1	1	6	7	9
Foreign controlled undertakings	..	..	0	0	1	6	7	8
Foreign companies (branches)	..	..	..	..	..	..	..	..
All undertakings	..	..	0	1	1	6	7	9
of which:								
Life	..	..	0	1	1	6	7	9
Domestic undertakings	..	..	0	1	1	6	7	9
Foreign controlled undertakings	..	..	0	0	1	6	7	8
Foreign companies (branches)	..	..	..	..	..	..	..	..
All undertakings	..	..	0	1	1	6	7	9
Non-life	..	..	..	0	..	..	..	..
Domestic undertakings	..	..	..	0	..	..	..	..
Foreign controlled undertakings	..	..	..	0	..	..	..	..
Foreign companies (branches)	..	..	..	..	..	..	..	..
All undertakings	..	..	..	0	..	..	..	..
Total								
Domestic undertakings	46	34	33	41	65	66	59	59
Foreign controlled undertakings	8	11	16	14	37	44	44	48
Foreign companies (branches)	17	19	..	..	..	..	..	..
All undertakings	64	53	33	41	65	66	59	59
1.4 Gross operating expenses								
Life								
Domestic undertakings	4	4	0	0	0	..	..	0
Foreign controlled undertakings	4	4	0	0	0	..	..	0
Foreign companies (branches)	..	..	..	..	..	..	..	..
All undertakings	4	4	0	0	0	..	..	0
Non-life								
Domestic undertakings	108	109	56	87	119	118	111	113
Foreign controlled undertakings	40	51	30	51	81	87	88	93
Foreign companies (branches)	..	..	..	..	..	..	..	..
All undertakings	108	109	56	87	119	118	111	113
Composite								
Domestic undertakings	..	..	4	5	5	17	18	19
Foreign controlled undertakings	..	..	4	4	5	16	18	18
Foreign companies (branches)	..	..	..	..	..	..	..	..
All undertakings	..	..	4	5	5	17	18	19
of which:								
Life	..	..	4	5	5	17	18	19
Domestic undertakings	..	..	4	5	5	17	18	19
Foreign controlled undertakings	..	..	4	4	5	16	18	18
Foreign companies (branches)	..	..	..	..	..	..	..	..
All undertakings	..	..	4	5	5	17	18	19
Non-life	..	..	..	0	..	..	..	..
Domestic undertakings	..	..	..	0	..	..	..	..
Foreign controlled undertakings	..	..	..	0	..	..	..	..
Foreign companies (branches)	..	..	..	..	..	..	..	..
All undertakings	..	..	..	0	..	..	..	..
Total								
Domestic undertakings	112	113	60	92	124	135	129	132
Foreign controlled undertakings	44	55	34	55	86	104	105	111
Foreign companies (branches)	..	..	..	..	..	..	..	..
All undertakings	112	113	60	92	124	135	129	132

Table 1. Selected aggregates *(cont.)*

Million EUR

	2014	2015	2016	2017	2018	2019	2020	2021
1.5 Insurance business written abroad by branches, gross premiums								
Life								
Branches and agencies	0	0	0	0	..	..	..	0
Subsidaries	..	..	..	..	..	..	..	0
Total	0	0	0	0	..	..	..	0
Non-life								
Branches and agencies	168	157	158	203	233	226	189	189
Subsidaries	..	..	..	..	..	..	..	..
Total	168	157	158	203	233	226	189	189
Composite								
Branches and agencies	..	..	0	0	..	69	70	72
Subsidaries	..	..	..	..	..	..	..	..
Total	..	..	0	0	..	69	70	72
of which:								
Life	..	..	0	0	..	69	70	72
Branches and agencies	..	..	0	0	..	69	70	72
Subsidaries	..	..	..	..	..	..	..	..
Total	..	..	0	0	..	69	70	72
Non-life	..	..	..	0	..	..	..	..
Branches and agencies	..	..	..	0	..	..	..	..
Subsidaries	..	..	..	..	..	..	..	..
Total	..	..	..	0	..	..	..	..
Total								
Branches and agencies	168	157	158	203	233	296	259	262
Subsidaries	..	..	..	..	..	..	..	0
Total	168	157	158	203	233	296	259	262

.. Not available

Note: Detailed metadata at: *http://metalinks.oecd.org/ins/20230516/eca0.*

Source: *OECD Insurance Statistics (database)*

LATVIA

Table 2. Number of companies and employees

	2014	2015	2016	2017	2018	2019	2020	2021
2.1 Number of companies								
Life								
Domestic undertakings	2	2	..	0	0	0	..	..
Foreign controlled undertakings	1	1	..	0	0	0	..	..
Foreign companies (branches)	5	4	..	0	0	0	..	..
All undertakings	7	6	..	0	0	..	..	..
Non-life								
Domestic undertakings	5	6	5	4	4	4	4	4
Foreign controlled undertakings	2	3	3	2	2	2	2	2
Foreign companies (branches)	9	10	8	7	7	8	7	7
All undertakings	14	16	13	11	11	12	11	11
Composite								
Domestic undertakings	0	0	2	2	2	2	2	2
Foreign controlled undertakings	0	0	1	1	1	1	1	1
Foreign companies (branches)	0	0	4	4	4	4	4	4
All undertakings	0	0	6	6	6	6	6	6
Reinsurance								
Domestic undertakings	0	0	..	0	..	..	..	..
Foreign controlled undertakings	0	0	..	0	..	..	..	..
Foreign companies (branches)	0	0	..	0	..	..	..	..
All undertakings	0	0	..	0	..	..	..	..
Total								
Domestic undertakings	7	8	7	6	6	6	6	6
Foreign controlled undertakings	3	4	4	3	3	3	3	3
Foreign companies (branches)	14	14	12	11	11	12	11	11
All undertakings	21	22	19	17	17	18	17	17
2.2 Number of employees								
Insurance undertakings	2 121	1 047	..	..	..	..	..	..
Intermediaries	773	905	..	..	..	..	..	..
Total	2 894	1 952	..	..	..	..	..	..

.. Not available
Note: Detailed metadata at: *http://metalinks.oecd.org/ins/20230516/eca0*.
Source: *OECD Insurance Statistics (database)*

LITHUANIA

Table 1. Selected aggregates

Million EUR

	2014	2015	2016	2017	2018	2019	2020	2021
1.1 Insurance business written in the reporting country								
1.1.1 Insurance business, by ownership								
Gross premiums								
Domestic undertakings	303	326	393	425	447	430	435	484
Foreign controlled undertakings	294	316	383	416	437	419	425	473
Foreign companies (branches)	298	319	317	367	432	516	520	557
All undertakings	601	645	710	793	878	946	955	1 041
Premiums ceded								
Domestic undertakings	8	8	21	27	29	23	22	28
Foreign controlled undertakings	8	8	21	27	29	23	22	28
Foreign companies (branches)	21	24	15	40	55	63	46	47
All undertakings	29	32	36	68	84	86	69	75
Net written premiums								
Domestic undertakings	295	318	372	398	418	407	413	456
Foreign controlled undertakings	285	308	362	388	408	397	403	445
Foreign companies (branches)	277	295	302	327	376	453	473	510
All undertakings	572	613	674	725	794	860	886	966
1.1.2 Insurance business on foreign risks, gross premiums								
Life	..	..	..	..	..	..	..	..
Non-life	..	..	..	..	..	..	..	..
Composite	..	..	..	..	..	..	..	..
of which:								
Life	..	..	..	..	..	..	..	..
Non-life	..	..	..	..	..	..	..	..
Total	..	..	..	..	..	..	..	..
1.1.3 Life insurance payments, by class, gross premiums								
Annuities	4	5	6	7	7	6	5	3
Unit linked	152	170	157	137	151	170	189	218
Other life insurance	59	60	84	88	90	94	96	98
Total life insurance	215	236	247	231	248	270	291	319
***of which:** Pension contracts*	..	..	1	..	..	..	..	..
1.1.4 Non-life insurance payments, by class, gross premiums								
Motor vehicle insurance	227	236	273	353	403	420	396	408
Marine, aviation and other transport insurance	2	2	2	2	2	1	1	1
Freight insurance	2	2	2	3	3	3	3	4
Fire and other property damage insurance	79	89	98	103	109	120	130	153
Pecuniary loss insurance	18	17	17	20	23	25	27	29
General liability insurance	20	20	20	21	22	24	24	28
Accident and health	37	42	49	56	65	78	79	95
***of which:** Health*	21	24	30	35	42	51	51	55
Other non-life insurance	1	1	2	3	3	4	4	4
Treaty reinsurance	..	..	..	0	0	0	0	0
Total non-life insurance	386	409	463	561	630	675	664	722
1.2 Gross claims payments								
Life								
Domestic undertakings	13	15	26	29	32	34	30	34
Foreign controlled undertakings	13	15	23	26	29	30	27	31
Foreign companies (branches)	47	42	45	56	48	45	68	74
All undertakings	60	57	71	85	80	79	98	108
Non-life								
Domestic undertakings	105	116	134	169	153	168	172	196
Foreign controlled undertakings	92	102	134	169	153	168	172	196
Foreign companies (branches)	111	113	117	126	158	184	187	194
All undertakings	216	229	251	295	311	353	360	390
Composite								
Domestic undertakings	35	40	43	65	46	20	21	22
Foreign controlled undertakings	33	38	43	65	46	20	21	22
Foreign companies (branches)	4	6	8	11	15	47	22	28
All undertakings	40	46	51	75	62	67	43	49
of which:								
Life	35	40	43	66	49	51	28	32
Domestic undertakings	32	36	39	60	42	15	18	18
Foreign controlled undertakings	30	34	39	60	42	15	18	18
Foreign companies (branches)	2	3	4	6	7	36	11	14
All undertakings	35	40	43	66	49	51	28	32
Non-life	5	6	8	9	13	16	14	18
Domestic undertakings	3	4	4	4	4	5	3	4
Foreign controlled undertakings	3	4	4	4	4	5	3	4
Foreign companies (branches)	2	2	4	5	9	11	11	14
All undertakings	5	6	8	9	13	16	14	18
Total								
Domestic undertakings	154	171	203	263	231	222	223	252
Foreign controlled undertakings	138	155	200	260	228	219	220	249
Foreign companies (branches)	163	161	170	193	221	277	278	295
All undertakings	316	332	373	456	453	499	501	547

LITHUANIA

Table 1. Selected aggregates *(cont.)*

Million EUR

	2014	2015	2016	2017	2018	2019	2020	2021
1.3 Commissions								
Life								
Domestic undertakings	0	0	0	0	0	0	0	0
Foreign controlled undertakings	0	0	0	0	0	0	0	0
Foreign companies (branches)	0	0	0	0	0	0	0	0
All undertakings	0	0	0	0	0	0	0	0
Non-life								
Domestic undertakings	1	0	2	5	7	5	5	5
Foreign controlled undertakings	1	0	2	5	7	5	5	5
Foreign companies (branches)	3	3	2	7	12	11	11	15
All undertakings	3	3	4	12	19	16	16	20
Composite								
Domestic undertakings	1	1	0	0	0	0	0	0
Foreign controlled undertakings	1	1	0	0	0	0	0	0
Foreign companies (branches)	0	1	1	1	1	1	1	2
All undertakings	1	1	1	1	2	2	2	2
of which:								
Life	..	1	1	1	2	2	2	2
Domestic undertakings	..	1	0	0	0	0	0	0
Foreign controlled undertakings	..	1	0	0	0	0	0	0
Foreign companies (branches)	..	1	1	1	1	1	1	2
All undertakings	..	1	1	1	2	2	2	2
Non-life	..	0	0	0	0	0	0	0
Domestic undertakings	..	0	0	0	0	0	0	0
Foreign controlled undertakings	..	0	0	0	0	0	0	0
Foreign companies (branches)	..	0	0	0	0	0	0	0
All undertakings	..	0	0	0	0	0	0	0
Total								
Domestic undertakings	1	1	3	5	7	6	6	5
Foreign controlled undertakings	1	1	3	5	7	6	6	5
Foreign companies (branches)	3	4	3	8	13	12	12	16
All undertakings	4	5	6	13	21	18	18	22
1.4 Gross operating expenses								
Life								
Domestic undertakings	9	12	16	16	16	17	18	19
Foreign controlled undertakings	9	12	14	14	15	15	15	16
Foreign companies (branches)	8	6	7	6	6	7	8	17
All undertakings	17	18	22	21	22	24	25	36
Non-life								
Domestic undertakings	71	97	87	90	94	98	101	103
Foreign controlled undertakings	68	94	85	89	92	96	99	101
Foreign companies (branches)	63	95	63	65	76	81	80	81
All undertakings	134	192	150	155	170	179	181	184
Composite								
Domestic undertakings	17	28	9	14	14	7	7	8
Foreign controlled undertakings	16	25	9	14	14	7	7	8
Foreign companies (branches)	9	29	12	13	14	23	23	20
All undertakings	27	56	22	26	28	30	30	28
of which:								
Life	26	55	20	24	25	27	27	25
Domestic undertakings	17	27	8	13	13	6	6	7
Foreign controlled undertakings	15	24	8	13	13	6	6	7
Foreign companies (branches)	9	28	12	11	12	21	21	18
All undertakings	26	55	20	24	25	27	27	25
Non-life	1	2	2	2	3	3	3	3
Domestic undertakings	1	1	1	1	1	1	1	1
Foreign controlled undertakings	1	1	1	1	1	1	1	1
Foreign companies (branches)	0	1	1	1	2	2	2	2
All undertakings	1	2	2	2	3	3	3	3
Total								
Domestic undertakings	97	137	111	120	124	122	125	130
Foreign controlled undertakings	93	131	108	116	121	118	121	125
Foreign companies (branches)	81	130	82	83	96	111	111	118
All undertakings	178	267	194	203	220	234	236	247

Table 1. Selected aggregates *(cont.)*

Million EUR

	2014	2015	2016	2017	2018	2019	2020	2021
1.5 Insurance business written abroad by branches, gross premiums								
Life								
Branches and agencies	0	0	0	0	0	0	0	0
Subsidaries	..	..	..	..	..	..	..	0
Total	0	0	0	0	0	0	0	0
Non-life								
Branches and agencies	17	40	65	115	142	150	167	207
Subsidaries	..	..	..	..	..	..	..	0
Total	17	40	65	115	142	150	167	207
Composite								
Branches and agencies	31	37	40	46	46	46	50	54
Subsidaries	..	..	..	..	..	..	..	0
Total	31	37	40	46	46	46	50	54
of which:								
Life	14	18	19	22	22	21	23	25
Branches and agencies	14	18	19	22	22	21	23	25
Subsidaries	..	..	..	..	..	..	..	0
Total	14	18	19	22	22	21	23	25
Non-life	17	20	21	24	24	25	26	30
Branches and agencies	17	20	21	24	24	25	26	30
Subsidaries	..	..	..	..	..	..	..	0
Total	17	20	21	24	24	25	26	30
Total								
Branches and agencies	48	77	105	161	188	196	217	261
Subsidaries	..	..	..	..	..	..	..	0
Total	48	77	105	161	188	196	217	261

.. Not available

Note: Detailed metadata at: *http://metalinks.oecd.org/ins/20230516/4ab7*.

Source: *OECD Insurance Statistics (database)*

Table 2. Number of companies and employees

	2014	2015	2016	2017	2018	2019	2020	2021
2.1 Number of companies								
Life								
Domestic undertakings	1	1	3	3	3	3	3	3
Foreign controlled undertakings	1	1	2	2	2	2	2	2
Foreign companies (branches)	3	3	2	2	2	2	3	3
All undertakings	4	4	5	5	5	5	6	6
Non-life								
Domestic undertakings	5	5	4	4	4	4	4	4
Foreign controlled undertakings	2	3	3	3	3	3	3	3
Foreign companies (branches)	10	10	9	9	8	8	8	7
All undertakings	15	15	13	13	12	12	12	11
Composite								
Domestic undertakings	4	4	2	2	2	1	1	1
Foreign controlled undertakings	3	3	2	2	2	1	1	1
Foreign companies (branches)	1	1	1	1	1	2	1	1
All undertakings	5	5	3	3	3	3	2	2
Reinsurance								
Domestic undertakings	..	..	..	..	..	..	0	0
Foreign controlled undertakings	..	..	..	..	..	..	0	0
Foreign companies (branches)	..	..	..	..	..	..	0	0
All undertakings	..	..	..	..	..	..	0	0
Total								
Domestic undertakings	10	10	9	9	9	8	8	8
Foreign controlled undertakings	6	7	7	7	7	6	6	6
Foreign companies (branches)	14	14	12	12	11	12	12	11
All undertakings	24	24	21	21	20	20	20	19
2.2 Number of employees								
Insurance undertakings	4 414	4 482	4 562	4 599	4 569	4 409	3 850	3 850
Intermediaries	1 433	1 441	1 480	1 463	1 459	1 480	1 429	1 429
Total	5 847	5 923	6 042	6 062	6 028	5 889	5 279	5 279

.. Not available

Note: Detailed metadata at: *http://metalinks.oecd.org/ins/20230516/4ab7*.

Source: *OECD Insurance Statistics (database)*

LUXEMBOURG

Table 1. Selected aggregates

Million EUR

	2014	2015	2016	2017	2018	2019	2020	2021
1.1 Insurance business written in the reporting country								
1.1.1 Insurance business, by ownership								
Gross premiums								
Domestic undertakings	21 712	19 100	18 259	21 446	20 702	23 692	19 810	26 809
Foreign controlled undertakings	20 356	17 075	13 690	18 728	18 360	21 280	14 361	19 067
Foreign companies (branches)	76	78	70	77	77	1 435	1 355	2 611
All undertakings	21 788	19 178	18 329	21 523	20 779	25 128	21 165	29 419
Premiums ceded								
Domestic undertakings	6 122	3 030	3 235	3 026	4 794	6 325	3 574	4 642
Foreign controlled undertakings	5 863	2 770	2 943	2 657	4 452	6 126	3 288	4 309
Foreign companies (branches)	33	26	31	27	33	456	475	534
All undertakings	6 155	3 056	3 267	3 053	4 827	6 781	4 050	5 175
Net written premiums								
Domestic undertakings	15 590	16 070	15 024	18 421	15 908	17 367	16 235	22 167
Foreign controlled undertakings	14 493	14 305	10 747	16 070	13 907	15 155	11 073	14 759
Foreign companies (branches)	43	52	39	50	44	980	880	2 077
All undertakings	15 633	16 122	15 063	18 470	15 952	18 347	17 115	24 244
1.1.2 Insurance business on foreign risks, gross premiums								
Life	18 455	16 383	15 071	18 182	17 356	19 705	16 131	22 671
Non-life	438	587	621	784	658	1 014	1 148	2 154
Composite	0	0	0	0	0	1 344	1 295	1 377
of which:								
Life	0	0	0	0	0	1 133	1 073	1 132
Non-life	0	0	0	0	0	211	222	245
Total	18 893	16 969	15 692	18 967	18 014	22 063	18 574	26 202
1.1.3 Life insurance payments, by class, gross premiums								
Annuities	..	..	..	..	..	..	..	..
Unit linked	11 086	12 874	11 949	15 426	12 966	14 616	13 063	18 994
Other life insurance	9 103	4 685	4 767	4 283	6 064	6 994	4 532	5 628
Total life insurance	20 190	17 559	16 716	19 709	19 030	21 610	17 595	24 621
***of which:** Pension contracts*	..	..	..	..	..	..	..	..
1.1.4 Non-life insurance payments, by class, gross premiums								
Motor vehicle insurance	..	..	..	..	..	..	..	..
Marine, aviation and other transport insurance	..	..	..	..	..	..	..	..
Freight insurance	..	..	..	..	..	..	..	..
Fire and other property damage insurance	..	..	..	..	..	..	..	..
Pecuniary loss insurance	..	..	..	..	..	..	..	..
General liability insurance	..	..	..	..	..	..	..	..
Accident and health	..	..	..	..	..	..	..	..
***of which:** Health*	..	..	..	..	..	..	..	..
Other non-life insurance	..	..	..	..	..	..	..	..
Treaty reinsurance	..	..	..	..	..	..	..	..
Total non-life insurance	1 339	1 476	1 554	1 767	1 707	2 339	2 462	3 637
1.2 Gross claims payments								
Life								
Domestic undertakings	10 597	9 995	11 802	12 002	11 103	11 861	13 703	22 804
Foreign controlled undertakings	10 214	9 032	11 035	11 291	10 262	10 534	10 591	19 801
Foreign companies (branches)	25	27	28	27	26	60	841	1 044
All undertakings	10 622	10 023	11 829	12 029	11 129	11 921	14 544	23 849
Non-life								
Domestic undertakings	809	900	860	961	987	1 192	1 363	2 969
Foreign controlled undertakings	428	512	766	500	488	552	843	1 781
Foreign companies (branches)	36	18	31	37	26	34	28	34
All undertakings	845	918	891	999	1 014	1 225	1 391	3 004
Composite								
Domestic undertakings	0	0	0	0	0	0	0	0
Foreign controlled undertakings	0	0	0	0	0	0	0	0
Foreign companies (branches)	133	17	8	8	9	754	158	-8 774
All undertakings	133	17	8	8	9	754	158	-8 774
of which:								
Life	130	17	8	8	9	624	4	-8 926
Domestic undertakings	0	0	0	0	0	0	0	0
Foreign controlled undertakings	0	0	0	0	0	0	0	0
Foreign companies (branches)	130	17	8	8	9	624	4	-8 926
All undertakings	130	17	8	8	9	624	4	-8 926
Non-life	3	0	0	0	0	130	154	152
Domestic undertakings	0	0	0	0	0	0	0	0
Foreign controlled undertakings	0	0	0	0	0	0	0	0
Foreign companies (branches)	3	0	0	0	0	130	154	152
All undertakings	3	0	0	0	0	130	154	152
Total								
Domestic undertakings	11 406	10 896	12 661	12 964	12 091	13 053	15 066	25 774
Foreign controlled undertakings	10 642	9 544	11 802	11 791	10 751	11 086	11 433	21 582
Foreign companies (branches)	195	62	66	72	61	848	1 027	-7 696
All undertakings	11 600	10 958	12 728	13 036	12 152	13 900	16 093	18 078

Table 1. Selected aggregates *(cont.)*

Million EUR

	2014	2015	2016	2017	2018	2019	2020	2021
1.3 Commissions								
Life								
Domestic undertakings	317	326	291	320	312	319	306	300
Foreign controlled undertakings	297	289	186	283	276	273	226	200
Foreign companies (branches)	0	0	0	0	0	0	0	0
All undertakings	317	326	292	320	312	319	306	300
Non-life								
Domestic undertakings	211	237	251	284	283	344	343	472
Foreign controlled undertakings	109	122	143	151	140	194	188	290
Foreign companies (branches)	9	9	9	8	7	9	8	7
All undertakings	221	246	260	292	290	353	351	479
Composite								
Domestic undertakings	0	0	0	0	0	0	0	0
Foreign controlled undertakings	0	0	0	0	0	0	0	0
Foreign companies (branches)	3	4	4	3	0	0	0	48
All undertakings	3	4	4	3	0	0	0	48
of which:								
Life	3	4	4	3	0	0	0	48
Domestic undertakings	0	0	0	0	0	0	0	0
Foreign controlled undertakings	0	0	0	0	0	0	0	0
Foreign companies (branches)	3	4	4	3	0	0	0	48
All undertakings	3	4	4	3	0	0	0	48
Non-life	0	0	0	0	0	0	0	0
Domestic undertakings	0	0	0	0	0	0	0	0
Foreign controlled undertakings	0	0	0	0	0	0	0	0
Foreign companies (branches)	0	0	0	0	0	0	0	0
All undertakings	0	0	0	0	0	0	0	0
Total								
Domestic undertakings	528	563	542	604	595	662	649	772
Foreign controlled undertakings	406	411	329	435	416	467	413	489
Foreign companies (branches)	13	14	14	11	7	9	8	55
All undertakings	541	576	556	615	602	672	657	828
1.4 Gross operating expenses								
Life								
Domestic undertakings	376	406	417	433	450	470	483	542
Foreign controlled undertakings	358	374	352	392	411	422	403	432
Foreign companies (branches)	1	0	1	1	1	0	30	30
All undertakings	376	406	418	433	450	470	513	572
Non-life								
Domestic undertakings	72	82	81	96	59	125	111	151
Foreign controlled undertakings	41	46	78	58	17	82	67	101
Foreign companies (branches)	2	2	3	3	5	6	4	6
All undertakings	74	84	84	99	64	131	116	157
Composite								
Domestic undertakings	0	0	0	0	0	0	0	0
Foreign controlled undertakings	0	0	0	0	0	0	..	0
Foreign companies (branches)	1	1	1	1	1	17	4	12
All undertakings	1	1	1	1	1	17	4	12
of which:								
Life	1	1	1	1	1	16	0	8
Domestic undertakings	0	0	0	0	0	0	0	0
Foreign controlled undertakings	0	0	0	0	0	0	..	0
Foreign companies (branches)	1	1	1	1	1	16	0	8
All undertakings	1	1	1	1	1	16	0	8
Non-life	0	0	0	0	0	1	3	4
Domestic undertakings	0	0	0	0	0	0	0	0
Foreign controlled undertakings	0	0	0	0	0	0	..	0
Foreign companies (branches)	0	0	0	0	0	1	3	4
All undertakings	0	0	0	0	0	1	3	4
Total								
Domestic undertakings	448	488	498	529	509	595	594	693
Foreign controlled undertakings	399	421	430	450	428	504	471	533
Foreign companies (branches)	4	3	4	5	6	23	38	48
All undertakings	451	491	502	534	515	618	632	741

Table 1. Selected aggregates *(cont.)*

Million EUR

	2014	2015	2016	2017	2018	2019	2020	2021
1.5 Insurance business written abroad by branches, gross premiums								
Life								
Branches and agencies	3 250	3 552	4 622	3 492	4 746	3 999	3 354	3 544
Subsidaries	..	..	..	..	..	..	..	..
Total	3 250	3 552	4 622	3 492	4 746	3 999	3 354	3 544
Non-life								
Branches and agencies	1 831	1 965	2 022	1 957	2 847	10 306	10 799	11 534
Subsidaries	..	..	..	..	..	..	..	..
Total	1 831	1 965	2 022	1 957	2 847	10 306	10 799	11 534
Composite								
Branches and agencies	0	0	0	0	0	0	0	0
Subsidaries	..	..	..	..	..	..	..	..
Total	0	0	0	0	0	0	0	0
of which:								
Life	0	0	0	0	0	0	0	0
Branches and agencies	0	0	0	0	0	0	0	0
Subsidaries	..	..	..	..	..	..	..	..
Total	0	0	0	0	0	0	0	0
Non-life	0	0	0	0	0	0	0	0
Branches and agencies	0	0	0	0	0	0	0	0
Subsidaries	..	..	..	..	..	..	..	..
Total	0	0	0	0	0	0	0	0
Total								
Branches and agencies	5 082	5 516	6 644	5 449	7 593	14 305	14 153	15 078
Subsidaries	..	..	..	..	..	..	..	..
Total	5 082	5 516	6 644	5 449	7 593	14 305	14 153	15 078

.. Not available
Note: Detailed metadata at: *http://metalinks.oecd.org/ins/20230516/5631.*
Source: *OECD Insurance Statistics (database)*

Table 2. Number of companies and employees

	2014	2015	2016	2017	2018	2019	2020	2021
2.1 Number of companies								
Life								
Domestic undertakings	44	43	40	39	38	36	33	32
Foreign controlled undertakings	39	38	34	35	30	30	28	27
Foreign companies (branches)	2	2	3	3	3	2	2	4
All undertakings	46	45	43	42	41	38	35	36
Non-life								
Domestic undertakings	34	32	33	34	41	42	40	39
Foreign controlled undertakings	8	21	24	25	33	31	30	30
Foreign companies (branches)	10	10	10	9	8	9	6	6
All undertakings	44	42	43	43	49	51	46	45
Composite								
Domestic undertakings	0	0	0	0	0	0	0	0
Foreign controlled undertakings	0	0	0	0	0	0	0	0
Foreign companies (branches)	3	3	3	2	3	3	3	3
All undertakings	3	3	3	2	3	3	3	3
Reinsurance								
Domestic undertakings	224	217	208	204	198	196	199	192
Foreign controlled undertakings	205	204	191	187	181	179	182	176
Foreign companies (branches)	0	0	0	0	0	0	0	0
All undertakings	224	217	208	204	198	196	199	192
Total								
Domestic undertakings	302	292	281	277	277	274	272	263
Foreign controlled undertakings	252	263	249	247	244	240	240	233
Foreign companies (branches)	15	15	16	14	14	14	11	13
All undertakings	317	307	297	291	291	288	283	276
2.2 Number of employees								
Insurance undertakings	6 057	6 484	6 484	7 446	8 034	10 295	13 113	13 129
Intermediaries	550	561	522	586	637	578	607	549
Total	6 607	7 045	7 006	8 032	8 671	10 873	13 720	13 678

Note: Detailed metadata at: *http://metalinks.oecd.org/ins/20230516/5631*.
Source: *OECD Insurance Statistics (database)*

MEXICO

Table 1. Selected aggregates

Million MXN

	2014	2015	2016	2017	2018	2019	2020	2021
1.1 Insurance business written in the reporting country								
1.1.1 Insurance business, by ownership								
Gross premiums								
Domestic undertakings	363 530	395 083	450 740	502 856	543 652	603 832	608 067	670 685
Foreign controlled undertakings	220 225	242 872	265 159	290 985	312 037	350 508	336 659	365 810
Foreign companies (branches)	..	..	..	..	..	..	..	..
All undertakings	363 530	395 083	450 740	502 856	543 652	603 832	608 067	670 685
Premiums ceded								
Domestic undertakings	58 378	67 135	70 420	93 577	91 472	112 667	109 313	121 602
Foreign controlled undertakings	29 932	40 217	40 674	58 977	51 768	68 212	58 064	69 094
Foreign companies (branches)	..	..	..	..	..	..	..	..
All undertakings	58 378	67 135	70 420	93 577	91 472	112 667	109 313	121 602
Net written premiums								
Domestic undertakings	305 152	327 947	380 320	409 279	452 180	491 165	498 754	549 084
Foreign controlled undertakings	190 293	202 655	224 485	232 008	260 270	282 295	278 595	296 716
Foreign companies (branches)	..	..	..	..	..	..	..	..
All undertakings	305 152	327 947	380 320	409 279	452 180	491 165	498 754	549 084
1.1.2 Insurance business on foreign risks, gross premiums								
Life	..	..	..	..	..	..	..	..
Non-life	..	..	..	..	..	..	..	..
Composite	..	..	..	..	..	..	..	..
of which:								
Life	..	..	..	..	..	..	..	..
Non-life	..	..	..	..	..	..	..	..
Total	..	..	..	..	..	..	..	..
1.1.3 Life insurance payments, by class, gross premiums								
Annuities	20 521	19 719	19 286	21 310	24 176	27 278	29 183	47 409
Unit linked	..	..	..	..	0	0	0	0
Other life insurance	148 624	162 199	189 860	193 587	218 641	243 178	245 057	252 710
Total life insurance	169 145	181 918	209 146	214 897	242 817	270 456	274 240	300 119
of which: *Pension contracts*	..	..	..	..	..	..	..	..
1.1.4 Non-life insurance payments, by class, gross premiums								
Motor vehicle insurance	68 735	75 858	91 375	103 014	110 405	115 377	102 231	108 462
Marine, aviation and other transport insurance	9 356	11 007	11 312	16 558	12 811	18 850	49 955	19 981
Freight insurance	..	..	..	..	..	..	..	..
Fire and other property damage insurance	12 232	13 815	14 497	18 115	37 929	46 830	5 591	58 290
Pecuniary loss insurance	501	947	1 131	12 278	1 774	1 933	14 643	2 623
General liability insurance	7 201	9 099	9 668	12 005	11 757	13 878	13 917	18 257
Accident and health	56 686	59 550	66 512	76 720	85 417	92 322	106 204	115 162
of which: *Health*	2 719	2 622	3 218	3 518	4 279	4 910	1 589	6 323
Other non-life insurance	38 511	42 081	45 976	48 006	39 687	42 678	39 316	46 261
Treaty reinsurance	..	..	..	..	..	..	..	..
Total non-life insurance	193 221	212 357	240 470	286 696	299 780	331 868	331 858	369 036
1.2 Gross claims payments								
Life								
Domestic undertakings	12 325	13 760	14 829	16 234	18 272	20 554	22 871	27 026
Foreign controlled undertakings	5 875	6 443	6 971	7 390	8 005	8 593	8 413	8 419
Foreign companies (branches)	..	..	..	..	..	..	..	..
All undertakings	12 325	13 760	14 829	16 234	18 272	20 554	22 871	27 026
Non-life								
Domestic undertakings	17 912	19 552	23 827	32 868	32 866	32 639	28 515	35 180
Foreign controlled undertakings	4 093	4 923	5 515	7 449	5 433	5 012	4 090	5 434
Foreign companies (branches)	..	..	..	..	..	..	..	..
All undertakings	17 912	19 552	23 827	32 868	32 866	32 639	28 515	35 180
Composite								
Domestic undertakings	148 932	162 803	185 481	204 354	224 193	256 776	258 111	295 758
Foreign controlled undertakings	104 822	109 465	125 575	136 316	151 138	179 902	169 907	191 331
Foreign companies (branches)	..	..	..	..	..	..	..	..
All undertakings	148 932	162 803	185 481	204 354	224 193	256 776	258 111	295 758
of which:								
Life	81 643	88 136	101 700	115 199	124 902	152 184	151 052	172 062
Domestic undertakings	81 643	88 136	101 700	115 199	124 902	152 184	151 052	172 062
Foreign controlled undertakings	67 855	70 802	81 029	89 726	97 155	122 938	111 557	124 174
Foreign companies (branches)	..	..	..	..	..	..	..	..
All undertakings	81 643	88 136	101 700	115 199	124 902	152 184	151 052	172 062
Non-life	67 289	74 667	83 781	89 154	99 291	104 592	107 060	123 696
Domestic undertakings	67 289	74 667	83 781	89 154	99 291	104 592	107 060	123 696
Foreign controlled undertakings	36 968	38 662	44 546	46 591	53 983	56 964	58 349	67 157
Foreign companies (branches)	..	..	..	..	..	..	..	..
All undertakings	67 289	74 667	83 781	89 154	99 291	104 592	107 060	123 696
Total								
Domestic undertakings	179 169	196 115	224 138	253 455	275 331	309 969	309 497	357 964
Foreign controlled undertakings	114 791	120 830	138 061	151 155	164 576	193 507	182 410	205 185
Foreign companies (branches)	..	..	..	..	..	..	..	..
All undertakings	179 169	196 115	224 138	253 455	275 331	309 969	309 497	357 964

MEXICO

Table 1. Selected aggregates *(cont.)*

Million MXN

	2014	2015	2016	2017	2018	2019	2020	2021
1.3 Commissions								
Life								
Domestic undertakings	749	1 045	1 155	..	..	..	..	..
Foreign controlled undertakings	74	192	247	..	..	..	..	..
Foreign companies (branches)	..	..	..	..	..	..	..	..
All undertakings	749	1 045	1 155	..	..	..	..	..
Non-life								
Domestic undertakings	9 458	7 257	9 473	..	..	..	..	..
Foreign controlled undertakings	3 808	1 888	1 618	..	..	..	..	..
Foreign companies (branches)	..	..	..	..	..	..	..	..
All undertakings	9 458	7 257	9 473	..	..	..	..	..
Composite								
Domestic undertakings	49 973	48 713	56 225	..	..	..	..	..
Foreign controlled undertakings	31 616	30 146	33 073	..	..	..	..	..
Foreign companies (branches)	..	..	..	..	..	..	..	..
All undertakings	49 973	48 713	56 225	..	..	..	..	..
of which:								
Life	21 023	22 507	26 955	..	..	..	..	..
Domestic undertakings	21 023	22 507	26 955	..	..	..	..	..
Foreign controlled undertakings	17 514	14 838	17 151	..	..	..	..	..
Foreign companies (branches)	..	..	..	..	..	..	..	..
All undertakings	21 023	22 507	26 955	..	..	..	..	..
Non-life	28 950	26 206	29 270	..	..	..	..	..
Domestic undertakings	28 950	26 206	29 270	..	..	..	..	..
Foreign controlled undertakings	14 103	15 308	15 922	..	..	..	..	..
Foreign companies (branches)	..	..	..	..	..	..	..	..
All undertakings	28 950	26 206	29 270	..	..	..	..	..
Total								
Domestic undertakings	60 180	57 016	66 853	..	..	..	..	..
Foreign controlled undertakings	35 498	32 226	34 937	..	..	..	..	..
Foreign companies (branches)	..	..	..	..	..	..	..	..
All undertakings	60 180	57 016	66 853	..	..	..	..	..
1.4 Gross operating expenses								
Life								
Domestic undertakings	1 156	1 336	1 705	1 617	1 480	1 699	1 551	2 607
Foreign controlled undertakings	570	661	723	759	734	704	718	1 492
Foreign companies (branches)	..	..	..	..	..	..	..	..
All undertakings	1 156	1 336	1 705	1 617	1 480	1 699	1 551	2 607
Non-life								
Domestic undertakings	4 198	4 924	5 852	7 490	8 280	9 060	10 304	9 168
Foreign controlled undertakings	2 010	3 137	3 249	4 041	3 412	4 004	4 934	4 354
Foreign companies (branches)	..	..	..	..	..	..	..	..
All undertakings	4 198	4 924	5 852	7 490	8 280	9 060	10 304	9 168
Composite								
Domestic undertakings	16 621	18 736	21 447	23 147	25 162	24 951	27 589	25 779
Foreign controlled undertakings	10 470	12 270	13 297	13 037	15 216	14 640	17 031	16 049
Foreign companies (branches)	..	..	..	..	..	..	..	..
All undertakings	16 621	18 736	21 447	23 147	25 162	24 951	27 589	25 779
of which:								
Life	8 486	9 990	11 792	11 674	12 701	12 400	13 701	13 204
Domestic undertakings	8 486	9 990	11 792	11 674	12 701	12 400	13 701	13 204
Foreign controlled undertakings	6 273	7 388	8 480	7 981	8 964	8 466	9 798	9 744
Foreign companies (branches)	..	..	..	..	..	..	..	..
All undertakings	8 486	9 990	11 792	11 674	12 701	12 400	13 701	13 204
Non-life	8 135	8 746	9 655	11 473	12 461	12 551	13 887	12 576
Domestic undertakings	8 135	8 746	9 655	11 473	12 461	12 551	13 887	12 576
Foreign controlled undertakings	4 198	4 882	4 818	5 055	6 252	6 174	7 233	6 306
Foreign companies (branches)	..	..	..	..	..	..	..	..
All undertakings	8 135	8 746	9 655	11 473	12 461	12 551	13 887	12 576
Total								
Domestic undertakings	21 974	24 996	29 004	32 254	34 923	35 709	39 443	37 555
Foreign controlled undertakings	13 050	16 068	17 270	17 837	19 363	19 349	22 683	21 895
Foreign companies (branches)	..	..	..	..	..	..	..	..
All undertakings	21 974	24 996	29 004	32 254	34 923	35 709	39 443	37 555

Table 1. Selected aggregates *(cont.)*

Million MXN

	2014	2015	2016	2017	2018	2019	2020	2021
1.5 Insurance business written abroad by branches, gross premiums								
Life								
Branches and agencies	..	..	..	..	..	..	..	..
Subsidaries	..	..	..	..	..	..	..	..
Total	..	..	..	..	..	..	..	..
Non-life								
Branches and agencies	..	..	..	..	..	..	..	..
Subsidaries	..	..	..	..	..	..	..	..
Total	..	..	..	..	..	..	..	..
Composite								
Branches and agencies	..	..	..	..	..	..	..	..
Subsidaries	..	..	..	..	..	..	..	..
Total	..	..	..	..	..	..	..	..
of which:								
Life	..	..	..	..	..	..	..	..
Branches and agencies	..	..	..	..	..	..	..	..
Subsidaries	..	..	..	..	..	..	..	..
Total	..	..	..	..	..	..	..	..
Non-life	..	..	..	..	..	..	..	..
Branches and agencies	..	..	..	..	..	..	..	..
Subsidaries	..	..	..	..	..	..	..	..
Total	..	..	..	..	..	..	..	..
Total								
Branches and agencies	..	..	..	..	..	..	..	..
Subsidaries	..	..	..	..	..	..	..	..
Total	..	..	..	..	..	..	..	..

.. Not available

Note: Detailed metadata at: *http://metalinks.oecd.org/ins/20230516/0b20.*

Source: *OECD Insurance Statistics (database)*

Table 2. Number of companies and employees

	2014	2015	2016	2017	2018	2019	2020	2021
2.1 Number of companies								
Life								
Domestic undertakings	16	16	17	15	15	14	13	15
Foreign controlled undertakings	9	9	10	8	8	7	6	8
Foreign companies (branches)	..	..	..	..	..	..	..	..
All undertakings	16	16	17	15	15	14	13	15
Non-life								
Domestic undertakings	49	46	44	60	58	61	62	64
Foreign controlled undertakings	26	23	22	31	28	31	31	32
Foreign companies (branches)	..	..	..	..	..	..	..	..
All undertakings	49	46	44	60	58	61	62	64
Composite								
Domestic undertakings	38	37	37	38	36	35	35	32
Foreign controlled undertakings	22	21	20	21	20	19	19	16
Foreign companies (branches)	..	..	..	..	..	..	..	..
All undertakings	38	37	37	38	36	35	35	32
Reinsurance								
Domestic undertakings	2	3	2	2	2	2	2	2
Foreign controlled undertakings	0	0	0	0	..	..	..	..
Foreign companies (branches)	..	..	..	..	..	..	..	..
All undertakings	2	3	2	2	2	2	2	2
Total								
Domestic undertakings	105	102	100	115	111	112	112	113
Foreign controlled undertakings	57	53	52	60	56	57	56	56
Foreign companies (branches)	..	..	..	..	..	..	..	..
All undertakings	105	102	100	115	111	112	112	113
2.2 Number of employees								
Insurance undertakings	14 799	19 168	..	..	..	..	..	..
Intermediaries	51 780	55 005	57 900	61 695	..	..	..	..
Total	66 579	74 173	57 900	61 695	..	..	..	..

.. Not available

Note: Detailed metadata at: *http://metalinks.oecd.org/ins/20230516/0b20.*

Source: *OECD Insurance Statistics (database)*

NETHERLANDS

Table 1. Selected aggregates

Million EUR

	2014	2015	2016	2017	2018	2019	2020	2021
1.1 Insurance business written in the reporting country								
1.1.1 Insurance business, by ownership								
Gross premiums								
Domestic undertakings	36 523	33 708	69 887	71 228	73 667	..	..	80 064
Foreign controlled undertakings	2 969	5 812	4 102	4 371	3 429	..	..	..
Foreign companies (branches)	62	0	..	..	..	..	..	2 758
All undertakings	36 585	33 708	69 887	71 228	73 667	..	..	82 822
Premiums ceded								
Domestic undertakings	3 880	2 814	1 198	1 698	1 460	..	..	3 525
Foreign controlled undertakings	1 615	1 365	287	353	84	..	..	0
Foreign companies (branches)	0	0	..	..	..	..	..	528
All undertakings	3 880	2 814	1 198	1 698	1 460	..	..	4 052
Net written premiums								
Domestic undertakings	32 643	30 894	68 689	69 530	72 207	..	..	76 540
Foreign controlled undertakings	1 354	4 447	3 815	4 018	3 345	..	..	..
Foreign companies (branches)	62	0	..	..	..	..	..	2 230
All undertakings	32 705	30 894	68 689	69 530	72 207	..	..	78 770
1.1.2 Insurance business on foreign risks, gross premiums								
Life	..	..	269	273	300	..	..	..
Non-life	..	..	534	452	1 102	..	..	..
Composite total	..	..	..	252	501	..	..	..
Total	..	..	803	977	1 903	..	..	..
1.1.3 Life insurance payments, by class, gross premiums								
Annuities	10 806	9 035	0	0	0	..	..	..
Unit linked	6 504	5 533	5 262	4 553	4 296	..	..	..
Other life insurance	150	122	8 465	8 411	7 674	..	..	..
Total life insurance	17 460	14 690	13 727	12 964	11 970	..	..	..
of which: *Pension contracts*	5 552	5 208	334	157	38	..	..	..
1.1.4 Non-life insurance payments, by class, gross premiums								
Motor vehicle insurance	3 934	3 884	3 892	4 051	4 312	..	..	..
Marine, aviation and other transport insurance	435	404	361	283	273	..	..	..
Freight insurance	231	191	..	0	0	..	..	..
Fire and other property damage insurance	3 449	3 456	3 256	3 290	3 380	..	..	..
Pecuniary loss insurance	164	176	258	206	271	..	..	..
General liability insurance	1 064	1 033	882	883	919	..	..	..
Accident and health	7 867	7 851	46 459	47 499	50 393	..	..	..
of which: *Health*	..	..	45 064	46 044	48 900	..	..	..
Other non-life insurance	1 976	2 016	1 049	1 165	1 099	..	..	..
Treaty reinsurance	..	..	..	0	0	..	..	..
Total non-life insurance	19 120	19 011	56 157	57 377	60 647	..	..	..
1.2 Gross claims payments								
Life								
Domestic undertakings	25 487	22 576	20 919	25 124	20 129	..	..	..
Foreign controlled undertakings	1 136	4 504	4 203	4 286	3 640	..	..	..
Foreign companies (branches)	0	0	..	..	..	..	..	..
All undertakings	25 487	22 576	20 919	25 124	20 129	..	..	..
Non-life								
Domestic undertakings	13 666	13 806	50 966	51 936	53 872	..	..	..
Foreign controlled undertakings	867	1 937	1 053	844	693	..	..	..
Foreign companies (branches)	149	0	..	..	..	..	..	..
All undertakings	13 815	13 806	50 966	51 936	53 872	..	..	..
Composite, all undertakings	**..**	**..**	**..**	**473**	**481**	**..**	**..**	**..**
Total								
Domestic undertakings	39 153	36 382	71 885	77 533	74 482	..	..	..
Foreign controlled undertakings	2 003	6 441	5 256	5 130	4 333	..	..	..
Foreign companies (branches)	149	0	..	..	..	..	..	..
All undertakings	39 302	36 382	71 885	77 533	74 482	..	..	..
1.3 Commissions								
Life								
Domestic undertakings	190	158	..	..	..	..	..	..
Foreign controlled undertakings	17	49	..	..	..	..	..	..
Foreign companies (branches)	0	0	..	..	..	..	..	..
All undertakings	190	158	..	..	..	..	..	..
Non-life								
Domestic undertakings	2 713	2 663	..	..	..	..	..	..
Foreign controlled undertakings	282	464	..	..	..	..	..	..
Foreign companies (branches)	21	0	..	..	..	..	..	..
All undertakings	2 734	2 663	..	..	..	..	..	..
Composite, all undertakings	**..**	**..**	**..**	**..**	**..**	**..**	**..**	**..**
Total								
Domestic undertakings	2 903	2 821	..	..	..	..	..	..
Foreign controlled undertakings	299	513	..	..	..	..	..	..
Foreign companies (branches)	21	0	..	..	..	..	..	..
All undertakings	2 924	2 821	..	..	..	..	..	..

Table 1. Selected aggregates *(cont.)*

Million EUR

	2014	2015	2016	2017	2018	2019	2020	2021
1.4 Gross operating expenses								
Life								
Domestic undertakings	2 497	2 072	2 183	2 002	1 839	..	..	..
Foreign controlled undertakings	113	378	417	356	274	..	..	..
Foreign companies (branches)	0	0	..	..	..	..	..	..
All undertakings	2 497	2 072	2 183	2 002	1 839	..	..	..
Non-life								
Domestic undertakings	4 635	4 485	6 219	6 156	6 235	..	..	..
Foreign controlled undertakings	373	771	525	550	461	..	..	..
Foreign companies (branches)	23	0	..	..	..	..	..	..
All undertakings	4 658	4 485	6 219	6 156	6 235	..	..	..
Composite, all undertakings	**..**	**..**	**..**	**115**	**71**	**..**	**..**	**..**
Total								
Domestic undertakings	7 132	6 557	8 402	8 273	8 145	..	..	..
Foreign controlled undertakings	486	1 149	942	906	735	..	..	..
Foreign companies (branches)	23	0	..	..	..	..	..	..
All undertakings	7 155	6 557	8 402	8 273	8 145	..	..	..
1.5 Insurance business written abroad by branches, gross premiums								
Life								
Branches and agencies	276	..	253	260	291	..	..	..
Subsidaries	..	..	..	..	..	..	..	..
Total	276	267	253	260	291	..	..	..
Non-life								
Branches and agencies	1 289	..	175	163	153	..	..	..
Subsidaries	..	..	..	..	..	..	..	..
Total	1 289	1 487	175	163	153	..	..	..
Composite total	**..**	**..**	**..**	**0**	**477**	**..**	**..**	**..**
Total								
Branches and agencies	1 565	..	428	423	921	..	..	..
Subsidaries	..	..	..	..	..	..	..	..
Total	1 565	1 754	428	423	921	..	..	..

.. Not available

Note: Detailed metadata at: *http://metalinks.oecd.org/ins/20230516/2431*.

Source: OECD *Insurance Statistics (database)*

NETHERLANDS

Table 2. Number of companies and employees

	2014	2015	2016	2017	2018	2019	2020	2021
2.1 Number of companies								
Life								
Domestic undertakings	38	..	31	30	27	..	..	18
Foreign controlled undertakings	7	..	11	10	6	..	..	0
Foreign companies (branches)	0	..	..	..	..	..	..	0
All undertakings	38	..	31	30	27	..	..	18
Non-life								
Domestic undertakings	136	..	107	101	96	..	..	90
Foreign controlled undertakings	8	..	9	8	7	..	..	0
Foreign companies (branches)	2	..	..	..	..	..	..	0
All undertakings	138	..	107	101	96	..	..	90
Composite, all undertakings	**0**	**0**	**0**	**0**	..	..	..	**0**
Reinsurance								
Domestic undertakings	10	..	9	9	8	..	..	6
Foreign controlled undertakings	0	..	0	0	0	..	..	0
Foreign companies (branches)	0	..	..	..	..	..	..	0
All undertakings	10	..	9	9	8	..	..	6
Total								
Domestic undertakings	184	..	147	140	131	..	..	114
Foreign controlled undertakings	15	..	20	18	13	..	..	..
Foreign companies (branches)	2	..	..	..	..	..	..	..
All undertakings	186	..	147	140	131	..	..	..
2.2 Number of employees								
Insurance undertakings	..	..	..	..	..	..	..	..
Intermediaries	..	..	..	..	..	..	..	..
Total	..	..	..	..	..	..	..	..

.. Not available

Note: Detailed metadata at: *http://metalinks.oecd.org/ins/20230516/2431*.

Source: *OECD Insurance Statistics (database)*

NEW ZEALAND

Table 1. Selected aggregates

Million NZD

	2014	2015	2016	2017	2018	2019	2020	2021
1.1 Insurance business written in the reporting country								
1.1.1 Insurance business, by ownership								
Gross premiums								
Domestic undertakings	..	..	..	..	..	9 384	9 924	..
Foreign controlled undertakings	..	..	..	..	..	6 678	7 021	..
Foreign companies (branches)	..	..	..	..	..	1 634	1 506	..
All undertakings	6 460	6 678	6 828	7 240	..	11 017	11 430	..
Premiums ceded								
Domestic undertakings	..	..	..	..	..	2 548	2 946	..
Foreign controlled undertakings	..	..	..	..	..	2 148	2 518	..
Foreign companies (branches)	..	..	..	..	..	721	776	..
All undertakings	1 292	1 305	1 789	1 852	..	3 269	3 722	..
Net written premiums								
Domestic undertakings	..	..	..	..	..	6 836	6 979	..
Foreign controlled undertakings	..	..	..	..	..	4 530	4 502	..
Foreign companies (branches)	..	..	..	..	..	912	730	..
All undertakings	7 186	7 523	7 303	7 729	..	7 748	7 708	..
1.1.2 Insurance business on foreign risks, gross premiums								
Life	..	..	..	..	..	0	0	..
Non-life	..	..	..	..	..	0	0	..
Composite	..	..	..	..	..	0	0	..
of which:								
Life	..	..	..	..	..	0	0	..
Non-life	..	..	..	..	..	0	0	..
Total	..	..	..	..	..	0	0	..
1.1.3 Life insurance payments, by class, gross premiums								
Annuities	..	..	..	..	..	1	2	..
Unit linked	..	..	..	..	..	9	5	..
Other life insurance	..	..	..	..	..	2 587	2 593	..
Total life insurance	..	..	..	..	..	2 597	2 600	..
of which: *Pension contracts*	..	..	..	..	..	0	0	..
1.1.4 Non-life insurance payments, by class, gross premiums								
Motor vehicle insurance	..	..	..	..	..	2 154	2 271	..
Marine, aviation and other transport insurance	..	..	..	..	..	149	159	..
Freight insurance	..	..	..	..	..	..	..	..
Fire and other property damage insurance	..	..	..	..	..	3 388	3 602	..
Pecuniary loss insurance	..	..	..	..	..	..	..	..
General liability insurance	..	..	..	..	..	593	655	..
Accident and health	..	..	..	..	..	1 678	1 772	..
of which: *Health*	..	..	..	..	..	1 633	1 735	..
Other non-life insurance	..	..	..	..	..	455	366	..
Treaty reinsurance	..	..	..	..	..	..	..	..
Total non-life insurance	6 460	6 678	6 828	7 240	..	8 415	8 825	..
1.2 Gross claims payments								
Life								
Domestic undertakings	..	..	..	..	..	556	474	..
Foreign controlled undertakings	..	..	..	..	..	388	286	..
Foreign companies (branches)	..	..	..	..	..	355	340	..
All undertakings	1 399	1 544	1 598	1 579	..	911	814	..
Non-life								
Domestic undertakings	..	..	..	..	..	4 730	4 487	..
Foreign controlled undertakings	..	..	..	..	..	3 119	2 879	..
Foreign companies (branches)	..	..	..	..	..	588	588	..
All undertakings	5 642	6 302	4 864	6 662	..	5 318	5 075	..
Composite								
Domestic undertakings	..	..	..	..	..	755	939	..
Foreign controlled undertakings	..	..	..	..	..	590	741	..
Foreign companies (branches)	..	..	..	..	..	84	0	..
All undertakings	..	..	..	..	..	839	939	..
of which:								
Life	..	..	..	..	..	549	652	..
Domestic undertakings	..	..	..	..	..	478	652	..
Foreign controlled undertakings	..	..	..	..	..	372	512	..
Foreign companies (branches)	..	..	..	..	..	71	0	..
All undertakings	..	..	..	..	..	549	652	..
Non-life	..	..	..	..	..	291	287	..
Domestic undertakings	..	..	..	..	..	277	287	..
Foreign controlled undertakings	..	..	..	..	..	218	228	..
Foreign companies (branches)	..	..	..	..	..	13	0	..
All undertakings	..	..	..	..	..	291	287	..
Total								
Domestic undertakings	..	..	..	..	..	6 041	5 900	..
Foreign controlled undertakings	..	..	..	..	..	4 097	3 906	..
Foreign companies (branches)	..	..	..	..	..	1 027	928	..
All undertakings	7 041	7 846	6 462	8 241	..	7 068	6 828	..

Table 1. Selected aggregates *(cont.)*

Million NZD

	2014	2015	2016	2017	2018	2019	2020	2021
1.3 Commissions								
Life								
Domestic undertakings	..	..	..	..	..	169	139	..
Foreign controlled undertakings	..	..	..	..	..	105	78	..
Foreign companies (branches)	..	..	..	..	..	35	39	..
All undertakings	..	..	..	..	..	204	178	..
Non-life								
Domestic undertakings	..	..	..	..	..	659	677	..
Foreign controlled undertakings	..	..	..	..	..	618	633	..
Foreign companies (branches)	..	..	..	..	..	190	117	..
All undertakings	..	..	..	..	..	849	793	..
Composite								
Domestic undertakings	..	..	..	..	..	313	371	..
Foreign controlled undertakings	..	..	..	..	..	196	240	..
Foreign companies (branches)	..	..	..	..	..	31	0	..
All undertakings	..	..	..	..	..	343	371	..
of which:								
Life	..	..	..	..	..	267	291	..
Domestic undertakings	..	..	..	..	..	240	291	..
Foreign controlled undertakings	..	..	..	..	..	144	184	..
Foreign companies (branches)	..	..	..	..	..	27	0	..
All undertakings	..	..	..	..	..	267	291	..
Non-life	..	..	..	..	..	76	80	..
Domestic undertakings	..	..	..	..	..	73	80	..
Foreign controlled undertakings	..	..	..	..	..	52	56	..
Foreign companies (branches)	..	..	..	..	..	3	0	..
All undertakings	..	..	..	..	..	76	80	..
Total								
Domestic undertakings	..	..	..	..	..	1 140	1 187	..
Foreign controlled undertakings	..	..	..	..	..	918	951	..
Foreign companies (branches)	..	..	..	..	..	256	155	..
All undertakings	..	..	..	..	..	1 396	1 343	..
1.4 Gross operating expenses								
Life								
Domestic undertakings	..	..	..	..	..	291	189	..
Foreign controlled undertakings	..	..	..	..	..	206	105	..
Foreign companies (branches)	..	..	..	..	..	70	48	..
All undertakings	2 384	2 323	2 489	2 476	..	360	237	..
Non-life								
Domestic undertakings	..	..	..	..	..	989	1 097	..
Foreign controlled undertakings	..	..	..	..	..	655	703	..
Foreign companies (branches)	..	..	..	..	..	153	179	..
All undertakings	7 490	8 472	6 875	8 884	..	1 142	1 275	..
Composite								
Domestic undertakings	..	..	..	..	..	342	471	..
Foreign controlled undertakings	..	..	..	..	..	258	395	..
Foreign companies (branches)	..	..	..	..	..	38	0	..
All undertakings	..	..	..	..	..	380	471	..
of which:								
Life	..	..	..	..	..	294	383	..
Domestic undertakings	..	..	..	..	..	261	383	..
Foreign controlled undertakings	..	..	..	..	..	200	327	..
Foreign companies (branches)	..	..	..	..	..	33	0	..
All undertakings	..	..	..	..	..	294	383	..
Non-life	..	..	..	..	..	86	88	..
Domestic undertakings	..	..	..	..	..	81	88	..
Foreign controlled undertakings	..	..	..	..	..	58	67	..
Foreign companies (branches)	..	..	..	..	..	5	0	..
All undertakings	..	..	..	..	..	86	88	..
Total								
Domestic undertakings	..	..	..	..	..	1 622	1 757	..
Foreign controlled undertakings	..	..	..	..	..	1 119	1 202	..
Foreign companies (branches)	..	..	..	..	..	261	226	..
All undertakings	9 874	10 795	9 364	11 360	..	1 882	1 983	..

NEW ZEALAND

Table 1. Selected aggregates *(cont.)*

Million NZD

	2014	2015	2016	2017	2018	2019	2020	2021
1.5 Insurance business written abroad by branches, gross premiums								
Life								
Branches and agencies	..	..	..	..	..	0	..	0
Subsidaries	..	..	..	..	..	..	..	..
Total	..	..	..	..	..	0	..	0
Non-life								
Branches and agencies	..	..	..	..	..	22	..	16
Subsidaries	..	..	..	..	..	..	..	..
Total	..	..	..	..	..	22	..	16
Composite								
Branches and agencies	..	..	..	..	..	0	..	0
Subsidaries	..	..	..	..	..	..	..	..
Total	..	..	..	..	..	0	..	0
of which:								
Life	..	..	..	..	..	0	..	0
Branches and agencies	..	..	..	..	..	0	..	0
Subsidaries	..	..	..	..	..	..	..	..
Total	..	..	..	..	..	0	..	0
Non-life	..	..	..	..	..	0	..	0
Branches and agencies	..	..	..	..	..	0	..	0
Subsidaries	..	..	..	..	..	..	..	..
Total	..	..	..	..	..	0	..	0
Total								
Branches and agencies	..	..	..	..	..	22	..	16
Subsidaries	..	..	..	..	..	..	..	..
Total	..	..	..	..	..	22	..	16

.. Not available

Note: Detailed metadata at: *http://metalinks.oecd.org/ins/20230516/88fc.*

Source: OECD *Insurance Statistics (database)*

NEW ZEALAND

Table 2. Number of companies and employees

	2014	2015	2016	2017	2018	2019	2020	2021
2.1 Number of companies								
Life								
Domestic undertakings	..	..	..	..	..	14	13	..
Foreign controlled undertakings	..	..	..	..	..	6	5	..
Foreign companies (branches)	..	..	..	..	..	3	3	..
All undertakings	43	30	30	30	..	17	16	..
Non-life								
Domestic undertakings	..	..	..	..	..	31	31	..
Foreign controlled undertakings	..	..	..	..	..	9	8	..
Foreign companies (branches)	..	..	..	..	..	20	20	..
All undertakings	145	102	90	87	..	51	51	..
Composite								
Domestic undertakings	..	..	..	..	..	10	10	..
Foreign controlled undertakings	..	..	..	..	..	3	3	..
Foreign companies (branches)	..	..	..	..	..	1	0	..
All undertakings	..	..	..	..	..	11	10	..
Reinsurance								
Domestic undertakings	..	..	..	..	..	0	1	..
Foreign controlled undertakings	..	..	..	..	..	0	1	..
Foreign companies (branches)	..	..	..	..	..	9	9	..
All undertakings	..	..	..	..	..	9	10	..
Total								
Domestic undertakings	..	..	..	..	..	55	55	..
Foreign controlled undertakings	..	..	..	..	..	18	17	..
Foreign companies (branches)	..	..	..	..	..	32	31	..
All undertakings	188	132	120	117	..	87	86	..
2.2 Number of employees								
Insurance undertakings	10 720	10 680	..	..	..	..	..	..
Intermediaries	..	..	..	..	..	..	..	..
Total	..	..	..	..	..	..	..	..

.. Not available

Note: Detailed metadata at: *http://metalinks.oecd.org/ins/20230516/88fc*.

Source: *OECD Insurance Statistics (database)*

NORWAY

Table 1. Selected aggregates

Million NOK

	2014	2015	2016	2017	2018	2019	2020	2021
1.1 Insurance business written in the reporting country								
1.1.1 Insurance business, by ownership								
Gross premiums								
Domestic undertakings	134 884	135 864	138 612	139 748	148 945	161 842	166 238	199 136
Foreign controlled undertakings	11 029	13 195	..	..	..	..	..	..
Foreign companies (branches)	31 867	30 638	31 150	29 049	29 917	32 324	34 607	37 377
All undertakings	166 751	166 502	169 762	168 797	178 862	194 166	200 845	236 513
Premiums ceded								
Domestic undertakings	6 891	7 973	7 053	7 061	7 109	6 671	7 364	7 551
Foreign controlled undertakings	198	218	..	..	..	..	..	..
Foreign companies (branches)	4 653	4 976	5 362	4 814	4 868	5 613	6 664	7 017
All undertakings	11 544	12 950	12 415	11 876	11 976	12 284	14 028	14 568
Net written premiums								
Domestic undertakings	127 993	127 890	131 559	132 686	141 836	155 171	158 874	191 585
Foreign controlled undertakings	10 832	12 978	..	..	..	..	..	..
Foreign companies (branches)	27 213	25 662	25 788	24 235	25 049	26 711	27 943	30 360
All undertakings	155 206	153 552	157 347	156 921	166 885	181 882	186 817	221 945
1.1.2 Insurance business on foreign risks, gross premiums								
Life	..	9	7	6	4 144	2	3	2
Non-life	11 468	11 250	10 855	10 417	10 989	12 310	16 571	15 720
Composite total	..	..	..	..	..	..	..	..
Total	11 468	11 260	10 862	10 422	15 133	12 313	16 573	15 722
1.1.3 Life insurance payments, by class, gross premiums								
Annuities	..	..	..	..	..	..	..	..
Unit linked	..	..	..	..	..	..	..	..
Other life insurance	..	..	..	..	..	..	..	..
Total life insurance	92 185	91 794	94 093	93 577	99 961	108 693	106 179	137 493
***of which:** Pension contracts*	..	..	..	..	..	..	..	..
1.1.4 Non-life insurance payments, by class, gross premiums								
Motor vehicle insurance	20 378	20 706	20 897	21 029	22 316	24 811	26 390	28 507
Marine, aviation and other transport insurance	6 574	5 201	15 291	5 292	5 203	11 270	16 064	15 988
Freight insurance	..	..	0	..	..	..	..	..
Fire and other property damage insurance	18 195	19 041	23 135	22 553	23 487	25 120	26 456	28 109
Pecuniary loss insurance	127	97	432	92	98	..	375	256
General liability insurance	1 695	1 637	2 000	1 774	1 980	3 276	3 663	3 951
Accident and health	5 608	5 553	10 526	10 288	11 075	12 004	11 951	12 886
***of which:** Health*	..	..	0	..	..	..	..	..
Other non-life insurance	21 989	13 048	7 085	6 088	12 644	8 992	9 766	9 322
Treaty reinsurance	..	..	0	..	2 099	..	..	..
Total non-life insurance	74 566	65 283	79 366	67 116	78 901	85 472	94 666	99 020
1.2 Gross claims payments								
Life								
Domestic undertakings	45 742	49 007	51 548	54 419	58 887	60 593	64 574	67 887
Foreign controlled undertakings	3 150	4 796	.. c	..	..	.. c	..	..
Foreign companies (branches)	476	235	288	281	298	288	261	270
All undertakings	46 218	49 242	51 836	54 700	59 185	60 881	64 836	68 157
Non-life								
Domestic undertakings	30 742	34 587	32 537	31 896	34 370	37 564	38 993	40 452
Foreign controlled undertakings	.. c	.. c	.. c	..	..	.. c	..	..
Foreign companies (branches)	22 287	21 584	21 146	20 655	20 427	23 006	24 786	42 172
All undertakings	53 030	56 170	53 683	52 550	54 797	60 569	63 779	82 624
Composite, all undertakings	..	..	..	..	..	..	..	..
Total								
Domestic undertakings	76 485	83 593	84 085	86 315	93 257	98 157	103 567	108 339
Foreign controlled undertakings	3 150	4 796	..	..	..	..	..	..
Foreign companies (branches)	22 763	21 819	21 434	20 935	20 725	23 294	25 047	42 442
All undertakings	99 248	105 413	105 519	107 250	113 983	121 451	128 615	150 781
1.3 Commissions								
Life								
Domestic undertakings	839	916	890	783	737	913	990	1 121
Foreign controlled undertakings	202	227	.. c	.. c	.. c	.. c	.. c	.. c
Foreign companies (branches)	0	..	..	..	..	..	..	..
All undertakings	839	916	890	783	737	913	990	1 121
Non-life								
Domestic undertakings	2 204	2 119	1 956	2 105	2 309	2 684	3 248	2 990
Foreign controlled undertakings	.. c	..	.. c	.. c	.. c	.. c	.. c	.. c
Foreign companies (branches)	1 099	1 107	950	915	916	952	1 013	1 424
All undertakings	3 303	3 226	2 906	3 020	3 224	3 636	4 260	4 414
Composite, all undertakings	..	..	..	..	..	..	..	..
Total								
Domestic undertakings	3 043	3 035	2 846	2 889	3 046	3 597	4 238	4 111
Foreign controlled undertakings	202	227	..	..	..	..	..	..
Foreign companies (branches)	1 099	1 107	950	915	916	952	1 013	1 424
All undertakings	4 142	4 142	3 797	3 804	3 961	4 549	5 250	5 535

Table 1. Selected aggregates *(cont.)*

Million NOK

	2014	2015	2016	2017	2018	2019	2020	2021
1.4 Gross operating expenses								
Life								
Domestic undertakings	7 205	7 383	7 750	7 380	7 817	8 313	8 492	8 783
Foreign controlled undertakings	807	765	.. c	..	..	..	.. c	.. c
Foreign companies (branches)	162	..	157	143	126	83	85	239
All undertakings	7 367	7 383	7 907	7 523	7 943	8 396	8 577	9 022
Non-life								
Domestic undertakings	6 585	6 138	6 139	6 956	11 045	8 474	9 700	9 302
Foreign controlled undertakings	.. c	.. c	.. c	..	..	..	.. c	.. c
Foreign companies (branches)	5 318	5 574	5 465	4 732	5 207	4 862	5 206	5 358
All undertakings	11 903	11 712	11 605	11 688	16 252	13 336	14 907	14 660
Composite, all undertakings	..	..	..	..	..	..	..	..
Total								
Domestic undertakings	13 790	13 521	13 889	14 336	18 862	16 787	18 192	18 085
Foreign controlled undertakings	807	765	..	..	..	..	..	..
Foreign companies (branches)	5 480	5 574	5 623	4 875	5 333	4 945	5 292	5 597
All undertakings	19 270	19 095	19 512	19 211	24 195	21 732	23 484	23 682
1.5 Insurance business written abroad by branches, gross premiums								
Life								
Branches and agencies	..	..	..	..	..	..	..	..
Subsidaries	..	..	..	..	..	..	..	..
Total	..	..	..	..	..	..	..	..
Non-life								
Branches and agencies	4 636	1 569	7 141	2 493	2 431	4 073	6 351	3 905
Subsidaries	.. c	..	..	..	..	..	..	..
Total	4 636	1 569	7 141	2 493	2 431	4 073	6 351	3 905
Composite total	..	..	..	..	..	..	..	..
Total								
Branches and agencies	4 636	1 569	7 141	2 493	2 431	4 073	6 351	3 905
Subsidaries	..	..	..	..	..	..	..	..
Total	4 636	1 569	7 141	2 493	2 431	4 073	6 351	3 905

.. Not available; c Confidential data
Note: Detailed metadata at: *http://metalinks.oecd.org/ins/20230516/a87f*.
Source: *OECD Insurance Statistics (database)*

Table 2. Number of companies and employees

	2014	2015	2016	2017	2018	2019	2020	2021
2.1 Number of companies								
Life								
Domestic undertakings	10	10	10	13	12	11	12	11
Foreign controlled undertakings	2	2	2	3	3	3	3	3
Foreign companies (branches)	7	7	7	6	6	6	6	9
All undertakings	17	17	17	19	18	17	18	20
Non-life								
Domestic undertakings	59	58	59	58	56	55	52	49
Foreign controlled undertakings	1	2	2	2	1	1	2	2
Foreign companies (branches)	22	21	23	23	21	24	24	25
All undertakings	81	79	82	81	77	79	76	74
Composite, all undertakings	**0**	**0**	..	..	..	..	..	..
Reinsurance								
Domestic undertakings	..	..	..	..	..	..	..	..
Foreign controlled undertakings	..	..	..	..	..	..	..	..
Foreign companies (branches)	..	..	..	..	..	..	..	..
All undertakings	..	..	..	..	..	..	..	..
Total								
Domestic undertakings	69	68	69	71	68	66	64	60
Foreign controlled undertakings	3	4	4	5	4	4	5	5
Foreign companies (branches)	29	28	30	29	27	30	30	34
All undertakings	98	96	99	100	95	96	94	94
2.2 Number of employees								
Insurance undertakings	..	..	..	..	..	..	..	..
Intermediaries	..	..	..	..	..	..	..	..
Total	..	..	..	..	..	..	..	..

.. Not available

Note: Detailed metadata at: *http://metalinks.oecd.org/ins/20230516/a87f*.

Source: *OECD Insurance Statistics (database)*

POLAND

Table 1. Selected aggregates

Million PLN

	2014	2015	2016	2017	2018	2019	2020	2021
1.1 Insurance business written in the reporting country								
1.1.1 Insurance business, by ownership								
Gross premiums								
Domestic undertakings	54 927	54 804	56 039	62 339	62 161	63 838	63 432	69 215
Foreign controlled undertakings	30 425	30 801	31 961	33 189	33 452	35 129	35 375	26 481
Foreign companies (branches)	..	..	..	..	..	..	..	..
All undertakings	54 927	54 804	56 039	62 339	62 161	63 838	63 432	69 215
Premiums ceded								
Domestic undertakings	4 170	5 197	6 765	7 216	7 235	7 940	8 332	10 140
Foreign controlled undertakings	3 533	4 355	4 798	4 664	4 396	4 768	5 171	3 827
Foreign companies (branches)	..	..	..	..	..	..	..	..
All undertakings	4 170	5 197	6 765	7 216	7 235	7 940	8 332	10 140
Net written premiums								
Domestic undertakings	50 757	49 606	49 274	55 123	54 927	55 898	55 100	59 075
Foreign controlled undertakings	26 892	26 446	27 163	28 525	29 057	30 361	30 204	22 654
Foreign companies (branches)	..	..	..	..	..	..	..	..
All undertakings	50 757	49 606	49 274	55 123	54 927	55 898	55 100	59 075
1.1.2 Insurance business on foreign risks, gross premiums								
Life	..	..	..	118	100	215	..	..
Non-life	..	..	..	181	255	422	..	..
Composite total	..	..	..	..	..	..	..	..
Total	..	..	..	299	355	637	..	..
1.1.3 Life insurance payments, by class, gross premiums								
Annuities	114	131	138	0	0	0	0	0
Unit linked	12 600	12 996	10 325	10 955	7 487	6 440	5 589	5 416
Other life insurance	15 933	14 377	13 370	13 583	14 216	14 187	14 380	15 812
Total life insurance	28 646	27 505	23 833	24 539	21 702	20 627	19 970	21 228
***of which:** Pension contracts*	356	356	..	243	230	962	214	234
1.1.4 Non-life insurance payments, by class, gross premiums								
Motor vehicle insurance	13 397	13 910	18 744	23 249	24 295	24 638	24 483	25 680
Marine, aviation and other transport insurance	275	210	185	271	319	435	412	440
Freight insurance	126	116	120	..	..	0	..	..
Fire and other property damage insurance	5 715	5 938	6 246	6 877	7 618	8 249	8 890	10 477
Pecuniary loss insurance	2 149	1 893	1 805	1 713	1 812	2 203	2 037	2 483
General liability insurance	1 964	2 134	1 915	2 064	2 297	2 518	2 719	3 022
Accident and health	2 007	2 273	2 222	2 347	2 715	2 972	3 480	4 195
***of which:** Health*	656	613	618	561	872	942	673	950
Other non-life insurance	627	804	947	1 256	1 403	2 197	1 441	1 689
Treaty reinsurance	..	..	..	..	..	0	..	..
Total non-life insurance	26 260	27 278	32 182	37 777	40 459	43 211	43 462	47 987
1.2 Gross claims payments								
Life								
Domestic undertakings	20 360	19 358	18 284	20 315	21 401	18 306	17 468	18 789
Foreign controlled undertakings	9 783	8 795	9 543	9 295	10 029	8 825	7 843	3 835
Foreign companies (branches)	..	..	..	..	..	..	..	..
All undertakings	20 360	19 358	18 284	20 315	21 401	18 306	17 468	18 789
Non-life								
Domestic undertakings	13 811	15 488	18 393	19 931	21 011	22 605	25 304	25 585
Foreign controlled undertakings	8 579	9 515	10 911	11 453	12 435	13 797	15 109	12 061
Foreign companies (branches)	..	..	..	..	..	..	..	..
All undertakings	13 811	15 488	18 393	19 931	21 011	22 605	25 304	25 585
Composite, all undertakings	..	..	..	..	..	..	..	..
Total								
Domestic undertakings	34 171	34 846	36 677	40 246	42 412	40 911	42 771	44 375
Foreign controlled undertakings	18 363	18 310	20 454	20 748	22 464	22 622	22 952	15 896
Foreign companies (branches)	..	..	..	..	..	..	..	..
All undertakings	34 171	34 846	36 677	40 246	42 412	40 911	42 771	44 375
1.3 Commissions								
Life								
Domestic undertakings	203	231	222	183	2 854	2 719	3 327	3 654
Foreign controlled undertakings	191	223	218	179	1 754	1 594	2 014	845
Foreign companies (branches)	..	..	..	..	..	..	..	..
All undertakings	203	231	222	183	2 854	2 719	3 327	3 654
Non-life								
Domestic undertakings	651	719	1 115	1 545	6 720	7 131	8 719	9 278
Foreign controlled undertakings	594	657	929	1 122	4 641	4 826	5 495	4 432
Foreign companies (branches)	..	..	..	..	..	..	..	..
All undertakings	651	719	1 115	1 545	6 720	7 131	8 719	9 278
Composite, all undertakings	..	..	..	..	..	..	..	..
Total								
Domestic undertakings	854	950	1 337	1 727	9 574	9 850	12 046	12 932
Foreign controlled undertakings	785	880	1 147	1 301	6 396	6 420	7 509	5 278
Foreign companies (branches)	..	..	..	..	..	..	..	..
All undertakings	854	950	1 337	1 727	9 574	9 850	12 046	12 932

POLAND

Table 1. Selected aggregates *(cont.)*

Million PLN

	2014	2015	2016	2017	2018	2019	2020	2021
1.4 Gross operating expenses								
Life								
Domestic undertakings	6 588	6 476	5 647	5 963	5 697	5 615	5 194	5 600
Foreign controlled undertakings	4 369	4 182	3 797	3 491	3 276	3 093	2 955	1 329
Foreign companies (branches)	..	..	..	..	..	..	..	..
All undertakings	6 588	6 476	5 647	5 963	5 697	5 615	5 194	5 600
Non-life								
Domestic undertakings	8 018	8 335	9 104	12 793	14 073	14 974	12 771	13 494
Foreign controlled undertakings	5 135	5 569	5 978	7 938	8 744	9 193	7 781	6 316
Foreign companies (branches)	..	..	..	..	..	..	..	..
All undertakings	8 018	8 335	9 104	12 793	14 073	14 974	12 771	13 494
Composite, all undertakings	..	..	..	..	..	..	..	..
Total								
Domestic undertakings	14 606	14 811	14 751	18 756	19 770	20 589	17 966	19 094
Foreign controlled undertakings	9 504	9 751	9 776	11 429	12 021	12 286	10 736	7 644
Foreign companies (branches)	..	..	..	..	..	..	..	..
All undertakings	14 606	14 811	14 751	18 756	19 770	20 589	17 966	19 094
1.5 Insurance business written abroad by branches, gross premiums								
Life								
Branches and agencies	79	92	..	95	80	99	118	136
Subsidaries	..	..	..	..	..	..	..	..
Total	79	92	..	95	80	99	118	136
Non-life								
Branches and agencies	98	116	..	..	0	0	0	0
Subsidaries	..	..	..	..	..	..	..	..
Total	98	116	..	..	0	0	0	0
Composite total	..	..	..	..	..	..	..	..
Total								
Branches and agencies	177	208	..	95	80	99	118	136
Subsidaries	..	..	..	..	..	..	..	..
Total	177	208	..	95	80	99	118	136

.. Not available

Note: Detailed metadata at: *http://metalinks.oecd.org/ins/20230516/7102.*

Source: *OECD Insurance Statistics (database)*

Table 2. Number of companies and employees

	2014	2015	2016	2017	2018	2019	2020	2021
2.1 Number of companies								
Life								
Domestic undertakings	26	28	27	27	26	25	26	25
Foreign controlled undertakings	19	21	21	20	18	17	18	9
Foreign companies (branches)	..	..	..	..	..	..	..	..
All undertakings	26	28	27	27	26	25	26	25
Non-life								
Domestic undertakings	30	32	33	33	33	33	32	29
Foreign controlled undertakings	19	22	20	19	19	19	18	9
Foreign companies (branches)	..	..	..	..	..	..	..	..
All undertakings	30	32	33	33	33	33	32	29
Composite, all undertakings	**0**	**0**	**0**	..	..	..	..	..
Reinsurance								
Domestic undertakings	1	1	1	1	1	1	1	1
Foreign controlled undertakings	1	1	1	1	1	1	1	0
Foreign companies (branches)	..	..	..	..	..	..	..	..
All undertakings	1	1	1	1	1	1	1	1
Total								
Domestic undertakings	57	61	61	61	60	59	59	55
Foreign controlled undertakings	39	44	42	40	38	37	37	18
Foreign companies (branches)	..	..	..	..	..	..	..	..
All undertakings	57	61	61	61	60	59	59	55
2.2 Number of employees								
Insurance undertakings	35 922	35 282	..	..	..	42 287	42 976	..
Intermediaries	58 004	49 126	..	..	..	..	..	..
Total	93 926	84 408	..	..	..	42 287	42 976	..

.. Not available

Note: Detailed metadata at: *http://metalinks.oecd.org/ins/20230516/7102*.

Source: *OECD Insurance Statistics (database)*

PORTUGAL

Table 1. Selected aggregates

Million EUR

	2014	2015	2016	2017	2018	2019	2020	2021
1.1 Insurance business written in the reporting country								
1.1.1 Insurance business, by ownership								
Gross premiums								
Domestic undertakings	14 051	12 568	10 913	11 455	12 590	11 915	9 674	13 167
Foreign controlled undertakings	8 737	8 890	9 048	10 640	11 441	10 457	8 804	12 009
Foreign companies (branches)	0	0	0	0	0	0	0	0
All undertakings	14 051	12 568	10 913	11 455	12 590	11 915	9 674	13 167
Premiums ceded								
Domestic undertakings	1 118	1 194	1 214	1 307	1 338	1 638	1 771	1 995
Foreign controlled undertakings	836	924	992	1 180	1 209	1 505	1 667	1 881
Foreign companies (branches)	0	0	0	0	0	0	0	0
All undertakings	1 118	1 194	1 214	1 307	1 338	1 638	1 771	1 995
Net written premiums								
Domestic undertakings	12 933	11 374	9 698	10 148	11 252	10 277	7 903	11 173
Foreign controlled undertakings	7 902	7 966	8 056	9 460	10 232	8 952	7 137	10 128
Foreign companies (branches)	0	0	0	0	0	0	0	0
All undertakings	12 933	11 374	9 698	10 148	11 252	10 277	7 903	11 173
1.1.2 Insurance business on foreign risks, gross premiums								
Life	13	8	11	8	0	0	0	0
Non-life	13	13	4	7	8	15	18	22
Composite	92	107	127	129	195	252	119	137
of which:								
Life	53	63	70	74	132	183	42	34
Non-life	39	44	57	55	63	69	77	103
Total	118	129	142	144	203	267	137	159
1.1.3 Life insurance payments, by class, gross premiums								
Annuities	64	109	142	183	142	40	18	12
Unit linked	1 966	2 119	1 655	2 077	1 703	1 647	1 852	4 570
Other life insurance	8 220	6 254	4 708	4 450	5 934	5 072	2 421	2 845
Total life insurance	10 249	8 481	6 504	6 710	7 779	6 759	4 291	7 427
***of which:** Pension contracts*	..	..	..	..	..	..	..	..
1.1.4 Non-life insurance payments, by class, gross premiums								
Motor vehicle insurance	1 256	1 316	1 399	1 482	1 429	1 517	1 570	1 581
Marine, aviation and other transport insurance	29	28	25	27	26	29	30	35
Freight insurance	24	23	22	22	0	21	19	19
Fire and other property damage insurance	699	745	771	795	764	820	860	927
Pecuniary loss insurance	70	73	84	83	47	95	98	102
General liability insurance	87	94	99	102	101	117	128	147
Accident and health	1 452	1 602	1 783	1 999	2 141	2 354	2 466	2 706
***of which:** Health*	896	973	1 084	1 208	1 307	1 429	1 540	1 699
Other non-life insurance	183	205	225	235	239	201	212	223
Treaty reinsurance	0	0	0	0	..	..	..	..
Total non-life insurance	3 802	4 086	4 408	4 745	4 747	5 155	5 383	5 740
1.2 Gross claims payments								
Life								
Domestic undertakings	5 254	6 133	6 568	3 940	3 306	3 141	4 695	4 957
Foreign controlled undertakings	2 667	2 724	2 252	2 853	2 749	2 547	4 605	4 672
Foreign companies (branches)	0	0	0	0	0	0	0	0
All undertakings	5 254	6 133	6 568	3 940	3 306	3 141	4 695	4 957
Non-life								
Domestic undertakings	1 407	1 520	1 336	1 413	1 530	1 550	1 409	1 533
Foreign controlled undertakings	1 174	1 278	1 070	1 130	1 200	1 246	1 133	1 247
Foreign companies (branches)	0	0	0	0	0	0	0	0
All undertakings	1 407	1 520	1 336	1 413	1 530	1 550	1 409	1 533
Composite								
Domestic undertakings	5 201	5 128	4 554	4 230	5 086	4 341	4 150	4 915
Foreign controlled undertakings	3 991	3 922	4 501	4 180	4 606	3 877	3 847	4 842
Foreign companies (branches)	0	0	0	0	0	0	0	0
All undertakings	5 201	5 128	4 554	4 230	5 086	4 341	4 150	4 915
of which:								
Life	3 895	3 840	2 867	2 479	3 320	2 568	2 485	3 105
Domestic undertakings	3 895	3 840	2 867	2 479	3 320	2 568	2 485	3 105
Foreign controlled undertakings	2 904	2 839	2 815	2 431	2 843	2 106	2 183	3 035
Foreign companies (branches)	0	0	0	0	0	0	0	0
All undertakings	3 895	3 840	2 867	2 479	3 320	2 568	2 485	3 105
Non-life	1 306	1 288	1 687	1 751	1 766	1 774	1 665	1 809
Domestic undertakings	1 306	1 288	1 687	1 751	1 766	1 774	1 665	1 809
Foreign controlled undertakings	1 087	1 083	1 686	1 749	1 763	1 771	1 664	1 807
Foreign companies (branches)	0	0	0	0	0	0	0	0
All undertakings	1 306	1 288	1 687	1 751	1 766	1 774	1 665	1 809
Total								
Domestic undertakings	11 861	12 782	12 458	9 582	9 922	9 032	10 254	11 404
Foreign controlled undertakings	7 832	7 923	7 822	8 163	8 555	7 670	9 585	10 761
Foreign companies (branches)	0	0	0	0	0	0	0	0
All undertakings	11 861	12 782	12 458	9 582	9 922	9 032	10 254	11 404

PORTUGAL

Table 1. Selected aggregates *(cont.)*

Million EUR

	2014	2015	2016	2017	2018	2019	2020	2021
1.3 Commissions								
Life								
Domestic undertakings	40	77	105	103	89	132	132	152
Foreign controlled undertakings	15	41	42	85	78	116	126	136
Foreign companies (branches)	0	0	0	0	0	0	0	0
All undertakings	40	77	105	103	89	132	132	152
Non-life								
Domestic undertakings	153	178	164	183	194	220	214	229
Foreign controlled undertakings	117	133	98	115	124	141	136	144
Foreign companies (branches)	0	0	0	0	0	0	0	0
All undertakings	153	178	164	183	194	220	214	229
Composite								
Domestic undertakings	301	295	286	351	350	393	416	438
Foreign controlled undertakings	208	222	283	344	333	373	394	429
Foreign companies (branches)	0	0	0	0	0	0	0	0
All undertakings	301	295	286	351	350	393	416	438
of which:								
Life	100	82	49	58	75	86	94	78
Domestic undertakings	100	82	49	58	75	86	94	78
Foreign controlled undertakings	42	44	47	52	58	66	73	70
Foreign companies (branches)	0	0	0	0	0	0	0	0
All undertakings	100	82	49	58	75	86	94	78
Non-life	201	214	237	293	275	307	322	360
Domestic undertakings	201	214	237	293	275	307	322	360
Foreign controlled undertakings	165	178	236	291	275	306	321	359
Foreign companies (branches)	0	0	0	0	0	0	0	0
All undertakings	201	214	237	293	275	307	322	360
Total								
Domestic undertakings	493	550	554	637	633	745	762	818
Foreign controlled undertakings	339	396	423	543	534	630	657	709
Foreign companies (branches)	0	0	0	0	0	0	0	0
All undertakings	493	550	554	637	633	745	762	818
1.4 Gross operating expenses								
Life								
Domestic undertakings	212	244	300	298	280	289	291	336
Foreign controlled undertakings	136	163	168	248	246	254	280	301
Foreign companies (branches)	0	0	0	0	0	0	0	0
All undertakings	212	244	300	298	280	289	291	336
Non-life								
Domestic undertakings	495	550	467	494	513	549	539	571
Foreign controlled undertakings	398	441	357	388	402	430	414	439
Foreign companies (branches)	0	0	0	0	0	0	0	0
All undertakings	495	550	467	494	513	549	539	571
Composite								
Domestic undertakings	717	720	711	851	823	859	928	977
Foreign controlled undertakings	541	571	702	839	790	821	886	957
Foreign companies (branches)	0	0	0	0	0	0	0	0
All undertakings	717	720	711	851	823	859	928	977
of which:								
Life	230	222	148	173	206	207	222	211
Domestic undertakings	230	222	148	173	206	207	222	211
Foreign controlled undertakings	125	145	140	162	175	170	181	194
Foreign companies (branches)	0	0	0	0	0	0	0	0
All undertakings	230	222	148	173	206	207	222	211
Non-life	487	497	562	678	617	652	706	767
Domestic undertakings	487	497	562	678	617	652	706	767
Foreign controlled undertakings	416	427	562	677	615	651	705	763
Foreign companies (branches)	0	0	0	0	0	0	0	0
All undertakings	487	497	562	678	617	652	706	767
Total								
Domestic undertakings	1 425	1 513	1 478	1 643	1 615	1 697	1 759	1 884
Foreign controlled undertakings	1 076	1 176	1 227	1 474	1 438	1 505	1 581	1 697
Foreign companies (branches)	0	0	0	0	0	0	0	0
All undertakings	1 425	1 513	1 478	1 643	1 615	1 697	1 759	1 884

Table 1. Selected aggregates *(cont.)*

Million EUR

	2014	2015	2016	2017	2018	2019	2020	2021
1.5 Insurance business written abroad by branches, gross premiums								
Life								
Branches and agencies	13	8	11	8	0	0	0	0
Subsidaries	0	0	0	0	0	0	0	0
Total	13	8	11	8	0	0	0	0
Non-life								
Branches and agencies	12	12	1	3	0	6	14	17
Subsidaries	0	0	0	0	0	0	0	0
Total	12	12	1	3	0	6	14	17
Composite								
Branches and agencies	92	107	127	129	195	252	119	137
Subsidaries	0	0	0	0	0	0	0	0
Total	92	107	127	129	195	252	119	137
of which:								
Life	53	63	70	74	132	183	42	34
Branches and agencies	53	63	70	74	132	183	42	34
Subsidaries	0	0	0	0	0	0	0	0
Total	53	63	70	74	132	183	42	34
Non-life	39	44	57	55	63	69	77	103
Branches and agencies	39	44	57	55	63	69	77	103
Subsidaries	0	0	0	0	0	0	0	0
Total	39	44	57	55	63	69	77	103
Total								
Branches and agencies	117	128	138	140	195	258	134	154
Subsidaries	0	0	0	0	0	0	0	0
Total	117	128	138	140	195	258	134	154

.. Not available

Note: Detailed metadata at: *http://metalinks.oecd.org/ins/20230516/20ef.*

Source: *OECD Insurance Statistics (database)*

Table 2. Number of companies and employees

	2014	2015	2016	2017	2018	2019	2020	2021
2.1 Number of companies								
Life								
Domestic undertakings	16	16	14	13	12	12	11	12
Foreign controlled undertakings	10	10	9	9	10	10	10	10
Foreign companies (branches)	5	5	4	4	5	0	0	0
All undertakings	21	21	18	17	17	12	11	12
Non-life								
Domestic undertakings	21	24	23	23	23	22	21	21
Foreign controlled undertakings	15	16	15	15	16	15	14	14
Foreign companies (branches)	23	21	19	19	23	0	0	0
All undertakings	44	45	42	42	46	22	21	21
Composite								
Domestic undertakings	5	5	5	6	5	5	5	4
Foreign controlled undertakings	3	3	4	4	3	3	3	3
Foreign companies (branches)	6	7	7	7	9	0	0	0
All undertakings	11	12	12	13	14	5	5	4
Reinsurance								
Domestic undertakings	1	1	1	1	1	1	1	1
Foreign controlled undertakings	1	1	1	1	1	1	1	1
Foreign companies (branches)	0	0	0	0	0	0	0	0
All undertakings	1	1	1	1	1	1	1	1
Total								
Domestic undertakings	43	46	43	43	41	40	38	38
Foreign controlled undertakings	29	30	29	29	30	29	28	28
Foreign companies (branches)	34	33	30	30	37	0	0	0
All undertakings	77	79	73	73	78	40	38	38
2.2 Number of employees								
Insurance undertakings	9 252	9 441	9 387	9 381	8 781	8 781	8 566	8 845
Intermediaries	23 465	22 738	21 426	20 258	18 999	16 763	15 831	11 932
Total	32 717	32 179	30 813	29 639	27 780	25 544	24 397	20 777

Note: Detailed metadata at: *http://metalinks.oecd.org/ins/20230516/20ef.*
Source: *OECD Insurance Statistics (database)*

SLOVAK REPUBLIC

Table 1. Selected aggregates

Million EUR

	2014	2015	2016	2017	2018	2019	2020	2021
1.1 Insurance business written in the reporting country								
1.1.1 Insurance business, by ownership								
Gross premiums								
Domestic undertakings	2 106	2 020	..	4 186	..	2 304	2 224	1 839
Foreign controlled undertakings	1 918	1 827	..	..	..	2 044	2 037	1 671
Foreign companies (branches)	142	143	..	282	..	287	282	470
All undertakings	2 248	2 163	..	4 468	..	2 522	2 444	2 309
Premiums ceded								
Domestic undertakings	314	319	..	319	..	363	-258	246
Foreign controlled undertakings	283	287	..	..	..	280	-277	180
Foreign companies (branches)	17	17	..	31	..	30	30	89
All undertakings	331	336	..	350	..	365	-255	335
Net written premiums								
Domestic undertakings	1 792	1 701	..	3 868	..	1 941	1 877	1 593
Foreign controlled undertakings	1 635	1 540	..	..	..	1 765	1 755	1 490
Foreign companies (branches)	126	126	..	250	..	258	252	381
All undertakings	1 917	1 827	..	4 118	..	2 157	2 095	1 974
1.1.2 Insurance business on foreign risks, gross premiums								
Life	..	..	..	..	..	..	..	53
Non-life	..	..	..	..	..	..	..	..
Composite	..	..	..	..	..	..	..	8
of which:								
Life	..	..	..	..	..	..	..	1
Non-life	..	..	..	..	..	..	..	7
Total	..	..	..	..	..	..	..	61
1.1.3 Life insurance payments, by class, gross premiums								
Annuities	623	586	..	2	..	1	0	0
Unit linked	417	351	..	166	..	253	145	219
Other life insurance	180	171	..	950	..	947	844	1 859
Total life insurance	1 220	1 108	..	1 119	..	1 202	989	2 079
of which: *Pension contracts*	12	12	..	..	..	..	..	..
1.1.4 Non-life insurance payments, by class, gross premiums								
Motor vehicle insurance	532	547	..	309	..	704	735	303
Marine, aviation and other transport insurance	6	6	..	10	..	12	0	7
Freight insurance	8	8	..	..	..	..	0	0
Fire and other property damage insurance	257	257	..	276	..	297	310	232
Pecuniary loss insurance	33	34	..	11	..	..	2	12
General liability insurance	78	78	..	80	..	79	80	65
Accident and health	49	44	..	..	..	..	106	121
of which: *Health*	2	3	..	..	..	..	8	5
Other non-life insurance	35	39	..	397	..	100	-185	531
Treaty reinsurance	32	42	..	..	..	..	0	..
Total non-life insurance	1 028	1 055	..	1 083	..	1 366	1 046	1 272
1.2 Gross claims payments								
Life								
Domestic undertakings	107	98	186	76	..	74	74	91
Foreign controlled undertakings	107	98	..	73	..	71	63	74
Foreign companies (branches)	0	2	..	117	..	102	93	89
All undertakings	108	100	..	193	..	176	167	180
Non-life								
Domestic undertakings	0	0	..	..	..	..	..	..
Foreign controlled undertakings	0	0	..	..	..	..	..	..
Foreign companies (branches)	29	32	..	21	..	18	21	16
All undertakings	29	32	..	..	..	18	..	16
Composite								
Domestic undertakings	1 084	1 057	2 291	..	..	..	655	929
Foreign controlled undertakings	948	911	1 909	76	..	1 171	1 040	842
Foreign companies (branches)	16	16	..	21	..	46	33	121
All undertakings	1 099	1 073	..	..	..	1 367	688	1 050
of which:								
Life	646	575	..	..	..	747	206	529
Domestic undertakings	634	563	1 794	..	..	..	178	478
Foreign controlled undertakings	533	457	1 459	72	..	615	520	435
Foreign companies (branches)	12	12	..	17	..	37	28	50
All undertakings	646	575	..	..	..	747	206	529
Non-life	453	497	..	..	..	620	482	521
Domestic undertakings	450	494	497	..	..	..	477	451
Foreign controlled undertakings	415	454	450	4	..	555	520	406
Foreign companies (branches)	3	3	..	5	..	9	5	70
All undertakings	453	497	..	..	..	620	482	521
Total								
Domestic undertakings	1 191	1 155	2 477	76	..	74	729	1 020
Foreign controlled undertakings	1 055	1 010	1 909	149	..	1 242	1 103	916
Foreign companies (branches)	44	49	..	159	..	166	147	226
All undertakings	1 236	1 205	..	193	..	1 561	855	1 246

SLOVAK REPUBLIC

Table 1. Selected aggregates *(cont.)*

Million EUR

	2014	2015	2016	2017	2018	2019	2020	2021
1.3 Commissions								
Life								
Domestic undertakings	33	37	..	..	..	..	..	..
Foreign controlled undertakings	33	37	..	..	..	..	..	..
Foreign companies (branches)	1	2	..	23	..	26	29	31
All undertakings	34	39	..	..	..	..	29	31
Non-life								
Domestic undertakings	0	0	..	..	..	..	..	..
Foreign controlled undertakings	0	0	..	..	..	..	..	..
Foreign companies (branches)	15	18	..	21	..	22	23	14
All undertakings	15	18	..	..	..	..	23	14
Composite								
Domestic undertakings	259	250	..	..	..	..	..	..
Foreign controlled undertakings	244	233	..	..	..	..	..	..
Foreign companies (branches)	4	16	..	20	..	22	24	47
All undertakings	264	266	..	..	..	..	24	47
of which:								
Life	95	89	..	..	..	..	21	17
Domestic undertakings	95	77	..	..	..	..	..	..
Foreign controlled undertakings	91	73	..	..	..	..	..	..
Foreign companies (branches)	0	12	..	13	..	12	21	17
All undertakings	95	89	..	..	..	..	21	17
Non-life	168	177	..	..	..	..	3	30
Domestic undertakings	164	173	..	..	..	..	..	..
Foreign controlled undertakings	153	160	..	..	..	..	..	..
Foreign companies (branches)	4	5	..	7	..	10	3	30
All undertakings	168	177	..	..	..	..	3	30
Total								
Domestic undertakings	292	287	..	..	..	..	..	..
Foreign controlled undertakings	277	270	..	..	..	..	..	..
Foreign companies (branches)	21	36	..	64	..	71	75	93
All undertakings	313	323	..	..	..	..	75	93
1.4 Gross operating expenses								
Life								
Domestic undertakings	63	72	..	55	..	107 361 381	106	102
Foreign controlled undertakings	63	72	..	..	..	53 819 969	62	61
Foreign companies (branches)	2	3	..	51	..	58	64	68
All undertakings	65	75	..	105	..	165	169	170
Non-life								
Domestic undertakings	0	0	..	..	..	..	..	..
Foreign controlled undertakings	0	0	..	..	..	..	..	..
Foreign companies (branches)	31	32	..	41	..	39	39	30
All undertakings	31	32	..	41	..	39	..	..
Composite								
Domestic undertakings	529	505	..	502	..	641 249 475	655	510
Foreign controlled undertakings	498	472	..	..	..	..	609	475
Foreign companies (branches)	7	25	..	29	..	32	35	87
All undertakings	536	531	..	531	..	673	690	597
of which:								
Life	212	187	..	179	..	191	208	167
Domestic undertakings	212	170	..	161	..	173 023 120	178	134
Foreign controlled undertakings	202	160	..	..	..	..	165	129
Foreign companies (branches)	1	17	..	19	..	18	29	33
All undertakings	212	187	..	179	..	191	208	167
Non-life	324	344	..	351	..	482	482	429
Domestic undertakings	317	336	..	341	..	468 226 356	477	376
Foreign controlled undertakings	295	312	..	..	..	..	444	346
Foreign companies (branches)	6	8	..	10	..	14	5	54
All undertakings	324	344	..	351	..	482	482	429
Total								
Domestic undertakings	592	578	..	556	..	748 610 856	761	612
Foreign controlled undertakings	561	544	..	..	..	53 819 969	671	536
Foreign companies (branches)	40	60	..	121	..	129	138	185
All undertakings	632	638	..	677	..	877	859	767

Table 1. Selected aggregates *(cont.)*

Million EUR

	2014	2015	2016	2017	2018	2019	2020	2021
1.5 Insurance business written abroad by branches, gross premiums								
Life								
Branches and agencies	0	1	..	..	..	..	..	..
Subsidaries	1	5	..	..	..	..	..	..
Total	1	6	..	..	..	..	..	..
Non-life								
Branches and agencies	0	0	..	..	..	..	..	..
Subsidaries	0	0	..	..	..	..	..	..
Total	0	0	..	..	..	..	..	..
Composite								
Branches and agencies	2	2	..	..	..	..	..	..
Subsidaries	4	6	..	..	..	..	..	..
Total	6	8	..	..	..	..	..	..
of which:								
Life	0	0	..	..	..	..	..	..
Branches and agencies	0	0	..	..	..	..	..	..
Subsidaries	0	0	..	..	..	..	..	..
Total	0	0	..	..	..	..	..	..
Non-life	6	8	..	..	..	..	..	..
Branches and agencies	2	2	..	..	..	..	..	..
Subsidaries	4	6	..	..	..	..	..	..
Total	6	8	..	..	..	..	..	..
Total								
Branches and agencies	2	3	..	..	..	..	..	..
Subsidaries	5	10	..	..	..	..	..	..
Total	7	14	..	..	..	..	..	..

.. Not available

Note: Detailed metadata at: *http://metalinks.oecd.org/ins/20230516/7ab7*.

Source: *OECD Insurance Statistics (database)*

Table 2. Number of companies and employees

	2014	2015	2016	2017	2018	2019	2020	2021
2.1 Number of companies								
Life								
Domestic undertakings	5	5	3	3	..	3	2	2
Foreign controlled undertakings	5	5	3	2	..	2	1	1
Foreign companies (branches)	1	1	2	2	..	..	5	2
All undertakings	6	6	5	5	..	5	7	4
Non-life								
Domestic undertakings	0	0	0	0	..	0	0	0
Foreign controlled undertakings	0	0	0	0	..	0	0	0
Foreign companies (branches)	17	17	19	19	..	..	13	13
All undertakings	17	17	19	19	..	0	13	13
Composite								
Domestic undertakings	12	12	12	12	..	10	10	7
Foreign controlled undertakings	10	10	12	10	..	8	8	6
Foreign companies (branches)	2	2	18	2	..	..	12	3
All undertakings	14	14	30	14	..	18	22	10
Reinsurance								
Domestic undertakings	0	0	0	0	..	0	0	0
Foreign controlled undertakings	0	0	0	0	..	0	0	0
Foreign companies (branches)	1	1	0	0	..	..	0	0
All undertakings	1	1	0	0	..	0	0	0
Total								
Domestic undertakings	17	17	15	15	..	13	12	9
Foreign controlled undertakings	15	15	15	12	..	10	9	7
Foreign companies (branches)	21	21	39	23	..	..	30	18
All undertakings	38	38	54	38	..	..	42	27
2.2 Number of employees								
Insurance undertakings	5 937	..	..	..	..	..	..	..
Intermediaries	1 358	..	..	..	..	25 066	..	..
Total	7 295	..	..	..	..	..	..	..

.. Not available

Note: Detailed metadata at: *http://metalinks.oecd.org/ins/20230516/7ab7*.

Source: *OECD Insurance Statistics (database)*

SLOVENIA

Table 1. Selected aggregates

Million EUR

	2014	2015	2016	2017	2018	2019	2020	2021
1.1 Insurance business written in the reporting country								
1.1.1 Insurance business, by ownership								
Gross premiums								
Domestic undertakings	2 095	2 150	2 182	2 298	2 424	2 647	2 734	2 876
Foreign controlled undertakings	166	172	180	186	191	522	534	564
Foreign companies (branches)	..	..	..	..	..	..	..	..
All undertakings	2 095	2 150	2 182	2 298	2 424	2 647	2 734	2 876
Premiums ceded								
Domestic undertakings	274	256	269	310	320	377	335	437
Foreign controlled undertakings	28	33	39	42	42	65	73	58
Foreign companies (branches)	..	..	..	..	..	..	..	..
All undertakings	274	256	269	310	320	377	335	437
Net written premiums								
Domestic undertakings	1 821	1 894	1 914	1 988	2 105	2 270	2 399	2 438
Foreign controlled undertakings	137	139	141	144	149	457	461	505
Foreign companies (branches)	..	..	..	..	..	..	..	..
All undertakings	1 821	1 894	1 914	1 988	2 105	2 270	2 399	2 438
1.1.2 Insurance business on foreign risks, gross premiums								
Life	..	..	..	..	..	..	..	..
Non-life	0	0	..	..	..	..	..	..
Composite	1	1	..	..	..	..	..	..
of which:								
Life	0	1	..	..	..	..	..	..
Non-life	1	0	..	..	..	..	..	..
Total	2	2	..	..	..	..	..	..
1.1.3 Life insurance payments, by class, gross premiums								
Annuities	..	..	..	..	..	..	..	..
Unit linked	195	215	213	223	225	258	247	283
Other life insurance	284	283	279	293	301	293	275	289
Total life insurance	479	498	492	516	526	551	522	571
of which: *Pension contracts*	37	37	39	41	41	50	53	50
1.1.4 Non-life insurance payments, by class, gross premiums								
Motor vehicle insurance	495	484	499	539	590	659	668	698
Marine, aviation and other transport insurance	16	18	18	19	21	24	40	34
Freight insurance	13	15	16	16	16	13	14	17
Fire and other property damage insurance	372	393	405	415	439	470	511	569
Pecuniary loss insurance	56	62	62	64	60	62	55	58
General liability insurance	65	64	72	73	79	87	96	92
Accident and health	574	591	591	623	661	738	784	790
of which: *Health*	470	484	489	522	556	628	673	674
Other non-life insurance	24	25	28	33	34	42	44	47
Treaty reinsurance	0	0	0	0	0	0	0	0
Total non-life insurance	1 616	1 652	1 690	1 782	1 898	2 096	2 212	2 304
1.2 Gross claims payments								
Life								
Domestic undertakings	36	52	50	46	..	..	..	0
Foreign controlled undertakings	1	0	2	..	..	..	..	..
Foreign companies (branches)	..	..	..	..	..	..	..	..
All undertakings	36	52	50	46	..	..	..	0
Non-life								
Domestic undertakings	449	499	491	532	556	595	638	628
Foreign controlled undertakings	..	1	0	..	0	6	4	2
Foreign companies (branches)	..	..	..	..	..	..	..	..
All undertakings	449	499	491	532	556	595	638	628
Composite								
Domestic undertakings	941	911	903	995	1 115	1 132	1 126	1 136
Foreign controlled undertakings	90	91	95	104	111	326	342	356
Foreign companies (branches)	..	..	..	..	..	..	..	..
All undertakings	941	911	903	995	1 115	1 132	1 126	1 136
of which:								
Life	304	305	314	347	402	424	439	426
Domestic undertakings	304	305	314	347	402	424	439	426
Foreign controlled undertakings	50	51	50	50	49	94	114	112
Foreign companies (branches)	..	..	..	..	..	..	..	..
All undertakings	304	305	314	347	402	424	439	426
Non-life	637	606	590	648	713	708	687	710
Domestic undertakings	637	606	590	648	713	708	687	710
Foreign controlled undertakings	41	40	45	54	62	232	228	244
Foreign companies (branches)	..	..	..	..	..	..	..	..
All undertakings	637	606	590	648	713	708	687	710
Total								
Domestic undertakings	1 426	1 461	1 445	1 573	1 670	1 727	1 764	1 764
Foreign controlled undertakings	91	91	97	104	111	331	346	358
Foreign companies (branches)	..	..	..	..	..	..	..	..
All undertakings	1 426	1 461	1 445	1 573	1 670	1 727	1 764	1 764

Table 1. Selected aggregates *(cont.)*

Million EUR

	2014	2015	2016	2017	2018	2019	2020	2021
1.3 Commissions								
Life								
Domestic undertakings	3	3	3	4	..	..	..	..
Foreign controlled undertakings	0	0	0	..	..	..	..	..
Foreign companies (branches)	..	..	..	..	..	..	..	..
All undertakings	3	3	3	4	..	..	..	..
Non-life								
Domestic undertakings	7	8	7	8	9	1	5	5
Foreign controlled undertakings	..	0	0	..	0	0	0	1
Foreign companies (branches)	..	..	..	..	..	..	..	..
All undertakings	7	8	7	8	9	1	5	5
Composite								
Domestic undertakings	86	89	86	92	104	115	120	121
Foreign controlled undertakings	20	21	28	22	23	49	48	47
Foreign companies (branches)	..	..	..	..	..	..	..	..
All undertakings	86	89	86	92	104	115	120	121
of which:								
Life	32	34	32	32	35	34	33	36
Domestic undertakings	32	34	32	32	35	34	33	36
Foreign controlled undertakings	10	10	15	9	9	13	13	13
Foreign companies (branches)	..	..	..	..	..	..	..	..
All undertakings	32	34	32	32	35	34	33	36
Non-life	54	56	54	60	68	81	87	84
Domestic undertakings	54	56	54	60	68	81	87	84
Foreign controlled undertakings	10	11	13	13	14	36	35	34
Foreign companies (branches)	..	..	..	..	..	..	..	..
All undertakings	54	56	54	60	68	81	87	84
Total								
Domestic undertakings	96	100	96	104	112	116	125	126
Foreign controlled undertakings	20	21	28	22	23	49	48	47
Foreign companies (branches)	..	..	..	..	..	..	..	..
All undertakings	96	100	96	104	112	116	125	126
1.4 Gross operating expenses								
Life								
Domestic undertakings	15	16	12	15	..	..	0	1
Foreign controlled undertakings	1	1	1	..	..	..	..	..
Foreign companies (branches)	..	..	..	..	..	..	..	..
All undertakings	15	16	12	15	..	..	0	1
Non-life								
Domestic undertakings	86	90	97	97	105	112	109	119
Foreign controlled undertakings	..	0	1	..	1	6	6	6
Foreign companies (branches)	..	..	..	..	..	..	..	..
All undertakings	86	90	97	97	105	112	109	119
Composite								
Domestic undertakings	362	368	378	388	418	442	426	461
Foreign controlled undertakings	57	60	60	66	68	146	140	139
Foreign companies (branches)	..	..	..	..	..	..	..	..
All undertakings	362	368	378	388	418	442	426	461
of which:								
Life	99	100	99	102	116	118	100	119
Domestic undertakings	99	100	99	102	116	118	100	119
Foreign controlled undertakings	27	28	26	27	27	43	37	39
Foreign companies (branches)	..	..	..	..	..	..	..	..
All undertakings	99	100	99	102	116	118	100	119
Non-life	263	268	279	286	302	324	326	341
Domestic undertakings	263	268	279	286	302	324	326	341
Foreign controlled undertakings	30	32	33	39	41	103	103	101
Foreign companies (branches)	..	..	..	..	..	..	..	..
All undertakings	263	268	279	286	302	324	326	341
Total								
Domestic undertakings	462	474	487	500	523	553	535	581
Foreign controlled undertakings	59	62	62	66	69	152	146	146
Foreign companies (branches)	..	..	..	..	..	..	..	..
All undertakings	462	474	487	500	523	553	535	581

SLOVENIA

Table 1. Selected aggregates *(cont.)*

Million EUR

	2014	2015	2016	2017	2018	2019	2020	2021
1.5 Insurance business written abroad by branches, gross premiums								
Life								
Branches and agencies	..	..	..	..	..	..	..	..
Subsidaries	..	..	..	..	..	..	..	..
Total	..	..	..	..	..	..	..	..
Non-life								
Branches and agencies	..	..	..	1	1	1	0	0
Subsidaries	..	..	..	..	..	..	..	..
Total	..	..	..	1	1	1	0	0
Composite								
Branches and agencies	..	2	..	31	44	65	77	56
Subsidaries	..	..	..	..	..	..	..	..
Total	..	2	..	31	44	65	77	56
of which:								
Life	..	2	..	6	7	7	3	..
Branches and agencies	..	2	..	6	7	7	3	..
Subsidaries	..	..	..	..	..	..	..	..
Total	..	2	..	6	7	7	3	..
Non-life	..	0	..	25	37	58	73	56
Branches and agencies	..	0	..	25	37	58	73	56
Subsidaries	..	..	..	..	..	..	..	..
Total	..	0	..	25	37	58	73	56
Total								
Branches and agencies	..	2	..	32	45	66	77	57
Subsidaries	..	..	..	..	..	..	..	..
Total	..	2	..	32	45	66	77	57

.. Not available

Note: Detailed metadata at: *http://metalinks.oecd.org/ins/20230516/2814.*

Source: *OECD Insurance Statistics (database)*

Table 2. Number of companies and employees

	2014	2015	2016	2017	2018	2019	2020	2021
2.1 Number of companies								
Life								
Domestic undertakings	3	3	3	2	0	0	1	1
Foreign controlled undertakings	1	1	1	0	0	0	0	0
Foreign companies (branches)	0	0	0	0	0	0	0	0
All undertakings	3	3	3	2	0	0	1	1
Non-life								
Domestic undertakings	3	4	4	4	4	4	4	4
Foreign controlled undertakings	0	0	0	0	1	2	2	2
Foreign companies (branches)	4	4	4	4	3	3	3	3
All undertakings	7	8	8	8	7	7	7	7
Composite								
Domestic undertakings	8	8	7	7	9	9	8	8
Foreign controlled undertakings	3	3	3	3	3	4	3	3
Foreign companies (branches)	2	2	2	2	4	4	3	4
All undertakings	10	10	9	9	13	13	11	12
Reinsurance								
Domestic undertakings	2	2	2	2	2	2	2	2
Foreign controlled undertakings	0	0	0	0	0	0	0	0
Foreign companies (branches)	0	0	0	0	0	0	0	0
All undertakings	2	2	2	2	2	2	2	2
Total								
Domestic undertakings	16	17	16	15	15	15	15	15
Foreign controlled undertakings	4	4	4	3	4	6	5	5
Foreign companies (branches)	6	6	6	6	7	7	6	7
All undertakings	22	23	22	21	22	22	21	22
2.2 Number of employees								
Insurance undertakings	..	..	..	..	..	..	..	..
Intermediaries	..	..	..	..	..	..	..	..
Total	..	..	..	..	..	..	..	..

.. Not available

Note: Detailed metadata at: *http://metalinks.oecd.org/ins/20230516/2814.*

Source: *OECD Insurance Statistics (database)*

SPAIN

Table 1. Selected aggregates

Million EUR

	2014	2015	2016	2017	2018	2019	2020	2021
1.1 Insurance business written in the reporting country								
1.1.1 Insurance business, by ownership								
Gross premiums								
Domestic undertakings	57 662	59 048	66 541	65 719	66 538	66 197	62 625	64 658
Foreign controlled undertakings	12 542	11 038	..	..	..	..	..	..
Foreign companies (branches)	0	0	..	..	..	..	..	..
All undertakings	57 662	59 048	66 541	65 719	66 538	66 197	62 625	64 658
Premiums ceded								
Domestic undertakings	5 019	5 161	6 014	6 206	6 020	6 885	10 174	7 596
Foreign controlled undertakings	923	736	..	..	..	..	..	..
Foreign companies (branches)	0	0	..	..	..	..	..	..
All undertakings	5 019	5 161	6 014	6 206	6 020	6 885	10 174	7 596
Net written premiums								
Domestic undertakings	52 643	53 886	60 527	59 513	60 518	59 312	52 451	57 062
Foreign controlled undertakings	11 620	10 301	..	..	..	..	..	..
Foreign companies (branches)	0	0	..	..	..	..	..	..
All undertakings	52 643	53 886	60 527	59 513	60 518	59 312	52 451	57 062
1.1.2 Insurance business on foreign risks, gross premiums								
Life	7	11	13	9	11	0	0	0
Non-life	73	59	45	20	3	326	362	411
Composite	44	61	49	26	147	150	110	94
of which:								
Life	34	46	35	2	28	46	36	33
Non-life	9	15	14	24	119	104	73	60
Total	123	130	107	55	160	476	472	505
1.1.3 Life insurance payments, by class, gross premiums								
Annuities	6 406	5 881	8 746	8 318	7 583	7 053	3 707	5 521
Unit linked	2 816	2 721	2 981	4 431	4 432	4 842	4 837	6 019
Other life insurance	16 021	17 128	19 330	16 270	16 559	15 144	12 961	11 682
Total life insurance	25 244	25 730	31 056	29 019	28 574	27 039	21 505	23 222
***of which:** Pension contracts*	..	..	..	..	..	..	..	..
1.1.4 Non-life insurance payments, by class, gross premiums								
Motor vehicle insurance	9 445	9 695	10 451	10 918	11 212	11 734	11 527	11 478
Marine, aviation and other transport insurance	361	369	369	367	389	409	466	498
Freight insurance	268	261	270	281	301	320	330	328
Fire and other property damage insurance	2 315	2 610	2 895	2 770	3 425	3 379	3 521	3 858
Pecuniary loss insurance	178	208	283	247	252	221	200	260
General liability insurance	1 009	1 011	1 049	1 100	1 181	1 300	1 268	1 366
Accident and health	8 227	8 449	8 879	9 329	9 744	10 057	10 539	11 034
***of which:** Health*	7 356	7 536	7 902	8 224	8 652	8 997	9 488	9 980
Other non-life insurance	10 558	10 729	11 001	11 264	11 029	11 281	11 521	12 105
Treaty reinsurance	0	0	0	..	..	..	..	..
Total non-life insurance	32 362	33 332	35 197	36 275	37 532	38 702	39 372	40 926
1.2 Gross claims payments								
Life								
Domestic undertakings	16 777	18 872	3 070	3 685	3 096	2 488	2 584	2 463
Foreign controlled undertakings	1 688	1 582	..	..	..	..	..	..
Foreign companies (branches)	0	0	..	..	..	..	..	..
All undertakings	16 777	18 872	3 070	3 685	3 096	2 488	2 584	2 463
Non-life								
Domestic undertakings	9 250	9 593	9 453	10 280	9 702	9 940	9 650	10 810
Foreign controlled undertakings	3 890	2 592	..	..	..	..	..	..
Foreign companies (branches)	0	0	..	..	..	..	..	..
All undertakings	9 250	9 593	9 453	10 280	9 702	9 940	9 650	10 810
Composite								
Domestic undertakings	21 596	20 659	32 425	35 292	35 464	37 506	35 799	37 966
Foreign controlled undertakings	5 230	5 136	..	..	..	..	..	..
Foreign companies (branches)	0	0	..	..	..	..	..	..
All undertakings	21 596	20 659	32 425	35 292	35 464	37 506	35 799	37 966
of which:								
Life	9 986	8 948	20 670	22 722	21 474	23 064	22 136	23 930
Domestic undertakings	9 986	8 948	20 670	22 722	21 474	23 064	22 136	23 930
Foreign controlled undertakings	2 497	2 292	..	..	..	..	..	..
Foreign companies (branches)	0	0	..	..	..	..	..	..
All undertakings	9 986	8 948	20 670	22 722	21 474	23 064	22 136	23 930
Non-life	11 610	11 711	11 755	12 571	13 989	14 442	13 663	14 036
Domestic undertakings	11 610	11 711	11 755	12 571	13 989	14 442	13 663	14 036
Foreign controlled undertakings	2 733	2 843	..	..	..	..	..	..
Foreign companies (branches)	0	0	..	..	..	..	..	..
All undertakings	11 610	11 711	11 755	12 571	13 989	14 442	13 663	14 036
Total								
Domestic undertakings	47 622	49 125	44 947	49 258	48 262	49 934	48 032	51 239
Foreign controlled undertakings	10 809	9 310	..	..	..	..	..	..
Foreign companies (branches)	0	0	..	..	..	..	..	..
All undertakings	47 622	49 125	44 947	49 258	48 262	49 934	48 032	51 239

SPAIN

Table 1. Selected aggregates *(cont.)*

Million EUR

	2014	2015	2016	2017	2018	2019	2020	2021
1.3 Commissions								
Life								
Domestic undertakings	660	712	234	257	273	225	252	294
Foreign controlled undertakings	86	71	..	..	..	..	..	..
Foreign companies (branches)	0	0	..	..	..	..	..	..
All undertakings	660	712	234	257	273	225	252	294
Non-life								
Domestic undertakings	1 472	1 436	1 433	1 522	1 524	1 565	1 599	1 686
Foreign controlled undertakings	642	517	..	..	..	..	..	..
Foreign companies (branches)	0	0	..	..	..	..	..	..
All undertakings	1 472	1 436	1 433	1 522	1 524	1 565	1 599	1 686
Composite								
Domestic undertakings	2 270	2 635	3 328	4 629	3 786	3 897	3 947	4 047
Foreign controlled undertakings	669	710	..	..	..	..	..	..
Foreign companies (branches)	0	0	..	..	..	..	..	..
All undertakings	2 270	2 635	3 328	4 629	3 786	3 897	3 947	4 047
of which:								
Life	418	379	979	1 185	1 114	1 169	1 174	1 272
Domestic undertakings	418	379	979	1 185	1 114	1 169	1 174	1 272
Foreign controlled undertakings	94	103	..	..	..	..	..	..
Foreign companies (branches)	0	0	..	..	..	..	..	..
All undertakings	418	379	979	1 185	1 114	1 169	1 174	1 272
Non-life	1 852	2 255	2 349	3 444	2 672	2 728	2 773	2 775
Domestic undertakings	1 852	2 255	2 349	3 444	2 672	2 728	2 773	2 775
Foreign controlled undertakings	576	607	..	..	..	..	..	..
Foreign companies (branches)	0	0	..	..	..	..	..	..
All undertakings	1 852	2 255	2 349	3 444	2 672	2 728	2 773	2 775
Total								
Domestic undertakings	4 403	4 782	4 995	6 408	5 583	5 687	5 798	6 027
Foreign controlled undertakings	1 398	1 298	..	..	..	..	..	..
Foreign companies (branches)	0	0	..	..	..	..	..	..
All undertakings	4 403	4 782	4 995	6 408	5 583	5 687	5 798	6 027
1.4 Gross operating expenses								
Life								
Domestic undertakings	994	1 075	425	455	484	409	419	446
Foreign controlled undertakings	190	192	..	..	..	..	..	..
Foreign companies (branches)	..	..	..	..	..	..	..	..
All undertakings	994	1 075	425	455	484	409	419	446
Non-life								
Domestic undertakings	2 880	2 832	2 876	3 081	3 065	3 092	3 194	3 544
Foreign controlled undertakings	1 289	947	..	..	..	..	..	..
Foreign companies (branches)	..	..	..	..	..	..	..	..
All undertakings	2 880	2 832	2 876	3 081	3 065	3 092	3 194	3 544
Composite								
Domestic undertakings	5 034	5 250	6 332	6 550	6 855	7 166	7 420	7 421
Foreign controlled undertakings	1 070	1 100	..	..	..	..	..	..
Foreign companies (branches)	..	4	..	..	..	..	..	..
All undertakings	5 034	5 254	6 332	6 550	6 855	7 166	7 420	7 421
of which:								
Life	797	729	1 489	1 546	1 677	1 816	1 789	1 887
Domestic undertakings	797	729	1 489	1 546	1 677	1 816	1 789	1 887
Foreign controlled undertakings	178	186	..	..	..	..	..	..
Foreign companies (branches)	..	..	..	..	..	..	..	..
All undertakings	797	729	1 489	1 546	1 677	1 816	1 789	1 887
Non-life	4 237	4 525	4 843	5 004	5 178	5 350	5 632	5 534
Domestic undertakings	4 237	4 521	4 843	5 004	5 178	5 350	5 632	5 534
Foreign controlled undertakings	892	913	..	..	..	..	..	..
Foreign companies (branches)	0	4	..	..	..	..	..	..
All undertakings	4 237	4 525	4 843	5 004	5 178	5 350	5 632	5 534
Total								
Domestic undertakings	8 907	9 157	9 633	10 087	10 405	10 667	11 033	11 412
Foreign controlled undertakings	2 549	2 239	..	..	..	..	..	..
Foreign companies (branches)	..	4	..	..	..	..	..	..
All undertakings	8 907	9 161	9 633	10 087	10 405	10 667	11 033	11 412

Table 1. Selected aggregates *(cont.)*

Million EUR

	2014	2015	2016	2017	2018	2019	2020	2021
1.5 Insurance business written abroad by branches, gross premiums								
Life								
Branches and agencies	0	0	0	0	1	0	0	0
Subsidaries	..	..	..	..	..	..	..	..
Total	..	..	0	0	1	0	0	0
Non-life								
Branches and agencies	654	701	1 694	1 841	1 537	1 606	1 381	1 568
Subsidaries	..	..	..	..	..	..	..	..
Total	..	..	1 694	1 841	1 537	1 606	1 381	1 568
Composite								
Branches and agencies	1 286	1 361	1 262	1 385	2 155	2 184	2 113	2 330
Subsidaries	..	..	..	..	..	..	..	..
Total	..	..	1 262	1 385	2 155	2 184	2 113	2 330
of which:								
Life	..	..	518	574	812	661	527	675
Branches and agencies	559	694	518	574	812	661	527	675
Subsidaries	..	..	..	..	..	..	..	..
Total	..	..	518	574	812	661	527	675
Non-life	..	..	744	812	1 344	1 523	1 586	1 654
Branches and agencies	728	667	744	812	1 344	1 523	1 586	1 654
Subsidaries	..	..	..	..	..	..	..	..
Total	..	..	744	812	1 344	1 523	1 586	1 654
Total								
Branches and agencies	1 940	2 062	2 955	3 226	3 693	3 790	3 494	3 898
Subsidaries	..	..	..	..	..	..	..	..
Total	..	..	2 955	3 226	3 693	3 790	3 494	3 898

.. Not available
Note: Detailed metadata at: *http://metalinks.oecd.org/ins/20230516/746c.*
Source: *OECD Insurance Statistics (database)*

SPAIN

Table 2. Number of companies and employees

	2014	2015	2016	2017	2018	2019	2020	2021
2.1 Number of companies								
Life								
Domestic undertakings	79	78	32	32	29	26	27	27
Foreign controlled undertakings	9	8	..	..	..	..	..	..
Foreign companies (branches)	0	0	..	..	..	..	..	..
All undertakings	79	78	32	32	29	26	27	27
Non-life								
Domestic undertakings	127	118	121	111	105	100	101	101
Foreign controlled undertakings	19	17	..	..	..	..	..	..
Foreign companies (branches)	0	1	..	..	..	..	..	..
All undertakings	127	119	121	111	105	100	101	101
Composite								
Domestic undertakings	45	41	75	74	74	74	71	68
Foreign controlled undertakings	8	8	..	..	..	..	..	..
Foreign companies (branches)	1	0	..	..	..	..	..	..
All undertakings	46	41	75	74	74	74	71	68
Reinsurance								
Domestic undertakings	3	3	3	3	3	4	4	4
Foreign controlled undertakings	0	0	..	..	..	..	..	..
Foreign companies (branches)	0	0	..	..	..	..	..	..
All undertakings	3	3	3	3	3	4	4	4
Total								
Domestic undertakings	254	240	231	220	211	204	203	200
Foreign controlled undertakings	36	33	..	..	..	..	..	..
Foreign companies (branches)	1	1	..	..	..	..	..	..
All undertakings	255	241	231	220	211	204	203	200
2.2 Number of employees								
Insurance undertakings	45 535	45 218	47 453	47 498	47 380	48 194	49 475	46 970
Intermediaries	129 549	..	..	..	..	..	..	..
Total	175 084	..	..	..	..	..	..	..

.. Not available

Note: Detailed metadata at: *http://metalinks.oecd.org/ins/20230516/746c.*

Source: *OECD Insurance Statistics (database)*

SWEDEN

Table 1. Selected aggregates

Million SEK

	2014	2015	2016	2017	2018	2019	2020	2021
1.1 Insurance business written in the reporting country								
1.1.1 Insurance business, by ownership								
Gross premiums								
Domestic undertakings	332 028	339 533	334 834	379 418	426 318	460 661	508 591	626 919
Foreign controlled undertakings	66 041	62 537	67 208	78 911	97 388	101 544	..	139 828
Foreign companies (branches)	10 260	..	..	..	..	..	..	..
All undertakings	342 288	339 533	334 834	379 418	426 318	460 661	508 591	626 919
Premiums ceded								
Domestic undertakings	15 157	10 306	9 139	10 693	11 095	14 223	..	18 256
Foreign controlled undertakings	3 870	4 441	4 296	5 538	6 138	8 471	..	11 859
Foreign companies (branches)	..	..	..	..	..	..	..	..
All undertakings	15 157	10 306	9 139	10 693	11 095	14 223	..	18 256
Net written premiums								
Domestic undertakings	316 871	329 227	325 695	368 725	415 223	446 438	..	608 663
Foreign controlled undertakings	62 171	58 096	62 912	73 373	91 250	93 073	..	127 969
Foreign companies (branches)	10 260	..	..	..	..	..	..	..
All undertakings	327 131	329 227	325 695	368 725	415 223	446 438	..	608 663
1.1.2 Insurance business on foreign risks, gross premiums								
Life	581	667	60	58	58	59	..	124
Non-life	28 134	27 121	26 941	30 482	40 549	44 517	..	46 857
Composite total	..	..	..	..	..	..	..	..
Total	28 715	27 788	27 001	30 540	40 607	44 576	..	46 981
1.1.3 Life insurance payments, by class, gross premiums								
Annuities	205 927	169 626	94 037	107 773	126 049	139 221	..	142 845
Unit linked	2 366	75 221	85 696	97 951	107 143	106 859	..	162 764
Other life insurance	29 900	3 957	71 084	82 841	89 138	102 063	..	198 268
Total life insurance	238 192	248 804	250 817	288 565	322 330	348 143	..	503 877
***of which:** Pension contracts*	..	..	..	..	..	..	..	..
1.1.4 Non-life insurance payments, by class, gross premiums								
Motor vehicle insurance	30 360	21 348	..	..	..	..	..	..
Marine, aviation and other transport insurance	2 627	749	..	..	..	..	..	..
Freight insurance	..	..	..	..	..	..	..	..
Fire and other property damage insurance	29 146	36 720	..	..	..	..	..	..
Pecuniary loss insurance	459	1 070	..	..	..	..	..	..
General liability insurance	4 045	4 119	..	..	..	..	..	..
Accident and health	5 674	5 155	..	..	..	..	..	..
***of which:** Health*	..	..	..	..	..	..	..	..
Other non-life insurance	9 165	21 483	..	..	..	..	..	..
Treaty reinsurance	13 811	..	..	..	..	..	..	..
Total non-life insurance	95 287	90 644	83 954	90 800	103 940	112 479	..	123 012
1.2 Gross claims payments								
Life								
Domestic undertakings	60 930	64 815	76 869	76 390	77 434	73 104	..	92 388
Foreign controlled undertakings	6 055	5 719	5 852	5 784	5 704	5 652	..	6 592
Foreign companies (branches)	5 999	..	..	..	..	..	..	..
All undertakings	66 929	64 815	76 869	76 390	77 434	73 104	..	92 388
Non-life								
Domestic undertakings	75 805	64 537	65 941	66 635	77 278	82 672	..	156 945
Foreign controlled undertakings	31 024	23 701	22 495	25 544	32 791	33 257	..	31 827
Foreign companies (branches)	5 328	..	..	..	..	..	..	..
All undertakings	81 133	64 537	65 941	66 635	77 278	82 672	..	156 945
Composite, all undertakings	..	..	..	..	..	..	..	..
Total								
Domestic undertakings	136 735	129 352	142 810	143 025	154 712	155 776	..	249 333
Foreign controlled undertakings	37 079	29 420	28 347	31 328	38 495	38 909	..	38 419
Foreign companies (branches)	11 327	..	..	..	..	..	..	..
All undertakings	148 062	129 352	142 810	143 025	154 712	155 776	..	249 333
1.3 Commissions								
Life								
Domestic undertakings	4 167	3 782	3 063	3 545	3 494	3 648	..	4 976
Foreign controlled undertakings	1 302	610	274	589	587	567	..	641
Foreign companies (branches)	121	..	..	..	..	..	..	..
All undertakings	4 288	3 782	3 063	3 545	3 494	3 648	..	4 976
Non-life								
Domestic undertakings	4 168	4 264	3 848	3 953	3 711	4 280	..	4 195
Foreign controlled undertakings	2 049	2 589	2 362	2 482	2 634	2 711	..	2 116
Foreign companies (branches)	786	..	..	..	..	..	..	..
All undertakings	4 954	4 264	3 848	3 953	3 711	4 280	..	4 195
Composite, all undertakings	..	..	..	..	..	..	..	..
Total								
Domestic undertakings	8 335	8 046	6 911	7 498	7 205	7 928	..	9 171
Foreign controlled undertakings	3 351	3 199	2 636	3 071	3 221	3 278	..	2 757
Foreign companies (branches)	907	..	..	..	..	..	..	..
All undertakings	9 242	8 046	6 911	7 498	7 205	7 928	..	9 171

Table 1. Selected aggregates *(cont.)*

Million SEK

	2014	2015	2016	2017	2018	2019	2020	2021
1.4 Gross operating expenses								
Life								
Domestic undertakings	12 738	13 573	12 617	13 248	15 095	13 651	..	15 068
Foreign controlled undertakings	3 639	2 122	1 297	1 918	1 901	1 944	..	2 041
Foreign companies (branches)	..	..	..	..	..	..	..	..
All undertakings	12 738	13 573	12 617	13 248	15 095	13 651	..	15 068
Non-life								
Domestic undertakings	16 878	16 854	15 781	15 863	18 250	19 503	..	20 539
Foreign controlled undertakings	8 238	7 704	7 205	7 691	9 496	10 114	..	10 055
Foreign companies (branches)	..	..	..	..	..	..	..	..
All undertakings	16 878	16 854	15 781	15 863	18 250	19 503	..	20 539
Composite, all undertakings	..	..	..	..	..	..	..	..
Total								
Domestic undertakings	29 616	30 427	28 398	29 111	33 345	33 154	..	35 607
Foreign controlled undertakings	11 877	9 826	8 502	9 609	11 397	12 058	..	12 096
Foreign companies (branches)	..	..	..	..	..	..	..	..
All undertakings	29 616	30 427	28 398	29 111	33 345	33 154	..	35 607
1.5 Insurance business written abroad by branches, gross premiums								
Life								
Branches and agencies	243	279	347	347	447	421	..	..
Subsidaries	..	..	..	..	..	..	..	..
Total	243	279	347	347	447	421	..	..
Non-life								
Branches and agencies	18 630	18 207	24 226	24 226	34 479	33 631	..	..
Subsidaries	..	..	..	..	..	..	..	..
Total	18 630	18 207	24 226	24 226	34 479	33 631	..	..
Composite total	..	..	..	..	..	..	..	..
Total								
Branches and agencies	18 873	18 486	24 573	24 573	34 926	34 052	..	..
Subsidaries	..	..	..	..	..	..	..	..
Total	18 873	18 486	24 573	24 573	34 926	34 052	..	..

.. Not available

Note: Detailed metadata at: *http://metalinks.oecd.org/ins/20230516/2e5e.*

Source: *OECD Insurance Statistics (database)*

Table 2. Number of companies and employees

	2014	2015	2016	2017	2018	2019	2020	2021
2.1 Number of companies								
Life								
Domestic undertakings	39	38	37	36	35	37	..	42
Foreign controlled undertakings	8	8	6	6	4	4	..	..
Foreign companies (branches)	6	8	6	4	4	4	..	..
All undertakings	45	46	43	46	39	41	..	42
Non-life								
Domestic undertakings	130	127	120	117	127	127	..	111
Foreign controlled undertakings	34	24	14	15	8	8	..	..
Foreign companies (branches)	28	33	31	25	9	9	..	..
All undertakings	158	160	151	157	136	136	..	111
Composite, all undertakings	**0**	**0**	**0**	..	..	..	..	..
Reinsurance								
Domestic undertakings	1	1	0	..	..	..	..	..
Foreign controlled undertakings	0	1	0	..	..	..	..	..
Foreign companies (branches)	0	0	..	..	..	..	..	..
All undertakings	1	1	..	..	..	..	..	..
Total								
Domestic undertakings	170	166	157	153	162	164	..	153
Foreign controlled undertakings	42	33	20	21	12	12	..	..
Foreign companies (branches)	34	41	37	29	13	13	..	..
All undertakings	204	207	194	203	175	176	..	153
2.2 Number of employees								
Insurance undertakings	19 573	18 792	20 600	21 900	20 865	22 000	..	..
Intermediaries	3 849	3 235	3 540	3 585	3 789	1 245	..	..
Total	23 422	22 027	..	25 485	24 654	23 245	..	..

.. Not available

Note: Detailed metadata at: *http://metalinks.oecd.org/ins/20230516/2e5e.*

Source: *OECD Insurance Statistics (database)*

SWITZERLAND

Table 1. Selected aggregates

Million CHF

	2014	2015	2016	2017	2018	2019	2020	2021
1.1 Insurance business written in the reporting country								
1.1.1 Insurance business, by ownership								
Gross premiums								
Domestic undertakings	66 312	65 628	63 975	63 967	65 722	67 482	63 005	62 934
Foreign controlled undertakings	14 214	13 846	12 578	11 699	12 241	7 760	6 618	6 388
Foreign companies (branches)	1 923	2 091	2 522	2 768	2 198	2 064	1 821	1 884
All undertakings	68 235	67 720	66 497	66 735	67 920	69 546	64 826	64 818
Premiums ceded								
Domestic undertakings	4 346	4 141	3 363	4 085	4 283	4 600	4 262	4 578
Foreign controlled undertakings	831	731	506	502	613	548	200	203
Foreign companies (branches)	533	553	813	874	776	772	887	863
All undertakings	4 879	4 694	4 176	4 959	5 059	5 372	5 149	5 441
Net written premiums								
Domestic undertakings	61 966	61 487	60 612	59 882	61 439	62 882	58 743	58 356
Foreign controlled undertakings	13 383	13 115	12 072	11 197	11 628	7 212	6 418	6 185
Foreign companies (branches)	1 390	1 539	1 709	1 894	1 422	1 292	934	1 021
All undertakings	63 356	63 026	62 321	61 776	62 861	64 174	59 677	59 377
1.1.2 Insurance business on foreign risks, gross premiums								
Life	..	..	..	..	..	..	..	..
Non-life	..	..	..	..	..	..	..	..
Composite total	..	..	..	..	..	..	..	..
Total	..	..	..	..	..	..	..	..
1.1.3 Life insurance payments, by class, gross premiums								
Annuities	441	495	428	317	246	281	245	230
Unit linked	1 730	1 755	1 738	1 861	1 947	2 202	2 190	2 518
Other life insurance	30 478	30 359	28 518	27 445	27 607	27 514	22 253	20 426
Total life insurance	32 649	32 609	30 684	29 623	29 800	29 997	24 688	23 174
***of which:** Pension contracts*	..	..	..	..	..	..	..	..
1.1.4 Non-life insurance payments, by class, gross premiums								
Motor vehicle insurance	6 580	6 595	6 598	6 742	6 804	6 909	7 137	6 890
Marine, aviation and other transport insurance	876	732	657	681	635	724	755	742
Freight insurance	..	..	..	..	..	..	..	..
Fire and other property damage insurance	8 123	7 909	7 411	7 397	7 804	8 297	8 413	9 001
Pecuniary loss insurance	1 096	897	1 095	1 108	1 055	1 024	958	1 221
General liability insurance	3 658	3 562	3 293	3 447	3 416	3 768	3 834	4 232
Accident and health	13 414	13 387	14 585	15 626	16 692	17 240	17 397	17 908
***of which:** Health*	9 934	10 266	10 606	11 361	11 901	12 099	12 358	12 723
Other non-life insurance	1 378	1 525	1 649	1 715	1 361	1 214	1 292	1 220
Treaty reinsurance	..	..	..	..	..	..	..	..
Total non-life insurance	35 125	34 607	35 288	36 716	37 767	39 176	39 786	41 214
1.2 Gross claims payments								
Life								
Domestic undertakings	27 943	27 794	29 083	29 352	44 908	58 408	28 395	27 013
Foreign controlled undertakings	7 917	8 123	8 578	8 159	11 255	29 424	3 963	4 807
Foreign companies (branches)	3	3	3	3	7	4	15	18
All undertakings	27 946	27 797	29 086	29 355	44 915	58 412	28 410	27 031
Non-life								
Domestic undertakings	20 149	20 621	20 498	20 716	42 021	44 831	24 267	24 505
Foreign controlled undertakings	2 281	2 671	2 471	2 299	4 534	4 308	2 377	2 685
Foreign companies (branches)	874	902	1 105	1 164	1 219	1 006	1 042	1 017
All undertakings	21 023	21 523	21 603	21 880	43 240	45 837	25 309	25 522
Composite, all undertakings	..	..	..	..	..	..	..	..
Total								
Domestic undertakings	48 092	48 415	49 581	50 068	86 929	103 239	52 662	51 518
Foreign controlled undertakings	10 198	10 794	11 049	10 458	15 789	33 732	6 340	7 492
Foreign companies (branches)	877	905	1 108	1 167	1 226	1 010	1 057	1 035
All undertakings	48 969	49 320	50 689	51 235	88 155	104 249	53 719	52 553
1.3 Commissions								
Life								
Domestic undertakings	920	856	856	836	829	850	891	971
Foreign controlled undertakings	114	169	169	163	163	139	159	184
Foreign companies (branches)	0	0	1	1	1	1	1	1
All undertakings	920	856	857	837	830	851	892	972
Non-life								
Domestic undertakings	1 597	2 188	2 289	2 078	1 403	2 410	2 471	2 344
Foreign controlled undertakings	381	441	450	453	458	469	488	520
Foreign companies (branches)	91	78	65	24	72	66	26	57
All undertakings	1 688	2 266	2 354	2 102	1 475	2 476	2 497	2 401
Composite, all undertakings	..	..	..	..	..	..	..	..
Total								
Domestic undertakings	2 517	3 044	3 145	2 914	2 232	3 260	3 362	3 315
Foreign controlled undertakings	495	610	619	616	621	608	647	704
Foreign companies (branches)	91	78	66	25	73	67	27	58
All undertakings	2 608	3 122	3 211	2 939	2 305	3 327	3 389	3 373

Table 1. Selected aggregates *(cont.)*

Million CHF

	2014	2015	2016	2017	2018	2019	2020	2021
1.4 Gross operating expenses								
Life								
Domestic undertakings	1 364	1 078	1 085	1 091	1 117	1 097	1 110	1 119
Foreign controlled undertakings	209	156	156	160	186	186	171	1 758
Foreign companies (branches)	2	1	1	2	3	1	2	1
All undertakings	1 366	1 079	1 086	1 093	1 120	1 098	1 112	1 120
Non-life								
Domestic undertakings	5 520	2 975	2 981	3 185	3 388	3 590	3 693	3 779
Foreign controlled undertakings	420	341	310	316	353	337	318	337
Foreign companies (branches)	108	103	215	195	186	157	153	162
All undertakings	5 628	3 078	3 196	3 380	3 574	3 747	3 846	3 941
Composite, all undertakings	..	..	..	..	..	..	..	..
Total								
Domestic undertakings	6 884	4 053	4 066	4 276	4 505	4 687	4 803	4 898
Foreign controlled undertakings	629	497	466	476	539	523	489	2 095
Foreign companies (branches)	110	104	216	197	189	158	155	163
All undertakings	6 994	4 157	4 282	4 473	4 694	4 845	4 958	5 061
1.5 Insurance business written abroad by branches, gross premiums								
Life								
Branches and agencies	1 794	1 604	1 567	1 613	1 653	1 717	1 792	1 467
Subsidaries	..	..	..	..	..	..	..	..
Total	1 794	1 604	1 567	1 613	1 653	1 717	1 792	1 467
Non-life								
Branches and agencies	15 331	14 100	12 578	12 689	6 664	6 089	6 428	6 883
Subsidaries	..	..	..	..	..	..	..	..
Total	15 331	14 100	12 578	12 689	6 664	6 089	6 428	6 883
Composite total	..	..	..	..	..	..	..	..
Total								
Branches and agencies	17 125	15 704	14 145	14 302	8 317	7 806	8 220	8 350
Subsidaries	..	..	..	..	..	..	..	..
Total	17 125	15 704	14 145	14 302	8 317	7 806	8 220	8 350

.. Not available
Note: Detailed metadata at: *http://metalinks.oecd.org/ins/20230516/63d1*.
Source: *OECD Insurance Statistics (database)*

Table 2. Number of companies and employees

	2014	2015	2016	2017	2018	2019	2020	2021
2.1 Number of companies								
Life								
Domestic undertakings	18	17	16	16	16	16	16	14
Foreign controlled undertakings	1	1	1	1	1	1	1	1
Foreign companies (branches)	3	3	3	3	3	3	3	3
All undertakings	21	20	19	19	19	19	19	17
Non-life								
Domestic undertakings	79	76	74	73	70	72	69	70
Foreign controlled undertakings	6	6	5	5	5	5	5	5
Foreign companies (branches)	48	46	46	45	44	46	47	48
All undertakings	127	122	120	118	114	118	116	118
Composite, all undertakings	**0**	**0**	**0**	..	..	..	..	..
Reinsurance								
Domestic undertakings	62	59	55	55	54	50	50	48
Foreign controlled undertakings	7	7	7	6	6	6	6	6
Foreign companies (branches)	..	..	..	..	..	..	..	..
All undertakings	62	59	55	55	54	50	50	48
Total								
Domestic undertakings	159	152	145	144	140	138	135	132
Foreign controlled undertakings	14	14	13	12	12	12	12	12
Foreign companies (branches)	51	49	49	48	47	49	50	51
All undertakings	210	201	194	192	187	187	185	183
2.2 Number of employees								
Insurance undertakings	..	..	..	..	..	..	..	..
Intermediaries	..	..	..	..	..	..	..	..
Total	..	..	..	..	..	..	..	..

.. Not available

Note: Detailed metadata at: *http://metalinks.oecd.org/ins/20230516/63d1*.

Source: *OECD Insurance Statistics (database)*

TÜRKIYE

Table 1. Selected aggregates

Million TRY

	2014	2015	2016	2017	2018	2019	2020	2021
1.1 Insurance business written in the reporting country								
1.1.1 Insurance business, by ownership								
Gross premiums								
Domestic undertakings	26 872	31 903	41 280	47 495	54 416	68 247	84 802	108 990
Foreign controlled undertakings	15 528	20 981	25 640	26 984	29 792	35 819	41 950	53 028
Foreign companies (branches)	77	126	152	201	304	553	805	974
All undertakings	26 949	32 029	41 431	47 696	54 720	68 800	85 607	109 965
Premiums ceded								
Domestic undertakings	6 686	7 984	9 816	13 268	15 814	19 346	22 795	32 835
Foreign controlled undertakings	3 510	4 773	5 482	6 672	7 850	8 518	9 719	14 193
Foreign companies (branches)	57	74	76	96	131	288	505	466
All undertakings	6 743	8 059	9 892	13 364	15 945	19 634	23 300	33 301
Net written premiums								
Domestic undertakings	20 186	23 919	31 464	34 227	38 601	48 901	60 416	76 155
Foreign controlled undertakings	12 018	16 208	20 158	20 312	21 942	27 300	31 549	38 835
Foreign companies (branches)	20	52	76	105	173	265	300	508
All undertakings	20 206	23 971	31 540	34 332	38 774	49 166	60 716	76 663
1.1.2 Insurance business on foreign risks, gross premiums								
Life	3 280	..	6 166	..	..	..	..	..
Non-life	22 711	..	34 322	..	..	..	..	..
Composite	958	..	943	..	..	..	..	..
of which:								
Life	24	..	19	..	..	..	..	..
Non-life	934	..	924	..	..	..	..	..
Total	26 948	..	41 431	..	..	..	..	..
1.1.3 Life insurance payments, by class, gross premiums								
Annuities	..	..	..	..	..	..	..	..
Unit linked	..	..	..	..	..	..	..	..
Other life insurance	..	..	..	..	..	..	..	..
Total life insurance	3 895	3 720	5 916	6 766	6 835	13 340	14 291	17 372
***of which:** Pension contracts*	..	..	..	..	..	..	..	..
1.1.4 Non-life insurance payments, by class, gross premiums								
Motor vehicle insurance	10 648	13 102	19 156	19 981	23 614	26 466	31 232	37 612
Marine, aviation and other transport insurance	321	423	455	490	706	929	1 348	2 106
Freight insurance	530	580	585	652	828	922	1 204	1 844
Fire and other property damage insurance	6 992	8 105	9 032	10 101	12 208	14 193	18 548	25 088
Pecuniary loss insurance	318	443	439	549	666	901	1 071	1 904
General liability insurance	679	811	863	1 028	1 389	1 698	2 190	3 217
Accident and health	4 010	4 685	4 582	6 708	8 051	9 798	12 333	15 522
***of which:** Health*	0	0	..	5 025	6 245	8 190	10 096	13 078
Other non-life insurance	147	99	134	226	167	197	225	306
Treaty reinsurance	..	0	..	..	..	..	..	..
Total non-life insurance	23 645	28 249	35 246	39 735	47 628	55 104	68 152	87 599
1.2 Gross claims payments								
Life								
Domestic undertakings	2 085	2 557	2 957	3 293	3 609	4 776	5 461	6 451
Foreign controlled undertakings	760	1 194	1 485	1 757	2 061	2 685	3 074	3 907
Foreign companies (branches)	..	..	0	..	0	..	0	..
All undertakings	2 085	2 557	2 957	3 293	3 609	4 776	5 461	6 451
Non-life								
Domestic undertakings	11 314	13 322	15 041	18 341	23 049	27 354	27 473	40 712
Foreign controlled undertakings	7 496	8 700	-9 940	11 648	13 543	15 282	15 007	21 323
Foreign companies (branches)	10	34	128	77	121	86	90	94
All undertakings	11 325	13 356	15 168	18 417	23 170	27 440	27 563	40 807
Composite								
Domestic undertakings	592	664	572	617	771	..	1 321	2 157
Foreign controlled undertakings	..	..	..	1	5	..	32	84
Foreign companies (branches)	..	..	..	..	..	..	..	..
All undertakings	592	664	572	617	771	..	1 333	2 157
of which:								
Life	11	6	9	15	7	..	11	12
Domestic undertakings	11	6	9	15	7	..	11	12
Foreign controlled undertakings	..	..	..	0	0	..	0	..
Foreign companies (branches)	..	..	..	..	..	..	..	..
All undertakings	11	6	9	15	7	..	11	12
Non-life	581	657	564	602	764	..	1 321	2 145
Domestic undertakings	581	657	564	602	764	..	1 321	2 145
Foreign controlled undertakings	..	..	..	1	5	..	32	84
Foreign companies (branches)	..	..	..	..	..	..	..	..
All undertakings	581	657	564	602	764	..	1 321	2 145
Total								
Domestic undertakings	13 991	16 543	18 570	22 251	27 430	32 130	34 255	49 320
Foreign controlled undertakings	8 256	9 894	-8 455	13 406	15 609	17 967	18 113	25 313
Foreign companies (branches)	10	34	128	77	121	86	90	94
All undertakings	14 001	16 578	18 698	22 328	27 551	32 216	34 357	49 415

Table 1. Selected aggregates *(cont.)*

Million TRY

	2014	2015	2016	2017	2018	2019	2020	2021
1.3 Commissions								
Life								
Domestic undertakings	..	..	..	..	..	..	..	..
Foreign controlled undertakings	..	..	..	..	..	..	..	..
Foreign companies (branches)	..	..	..	..	..	..	..	..
All undertakings	..	..	..	..	..	..	..	..
Non-life								
Domestic undertakings	..	..	..	..	..	..	..	..
Foreign controlled undertakings	..	..	..	..	..	..	..	..
Foreign companies (branches)	..	..	..	..	..	..	..	..
All undertakings	..	..	..	..	..	..	..	..
Composite								
Domestic undertakings	..	..	..	..	..	..	..	..
Foreign controlled undertakings	..	..	..	..	..	..	..	..
Foreign companies (branches)	..	..	..	..	..	..	..	..
All undertakings	..	..	..	..	..	..	..	..
of which:								
Life	..	..	..	..	..	..	..	..
Domestic undertakings	..	..	..	..	..	..	..	..
Foreign controlled undertakings	..	..	..	..	..	..	..	..
Foreign companies (branches)	..	..	..	..	..	..	..	..
All undertakings	..	..	..	..	..	..	..	..
Non-life	..	..	..	..	..	..	..	..
Domestic undertakings	..	..	..	..	..	..	..	..
Foreign controlled undertakings	..	..	..	..	..	..	..	..
Foreign companies (branches)	..	..	..	..	..	..	..	..
All undertakings	..	..	..	..	..	..	..	..
Total								
Domestic undertakings	..	..	..	..	..	..	..	..
Foreign controlled undertakings	..	..	..	..	..	..	..	..
Foreign companies (branches)	..	..	..	..	..	..	..	..
All undertakings	..	..	..	..	..	..	..	..
1.4 Gross operating expenses								
Life								
Domestic undertakings	1 198	1 595	1 970	2 644	2 961	4 103	5 307	6 410
Foreign controlled undertakings	765	1 033	1 241	1 724	1 926	2 376	3 025	3 778
Foreign companies (branches)	..	..	..	..	..	..	..	..
All undertakings	1 198	1 595	1 970	2 644	2 961	4 103	5 307	6 410
Non-life								
Domestic undertakings	4 309	4 648	5 579	6 263	6 689	8 211	9 770	11 919
Foreign controlled undertakings	2 944	3 110	3 847	4 170	4 183	4 821	5 700	6 607
Foreign companies (branches)	20	24	26	30	44	122	159	225
All undertakings	4 329	4 672	5 604	6 293	6 733	8 333	9 929	12 144
Composite								
Domestic undertakings	..	309	316	333	436	..	772	1 181
Foreign controlled undertakings	..	..	5	2	3	..	6	7
Foreign companies (branches)	..	..	..	..	..	..	..	..
All undertakings	289	309	316	333	436	..	772	1 181
of which:								
Life	8	10	10	5	8	..	13	3
Domestic undertakings	..	10	10	5	8	..	13	3
Foreign controlled undertakings	..	..	..	0	0	..	0	..
Foreign companies (branches)	..	..	..	..	..	..	..	..
All undertakings	8	10	10	5	8	..	13	3
Non-life	281	299	306	328	429	..	759	1 178
Domestic undertakings	..	299	306	328	429	..	759	1 178
Foreign controlled undertakings	..	..	5	2	3	..	6	7
Foreign companies (branches)	..	..	..	..	..	..	..	..
All undertakings	281	299	306	328	429	..	759	1 178
Total								
Domestic undertakings	5 507	6 552	7 865	9 240	10 087	12 314	15 849	19 510
Foreign controlled undertakings	3 708	4 143	5 092	5 895	6 112	7 197	8 731	10 392
Foreign companies (branches)	20	24	26	30	44	122	159	225
All undertakings	5 816	6 576	7 890	9 270	10 130	12 436	16 008	19 735

TÜRKIYE

Table 1. Selected aggregates *(cont.)*

Million TRY

	2014	2015	2016	2017	2018	2019	2020	2021
1.5 Insurance business written abroad by branches, gross premiums								
Life								
Branches and agencies	..	..	..	..	..	..	..	..
Subsidaries	..	..	..	..	..	..	..	..
Total	..	..	..	..	..	..	..	..
Non-life								
Branches and agencies	..	..	..	..	..	..	..	..
Subsidaries	..	..	..	..	..	..	..	..
Total	..	..	..	..	..	..	..	..
Composite								
Branches and agencies	..	..	..	..	..	..	..	..
Subsidaries	..	..	..	..	..	..	..	..
Total	..	..	..	..	..	..	..	..
of which:								
Life	..	..	..	..	..	..	..	..
Branches and agencies	..	..	..	..	..	..	..	..
Subsidaries	..	..	..	..	..	..	..	..
Total	..	..	..	..	..	..	..	..
Non-life	..	..	..	..	..	..	..	..
Branches and agencies	..	..	..	..	..	..	..	..
Subsidaries	..	..	..	..	..	..	..	..
Total	..	..	..	..	..	..	..	..
Total								
Branches and agencies	..	..	..	..	..	..	..	..
Subsidaries	..	..	..	..	..	..	..	..
Total	..	..	..	..	..	..	..	..

.. Not available
Note: Detailed metadata at: *http://metalinks.oecd.org/ins/20230516/db01.*
Source: *OECD Insurance Statistics (database)*

TÜRKIYE

Table 2. Number of companies and employees

	2014	2015	2016	2017	2018	2019	2020	2021
2.1 Number of companies								
Life								
Domestic undertakings	25	23	22	22	22	22	21	21
Foreign controlled undertakings	16	15	15	15	15	15	15	15
Foreign companies (branches)	0	..	0	0	..	..	..	0
All undertakings	25	23	22	22	22	22	21	21
Non-life								
Domestic undertakings	36	36	35	37	36	37	37	39
Foreign controlled undertakings	24	22	23	23	20	19	18	17
Foreign companies (branches)	2	2	2	2	2	2	2	2
All undertakings	38	38	37	39	38	39	39	41
Composite								
Domestic undertakings	0	..	0	0	0	..	3	0
Foreign controlled undertakings	0	..	0	0	0	..	1	0
Foreign companies (branches)	0	..	0	0	0	..	..	0
All undertakings	0	..	0	0	0	..	3	0
Reinsurance								
Domestic undertakings	1	1	2	2	2	3	..	3
Foreign controlled undertakings	0	..	1	1	1	1	..	1
Foreign companies (branches)	0	..	0	0	0	..	..	0
All undertakings	1	1	2	2	2	3	..	3
Total								
Domestic undertakings	62	60	59	61	62	62	61	63
Foreign controlled undertakings	40	37	39	39	38	35	35	33
Foreign companies (branches)	2	2	2	2	2	2	2	2
All undertakings	64	62	61	63	62	64	63	65
2.2 Number of employees								
Insurance undertakings	19 305	19 274	19 240	19 883	19 117	14 228	..	20 502
Intermediaries	15 587	18 931	35 992	40 231	20 605	40 000	..	..
Total	34 892	38 205	55 232	60 114	39 722	54 228	..	20 502

.. Not available

Note: Detailed metadata at: *http://metalinks.oecd.org/ins/20230516/db01*.

Source: *OECD Insurance Statistics (database)*

UNITED KINGDOM

Table 1. Selected aggregates

Million GBP

	2014	2015	2016	2017	2018	2019	2020	2021
1.1 Insurance business written in the reporting country								
1.1.1 Insurance business, by ownership								
Gross premiums								
Domestic undertakings	219 832	217 673	298 817	306 378	352 555	327 326	296 715	322 900
Foreign controlled undertakings	57 959	58 471	..	..	..	..	..	..
Foreign companies (branches)	2 407	2 741	247	473	498	592	429	958
All undertakings	222 239	220 414	299 064	306 851	353 053	327 918	297 144	323 858
Premiums ceded								
Domestic undertakings	33 780	24 299	68 763	36 957	68 169	63 873	57 635	60 982
Foreign controlled undertakings	11 048	10 801	0	..	..	..	..	..
Foreign companies (branches)	47	52	115	199	207	213	117	922
All undertakings	33 827	24 351	68 878	37 156	68 376	64 087	57 752	61 904
Net written premiums								
Domestic undertakings	186 052	193 374	230 054	269 421	284 386	263 453	239 080	261 918
Foreign controlled undertakings	46 911	47 670	..	..	..	..	..	..
Foreign companies (branches)	2 361	2 689	132	273	291	378	312	36
All undertakings	188 412	196 062	230 186	269 695	284 677	263 831	239 392	261 954
1.1.2 Insurance business on foreign risks, gross premiums								
Life	..	..	..	..	..	..	..	..
Non-life	..	..	..	..	..	..	..	..
Composite	..	..	..	..	..	..	..	..
of which:								
Life	..	..	..	..	..	..	..	..
Non-life	..	..	..	..	..	..	..	..
Total	..	..	..	..	..	..	..	..
1.1.3 Life insurance payments, by class, gross premiums								
Annuities	22 295	17 278	..	..	..	..	..	75
Unit linked	114 296	117 452	..	..	..	..	124 462	144 965
Other life insurance	11 834	10 622	..	..	..	..	52 702	49 343
Total life insurance	148 425	145 353	121 964	189 651	206 896	200 336	177 164	194 383
of which: *Pension contracts*	132 542	128 601	..	..	..	..	..	..
1.1.4 Non-life insurance payments, by class, gross premiums								
Motor vehicle insurance	12 069	12 883	18 956	16 011	15 520	16 285	14 374	14 014
Marine, aviation and other transport insurance	3 098	2 604	9 395	10 521	10 636	9 687	9 908	10 236
Freight insurance	885	808	..	0	..	..	..	..
Fire and other property damage insurance	15 969	15 544	30 491	32 412	33 815	30 639	31 408	34 319
Pecuniary loss insurance	5 966	5 791	5 064	5 922	6 018	4 561	4 016	4 463
General liability insurance	10 593	10 308	16 201	18 254	18 635	17 155	17 570	22 151
Accident and health	7 662	7 821	10 872	9 591	15 548	8 971	8 035	8 422
of which: *Health*	..	..	8 287	7 574	11 055	7 345	6 723	7 036
Other non-life insurance	2 962	3 177	2 407	2 341	2 497	2 436	2 289	1 966
Treaty reinsurance	..	..	..	..	..	..	..	..
Total non-life insurance	59 206	58 936	93 387	102 627	102 669	89 735	87 600	95 571
1.2 Gross claims payments								
Life								
Domestic undertakings	161 503	172 514	131 443	245 168	280 644	238 118	205 592	240 836
Foreign controlled undertakings	26 653	29 078	..	..	..	..	..	..
Foreign companies (branches)	4	5	..	..	..	..	..	..
All undertakings	161 507	172 518	131 443	245 168	280 644	238 118	205 592	240 836
Non-life								
Domestic undertakings	32 079	30 897	30 260	15 238	14 938	10 613	12 074	12 247
Foreign controlled undertakings	17 062	16 387	..	..	..	..	..	..
Foreign companies (branches)	1 469	1 871	43	437	280	498	359	625
All undertakings	33 548	32 768	30 303	15 675	15 430	11 111	12 433	12 872
Composite								
Domestic undertakings	22 527	23 077	50 234	64 507	63 455	63 441	61 383	58 331
Foreign controlled undertakings	2 170	2 734	..	..	..	..	..	..
Foreign companies (branches)	0	0	..	..	..	..	..	..
All undertakings	22 527	23 077	50 234	64 507	63 455	63 441	61 383	58 331
of which:								
Life	21 254	21 794	23 337	14 055	15 285	15 686	14 271	14 747
Domestic undertakings	21 254	21 794	23 337	14 055	15 285	15 686	14 271	14 747
Foreign controlled undertakings	1 876	2 413	..	..	..	..	..	..
Foreign companies (branches)	0	0	..	..	..	..	..	..
All undertakings	21 254	21 794	23 337	14 055	15 285	15 686	14 271	14 747
Non-life	1 273	1 283	26 897	50 452	48 169	47 754	47 112	43 584
Domestic undertakings	1 273	1 283	26 897	50 452	48 169	47 754	47 112	43 584
Foreign controlled undertakings	294	321	..	..	..	..	..	..
Foreign companies (branches)	0	0	..	..	..	..	..	..
All undertakings	1 273	1 283	26 897	50 452	48 169	47 754	47 112	43 584
Total								
Domestic undertakings	216 108	226 488	211 938	324 912	359 037	312 171	279 049	311 414
Foreign controlled undertakings	45 885	48 198	..	..	..	..	..	..
Foreign companies (branches)	1 474	1 875	43	437	280	498	359	625
All undertakings	217 582	228 363	211 981	325 350	359 529	312 669	279 408	312 039

Table 1. Selected aggregates *(cont.)*

Million GBP

	2014	2015	2016	2017	2018	2019	2020	2021
1.3 Commissions								
Life								
Domestic undertakings	..	..	..	..	..	..	..	..
Foreign controlled undertakings	..	..	..	..	..	..	..	..
Foreign companies (branches)	..	..	..	..	..	..	..	..
All undertakings	..	..	..	..	..	..	..	..
Non-life								
Domestic undertakings	..	..	..	..	..	..	..	..
Foreign controlled undertakings	..	..	..	..	..	..	..	..
Foreign companies (branches)	..	..	..	..	..	..	..	..
All undertakings	..	..	..	..	..	..	..	..
Composite								
Domestic undertakings	..	..	..	..	..	..	..	..
Foreign controlled undertakings	..	..	..	..	..	..	..	..
Foreign companies (branches)	..	..	..	..	..	..	..	..
All undertakings	..	..	..	..	..	..	..	..
of which:								
Life	..	..	..	..	..	..	..	..
Domestic undertakings	..	..	..	..	..	..	..	..
Foreign controlled undertakings	..	..	..	..	..	..	..	..
Foreign companies (branches)	..	..	..	..	..	..	..	..
All undertakings	..	..	..	..	..	..	..	..
Non-life	..	..	..	..	..	..	..	..
Domestic undertakings	..	..	..	..	..	..	..	..
Foreign controlled undertakings	..	..	..	..	..	..	..	..
Foreign companies (branches)	..	..	..	..	..	..	..	..
All undertakings	..	..	..	..	..	..	..	..
Total								
Domestic undertakings	..	..	..	..	..	..	..	..
Foreign controlled undertakings	..	..	..	..	..	..	..	..
Foreign companies (branches)	..	..	..	..	..	..	..	..
All undertakings	..	..	..	..	..	..	..	..
1.4 Gross operating expenses								
Life								
Domestic undertakings	6 694	6 794	8 085	10 917	10 794	9 766	9 259	9 787
Foreign controlled undertakings	929	850	..	..	..	..	..	..
Foreign companies (branches)	1	1	..	..	..	..	..	..
All undertakings	6 695	6 795	8 085	10 917	10 794	9 766	9 259	9 787
Non-life								
Domestic undertakings	6 782	6 639	15 414	8 440	8 495	5 793	6 444	6 995
Foreign controlled undertakings	3 549	3 562	..	..	..	..	..	..
Foreign companies (branches)	174	186	59	117	119	138	107	192
All undertakings	6 956	6 825	15 474	8 569	8 614	6 346	6 551	7 187
Composite								
Domestic undertakings	2 127	2 325	16 675	24 078	25 164	24 209	23 702	23 585
Foreign controlled undertakings	277	328	..	..	..	..	..	..
Foreign companies (branches)	0	0	..	..	..	..	..	..
All undertakings	2 127	2 325	16 675	24 078	25 164	24 209	23 702	23 585
of which:								
Life	1 874	2 038	3 140	579	1 608	2 015	1 660	1 755
Domestic undertakings	1 874	2 038	3 140	579	1 608	2 015	1 660	1 755
Foreign controlled undertakings	185	211	..	..	..	..	..	..
Foreign companies (branches)	0	0	..	..	..	..	..	..
All undertakings	1 874	2 038	3 140	579	1 608	2 015	1 660	1 755
Non-life	252	287	13 535	23 499	23 556	22 195	22 042	21 830
Domestic undertakings	252	287	13 535	23 499	23 556	22 195	22 042	21 830
Foreign controlled undertakings	92	117	..	..	..	..	..	..
Foreign companies (branches)	0	0	..	..	..	..	..	..
All undertakings	252	287	13 535	23 499	23 556	22 195	22 042	21 830
Total								
Domestic undertakings	15 602	15 759	40 174	43 435	44 453	39 768	39 405	40 367
Foreign controlled undertakings	4 754	4 740	..	..	..	..	..	..
Foreign companies (branches)	175	187	59	117	119	138	107	192
All undertakings	15 777	15 946	40 234	43 564	44 572	40 322	39 512	40 559

UNITED KINGDOM

Table 1. Selected aggregates *(cont.)*

Million GBP

	2014	2015	2016	2017	2018	2019	2020	2021
1.5 Insurance business written abroad by branches, gross premiums								
Life								
Branches and agencies	..	..	..	..	..	..	..	..
Subsidaries	..	..	..	..	..	..	..	..
Total	..	..	..	..	..	..	..	..
Non-life								
Branches and agencies	..	..	..	..	..	..	..	..
Subsidaries	..	..	..	..	..	..	..	..
Total	..	..	..	..	..	..	..	..
Composite								
Branches and agencies	..	..	..	..	..	..	..	..
Subsidaries	..	..	..	..	..	..	..	..
Total	..	..	..	..	..	..	..	..
of which:								
Life	..	..	..	..	..	..	..	..
Branches and agencies	..	..	..	..	..	..	..	..
Subsidaries	..	..	..	..	..	..	..	..
Total	..	..	..	..	..	..	..	..
Non-life	..	..	..	..	..	..	..	..
Branches and agencies	..	..	..	..	..	..	..	..
Subsidaries	..	..	..	..	..	..	..	..
Total	..	..	..	..	..	..	..	..
Total								
Branches and agencies	..	..	..	..	..	..	..	..
Subsidaries	..	..	..	..	..	..	..	..
Total	..	..	..	..	..	..	..	..

.. Not available
Note: Detailed metadata at: *http://metalinks.oecd.org/ins/20230516/deea.*
Source: *OECD Insurance Statistics (database)*

UNITED KINGDOM

Table 2. Number of companies and employees

	2014	2015	2016	2017	2018	2019	2020	2021
2.1 Number of companies								
Life								
Domestic undertakings	181	181	74	75	69	70	69	67
Foreign controlled undertakings	14	14	..	..	..	..	..	..
Foreign companies (branches)	1	1	1	1	0	1	2	2
All undertakings	182	182	75	76	69	71	71	69
Non-life								
Domestic undertakings	214	209	168	165	153	179	137	128
Foreign controlled undertakings	92	89	..	..	..	..	..	..
Foreign companies (branches)	12	7	13	11	12	14	11	16
All undertakings	226	216	181	176	165	193	148	144
Composite								
Domestic undertakings	25	25	21	22	19	15	37	37
Foreign controlled undertakings	8	8	..	..	..	..	..	..
Foreign companies (branches)	2	2	1	1	1	1	..	..
All undertakings	27	27	22	23	20	16	37	37
Reinsurance								
Domestic undertakings	29	26	16	19	17	14	24	19
Foreign controlled undertakings	16	13	..	..	..	..	..	..
Foreign companies (branches)	2	3	0	0	1	0	..	4
All undertakings	31	29	16	19	18	14	24	23
Total								
Domestic undertakings	449	441	279	281	258	278	267	251
Foreign controlled undertakings	130	124	..	..	..	..	..	..
Foreign companies (branches)	17	13	15	13	14	16	13	22
All undertakings	466	454	294	294	272	294	280	273
2.2 Number of employees								
Insurance undertakings	..	..	..	..	..	..	..	..
Intermediaries	..	..	..	..	..	..	..	..
Total	..	..	..	..	..	..	..	..

.. Not available

Note: Detailed metadata at: *http://metalinks.oecd.org/ins/20230516/deea.*

Source: *OECD Insurance Statistics (database)*

UNITED STATES

Table 1. Selected aggregates

Million USD

	2014	2015	2016	2017	2018	2019	2020	2021
1.1 Insurance business written in the reporting country								
1.1.1 Insurance business, by ownership								
Gross premiums								
Domestic undertakings	2 430 627	2 619 954	2 702 786	2 835 259	2 631 364	2 773 179	2 934 215	3 241 939
Foreign controlled undertakings	330 660	324 083	393 449	401 025	273 750	320 958	446 072	469 418
Foreign companies (branches)	696	1 129	1 007	1 034	920	737	614	776
All undertakings	2 431 323	2 621 083	2 703 793	2 836 293	2 632 284	2 773 916	2 934 829	3 242 715
Premiums ceded								
Domestic undertakings	609 531	713 961	743 307	810 265	429 234	430 891	495 526	605 389
Foreign controlled undertakings	134 223	139 675	195 708	226 256	108 845	175 820	216 189	206 399
Foreign companies (branches)	287	252	260	274	307	502	314	309
All undertakings	609 818	714 213	743 567	810 539	429 541	431 393	495 840	605 698
Net written premiums								
Domestic undertakings	1 821 096	1 905 993	1 959 479	2 024 995	2 202 129	2 342 288	2 438 689	2 636 550
Foreign controlled undertakings	196 437	184 408	197 742	174 769	164 906	145 138	229 883	263 019
Foreign companies (branches)	409	877	747	760	613	236	299	467
All undertakings	1 821 505	1 906 870	1 960 226	2 025 755	2 202 742	2 342 524	2 438 988	2 637 017
1.1.2 Insurance business on foreign risks, gross premiums								
Life	..	..	..	..	..	..	..	..
Non-life	..	..	..	..	..	..	..	..
Composite total	..	..	..	..	..	..	..	..
Total	..	..	..	..	..	..	..	..
1.1.3 Life insurance payments, by class, gross premiums								
Annuities	261 327	264 944	254 313	247 002	277 044	302 021	291 087	325 904
Unit linked	..	..	..	..	..	..	..	..
Other life insurance	527 280	561 674	581 948	612 083	632 578	666 265	743 257	786 659
Total life insurance	788 607	826 618	836 261	859 085	909 623	968 286	1 034 344	1 112 563
***of which:** Pension contracts*	..	..	..	..	..	..	..	..
1.1.4 Non-life insurance payments, by class, gross premiums								
Motor vehicle insurance	379 889	393 897	422 808	459 200	297 284	309 499	306 075	326 875
Marine, aviation and other transport insurance	3 070	2 911	4 815	2 732	2 187	2 340	2 976	3 289
Freight insurance	36 319	39 175	41 305	43 059	30 091	34 733	32 768	37 255
Fire and other property damage insurance	243 389	248 174	250 765	258 294	174 853	191 502	204 442	227 177
Pecuniary loss insurance	33 690	36 271	38 699	41 003	36 874	38 337	25 232	50 846
General liability insurance	204 069	208 722	211 362	218 298	144 286	160 208	176 819	206 933
Accident and health	646 938	714 394	761 509	799 804	803 339	852 838	922 498	999 038
***of which:** Health*	..	..	..	..	..	..	..	..
Other non-life insurance	3 780	3 728	3 921	4 493	3 716	3 720	3 361	8 400
Treaty reinsurance	0	0	0	..	..	..	..	..
Total non-life insurance	1 551 144	1 647 272	1 735 184	1 826 883	1 492 630	1 593 177	1 674 171	1 859 813
1.2 Gross claims payments								
Life								
Domestic undertakings	357 201	376 240	396 611	416 664	436 219	461 577	483 571	528 444
Foreign controlled undertakings	69 748	68 967	79 082	86 000	92 293	89 797	97 486	107 418
Foreign companies (branches)	0	0	0	0	0	0	0	0
All undertakings	357 201	376 240	396 611	416 664	436 219	461 577	483 571	528 444
Non-life								
Domestic undertakings	980 750	1 077 317	1 145 423	1 228 757	1 055 839	1 112 688	1 131 976	1 265 084
Foreign controlled undertakings	76 540	79 309	84 878	95 499	71 727	70 810	1 813	83 554
Foreign companies (branches)	240	359	504	609	649	661	337	427
All undertakings	980 990	1 077 676	1 145 927	1 229 366	1 056 488	1 113 349	1 134 126	1 265 511
Composite, all undertakings	..	..	..	..	..	..	..	..
Total								
Domestic undertakings	1 337 951	1 453 557	1 542 034	1 645 421	1 492 058	1 574 265	1 615 547	1 793 528
Foreign controlled undertakings	146 288	148 276	163 960	181 499	164 020	160 607	99 299	190 972
Foreign companies (branches)	240	359	504	609	649	661	337	427
All undertakings	1 338 191	1 453 916	1 542 538	1 646 030	1 492 707	1 574 926	1 617 697	1 793 955
1.3 Commissions								
Life								
Domestic undertakings	53 082	56 784	67 963	59 387	..	71 982	62 551	67 283
Foreign controlled undertakings	11 165	10 339	10 639	10 700	..	9 946	9 561	10 640
Foreign companies (branches)	0	0	0	0	..	0	0	0
All undertakings	53 082	56 784	67 963	59 387	..	71 982	62 551	67 283
Non-life								
Domestic undertakings	..	..	..	..	..	..	..	..
Foreign controlled undertakings	..	..	..	..	..	..	..	..
Foreign companies (branches)	..	..	..	..	..	..	..	..
All undertakings	..	..	..	..	..	..	..	..
Composite, all undertakings	..	..	..	..	..	..	..	..
Total								
Domestic undertakings	53 082	56 784	67 963	59 387	..	71 982	62 551	67 283
Foreign controlled undertakings	11 165	10 339	10 639	10 700	..	9 946	9 561	10 640
Foreign companies (branches)	0	0	0	0	..	0	0	0
All undertakings	53 082	56 784	67 963	59 387	..	71 982	62 551	67 283

Table 1. Selected aggregates *(cont.)*

Million USD

	2014	2015	2016	2017	2018	2019	2020	2021
1.4 Gross operating expenses								
Life								
Domestic undertakings	67 225	68 488	69 722	75 161	75 904	78 079	77 600	81 086
Foreign controlled undertakings	10 285	9 952	11 175	11 838	12 374	10 951	11 685	12 559
Foreign companies (branches)	0	0	..	..	0	0	0	0
All undertakings	67 225	68 488	69 722	75 161	75 904	78 079	77 600	81 086
Non-life								
Domestic undertakings	281 766	298 911	308 839	310 003	343 131	339 686	373 651	380 385
Foreign controlled undertakings	23 274	23 035	26 711	26 891	31 608	30 224	47 514	39 078
Foreign companies (branches)	194	410	354	360	300	146	195	149
All undertakings	281 960	299 321	309 193	310 363	343 431	339 832	373 846	380 534
Composite, all undertakings	..	..	..	..	..	..	..	..
Total								
Domestic undertakings	348 991	367 399	378 561	385 164	419 035	417 765	451 251	461 471
Foreign controlled undertakings	33 559	32 987	37 886	38 729	43 982	41 175	59 199	51 637
Foreign companies (branches)	194	410	354	360	300	146	195	149
All undertakings	349 185	367 809	378 915	385 524	419 335	417 911	451 446	461 620
1.5 Insurance business written abroad by branches, gross premiums								
Life								
Branches and agencies	..	..	..	..	..	..	..	..
Subsidaries	..	..	..	..	..	..	..	..
Total	..	..	..	..	..	..	..	..
Non-life								
Branches and agencies	..	..	..	..	..	..	..	..
Subsidaries	..	..	..	..	..	..	..	..
Total	..	..	..	..	..	..	..	..
Composite total	..	..	..	..	..	..	..	..
Total								
Branches and agencies	..	..	..	..	..	..	..	..
Subsidaries	..	..	..	..	..	..	..	..
Total	..	..	..	..	..	..	..	..

.. Not available

Note: Detailed metadata at: *http://metalinks.oecd.org/ins/20230516/3317*.

Source: *OECD Insurance Statistics (database)*

UNITED STATES

Table 2. Number of companies and employees

	2014	2015	2016	2017	2018	2019	2020	2021
2.1 Number of companies								
Life								
Domestic undertakings	1 031	1 030	738	735	715	728	708	725
Foreign controlled undertakings	158	158	168	157	157	149	145	147
Foreign companies (branches)	..	..	..	..	0	0	0	0
All undertakings	1 031	1 030	738	735	715	728	708	725
Non-life								
Domestic undertakings	3 404	3 185	3 205	3 419	3 430	3 471	3 404	3 814
Foreign controlled undertakings	404	390	418	405	399	388	373	372
Foreign companies (branches)	9	13	19	13	14	15	14	11
All undertakings	3 413	3 198	3 224	3 432	3 444	3 486	3 418	3 825
Composite, all undertakings	**0**	**0**	**0**	..	..	..	..	..
Reinsurance								
Domestic undertakings	234	354	221	228	235	228	..	..
Foreign controlled undertakings	64	76	52	44	48	48	..	..
Foreign companies (branches)	1	4	2	1	1	2	..	..
All undertakings	235	358	223	229	283	230	..	..
Total								
Domestic undertakings	4 669	4 569	4 164	4 382	4 380	4 427	..	4 539
Foreign controlled undertakings	626	624	638	606	604	585	..	519
Foreign companies (branches)	10	17	21	14	15	17	..	11
All undertakings	4 679	4 586	4 185	4 396	4 442	4 444	..	4 550
2.2 Number of employees								
Insurance undertakings	..	..	..	..	..	..	..	..
Intermediaries	..	..	..	..	..	..	..	..
Total	..	..	..	..	..	..	..	..

.. Not available

Note: Detailed metadata at: *http://metalinks.oecd.org/ins/20230516/3317*.

Source: *OECD Insurance Statistics (database)*

www.ingramcontent.com/pod-product-compliance
Ingram Content Group UK Ltd.
Pitfield, Milton Keynes, MK11 3LW, UK
UKHW051502290926
15471UKWH00008B/1365

9 789264 527447